Tucson

University of Oklahoma Press   Norman

TUCSON

THE LIFE AND TIMES OF AN AMERICAN CITY

By C. L. Sonnichsen

Maps by Donald H. Bufkin

BY C. L. SONNICHSEN

Billy King's Tombstone (Caldwell, 1942)
Roy Bean: Law West of the Pecos (New York, 1943)
Cowboys and Cattle Kings (Norman, 1950)
I'll Die Before I'll Run (New York, 1951)
Alias Billy the Kid (coauthor; Albuquerque, 1955)
Ten Texas Feuds (Albuquerque, 1957)
The Mescalero Apaches (Norman, 1958)
Tularosa: Last of the Frontier West (New York, 1960)
The El Paso Salt War (El Paso, 1961)
The Southwest in Life and Literature (New York, 1963)
Outlaw: Bill Mitchell, Alias Baldy Russell (Denver, 1964)
Pass of the North (El Paso, 1968)
The State National Bank of El Paso (coauthor; El Paso, 1971)
White Oaks, New Mexico (coauthor; Tucson, 1971)
Colonel Greene and the Copper Skyrocket (Tucson, 1974)
San Agustin: First Cathedral Church in Arizona (coauthor; Tucson, 1974)
From Hopalong to Hud (College Station, Texas, 1978)
The Grave of John Wesley Hardin (College Station, Texas, 1979)
The Ambidextrous Historian: Historical Writers and Writing in the American West (Norman, 1981)
Tucson: The Life and Times of an American City (Norman, 1982)

Library of Congress Cataloging in Publication Data

Sonnichsen, C. L. (Charles Leland), 1901–
    Tucson, the life and times of an American city.

    Includes bibliographical references and index.
    1. Tucson (Ariz.)—History.   I. Title.
F819.T957S66   1982   979.1'77   82–40329

This book is dedicated, with sympathy and understanding, to all those living elsewhere who would rather be in Tucson

Contents

Illustrations and Maps

Explanations and Acknowledgments

This book is an attempt to survey the life story of an old and colorful American city. Many chroniclers have dealt with its history in part, but few have looked at it as a whole. Bernice Cosulich's *Tucson* (1953) is a collection of newspaper feature stories, useful but limited, about events and personalities of pioneer times. John BretHarte's *Tucson: The Story of a Desert Pueblo* (1980), expertly written and rich in pictorial history, is limited in space and scope. Other volumes by good scholars and excellent writers (Dobyns, Fontana, McCarty, Brinckerhoff, Martin, Chambers, Haury, Myrick, Griffith, and many more) are directed at specific segments of Tucson's past, and the thousands of pages of description, analysis, and reminiscence carefully preserved in various archives have needed to be synthesized into a general survey.

The present overview aims to create such a synthesis, distilling the fruits gathered by a great many collectors and researchers, along with the available archival material, in a single volume and painting a coherent picture of the development of a great southwestern city from its beginning as a mud village in northern Mexico two centuries ago to its emergence as an American metropolis.

Such a book must necessarily accumulate obligations, too many to be adequately acknowledged, as a banker accumulates mortgages. One special debt which must be recognized, however, is to the staff of the Arizona Historical Society at its Tucson Heritage Center, where I have spent a pleasant and rewarding decade, beginning with Director Sidney B. Brinckerhoff and Assistant Director Donald H. Bufkin. Cartographer and urban historian Bufkin has placed me under special obligation through sometimes daily conversations and constant judicious encouragement and criticism. Indispensable also was the unremitting support of Librarian Margaret BretHarte and her associates Lori Davisson, Susan Peters, Barbara Bush, and others who have come and gone, without whose help the book would not have been written. Always ready to contribute were Publications Director A. Tracy Row, Assistant Editor Kenneth Nichols, and Special Assistant Karen Dahood, as were Archivist David Hoober, Chief of the Photography Section Susan Luebberman, Buehman Collection Curator Heather Hatch, Photo Specialist Joan Metzger, Public Relations Director Adina Wingate, and all the other generous people at the Heritage Center.

Unless otherwise noted, the photographs in this book are from the collections of the society.

I owe sincere thanks to the staff of the Tucson Public Library, G. Freeman Woods Branch, and to Donald Powell (former director) and Phyllis Ball, of the University of Arizona Special Collections. Tucsonans with long memories in the Tucson Literary Club helped at monthly meetings, especially Judge Evo DeConcini, Judge Richard Chambers, Dr. Richard A. Harvill, Dr. Lawrence Muir, Dr. William B. Steen, George Rosenberg, Leland Case, William P. Hazard, Richard Duffield, and the Reverend Jerry Wallace. Particularly helpful on many occasions were David F. Brinegar, former executive editor of the *Arizona Daily Star*; Mrs. James P. Moore, former director of the Arizona Historical Society; Dr. Bernard L. Fontana, historian, anthropologist, and philosopher; Charles W. Polzer, S.J., mission historian *par excellence*; and the late George W. Chambers and his wife, Mary, collectors of a treasure of Tucsoniana and supporters of all good historical enterprises.

Other contributors include Glenton Sykes, creator and collector of Tucson history for sixty years; Don Schellie, *Citizen* columnist and historical treasure hunter; Thomas F. Peterson, Jr., and the late Ann-Eve Mansfeld Johnson, dedicated preservers of Tucson's past; the late Bert M. Fireman, encyclopedia of Arizona history; specialists Henry F. Dobyns, John Gilchriese, Dr. James Officer, the late George Eckhart, Orville McPherson, and many others, some of them listed in "Sources" under "Interviews."

Useful research tools were provided by Geoffrey L. Peters ("Tucson Chronology, 1930–1980") and Douglas D. Martin (*An Arizona Chronology* in two volumes, *The Territorial Years* and *Statehood*—the latter edited by Patricia Paylore).

My wife, Carol, endured much and complained little during the years of research and writing and deserves a lioness's share of credit for the final product. Errors and inadequacies are, of course, my own.

Everyone mentioned, and everyone not mentioned, has helped make Tucson a great place to live and to write about.

C. L. SONNICHSEN

Tucson, Arizona

Tucson

Precarious Paradise: An Introduction

The metropolitan area of Tucson, Arizona (greater Tucson), is a community of half a million people (according to the census of 1980) set in the lower Sonoran Desert in a great basin surrounded by high mountain ranges. In many ways it is different from any other American city, but, like all other Sunbelt cities, it has been growing over the last century by great leaps and bounds. It is a popular winter resort, and the fugitives from the Frozen North who spent almost $4.5 billion in Arizona in 1978 left a fair share of their cash in what natives like to call the Old Pueblo. [1] Every month a new crop of immigrants arrives, and the area booms with new people, new industries, new shopping centers, and new subdivisions. The place must have something special to attract so many outsiders.

Opinions about it, however, are sharply divided. On the one hand, public-relations people and chamber-of-commerce boosters paint an ecstatic picture of a "young, vibrant community" generating "a tremendous amount of excitement" and "permeated with a spirit of anticipation." [2] Outside agencies give it top marks as a place to live—for instance, the Midwest Research Institute, based in Kansas City and presumably unbiased, gave a high rating in 1975 to Tucson's "quality of life" (whatever that means). [3] Desert lovers find the setting supremely attractive; newcomers report that their neighbors are aglow with western friendliness; long-time residents would not consider living anywhere else on earth. One wing of opinion rates the Tucson area as a somewhat spiny and superheated corner of Paradise.

They must be in the majority, since so many of them keep crowding in, and yet there are skeptics and unbelievers. Franz Douskey calls Tucson "a sprawling, amoebalike city carved like a disease from the abdomen of the Sonora Desert. . . . A geriatric ghetto." [4] In December, 1980, Dorothy Livadas, of Rochester, New York, voiced a similar view in a letter to the editor of the *Arizona Daily Star*:

After nearly three months in Tucson, one of the sunshine centers of the world, I am back in good, old, dull, Rochester with its sleety weather and slippery pavements, its biting cold and dirty old December snow. And I couldn't like it better. . . . There, sand is the building material; houses hug the ground and have about them an impermanence that is shattering to one accustomed to the solidity of Eastern cities. They are scattered all about like matchboxes blown around by the wind.[5]

How can one explain this ambivalence about an unusually interesting, friendly, and hospitable American town? The length of one's residence seems to be the determining factor. People come to Tucson because to them it is new and different and exciting, and when they get here, they want to change it to something they recognize. Tucson enthusiast Sherman Miller noted in *Tropic of Tucson* (1964) that "the first instinct of every newcomer is to grab the city by the throat, shake it until its teeth rattle, and make it behave just like the place they have come to get away from."[6] Anthropologist and philosopher Bernard Fontana adds that most new residents bring with them as much as possible of their home communities—grass, trees, housing styles, attitudes. If a man woke up in Tucson some morning and nobody told him where he was, he might think he was back in New York State. "It is as if one long avenue connected Schenectady to Tucson, almost as if one were the suburb of the other."[7]

This ambivalence, sometimes amounting to a love-hate relationship, explains the diversity of opinions about the town and accounts for a certain impatience sometimes exhibited by old residents toward the new. They are welcome for one good reason, says Edward Abbey. "We hate their guts but we want their money."[8]

The most amazing aspect of the situation is what happens to the dissatisfied immigrant after a few months. In a surprisingly short time he becomes a zealous convert, defensive about his new home, and joins the natives in asking, to quote Abbey again, "Who are all these people, anyhow? Where do they come from, all these damned foreigners overrunning our peaceful little hellhole of a state?" He has accepted the town and the desert as his own and wants to keep them just as they were the day he arrived. This desire of all comers to bring their roots with them and keep others from bringing in theirs is a special Tucson characteristic and accounts for many aspects of their attitudes, their life-styles, and their voting records.

It is obvious to them from the beginning, whether or not they approve of Tucson, that this community is a place apart, with a special background and a long history of its own. The basic fact, they learn, is its location in the hot and arid reaches of the Lower Sonoran Desert, remote from the great urban centers and, in many ways, from the mainstream of American life. It has always been a separate world. It was an oasis, far from other Indian cultures, a thousand years ago in the days of the Hohokam. It was an outpost in Spanish times. It was not far from the edge of the world when American Anglo-Saxons began settling on the Santa Cruz River. Even with the coming of the railroad, the airplane, and television, it remained insulated by distance and by special habits of mind from the East and Middle America. Much of the charm of Tucson, and much of its negative impact on newcomers, derives from this separateness.

Behind this separateness, however, is a fact which we ought to think about more often than we do: deserts were not meant for people. We were not planned for by the Great Planner; we were not provided for by the Great Provider; and our days, relatively speaking, may not be long in the land. Only our technological skills make survival possible for most of us (the Papagos do not need air conditioning or plumbing), and eventually we will have to make drastic changes in our life-style or find new ways to support it. The luxuriant green desert, which seems so beautiful and inviting to a newcomer from Wisconsin, was created to maintain a sparse population of coyotes, rattlesnakes, and Gila monsters, with some tolerance for a small, hardy collection of seminomadic Papagos and wide-ranging Apaches. A very limited acquaintance demonstrates that the desert is a cruel and lonely place where the deadly game of life and death goes on day and night between coyotes and rabbits, rattlesnakes and mice, roadrunners and quail. Life is precarious at best for the lower orders of the creation, and sometimes for human beings. A brief contact with a cholla makes the point. It is an obvious fact that, when southern Arizona was on the drawing board, plans for people were not made.

Indeed, it would seem that everything in this country was planned to repel human invasion—the intolerable summer sun, the limited water supply, the armored and resentful vegetation, the rocky soil, the vast distances. The desert dwellers are better prepared than we are to survive. Barrel cactus and prickly pear hold moisture inside their thick hides and can exist for many months without rain. The palo-verde cannot afford ordinary leaves and stores its chlorophyll in its bark. In such a difficult country settlers had to make do with little, undergo much, and expect the worst. In our day we are like people living in an artificial environment at the bottom of the sea or out in space. We stay alive, but we are bucking the odds, and the future is by no means secure. Survival, until recent years, has been a matter of adaptation and

endurance, and the earliest comers were probably forced out of more hospitable regions. They would not have come if they had had a choice, and their hardihood was thrust upon them.

It is not so with us. We use our resources as if they were inexhaustible, expand our industries and bid for immigrants as if we could afford them, and keep on building as if this were the promised land, flowing with milk, honey—and water. In a few decades, perhaps, it will all end, and we are hastening the day, rejoicing in every temporary gain, buying our prosperity on the installment plan—unmindful of the inexorable bill collector who is getting ready, even now, to call in our credit cards.

The ecologists, the conservationists, the hydrologists, the wildlife people, the environmentalists would like to send us back to the Middle West or transport us to some other planet, preferably in a distant galaxy. A city in the fragile desert environment is to them a monumental mistake, and the technology that keeps us here, in the bitter words of Edward Jeremiah Abbey, high priest of the cult, preserves only "that phosphorescent, putrefying glory (all the glory there is left) called Down Town, Night Time, Wonderville, U.S.A."[9]

Well, then, why *are* we here in this precarious paradise? Basically we are here because of the Santa Cruz, a stream so modest that travelers in the 1840s called it a creek. It flowed quietly northward from Mexico through a wide valley lined with trees and brush, spreading out into swampy areas where many creatures, including mosquitoes, abounded. Its fifty-mile course after it passed Tucson was mostly underground.

Human beings lived here a thousand

years ago—the earliest in pit houses, the later ones in simple shelters beside their fields. The river was their lifeline. In its own small way it did for southern Arizona what the Nile and the Danube did for Egypt and central Europe. About 800 arable acres were all the Tucson Basin could provide, but it was enough for a few hundred Indians and an equal number of Spaniards. There was no natural provision for half a million people.

The Spanish missionaries who saw it 300 years ago would not know the river now. It is a dry trough which runs through downtown Tucson, flowing only when the rains come. At such times, however, it can rage and ruin and take quick vengeance on the race which has crippled and almost destroyed it. Its banks have been used as an unofficial city dump, the shoulders and the stream bed itself disfigured by heaps of discarded building materials, automobile bodies, and miscellaneous junk. Concerned citizens at the end of the 1970s took serious steps toward the creation of a "river park" which would restore the bottomlands inside the city limits to beauty and usefulness, but as a living stream the Santa Cruz belongs to history.

Until the Americans came, it retained its identity and fulfilled its lifegiving function. When Samuel Reid saw it in 1858 in the course of his "tramp" through the Gadsden Purchase and Sonora, he described the valley near Tubac as "several miles wide and highly fertile. Cottonwood

and mesquite of good size are abundant. . . . If you will portray in your imagination a bottom covered with tall golden grass . . . divided by a meandering stream a dozen yards wide and as many inches deep." [10] Julius Froebel followed its banks the next year and called it "a rapid brook, clear as crystal, and full of aquatic plants, fishes and tortoises of various kinds . . . flowing through a small meadow covered with shrubs." [11]

Because of the river the valley was a place where people would naturally come, and they did come—more and more of them. In later years cities like Tucson and Phoenix grew and flourished for reasons never dreamed of by the Indians and the Spaniards—proximity to mines and transcontinental travel routes, for example—but in the beginning water was the attraction. Four centuries after the arrival of the Spaniards, water is still the key to life in Tucson, and the future of the city is tied to it as salvation is tied to faith.

Thus the old problems—climate, water, and people—are still with us, and new ones like pollution, urban sprawl, and crime make existence in the beautiful valley more and more precarious. Where it will end is impossible to predict. Perhaps we can take care of the sun seekers who continue to invade the Southwest. Maybe the desert will reclaim its own.

Meanwhile we have 400 years of recorded history to try to understand, and a present situation which is interesting if not reassuring.

CHAPTER 1

Post Farthest Out

Four months after Paul Revere mounted his borrowed horse and set out on his famous midnight ride, Tucson, Arizona, was founded. The date was August 20, 1775. The founder was Don Hugo O'Conor (correctly spelled O'Connor), a red-headed, hyperactive Irishman who rode up from the presidio at Tubac to see about moving the post to a point farther north. Don Hugo had been charged with inspecting and realigning the array of presidios between Sonora and Texas, intended to keep the wild Indians on the north from raiding the Spanish settlements on the south.[1] The foothold of Europeans in the desert country was still precarious, and the problem of frontier defense had long been desperate. The fort at Tubac, forty miles up the Santa Cruz River from the site of Tucson, had been in existence since 1752, but even there, with soldiers for protection, survival was difficult and sometimes nearly impossible. As a result, the decision makers far away in Spain and Mexico City decided on a reorganization of the presidial system. A reshuffling of the cards might bring them better luck in their great gamble.

Don Hugo surveyed the terrain and made his choice. Historians assume that the site was near the center of present-day downtown Tucson, where the adobe walls of the fort finally rose eight years later, but it is possible that the first location was about four or five miles north, where the natives were concentrated in large numbers. Father Eusebio Francisco Kino had called this place San Agustín de Oiaur when he first visited the valley eighty years before. Archaeologists locate it near the Miracle Mile overpass across Interstate 10 on the east bank of the Santa Cruz. From this point the Indians' fields extended away to the west and south to a nook overshadowed by Tumamoc Hill in the vicinity of present-day Saint Mary's Hospital. In this vicinity was the eminence of volcanic rock which gave the community its name, *schookson* or *stjukson*, which translates as "at the foot of the black hill or mountain."[2]

Farther east and across the stream from downtown Tucson is a smaller hill, called Sentinel Peak because in Spanish times the villagers kept a watch there for raiding Apaches. Since 1916 it has been known as A Mountain in recognition of a peculiarly American ritual, the annual repainting of a giant *A* on the east slope by students of the

Father Eusebio Francisco Kino breaking trail. Diorama at the Tumacacori National Monument, Tumacacori, Arizona. Courtesy Arizona Historical Society, Tucson. Unless otherwise noted, subsequent illustrations are courtesy Arizona Historical Society.

University of Arizona—a group whose folkways and ceremonials are quite as curious as those of their native predecessors. A Mountain is said to be the "Black Mountain," though Tumamoc is bigger and blacker, because a fine spring issued from its base, providing, along with a smaller *ojito* across the river near the site of the future city, water for an Indian village. Here the native farmers built their sand dams and diverted the water into their irrigation ditches. Kino named the place San Cosme de Tucson, which indicates that Tucson was an area designation, not the name of a particular community. It may have been the permanent village where the Indians spent the fall and winter months before moving out in the spring and sum-

mer to shelters near their fields of corn and beans near San Agustín de Oiaur. Some historians find it logical to assume that O'Conor's first post was set up near the latter place.[3] Cautious scholars, however, will say only that "there is, so far as is known, no evidence to fix either the mission or the first presidio on the east or west bank of the Rio Santa Cruz."[4]

Having made his decision, whatever it was, O'Conor retraced his steps to Tubac and certified that "San Agustín de Toixon" offered "the requisite conditions of water, pasture, and wood," as well as "a perfect closing of the Apache frontier."[5]

There was much to be said for the Tucson location. It seemed to be favored by God and nature, in sharp contrast to the enormous wasteland which surrounded it. Soil, water, and climate were favorable, though the summers were hot. There was game; there was wood; there was pasture; and there were people—Indians whom the Spaniards called Papagos, or Bean People, who had been in the country for a very long time and were experts in desert living.[6]

Their numbers were considerable. On his second visit to them in 1698, Father Kino noted that San Agustín de Oiaur contained 177 houses and that he passed through "many cornfields, through rich fields of beans, watermelons and squash."[7] The community of Bac, eight miles south, was the mission headquarters for many years, and Tucson was only a *visita*, but their numbers were about the same. Kino's companion Juan Mateo Manje counted 900 Indians at Bac and 800 at Tucson in 1697. He called the area the best mission site in the region and visualized the two communities connected by a double row of shady cottonwoods with 2,000 happy people going about their business under the eyes of the missionary fathers.[8]

These Papagos belonged to the Piman stock with branches on the Gila River on the north and the San Pedro on the east. Scientists who have dug up their vanished villages, with anthropologist Charles DiPeso in the lead, have concluded that they had made an admirable adjustment to their difficult environment.[9]

The early Spaniards were not so charitable. Father Luis Velarde, for instance, writing in 1716, noted that they were "of good height and well featured," that they were hospitable and "lived in harmony together," that they were "valiant and daring" and gave the Apaches an occasional beating, but in his opinion their deficits outweighed

Desert Papagos beneath a naturally air-conditioned ramada.

their assets. Their understanding was "very small." They practiced plural marriage and easy divorce. They indulged periodically in ritualistic drunkenness, though Father Luis admitted that it lasted "only for two or three days" when the cactus fruit ripened. He would not concede that they had any religion. Their ceremonials were "magic," and he was contemptuous of their story of a great flood and their myth of a savior. "It is a long history," he said, "full of a thousand stupidities, so I omit it here, although it would not be disagreeable, due to the gracefulness of its style." His final judgment of the Papagos was that they were "dull."[10]

Their homeland was the enormous expanse of desert and mountain which the Spaniards called Pimería Alta, as distinguished from Pimería Baja farther south in Sonora. It was bounded, roughly, by the Colorado River on the west, the Gila on the north, and the San Pedro on the east. The Papago reservation west and northwest of Tucson is part of their original home. The Santa Cruz Valley was an oasis in this wasteland, but two centuries ago it was at the end of a long, long road. It was the ultimate frontier, the post farthest out, on the very edge of Christendom.[11]

Why, one wonders, did the Spaniards want to fight for their lives in this jumping-off place? They had what they considered very good reasons. In the first place they wanted to transform the local Indians into contented, tribute-paying, Christian vassals of the Spanish king, and they expected to do it in ten years. In the second place, they wished to protect the established Spanish settlements from raiding tribes. A third consideration was the safety of the northern route to California, which was about to be opened by Captain Juan Bautista de Anza, commander of the Tubac presidio. A fourth, somewhat less pressing, reason was preparation for potential incursions by other European powers, particularly the Russians, who were known to be moving in along the Pacific coast.[12]

The Apache raiders were not the only dangerous Indians. The Piman peoples themselves were a hazard and had been for almost a century. The southern Pimas plotted in 1681 to drive the Spaniards out. In 1684 "constant warfare" began; "the fear of open rebellion was rampant" in Sonora; and the Spaniards of the frontier "lived in mortal fear of the extensive Pima nation to the northwest."[13]

The Papagos in the Santa Cruz Valley were restless with the others. In 1744 the two missionary fathers at Bac considered their 400 Indian families "a bad lot" and complained that they would not stay in one place.[14] In his reports half a century before, Father Kino had not mentioned "their drunkenness, their orgies, their plural wives."[15] He had accepted them as they were. His successors did not follow his ex-

ample. "When a missionary moved in with them," according to historian John Kessell, "and began treating them as wards day in and day out, making them work when they would rather not, suppressing their ceremonials, and deriding their medicine men as witches, he understandably provoked their resentment."[16] From this point of view the mission establishments were "concentration camps,"[17] and, in the opinion of such specialists as Jack D. Forbes, the rebellious Indians of the Pimería were "freedom fighters."[18]

This point of view has become standard in our time. The missionary priest, we say, was "an official agent of the Spanish crown" in expanding the Spanish empire.[19] The focus was on the Indian, and the object was "to convert him, to civilize him, and to exploit him," according to Herbert Eugene Bolton, and the colonists who followed the missionaries subjected the natives to "practical slavery."[20] The missionaries themselves imposed their own doctrine on people who already had a religion adequate for their needs and were a disruptive influence in spite of "unfeigned religious motives."[21] "In this sense," say Daniel S. Matson and Bernard L. Fontana, "the role of the missionary has been the role of the aggressor. Simply to spread 'news of great joy' is one matter; to invade the most sacred precincts of another man's being, and thereby to defile him, is something else again. It seems to us there can be no greater form of violence than this."[22]

Spanish food supplies "must have looked very good to the Pimans," these authors admit, especially in lean years.[23] These fleshpots, however, could not justify the bondage imposed by the Europeans. Occasionally a film or television special portrays the saintly fathers ministering to their simple, happy congregations,[24] but the usual view nowadays is that of Charles DiPeso. To escape "bondage," he writes, "it remained for these ancient occupants to resolve whether or not they would remain on their lands and become slaves . . . or whether they would resist the alien invasion by tearing their roots from the land and running. . . . The sociopolitical circumstances created a great surge of hatred fostered by fear among both factions."[25]

Jesuit specialists in mission history have been slow to take issue with these critics. In 1979, however, Jesuit John Francis Bannon protested "an ill-concealed acceptance of the Black Legend mentality," and Charles W. Polzer, also a black robe, speaks for all missionaries, living and dead, in dedicating his *Rules and Precepts of the Jesuit Missions in Northwestern New Spain* to "the Blackrobes who lived by these rules and worked for a better day."[26]

The Indian "freedom fighters" made trouble from 1688 until the end of the mission system in the nineteenth century. The Southern Pimas in Sonora rose in 1751.[27] The Northern Pimas, whose contacts with priests and soldiers were not quite so close, joined in later and fled to the wilds. Finally, in 1752, peace-minded Spanish leaders persuaded them to go back to their villages. The Indians concentrated in greater numbers than before, possibly through fear of the Apaches, at San Cosme in the shadow of A Mountain.[28]

Once communication was reestablished between the Spaniards and the natives, the time seemed ripe to station a missionary permanently at Tucson. As a result, Father Gottfried Bernhardt Middendorff appeared on the scene. An unlikely candidate for service on the frontier, he was a frail, consumptive, dedicated German, thirty-three years old, learned in German and Latin, hardly fluent in Spanish, completely ignorant of Piman customs and language. He was there because the Spanish Jesuits were low in manpower and he had volunteered—one of a quartet of German friars who had crossed the ocean to serve in the desert outposts. Middendorff had weak lungs, hemorrhaged often, and must have been insecure and a little frightened. It was probably unfortunate that he had to rely heavily on Father Alonso I. B. Espinosa, his superior at San Xavier del Bac, who was as rigid as Kino had been accommodating.

Middendorff's parish, called Santa Catalina de Cuitabagu, had an interesting history. When Kino and Manje came through in the 1690s, Cuitabagu (which means "well where people gather mesquite beans") was twenty-five miles downriver north of the valley settlements.[29] Later it seems to have been pulled back to a location in the Cañada del Oro eight or ten miles north of Black Mountain and close to the Santa Catalina foothills, thereby gaining its saint's name. By the time of Middendorff's arrival it had been moved again and was probably close to San Agustín de Oiaur since the Jesuits liked to locate their missions in major Indian communities. If arrangements had been made for his arrival, they did not include provisions for housing, and the new priest and his escort of ten soldiers had to improvise shelters for themselves and their equipment.

It is not surprising that Middendorff lasted only four months. He describes his ordeal in one anguished paragraph:

I was fond of my catechumens and they reciprocated my affection with gifts of birds' eggs and wild fruits. But our mutual contentment did not last long because in the following May [1757] we were attacked in the night by about five hundred savage heathen and had to withdraw as best we could. I with my soldiers and various families fled to Mission San Xavier del Bac where we arrived at daybreak.[30]

Had Middendorff been able to hold out, the date of the founding of Tucson might have been pushed back eighteen years. When the new Pima revolt broke out in 1756, however, he was in its path and unable to build on his shaky foundations. The village of Santa Catalina de Cuitabagu, where he made his attempt, cannot now even be located.

Father Espinosa, the resident priest at Bac, may have pushed his natives a little too far and caused the explosion. The Indians, says Henry F. Dobyns, were "goaded into their own nativistic movement" at the time of the great October festival (a major ceremonial to this day) when Espinosa, a zealous, hardheaded black robe, determined to bring events into line with Christian ideals as he understood them.[31] Ritual intoxication, intended as prayer for rain, was his first objective. Many ollas of fermented cactus juice were brought in from secret desert manufactories and given to the people.[32] When Espinosa ordered the omission of this rite, his charges reacted violently. He escaped with his life, but the soldiers and civil authorities were much disturbed, especially when they learned that the Pimas on the Gila River on the north were involved. This warlike and well-organized group was useful in fighting Apaches, dangerous when hostile to the Spaniards.[33] A presidio at Tucson might help keep them in line, and that was one reason for O'Conor's decision to move the Tubac post in 1775. Another was the Apaches, raiders by profession, who moved about when and where they pleased, looking for plunder.

As the eighteenth century progressed, the Apaches became more and more aggressive. They stole the Spaniards' horses, thus becoming mobile. They recruited other Indians who wished to share in the booty.[34] In the 1760s the line of settlements along the Santa Cruz was holding out with the greatest difficulty. Nothing was safe, and no life was secure. Livestock had to be corralled at night. "Mission Indians and settlers alike were terrorized."[35]

Desperate for a remedy, the civil and military authorities tried a policy of concentration. On the San Pedro, east of the Santa Cruz, lived a group of Piman natives called Sobaipuris—good fighters who had given the Apaches some setbacks. In 1762, Captain Francisco Elías González, after considerable effort, persuaded the Sobaipuris to move to the Santa Cruz. He brought the largest group to Tucson and settled them somewhere near the Black Mountain. He called their community Señor San José de Tucson, "because the Sobaipuri settlement occurred on the feast of the Holy Patriarch." He could not foresee the confusion he would cause among later historians by adding another saint to the list of patrons of Tucson.[36]

Moving the Sobaipuris turned out to be a mistake. The hostile tribesmen now swept in without any restraint at all, and as a result the king and his advisers decided to attack the problem in a different way. The Marqués de Rubí was given a royal commission to inspect the northern frontier and recommend measures for an improved defense. He reached Tubac during the Christmas season of 1767, accompanied by an extraordinary engineer named Nicolás de Lafora, who kept a record of the trip. Rubí's proposals led to the New Regulations of 1772, under which the frontier presidios operated for the next fourteen years.[37] Rubí and Lafora agreed that the Tubac presidio, undermanned and unprotected by walls, should be relocated, and they recommended the Tucson site. Rubí noted that the Apaches raided Tubac while his inspection was going forward. [38]

The king approved Rubí's proposals on July 11, 1769, [39] but several years elapsed before the decree could be implemented and O'Conor could be sent to lay out the Tucson presidio. With 3,000 miles of ocean between the Old World and the New and 1,500 miles of difficult travel between Mexico City and the remote frontier, nothing could be done in a hurry. Patience was a necessary virtue in New Spain.

Meanwhile, an unexpected complication occurred. In 1767, King Charles III ordered the expulsion of the Jesuits from the Americas and replacement by the Franciscans. [40] His motives were complex, but he may have had a humanitarian impulse. This was the time of the Enlightenment, and Charles was influenced by reform-minded advisers who thought that the mission Indians were being repressed and enslaved. Never having seen a live Indian and completely unaware of conditions on the frontier, they were sure that kind treatment would bring these primitive people quickly into rapport with European ideas and standards—that even the hostile Apaches would see the error of their ways if they were offered friendship and treated with respect. The mission Indians were no longer to be classed as servants, children, or inferiors. They were to become independent, taxpaying subjects of the Spanish crown, on a par with the Spanish settlers, from whom they had always, at least in theory, been kept separate. [41]

The Jesuit fathers, on the other hand, were convinced that, unless a priest "could provide materially for his Indians and discipline them with authority, he stood little chance of converting them." [42] Civilization

could not be attained in one decade, or in many decades, they thought, and they were not ready to turn over their charges to the secular clergy and the civil authorities. The reformers decided that the Jesuits had to go.

With the greatest secrecy preparations were made to arrest the priests and deport them. There was no warning. When the soldiers appeared at the mission gates all across the land, the fathers were forced to gather up what they could and set out immediately for the nearest concentration point.

The few secular priests in that vast area tried to keep religion alive in the Indian villages after the expulsion, but the missions lost ground both spiritually and temporally. The Indians were told by the civil authorities that mission property now belonged to them, and looting began in some of the abandoned establishments. The Apaches attacked joyfully and vigorously. [43]

When the Franciscans arrived a year later, these conditions made their task harder, but not all of them were dismayed.

There was, for example, Father Francisco Tomás Hermenegildo Garcés Maestro (plain Father Francisco on ordinary occasions), who arrived at San Xavier del Bac in late June, 1768, and started his own campaign to repair the damage. He was a most extraordinary man. A country boy from Aragon, in Spain, he joined the Franciscans at fifteen, was ordained in 1763, and soon thereafter sailed for the New World. [44] At the College of the Holy Cross in Querétaro, the regional headquarters, he impressed his fellow Franciscans as "simple and artless," and they sometimes called him the "children's priest." He seemed an ideal choice to work with the least civilized of the Indians on the farthest frontier, and as it turned out, he was. He was not as pious as some; he got someone else to write his letters and reports when he could; he did not care about the pomp and ceremony of the church; but he did like people, including Indians. He ate their food; he studied their languages; he trusted them and went about among them with a couple of tribesmen as guides and interpreters; and he was content. A born explorer, he was off on an expedition into the wilds within two months of his arrival at Bac, provisioned only with "a little pinole, a little chocolate, and a few strips of dried beef." It was all he needed. "The Indians of one rancheria would escort me to the next," he said, "and everywhere they would provide for the interpreter and me from what they had. Such gifts from among such a people, and with me so poor, are extremely precious."[45]

He was especially interested in the *visita* of Tucson. On July 29, 1768, two weeks after his arrival, he sent a letter to Captain Juan Bautista de Anza, commanding at Tubac, a description of his experiences there. "They are very wild," he reported, and "without doctrine," but they "have not wanted any other priest but me. . . . They have already built me a little hut among their own. Three times I have been there and I have told them that . . . they are my children like those of San Xavier."[46]

Father Pedro Font, a companion on the California trail in 1776, left a priceless picture of this man whom the Indians called "the boy":

Father Garcés is so well suited to get along with the Indians and among them that he appears to be but an Indian himself. Like the Indians he is impassive in everything. He sits with them in the circle, or at night around the fire, with his legs crossed. There he will sit musing two or three hours or more, oblivious to all else, talking with much serenity and deliberation. And though the foods of the Indians are as nasty and dirty as those outlandish people themselves, the father eats them with great gusto, and says they are good for the stomach and delicious. In short, God has created him, as I see it, solely for the purpose of seeking out these unhappy, ignorant, and rustic people.[47]

Did Father Francisco's Roman Catholic conscience trouble him because he "enjoyed frontier life as much as he did?"[48] Henry F. Dobyns suspects that it did, but Garcés does not seem to have been a worrier.

Although they did not become "boon companions,"[49] Garcés and Anza were friends. They agreed that they lived in a "sad province," but they differed on what could be done about it. Anza thought that the Indians were making no progress and recommended dismantling the mission system, leaving the natives to "work for themselves and their own benefit."[50] Naturally Garcés disagreed, but he did complain bitterly to his superiors about his problems and frustrations.

The Apaches were his great problem. By 1769 they were carrying off the mission livestock almost at will. The villagers refused to organize and pursue them, and Garcés admitted sorrowfully that the raiders had finally "won the war of fear and held both Pimas and Spaniards in the palm of their hand."[51]

To complicate the situation, the Sobaipuris, brought in from the San Pedro in 1762, were restless, and some left Tucson to join their cousins on the Gila in 1770. Captain Anza was forced to hurry home from an expedition against the Seris far to the south to look into the matter. "Why," he asked the Tucson headmen, "did your people leave?"

"We have no protection from the Apaches."

"Then we will build a fort."

They still objected. "There is not enough food."

Here Garcés entered the negotiations and

Reenacting Anza's second expedition to California, 1976. Yginio Aguirre, center, as Captain Juan Bautista de Anza; Sidney B. Brinckerhoff, second from left, as Lieutenant Joseph Joachín Moraga. Courtesy Susan Luebberman.

promised more wheat from the mission supply. Since it seemed to be a good time for asking, the leaders added, "We have always wanted a church, but the missionary does nothing."

The priest and the soldier agreed that they should have that too, and that was the start of the most ambitious building program Tucson had seen up to that time—a community building and fortification. Garcés went off on a three-week jaunt to the Gila pueblos to help the Indians there get through an epidemic of measles and bring back the three families of Sobaipuri refugees. When he returned, an adobe defensive wall was rising, and on February 1, 1771, an adobe building with lookout towers was finished. The Apaches gave it their attention the day the last brick was laid, and they were

repulsed with the loss of two Papago boys and some livestock. In 1772, Garcés reported that a church was being erected in the fortified village. He called it San Agustín del Tucson.[52] From this time on, there was never any doubt that San Agustín was the patron saint.[53]

In these years, while the community was putting down roots on the west bank of the Santa Cruz and the wheels which would bring the presidio were slowly turning, Garcés and Anza were discussing a dream which they shared—the opening of a road to the infant Spanish settlements in California. Anza first proposed it to the viceroy in 1772. The venture was discussed and approved by everyone, including the king. In January, 1774, the expedition started from Tubac and arrived at San Diego on March

15

22. The route was changed at the last minute. Just before Anza reached Tubac to lead the little army, Apaches made off with the entire horse herd—130 head. Badly mounted as they were, the men could not risk losing any more of their precious livestock, so they swung southwest through northern Sonora, reaching the Yuma Crossing of the Colorado by way of the Camino del Diablo—the dry and difficult route which would claim the lives of incautious forty-niners seventy-five years later.

The successful completion of this venture opened the door for a larger one. On Monday, October 23, 1775, under skies that threatened rain, Anza's second expedition left Tubac, heading north. Three days later the men camped a few miles beyond Tucson.

The next day they started the long journey to the Gila, the Colorado, and the California coast. The founding of San Francisco followed.

The start was made only two months after O'Conor's choice for the site of the presidio, but as yet there was no sign of military activity. The wheels of the Spanish bureaucracy were slowly revolving, however. The viceroy approved transfer of the Tubac garrison, and O'Conor set a date for it—December 10, 1775. Probably there was some delay. Father Pedro Font, the historian of Anza's second expedition, says that in 1776 "the presidio of Tubac was transferred hither, where it remains still, and is called the Presidio of San Agustín del Tuquisón."[54]

CHAPTER 2

The Presidio and the Pueblito

Juan María Oliva, a career soldier who had risen from the ranks, was the acting post commander at Tucson in 1776.[1] Anza was far away and on the move, first to California and then to Mexico City to report his success and further his career. In 1777, Anza was appointed governor of New Mexico, and Oliva, his second-in-command, was in charge until his replacement arrived.[2] As a result the presidio at Tucson existed for some years only in theory. Oliva had been in the service for almost forty years, was sixty years old, and had been recommended in 1775 for retirement. Undoubtedly he was tired. Furthermore, he was barely able to write his name, and although he was a fine field commander, he was not good at handling the petty details of on-post command. If the fort was to be built, he and his soldiers would have to build it, and they seemed to be in no hurry.[3]

Oliva's second-in-command, Ensign Juan Felipe Belderrain, was even less effective. Son of the first commander of the Tubac post, grandson of Gabriel Mujica, Baron of Heider (an early governor of Sonora), this tall young Basque came from important people and probably owed his commission to their influence. He seems to have pre-

sumed on his position and made himself offensive to his social inferiors. Father Pedro Font, who kept a record of everything at the time of Anza's second expedition to California, flared up when the ensign made a joke about a recent Apache attack, including him among the young wastrels who did nothing but "dance, gamble, and wear many galloons" on their hats.[4] Furthermore, he was heavily in debt—had probably "borrowed" money intended for construction of the post.[5] Juan Felipe was a New World prodigal son. Two years later he was in the guardhouse meditating on his errors, at the lowest point in his career.

It was probably his fault, as much as Oliva's, that not a single brick had been laid at the site of the fort. The men were sleeping in tents, guarding the horse herd (which was pastured some distance from camp), and grumbling about their hard life and the feebleness of their force. Some of them left on detached duty almost as soon as they arrived. A dozen were sent to give what help they could to the people at Tubac, Tumacacori, and Calabasas, in the upper Santa Cruz Valley.[6] Others were detailed to escort important people; a few were on sick leave.

This was the situation on June 12, 1777,

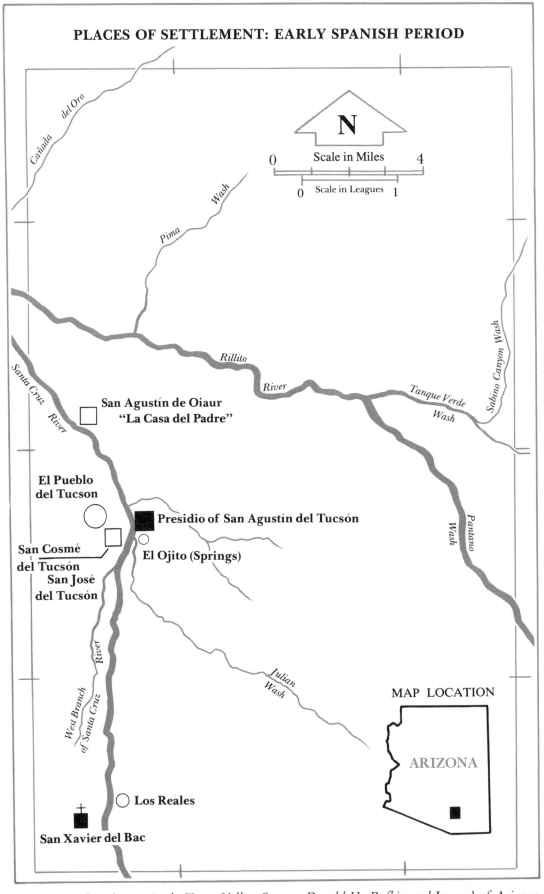

PLACES OF SETTLEMENT: EARLY SPANISH PERIOD

N

Scale in Miles
0   4

Scale in Leagues
0   1

Cañada del Oro

Pima Wash

Santa Cruz River

Rillito River

Sabino Canyon Wash

Tanque Verde Wash

San Agustín de Oiaur
"La Casa del Padre"

El Pueblo
del Tucson

Presidio of San Agustín del Tucsón

San Cosmé
del Tucsón

El Ojito (Springs)

San José
del Tucsón

Pantano Wash

West Branch of Santa Cruz River

Julian Wash

MAP LOCATION

ARIZONA

Los Reales

San Xavier del Bac

Early Spanish settlements in the Tucson Valley. Courtesy Donald H. Bufkin and Journal of Arizona History.

when the new commandant arrived. Captain Don Pedro de Allande y Saabedra was a Spanish nobleman in his mid-thirties, a widower with a grown son who served under him as a junior officer, a proud, precise, indomitable, demanding, irritable Spaniard whose honor was of supreme importance to him. At Guaymas in 1769 he had been confined to quarters when he quarreled with a fellow officer named Jose Antonio Vildosola over a game of cards and challenged him to prove his courage "with the point of his sword."[7]

Allande was as demanding as Oliva had been lax, and he was appalled by what he encountered at his new post. He reported to his superiors that his troops were without discipline and lacked even the means of subsistence; that the post, far from being built, was barely begun; and that there was no inventory to show how much government property had been lost, destroyed, or stolen.[8] Nevertheless, he soon had a post routine set up and the men under control. He even had them behind some semblance of a wall—an earthen breastwork surmounted by a wooden palisade.

The fort by now was at its downtown-Tucson site, across from the mission compound under Sentinel Peak and not far from the *ojito*, the small spring on the east bank of the river. Father Garcés wrote to Governor Alonso de Pineda on August 20, 1775, that the natives had "closed the old site of the Pueblo because of Apaches." The post may have been moved at the same time.[9]

Indian lands were already beginning to pass into the hands of the Spaniards. Presidio captains could make grants to soldiers and settlers (Allande made several), and a dozen families from Tubac left their exposed settlement and sought protection near the new presidio.[10] New buildings arose, including one occupied by Lieutenant José María Abate of the garrison, and more were probably under construction near the mission. One of the new adobe structures may have been a chapel inside Allande's stockade, where Friar Francisco Perdigon, a Franciscan assigned to the post, said mass and heard confessions.[11] The mission across the river was still a *visita* of the church at Bac, which was at this time the charge of Father Juan Bautista Belderrain, brother of Prodigal Son Juan Felipe. The mission and the presidio were only a few hundred yards apart, but they were divided by a pond or marsh in the riverbed and by two irrigation ditches. The area between the *acequias* was known as *la isla*, "the island."[12] Thus the "Two Majesties," as the Spaniards spoke of them, were in proper balance with the king's men on one side of the bridge across the riverbed and the ditches and God's representatives on the other.

In New Spain the Two Majesties did not always get along. Father Perdigon and Captain Allande could not abide each other. Each was jealous of his own powers and privileges, and Perdigon finally applied for a transfer,[13] leaving the captain and his soldiers to concentrate on preparing for the next assault by the Apaches.

Discipline was Allande's watchword. An inspector in 1779 reprimanded him for using "cruel and improper punishments to maintain discipline, and for employing soldiers and Indian scouts in his private business affairs."[14] The official did not recommend corrective action, probably noting that the commandant's harshness got results. At the end of his career at Tucson in 1786, however, Governor Jacobo Ugarte y Loyola in a letter to the viceroy remarked that Allande's "violent and valiant temperament makes it difficult to serve under him and that he has often been corrected for it." [15]

In 1779 only fifty-nine of the seventy-seven presidials were "effective" One of the ineffectives was former Ensign Juan Felipe Belderrain, who was serving time in the guardhouse, no longer able to dance and gamble and wear many galloons on his hat. He had been discharged on recommendation of O'Conor in 1776 and replaced by First Ensign Diego de la Oya, a native of Spain. [16] The other two ensigns were career soldiers, born in the New World. The Spanish caste system was clearly at work in Tucson. A Spanish nobleman was in charge. Criollos (Spaniards born in Mexico) ranked high and often achieved leadership. Men of lesser family could be promoted from the ranks, but the road was long and hard. At the same time, as Oakah L. Jones points out, on the frontier "class rivalry and distinction had little place except for statistical purposes." [17]

The men in the ranks were divided into two groups—the heavy cavalry, or *soldados de cuera*, so called from their leather-jacket armor, and a faster, lighter unit called a flying company intended for quick action and fast pursuit. The garrison included ten Indian scouts under a corporal. Classification of the men according to racial origin showed several types of mixed bloods. "Clearly," says Henry F. Dobyns, "racial mixture was well advanced in this garrison." [18]

The Tucson company in 1779, thanks to Allande's vigilance and drive, was in better shape than many others along the frontier. The men had been issued new uniforms in 1778. They were well drilled, and they could shoot: "The commandant general of the Frontier Provinces considered the Tucson unit the only one in Sonora well trained in the use of firearms." [19] They were also provided with the long lance, always effective

if the Indians could be brought to close quarters. Historians who paint gloomy pictures of the "chaotic discipline" and "inefficiency of administration within the presidios" [20] are not talking about Allande's troops at Tucson. His cavalry was as ready as their commander could make them for the campaigns just ahead.

The man who was to send them into action was a Frenchman who had risen to high rank in the Spanish army and had become the commandant general of the Interior Provinces of New Spain in 1776. Teodoro de Croix was a persistent, farseeing, enormously competent administrator who finally succeeded in organizing an effective campaign against the Apaches. His office carried with it powers almost equal to those of the viceroy, and he could have brought order out of the frontier chaos. He almost did—with the help of a few competent leaders, such as Allande, and their cavalrymen. [21]

His appointment was, in effect, an act of desperation. All across the northern provinces the Apaches and their allies and converts were murdering and robbing and burning almost at will. Croix, a last hope, was ready to mount a counterattack, but he could not make an all-out effort because Viceroy Antonio María de Bucareli y Ursúa, who controlled the funds, could not be persuaded that heroic measures were needed. When Croix tried to convince him that "great disasters" and eventual ruin were close at hand, he argued that things were not that bad. Even when he saw the statistics—1,674 persons murdered, 154 captured, 116 haciendas and ranches abandoned, and 68,256 head of livestock stolen, besides much unrecorded loss of life and property—he still delayed. [22]

The settlements on the Santa Cruz were a prime example of what was wrong. At one time the Tucson post was without meat, butter, and candles. In fact, the only commodity the presidio had enough of was Apaches.[23] In 1777 the Indians ran off the last of the cattle and horses belonging to the settlers at Tubac. In 1779 they began active warfare against the post at Tucson.

Croix told his captains to do the best they could. In May, acting on his orders, Allande made the first sortie in reprisal, leading seventy-nine soldiers and Piman auxiliaries (hired out of his own pocket) on an ineffectual search-and-destroy mission. In October the raiders countered by stealing five horses and a mule and eluding pursuit. On November 6 a large number (Allande said 350) approached the fort, but Allande led fifteen of his cavalrymen in a long running battle in which several Apaches were killed. The captain cut off the head of one, an important leader, placed it on the point of his lance, and thereby (he said) scared the remaining warriors into flight. The gruesome trophy was displayed over the presidio gate, and as time went on, others decorated the wall of the fort.[24] Whether this butchery had its intended effect on the Apaches is debatable.

Indians and Spaniards traded blows, each side losing men, in the final months of 1779.[25] As 1780 opened, the pace stepped up. Father Perdigon, the disgruntled post chaplain, was slain far to the south. There were killings at Tumacacori and villages farther away. In July, 1781, an Indian uprising at the Yuma Crossing took the lives of several people from Bac and Tucson, including that of the remarkable Father Garcés.[26] Then, on May 1, 1782, came the crucial battle which could have resulted in the destruction of Tucson—fort, mission, pueblo, and all. Henry F. Dobyns has published the fullest translation of the documents which tell the story.[27]

It was a typical quiet Tucson spring Sunday. Father Belderrain had come up from Bac to say mass in the mission chapel. Father Gabriel Franco, Perdigon's replacement, did the same at the presidio chapel and then strolled across the bridge to join the visitors at the mission. The twenty soldiers inside the fortification (the rest were away on detached duty or were out with the horse herd) were not expecting trouble, and neither were their officers. Lieutenant Abate, who lived in a house near the stockade, had slept late and at ten in the morning was just about to finish dressing. His commander, fortunately, was attending to some business near the entrance to the fort, where two of the post's small cannon were mounted. At that moment Abate's servant came running into the house shouting, "The Apaches! The Apaches are coming!"

Allande estimated later that there were 600 of them. They could have overrun the fort and the village, leaving few or no survivors, but they ran into stiff resistance. Abate went up to his roof and began shooting down the attackers, who had to take cover. Allande stood off the first attack at the entrance, which was not yet provided with a gate, with the help of one civilian and one soldier. "They shot the deponent's right leg through and through," Allande reported, despite which he killed two by his own hand after being wounded, continuing to direct from the bulwarks and the stockade (a soldier serving him as support) such a heavy fire that they were obliged to retire with heavy losses."

The final act of the drama came when, on Allande's order, a soldier climbed the embankment and touched off one of the cannon. The noise and smoke turned the tide, and the attack ceased.

Another stout defense was made at the

Cal Peters's visualization of the Presidio of San Agustín del Tucson.

bridge connecting the fort and the mission. When the firing started, Ensign Ygnacio Felix Usárraga was visiting the pueblo, accompanied by none other than the once-scandalous Juan Felipe Belderrain, who had reenlisted as a private soldier following his discharge from the service. This was a great descent for a man of his rank and pretensions, but it apparently did not cost him the regard or the companionship of the post officers. Both men were armed, and when the battle commenced, they headed for the bridge on the double. There they found themselves face to face with a great number of Apaches who were about to cross. "They tried forcefully to advance over the island to the pueblo," Usárraga reported later, but the two men were able to hold them off and eventually drive them back.

Juan Felipe's bravery at the bridge gave evidence of a change in his life and his attitudes. The records of the post inspection of 1783 show that his debts had been paid and that he had a credit of seventeen pesos in the presidio accounts. How he accomplished this miracle cannot now be known, but he was on his way to better days.[28]

It took some time for the community to recover from this harrowing experience, even longer than for Allande's wound to heal. One good result was the erection, at long last, of an adobe wall around the fort. It was paid for by Lieutenant Abate.[29] A ditch dug along the base provided the material for the adobe bricks, and formed a moat when it rained.[30] The walls, when completed, were three feet thick at the base and rose ten to twelve feet high around a quadrangle about 300 yards

The same area from the air in 1954. Courtesy Donald H. Bufkin.

on a side, making it one of the largest posts on the northern frontier. There was one main gate opening on the Camino Real (Royal Road), now Main Street in downtown Tucson, about where the county courthouse stands today, and there was a smaller entrance on the east side. Pennington Street, which lies along the south side of the courthouse, runs approximately at the base of the south wall of the old fortification.[31] The commandant's residence was inside, along with a guardhouse, a small chapel (paid for by Allande), storerooms, and offices. As time went on, houses were constructed for some of the soldiers, backed up against the wall. The roofs of these structures were the right height for use by sentries, the wall itself being used as a breastwork. Over the entrance was

Spanish presidial soldiers, with shields and leather jackets, under Indian attack. Watercolor by Jack Schlichting.

a platform for the small cannon, and there may have been a bastion at the northeast corner. Space was provided along the north wall for stabling part of the horse herd, but most of the time the animals were pastured out on the mesa, sometimes a considerable distance from the post.

There was never another attack as massive as the May Day encounter, but after that notable defense both sides stepped up the tempo of assault and pursuit. The Indians gained a measure of revenge on Christmas Day, 1782, when they rounded up and drove off the community's cattle herd—200 head. Allande's men set off in hot pursuit, led by Juan Antonio Oliva, son of the retired commandant (the captain's wound had not yet healed). The troop came back with the livestock and the heads of six slain Apaches.[32]

In 1783, Allande was ready to embark on

a major offensive, in accordance with the plans of Commandant General de Croix, and for the next five years he was a busy and effective field commander. He used Pima auxiliaries, sometimes paying them out of his own funds,[33] and hunted the enemy down in his own domain. He ranged through the Catalinas and the mountains beyond, killing warriors and taking prisoners, much to the satisfaction of his superiors, who recommended him for promotion.[34] Croix's objective was to wipe out every single Apache, and Allande was bringing him closer to his goal.

In 1784 he was ready to undertake a coordinated effort to sweep the entire desert empire of Apachería and finish the enemy in a mighty slaughter. Five columns penetrated the Apache homeland on the upper Gila, and once more Allande proved to be the most effective of the Spanish leaders. Again he was recommended for promotion, and this time someone was listening.[35]

His promotion to lieutenant colonel, however, created a problem for him. It might not have troubled anyone but a Spanish officer, but he asked for relief:

The deponent finds it impossible to continue this labor because of the wounds which he received in his right leg which have hurt the nerves, as well as because of the present aggravation of seeing the arms of this Province commanded by an Adjutant Inspector Don Roque de Medina, who has only the rank of captain.[36]

This complaint gained favorable consideration by the new governor, Jacobo Ugarte y Loyola, who allowed Allande to retire to Horcasitas, in Sonora, to regain his health while the king decided what to do with him. The last we hear of him, he is on his way to Mexico City with a retinue of servants, nine small children (all girls), and a new daughter born in Culiacán on March 15, 1788. He complained to the viceroy of "insults to person and position" as he contended with servants and innkeepers while approaching the capital in July.[37] Life was never easy for Allande, but he never gave in to it.

Meanwhile his old command fought the Apaches vigorously, keeping them on the run. The settlers were comparatively safe—at least safer than they had been—and were prospering.[38] When Bernardo de Gálvez became viceroy in 1785, however, the situation changed radically. De Croix had departed in 1783 without destroying all the Apaches. The commandancy had been divided into three parts, under the viceroy, creating problems for everybody. These and other considerations induced Gálvez to adopt a completely new strategy beginning in 1786.[39]

The Apaches were to be harried until they were ready to give in. Then they would be allowed to sue for peace, make treaties, and settle near the Spanish towns. Supplies were to be issued, including liquor and firearms. The crafty Gálvez specified, however, that the arms were to be of inferior quality and that the liquor was intended to enslave the natives.

The new policy worked. Hard-hitting forays brought the Apaches closer to capitulation, and by 1788 they were coming in to settle and be fed. As a result New Spain enjoyed twenty years of unprecedented peace and prosperity. For a while conversion of the tribesmen to Spanish ways seemed at least possible. Friar Diego Bringas of Bac noted at the end of the century that they knew all about drinking, gambling, prostitution, and obscene language, though he did not feel that this sort of proficiency was an indication of progress.[40]

Apaches began coming in to other communities as early as 1787, but Tucson did not acquire an Indian population until 1793, when Chief Nautil Nilché of the Arivaipa band, at home in the mountains along the Gila, brought in ninety-four men, women, and children for settlement. Later arrivals brought the total to 107. Captain Manuel de Echeagaray, the regional commander, provided them with beef, wheat, maize, cigarettes, and *panoche* (brown sugar cakes).[41] They built their wickiups beside the Santa Cruz at the northern end of the settlement, and there they lived for two decades, doing as little as possible to conform to the white man's work ethic but staying more or less out of trouble. Some of the Apache clans did not get along with each other, and in 1819 Commandant Antonio de Narbona sent one quarrelsome group to a new home at the fort and pueblo of Santa Cruz, a safe distance away in the Santa Cruz Valley.[42] As the Spaniards pursued holdouts in the mountains and more Indians came in, there were more dissensions, but they were always worked out,[43] and the country was comparatively free of trouble.

It was even possible to open up new avenues of trade and travel. Two serious attempts were made to find a road through the wilderness to New Mexico, the first in 1786 under Echeagaray; the second in 1795, led by Captain José de Zúñiga, the post commander at Tucson. The first ran out of provisions on the San Francisco River beyond the Gila and had to return.[44] Zúñiga, a veteran soldier in the Allande tradition,[45] led a force of 148 men as far as Zuñi, in New Mexico, but was unable to go any farther.[46]

It is worth noting here that Juan Felipe Belderrain went along with Zúñiga as an officer, having just been promoted to first ensign. His recovery from disgrace had been slow, but it had been sure, and it could only have been the result of diligence and determination.

The Tucson detachment returned on May 29, disappointed because it had failed to reach the New Mexico capital and because it had not been able to do much damage to the Apaches. The troop brought back only one captive warrior, four "others," and "five pairs of ears" removed from dead tribesmen.[47]

Zúñiga, who seems to have left the post in 1803, was followed by a succession of capable commanders, most of whom had grown up in the service. The fort was a busy place, with soldiers coming and going on escort duty and guard duty at Bac and other communities. The full complement was about a hundred men, but in 1817, says Dobyns, there were only fourteen regulars, one carabineer, and one corporal on duty. Nine men were in the hospital. The garrison was scarcely a skeleton force. Dobyns points out that there was still considerable "ethnic stratification" at the fort with persons of noble blood at the top and natives and mixed-bloods at the bottom. Neither on nor off the post was there anything that could be called a middle class—no professional people, a few merchants or traders, no large landowners.[48] The population, however, was growing slowly—77 persons in 1777, 300 in 1804, 500 in 1819,[49] counting only Spaniards.

A picture of the industrial base of the community can be gained in some detail from a report submitted in 1804 to the Real Consulado (a government bureau much like a chamber of commerce) by Commandant Zúñiga of the Tucson presidio. The total population, Spanish, native, and mixed, was 1,015. The people occupied an area less than two miles square. Their only mineral

resource was a lime pit. The only public work "truly worthy of report" in the whole region was the recently completed Church of San Xavier del Bac. The settlers grew corn, wheat, beans, and vegetables but no cotton. The Indians produced some cotton for their own use. The cattle herd numbered 3,500 head; the sheep flocks 2,600; the horse herd 1,200. Half the soap used locally was made in the pueblo, but "no brandy, whiskey or tequila is distilled. No gunpowder, chinaware or glass is manufactured." There was no saddlemaker, weaver, tanner, tailor, hatter, or shoemaker. Most of the men were engaged in agriculture or stock raising, but Zúñiga complained that they did as little work as possible. "I have observed," he said, "that there is very fertile land here. Why do the settlers not prosper when even neglected vineyards produce a bumper crop? They hardly allow the grape to mature before they are selling it."[50]

In spite of their lack of industry, or because of it, the Spaniards enjoyed life—or would have if the Apaches had let them. Little has been left to tell us about the day-to-day existence of those people at the turn of the century, but one old, old woman opened the door of memory a little way in 1873 when she was interviewed by former governor A. P. K. Safford and pioneer merchant Samuel Hughes for the *Arizona Citizen*. Mariana Díaz was more than one hundred years old at the time and had lived through the last half century of Spanish and Mexican control. "She referred to the pleasant times they used to have, when their wants were few and easily supplied, and told how they danced and played and enjoyed themselves." Crime, she said, was almost unknown. There was plenty of mescal, "But it was only on rare occasions that they drank to excess, and then they acted to each other like brothers." If it had not been for the Apaches, "they would not have known what trouble was." Her husband and many of her relatives had died in Indian attacks.[51]

Recent investigations tend to show that the Tucsonenses were not always kind to each other. In the year 1813, for example, María Ignacia Castelo was found murdered in her home at Bac. The prime suspect was her cowboy husband, Francisco Xavier Díaz, who took refuge in the chapel at Tucson. Father Pedro de Arriquibar, the chaplain, persuaded him to give himself up, and he was tried in a local court. He confessed to the murder but pleaded that the woman had had relations with "a Pima, named Juan from the Tucson Pueblito." Testimony showed that Francisco had beaten his wife regularly, that she had never shown the least sign "of even thinking about being unfaithful," and that Juan Francisco Pacheco, the supposed lover, had been in her house only once to ask for a drink of water. Kieran McCarty, who found and translated the trial transcript, was unable to determine the husband's sentence, but he thinks it probable that Díaz was garrotted in the latter part of 1818 at the Tucson presidio.[52]

At the end of the Spanish period, just before the revolution of 1821, Tucson was a moderately prosperous village in which Spaniards and Indians lived side by side, but the native population was slowly but steadily giving way to Hispanics and mixed-bloods. Retired soldiers were occupying fields which had once belonged to the Papagos, though they were not allowed to take possession of lands controlled by the mission. Other Spaniards had come up from the south in response to the settlement law of 1791, which set aside four square leagues around each presidio for settlers.[53] There was trouble between mission Indians and

settlers, giving a preview of problems that were to plague the community for many years to come.[54]

The people in this remote outpost seldom had contact with the outside world. Few of them could read or write, and books were scarce. The fathers did some teaching at the *convento*, but they were primarily interested in religious education and in developing the vocational skills of their students. The church calendar, with its saints' days and festivals, gave a special pattern to daily life, but it may have promoted rather than prevented the sinfulness of the ordinary citizens. Padre Arriquibar was so grieved by the wanton ways of his men and women that he "was almost ready to abandon the enterprise and retire to my convent."[55] Father Antonio de los Reyes, who became the first bishop of Sonora, said in 1772 that they were a rascally crew of opportunists without scruples or conscience.[56] In other words, they were human.

The most conspicuous sign of Tucson's growing importance was the *convento*, a massive two-story structure built sometime between 1797 and 1804 at or near the mission under Sentinel Peak. Father Juan Baptista Llorens, who in 1797 completed the great church at San Xavier del Bac begun by Father Belderrain, may have been responsible for its construction. It was gutted and abandoned when the missions were secularized in 1828, but its walls were still standing in the early years of the next century, and one of the great oversights of the municipal government of Tucson over the decades was its negligence in allowing this monument to be carried away, brick by brick, and finally disappear under a city dump.[57]

The most prominent representative of the church during the first two decades of the new century, and one of Tucson's most interesting and unusual human beings, was Father Pedro de Arriquibar, the post chaplain, a portly, fussy, sometimes distracted, but very responsible Spanish Franciscan, who began his work in the New World in Baja California in 1771. He came to Tumacacori, near Tubac, in 1774 or 1775 and was there when Anza set out for California on his first expedition. He remained until about 1780 in spite of Apache attacks which left practically nothing of value in his mission and village. At Caborca, in Sonora, where he labored from 1780 to 1794, he became a chaplain in the Spanish army and was transferred to the Tucson post a few years later. In 1797 he made an inventory of the furnishings of the presidio chapel and drew up a census of the 395 inhabitants of post and pueblo, excluding Indians.[58] Their descendants are still at home in Tucson.

Close to Father Arriquibar's heart was the family of Juan J. Ramírez and his wife, Manuela Sosa. They became friends in 1775, when duty brought Padre Pedro to Tumacacori to take care of the frightened little flock there. Juan was the son of old Crisóstomo Ramírez, who in 1776 took on the hopeless task of organizing a local militia company when the troops moved from nearby Tubac to Tucson. The son was listed on the mission records as "Spanish and interpreter," which may mean that he had learned the Piman language as a boy. There were five children, of whom Teodoro was Arriquibar's godson and favorite.[59] Three other children are mentioned in his will. There were many orphans in the Indian country.

Father Pedro needed someone to take care of him. He was always behind. His correspondence was often neglected, and he complained to his superiors about his multifarious duties. Twenty years later he was still complaining. "I have to do everything but ring the bells," he said. Once he forgot to record a baptism, thereby causing trouble for the child many years later when she wanted to get married.[60] Juan and Manuela were his refuge.

When in due time they died, the good priest took charge of all the children—something hardly possible on his little stipend—and that was why he became an army chaplain. He needed the salary. To make sure he was on safe ground, he secured a papal dispensation allowing him to keep and dispose of any goods he might acquire while holding this office. "I declare," he said, as his last days approached, "that during some forty years in which they have been under my care and in my company, I have reared the family of my late compadre Juan José Rámirez and Manuela Sosa, now dead. . . . I have not permitted them to be deprived of anything." Teodoro was still his favorite, his right hand, and his heir, "the guardian of my old age."[61]

An inventory of his possessions was included in his will. The property included a small house, a few clothes, fifty books (the largest and perhaps the only library in Tucson), forty head of cattle, twenty-seven horses and mules, and about 600 pesos in cash. It was enough to make Teodoro one of the wealthiest men in the village when it all became his on Father Pedro's death on September 17, 1820. It enable him to get married, set up a store inside the presidio walls, and become a collector of books and documents. He refused to let anyone else use them, or even look at them, but his neighbors forgave him. When he died of old age in Tucson at ninety-four in July, 1871, he was remembered as "an honored and faithful officer."[62] Father Pedro would have been proud.

CHAPTER 3

The Yanqui Invasion

To the Tucson *vecinos*—the neighbors, the people—in 1820, the outside world barely existed. When Mariana Díaz looked back over her hundred years of memory, she recalled that when she was growing up she had never heard of California.[1] The new ideas which were changing everything in Europe may have been echoed in Padre Arriquibar's little library, but not even he could foresee the great changes that were coming.

In Europe the French Revolution had come and gone. In the United States political fanatics had declared that all men were created free and equal and had thrown out their British overlords. The infection had spread to Mexico, and Father Miguel Hidalgo y Costilla's revolt had flared up in 1810, giving the underdogs, for a few months, hope of a better day.[2] The aristocrats in Spain and Mexico labored to prevent the spread of dangerous doctrines, and subversive ideas were slow to reach San Agustín de Tucson, where life went on as it always had with its sowing and reaping, its fiestas and dances, its tame Apaches huddled in their flimsy shelters north of the settlement, its wild Apaches in the Santa Catalinas, its occasional murders and adulteries.[3] Who

could dream of a revolution in such an environment? The tidal wave of history was moving, however, and the old days were almost over.

The Spanish king was no longer all-powerful. Napoleon had invaded the Peninsula and overthrown the monarchy, and with the weakening of the authority to which they had been subservient for centuries, the ruling class in Mexico began to think about independence from Spain. This ruling class was divided into two opposing groups—the gachupins (Spaniards born in Spain) and the creoles (Spaniards born in the New World). The gachupins assumed that their European origin entitled them to an extra measure of respect and to the highest social and political positions. The native-born colonials were by no means convinced that they deserved second place. The two groups were united on one point, however; a firm opposition to creeping democracy. God intended the government and the wealth to belong to men of blood and family. Hidalgo and his paisanos (countrymen) must be put down.

By 1820, when the Spanish Empire was breaking up, gachupins and creoles found themselves in opposition. The native-born

Spaniards were ready to strike a blow for liberty, which meant liberty to run the country themselves. The bishops and the church, alarmed by the growing unrest, were on their side, and events in Spain impelled them to action. Early in 1820 rebels in Spain had forced the king to set up a constitutional government and move toward democracy and social justice. Spanish anticlericals seized some church property. Liberals insisted on the liberation of political prisoners. In Mexico the churchmen and the hidalgos (nobles), horrified by these evidences of madness in the world, took matters into their own hands. Agustín Iturbide, a creole officer and landowner, was chosen to spearhead the revolt, and in September, 1821, he entered Mexico City and called himself—for a year—emperor of Mexico. His manifesto, the "Plan de Iguala," was subscribed to by many provincial authorities in the north, beginning with Intendant General Alexo García de Conde.[4] José Romero, in command at Tucson, undoubtedly signed with the rest.[5] For the next three decades the community carried on much as before, but the flag of Mexico flew above the walls, and the people of the village were *ciudadanos* (citizens) instead of *vecinos*.[6]

One important change involved the "Apaches de Paz" (peaceable Apaches), camped near the settlement. When the disturbances began in 1810, the economy of the country was disrupted. *Insurrectos* destroyed the haciendas and stole the cattle. The mines were abandoned and flooded. Food production fell off. It was hard to get anything done. As a result, there were no rations for the peaceable Apaches. Hungry and resentful, many of them went back to the wilds and resumed their old life of raiding. Twenty years of peace were over.[7]

Signs of disintegration were visible every-

where. The presidios fell into disrepair. Church buildings were neglected, especially after the missions were secularized in 1828, and the Tucson *convento* went with the rest. In 1843, when it was finally abandoned, Joaquín Quiroga, of Cucurpe, made an inspection and reported to his superiors in Guaymas that this once-handsome structure was without windows or doors and the roof was falling in. The orchard no longer bore fruit. The Indians had stopped paying rent for the land they worked. It was a sad spectacle.[8]

Even sadder was the decline of the native population in the Tucson Valley. Diseases brought by the Europeans had decimated the Papagos over the decades, and the birthrate had fallen below replacement level. Many individuals had been absorbed into the mestizo population. In the middle Santa Cruz Valley only two Indian communities survived—Bac and Tucson.[9]

The general breakdown included an interruption in the keeping of records and reports, and it is difficult to find out what was happening in Tucson at the end of the Mexican period. There is evidence, however, that the northern provinces were trying to break out of the isolation which had been their lot for more than a century. In 1822, Captain José Romero of the Tucson presidio received orders to open a mail route from the post to the settlements in California by way of the Gila Trail, which had been disused since 1781, when Padre Garcés was murdered at the Yuma Crossing. Before Romero took any action, however, a group from California under Padre Felix Caballero reached Tucson and went on to the capital at Arispe. In June, 1823, having received new orders, Romero finally put together an expedition and hit the trail. All went well until a too-friendly band of natives at the Yuma

Crossing helped the travelers build rafts, pushed them into the flooded river, and abandoned them in midstream. They managed to reach the west bank, where they watched helplessly while the happy warriors across the channel divided up their supplies, their horses, and even their clothes, which they had removed before they took to the water. Destitute and practically naked, they barely made it to Mission Santa Catalina, in Baja California. Romero had to mark time in California until the fall of 1825 on account of Indian outbreaks which made it impossible to provide him with an escort. He was in favor, naturally, of abandoning the Yuma Crossing, but it eventually was used by pilgrims of all kinds on their way to the West Coast.[10]

All these tokens of change in northern Mexico were important, but even more significant changes were just ahead, brought on by the arrival of a strange and alien group— the American traders and trappers, mountain men who were described by their countrymen as "intrepid" and "hardy" and by the Mexicans as "lawless" and "dangerous." Mexico's "protectionist wall" came down in 1821, and trade routes opened up between the Missouri settlements and New Mexico.[11] Hugh Glenn and Jacob Fowler, who led a caravan to Santa Fe in 1821, immediately took out a license to trap the headwaters of the Rio Grande in Colorado, and others followed.[12] In 1824 a government decree made fur hunting illegal but the traffic continued.[13] James Ohio Pattie trapped the "Helay" in 1825, bringing frontier Americans within two days' ride of Tucson. After Jedediah Smith pioneered a route to California from Utah, crossing the Colorado at Needles,[14] many trappers followed the Gila to the West Coast. So many of them entered the Gila country that in 1826 the Mexican

government took official notice and protested to Washington—without perceptible effect.

Four parties are known to have trapped the Arizona rivers in 1826–27, and there may have been more. Ceran St. Vrain spent four days at the Pima village north of Tucson. The Indians were not unfriendly, but they stole mules, blankets, and papers and finally sent off a messenger to Tucson to inform the commandant. Don Ignacio Pacheco sent eight men to bring in the intruders, but the Americans heard about the messenger and decamped three days before the soldiers arrived, postponing the first contact.

Other parties came to trap after 1826, fighting the Indians and sometimes stealing horses from them,[15] living off the country and coming near starvation in it. In 1831, David E. Jackson, on his way to the West Coast to buy mules for resale in the United States, took his party to Tucson. Among his men was J. J. Warner, who left an account of the journey. Had Warner known how much value posterity would place on a description of the town, he might have recorded his impressions. He had other things on his mind, however, and spent only six words on the post and community: "a military post and a small town."[16] The party stayed for some time, hoping to find a guide who knew the Gila Trail. When none could be found, they started without one, reached their goal, and returned with the mules.[17]

The outbreak of the Mexican War in 1846 gave the Tucsonenses their first look at American soldiers. They missed Stephen Watts Kearny, who passed through the Pima villages on his way to California,[18] but the young men of the famous Mormon Battalion marched straight through the town.

This unusual organization was sworn in

31

Careful soldier: Lieutenant Colonel Philip St. George Cooke. Courtesy Library of Congress.

at Council Bluffs, Iowa, with the encouragement of Brigham Young, the Mormon leader. He had several reasons for backing the project. Participation in the war effort could give his people some badly needed credit in Washington and would ensure the safe passage of several hundred of his men to the Far West, where he was planning to establish a permanent home for the faithful. Kearny assigned command to a stern and severe career officer, Lieutenant Colonel Philip St. George Cooke, who was not at all happy with his orders but accepted them like the good soldier he was and, in spite of initial misunderstandings and later hardships, brought his mission to a successful end. [19]

His expedition was the first to use wagons on a transcontinental journey, and he had to look for a route negotiable by his rumbling vehicles. He crossed southern New Mexico in November, 1846, leaving his name on

Cooke's Peak and Cooke's Spring, north of Deming. [20] At the southwestern corner of the future state he headed into Old Mexico, negotiated the difficult Guadalupe Pass (where he had to lower his wagons with ropes), paused at the now-deserted San Bernardino Ranch, later the home of Tombstone Sheriff John Slaughter, and headed northwest for the San Pedro. [21]

There were wild cattle in the river bottom and on December 11 several of the men with hunting rifles got permission to shoot some of them for meat. Wounded and furious, several bulls charged the column and sent the startled soldiers into a shooting spree which gained the engagement the title "Battle of the Bulls." It was the only battle the battalion fought on its way to California. [22]

The caravan camped at today's Benson before heading toward Tucson. Word of its approach was taken to Captain Antonio Comaduran at the presidio by a party of Apaches who were making mescal at a shack along the route. [23] Excitement grew in the village and in the fort. The captain's orders were to defend the post and not allow the Americans in without a fight, but his force consisted of only a hundred men, and he knew that resistance would be useless, perhaps suicidal. He decided to try diplomacy. He sent out three emissaries, one of them his son, with a message for Lieutenant Colonel Cooke. [24]

Meanwhile Cooke was making some decisions of his own. First he sent Stephen F. Foster, a young Yale graduate known as "Dr. Foster," who had requested the assignment, to move ahead of the column and spy out the land. [25] Then he assembled the battalion and put the men through a rigorous drill with their weapons. Finally he issued a set of instructions which read in part:

We came not to make war against Sonora, and less still to destroy an unimportant outpost of defense against Indians. But we will take the straight course before us and overcome all resistance. But shall I remind you that the American soldier ever shows justice and kindness to the unarmed and unresisting? The property of individuals you will hold sacred. The people of Sonora are not our enemies.[26]

At 8:00 A.M. on December 14, Cooke started his men up the long slope out of San Pedro Valley. Foster had not reappeared, and he was worried. He was still worried when he came to the Apache "stillhouse," about fifteen or twenty miles west, where he found Comaduran's messengers waiting for him.[27] A Mexican sergeant delivered the message—a request that Cooke not enter the town but go around it. Cooke sent back a reply assuring the Mexicans that "we were not their enemies but friends, who wanted to purchase flour, etc."[28] He heard that Foster was confined and guarded in Tucson and held several Mexicans as hostages for his safety. Foster returned at midnight the next day, December 16. Two officers accompanied him and continued Comaduran's diplomatic effort. Without replying to their suggestions, Cooke made one of his own— that the commander surrender two cavalry carbines and three lances as assurance of nonresistance.[29] The tension in Tucson undoubtedly rose when this proposal was delivered, but, although the commandant sent word he could not in honor submit to a surrender of arms,[30] he found a way out. He and his men evacuated the fort and marched to San Xavier, taking all public property with them. When the Americans entered the outskirts of the town, Cooke reminded his troops again that the United States was not at war with the people of Sonora[31] and then marched them through the village and halted them at a campsite on the other side. An Englishman who marched with the battalion remarked, with wry humor, that the Mexican soldiers had decamped "in time to save their bacon and ours too."[32]

Several of the soldiers kept journals of the long march, and they all paid tribute to the kindness and goodwill of the Tucsonenses. "The author remembers with much gratitude," wrote Sergeant Daniel Tyler, "the silver-haired Mexican, of perhaps more than three score years and ten, who, when signs of thirst were given, ran to the brook as fast as his tottering limbs could carry him, dipped up his water, and almost out of breath but with cheerful countenance, delivered the refreshing and much-needed draft." Robert W. Bliss must have had a similar experience. He wrote in his journal, "The people here are the most friendly and intelligent I have seen of all the Spaniards."[33]

Cooke himself encouraged good relations when he walked back from the camp to the village. "At first," says Daniel Tyler, "some of the women were much frightened, but, on receiving only kindness, from both officers and soldiers, their excitement was allayed, and they showed strong signs of gratitude."[34]

This contact, on December 17, 1846, was the first important face-to-face encounter in Tucson of Mexican and Yanqui, and kindness and courtesy prevailed. Later contacts were not always so pleasant, but basic respect between the "better" elements of both groups continued down through the years.

The next day the men rested and did a little trading with the townspeople, bringing away wheat, fruit, salt, and flour.[35] They made observations on how things were done in Mexico—grinding flour between millstones with a burro for motive power, for example.

On the seventeenth, Cooke reconnoitered in the direction of Bac but decided not to go all the way, thus sparing the Mexican force further embarrassment. He made the whole adventure sound like a courtesy call when he apologized in writing to Captain Comaduran for "having to break up your quarters at the post" and took pains to inform Governor Manuel Gándara of Sonora of his passage: "Be assured I do not come as an enemy of the people you represent; they have received only kindness at my hands."[36] On the eighteenth he left for the Gila and the trail to California.

The next contact with American troops was on a less high and idealistic plane. Sometime late in 1847 a command of sixty men, headed by one Lieutenant Schoonmaker, left Fort Bliss, near El Paso, Texas, with dispatches for General Kearny in California. Among them was a soldier named F. Adams, who recalled these events in 1889 for a Tucson reporter. The detachment reached Tucson in November, he recalled, planning to ride in boldly and take the fort. They rode boldly in, but the troops were safely inside the presidial compound. There was an exchange of shots, and one mule belonging to the Americans was killed. The invaders camped under the walls for four days. On the fifth day a detail of five men from Fort Bliss arrived with orders to abandon the expedition and return to the post.[37]

This episode, if it happened, would have been the lowest point in Mexican-American relations had it not been for the peculiar genius of Major Lawrence F. Graham, who late in 1848 led a column of United States troops from Monterrey, Mexico, to California, passing through Tucson en route.[38] The war had left few emotional or physical scars in this remote region, and the commandant at the presidio was prepared to extend what

hospitality he could. Early on the morning after the troops' arrival, he paid a courtesy call at the major's tent and found that Graham, already drunk, had staggered off to inspect the town.[39] Two soldiers left a record of the episode. One was Samuel E. ("Peloncillo Jack") Chamberlain, whose *My Confession* (subtitled *The Adventures of a Rogue*) was a publishing find of 1956. Sam was sketching the San Xavier Mission when Graham caught him at it, demanded to know what the hell he knew about art, threw the sketchbook in his face, and had him tied up and handcuffed. The next day Peloncillo Jack deserted with the intention of joining John Glanton and his notorious company of scalp hunters somewhere off to the west.[40]

A more responsible member of the command, Lieutenant Cave Johnson Couts, expressed himself freely in his journal, taking particular notice of the major's vices and vulgarities, remarking that on one occasion he looked "as stupid as liquor usually renders him."[41]

Contacts between the two peoples multiplied unexpectedly in the late 1840s, thanks to the discovery of gold in California and the consequent migration from the eastern states. "Once Cooke's wagon road had been marked," says historian Howard Lamar, "as many as 50,000 argonauts used it to reach the California gold fields in 1849 and 1850."[42] A large proportion of them came through Tucson, sometimes recording their impressions—usually bad—for posterity. From then on, Americans were no novelty on the dusty streets of the village, and they came in all shapes and sizes with a wide range of occupations. Many were cowboys and cattlemen. Ranchers in Texas realized that the horde of forty-niners would need more food than California could supply, and a number of them drove herds

Cave Johnson Couts, California-bound in 1848. Courtesy Huntington Library, San Marino, California.

through the desert country, defying the Apaches, and reached the coast. Migrating families took smaller herds with them. The traffic began as early as 1848,[43] and was still flourishing in 1854, when young James G. Bell went through with the outfit of John James, of San Antonio. Bell was a tenderfoot from Tennessee and was curious about everything he saw and heard. He even described the small bell hung at the right side of the entrance to the tiny church, dated 1807 and named for the Virgin of Guadalupe. With typical Anglo prejudice he noted the division of labor between men and women: "The women do the principal part of the work about the household; the men, long fellows with broad shoulders and no other part in proportion, seemed to be busily engaged in lounging."

The soldiers were "a set of ragamuffins," the layout of the town was "very irregular," and the local priest was "only reported to have been drunk *once* since our stay—two days."[44] Tucson had no redeeming features as far as Bell was concerned.

Almost everything written about Tucson from this period embodies the special prepossessions of mid-nineteenth-century citizens of the United States. The Mexicans are judged by the standards of Salem, Massachusetts, or Peoria, Illinois, and it never occurs to the reporters that the Tucson lifestyle was the product of a difficult time and place.

A typical observer was John E. Durivage, of the *New Orleans Daily Picayune.* He had a "bold and ardent nature" and a sense of humor. His dispatches, perhaps overdramatized, were full of life and human interest. He first saw Tucson on May 28, 1849, and it did not impress him. He was surprised by the "solemn grandeur" of the old church at Bac, by the "bright and intelligent Indians,"

and by the "rich and fertile land." Tucson, by contrast, was "a miserable old place garrisoned by about one hundred men." Flour and a small quantity of corn were the only edibles that could be had, though there was fruit in the abandoned orchard of the *convento.* And it was hot—so hot that the pores "are now reopened and perspiration flows at the slightest exertion."[45]

The people of the village were no longer afraid of, or much impressed by, these creatures from another world. The day after Durivage's party arrived, their camp was filled with Mexican women and Indians, "all eager to traffic and anxious to buy needles and thread." The Apaches were particularly repulsive to this southern gentleman, who described them as "cowardly and imbecile, . . . a miserable degraded set" exhibiting "that peculiarly squalid and filthy appearance usual when the wild man leaves his native hills, casts off his old habits and pursuits, and hovers around the haunts of civilization."[46]

Only two days behind Durivage came forty-niner A. B. Clarke, who stopped at the village to look for meat, bread, and flour. He noted the "contemptible appearance" of the Mexican troops and went on to Pacheco's blacksmith shop, where he bought four mule shoes for a dollar apiece. To his surprise, "the smith did not know how to put them on, although he was considered the best mechanic in town."[47]

At the blacksmith shop Clarke saw an unusual sight, an anvil made from a meteorite which had descended to earth somewhere in the Santa Rita Mountains. The history of this curiosity extended in later years all the way to the Smithsonian Institution and produced a good deal of writing.[48]

Four months later a twenty-four-year-old Texas boy named C. C. Cox arrived with his

John R. Bartlett's sketch of Tucson in 1852, the Convento at right. From Bartlett's Personal Narrative (New York: D. Appleton, 1854).

party and found himself involved in a brisk trading session. "Almost all articles of merchandise and especially dry goods are in great demand in Tosone. Some of our party have made handsome profits upon their little stocks of finery, trinckets &c." Cox notes also the beginning of social intercourse between natives and outsiders: "The town gave a fandango the night of our arrival in honor as was said of the Americans.—I did not attend but learn that it was an affair extra."

In that same month, September, 1849, Lorenzo D. Aldrich found that by now the natives were able to hold their own in trading sessions: "Here the Mexicans came to our camp to trade with cotton goods at 3s. per yard; and other articles after a proportionate rate." There was no doubt in the mind of either Cox or Aldrich that Tucson was full of "friendly people."[49]

It was inevitable, with all this trade going on, that some enterprising American would open a store. Robert Eccleston, who arrived on November 6, 1849, diary in hand, found one already in operation: "I brought a few little notions to trade with them, but they are up to trade and bid low. Torrey's opening his store also spoils trade in a small way. . . . Torrey is selling his goods, I hear, rapidly. He took in $400 in two hours the other day."[50]

There was a tentative quality about these early contacts, but in no time at all a growing colony of Americans had settled in Tucson. Mexican food and Mexican ideas became a part of their lives. Mexican women became their wives, and the Mexican heritage shaped the lives of their children. The influence of American customs and concepts on the Mexicans was, of course, just as far-reaching. In the 1850s, Tucson was becoming a biracial—perhaps better, triracial—community. It was not a bustling town yet, but it was beginning to stir.

The treaty which ended the war with Mexico was partly responsible. An official boundary between the two countries had to be established and agreed upon, and in July, 1849, commissioners representing the two nations met and began their joint activities. John W. Bartlett, the scholarly and artistic Connecticut bookseller who failed conspicuously as commissioner but left a remarkable record of his activities, reached Tucson on July 17, 1852, reported what he saw, and sketched the town from the slopes of A Mountain, giving us an important visual record.[51]

General Miguel Blanco was in command of 300 Indian-fighting troops at the presidio. With his officers he paid the commissioner a courtesy call—a visit somewhat dampened by a heavy rain and the fact that Bartlett's tent was too small to hold everybody—but the two leaders discussed their mutual interests and agreed that something had to be done about the Apaches. The general offered the services of his blacksmith for repairing the commission's wagons, and they parted amicably when Bartlett moved on.

Bartlett pictured life in Tucson in the 1850s as next to impossible. The Apaches, he said, had nearly depopulated the region and had forced the ranchers and farmers in outlying districts to abandon their lands and move to Tubac or Tucson. Even with this influx, however, the number of Tucson residents did not exceed 300. "The miserable population, confined to such narrow limits, barely gains a subsistence, and could not exist a year but for the protection of the troops," he reported; adding, with typical Anglo condescension:

The houses of Tucson are all of adobe, and the majority are in a state of ruin. No attention seems to be given to repair; but as soon as a dwelling becomes uninhabitable, it is deserted, the miserable tenants creeping into some other hovel where they may eke out their existence. We found three hundred soldiers on the place, although the average number for some years past has not exceeded twenty.[52]

Bartlett's views epitomize Anglo ideas of Mexico in his time, but it is worth noting that his pessimistic picture can be checked against the memories of local residents who were alive in the 1850s. In the 1920s several of them were interviewed, and none of them seems to have felt that his early life was barren and deprived. Cirilo Solano León, born in 1845, the son of a Mexican army lieutenant, remembered the presidio and the pueblito. His father built the church inside the walls. The family owned a farm west of the Camino Real (Main Street), got their drinking water at the spring, and lived like everybody else—perhaps a little better, since the Leóns were considered to be rich. The Apaches were a menace but were "afraid to come near" because of the troops.[53]

Hilario Gallego came along a little later (he was born in 1850), but he too had vivid recollections of the presidio and the Indians. He recalled Teodoro Ramírez's store and Juan Burruel's *cantina* inside the walls. Cirilo León, Juan Elías, and Ramón Pacheco had stores outside. Church services, with marriages and baptisms, were held once every four or five years. The dances, the entertainers from Sonora, the women washing clothes at the *acequia*, the soldiers and their families leaving for Sonora in wagons in 1856—all were clear in his mind:

When we needed provisions we made a lot of rag dolls and took them over to the Gila River where there were Pima and Maricopa Indian settlements and traded them for tepary beans, corn, wheat and black-eyed peas. From around home we gathered mesquite beans and dried them and then ground them into pinole. We ate the nopal [prickly pear] and the sahuaro fruit.

You see we had to learn to use things as they came. We had plenty of meat, game, cattle, etc. And we made our own candles out of the tallow. . . .

The first time we heard of coffee was when the Oury brothers came and gave some of the green coffee to the women to cook, saying "Cook us some coffee." They took it for granted that the women knew how to fix it. The women boiled it first but the kernels did not get soft; so they tried frying it and cooked it and cooked it. And they were still cooking it when Oury, the lawyer, came in and asked if the coffee was ready. One of the women looked at the frying grains and said: "Well, it's been cooking a long time but it seems awful tough yet." [54]

Juan I. Tellez was born in 1862, but he too remembered the Indians and the trouble they made. People dug ditches around their corrals to make it harder for raiders to take their livestock, and if the cattle were stolen in spite of all precautions, the men went in pursuit. "Men in those days did not know what fear was." Juan's father was quite wealthy, owning land and cattle, and had enough to send his son off to Lawrence, Kansas, to a school recommended by American pioneer Sam Hughes. [55]

Not one of these men talks about the hard lot of the natives or pictures them creeping from one ruined hovel to another, eking out an existence. They learned to "use things as they came," but they thought they had enough. What seemed like abject poverty to Bartlett added up to a pretty good life in the minds of the natives.

Negative concepts continued to exist in the minds of both groups. On the Anglo side those concepts went all the way back to the Black Legend of Spain, which declared that Spain and all its works were evil, and were reinforced by soldiers' tales of the Mexican War, by popular novelists, and by natural and inevitable human prejudice. The Anglos wrote off the Mexican males as cowardly and lazy. The women were judged to be different—industrious, loyal to their unworthy sons and spouses, and often lovely to look at. Lonely strangers enjoyed fantasizing about their preference for American men. These judgments were generally based on limited contacts with upper-class Mexicans, who guarded their privacy and their women from prying outsiders.

The Mexican life-style was seldom viewed with approval. The adobe house—comparatively cool in summer and warm in winter and well suited to the desert climate—became a symbol of Mexican backwardness and degeneracy. To a man brought up in a clapboarded New England farmhouse with glass windows and wooden floors, it was a primitive hovel. Women washing clothes beside the irrigation ditches and carrying water in ollas on their heads reminded some travelers of the Holy Land and its customs. [56] The blacksmith who did not know how to shoe a mule (he had never before been called on to shoe one); the food which bore no resemblance to a New England boiled dinner; the ragged soldiers in the presidio—all were unfamiliar to the newcomers and therefore suspect.

Since the Mexicans were not going anywhere and were not keeping travel diaries, their sentiments are not as well recorded, but the Mexican War, the forty-niners, and the Yankee invasion left them with some negative impressions also. The Americans at their worst were loud-mouthed, rude, domineering, and unclean—savages with a superiority complex. Cecil Robinson sums it all up as "the swagger, the braggadocio, the grand disdain, and the self-righteousness of the mountain man, explorer, Santa Fe trader, military man, journalist, or plain forty-niner."[57] The Americans were far from realizing what David J. Weber points out: "Mexicans on the far northern frontier developed commendable folk cultures and maintained themselves remarkably well in an area where literacy and education could be viewed only as luxuries until more elemental needs were met."[58]

The Gadsden Purchase, approved by Congress on June 29, 1854, was a major factor in the mingling of cultures. Washington wanted a southern railroad route, and as a result Mexico got $10 million, and the United States got nearly 30,000 square miles of new territory. Tucson was now an American town, and nine Americans raised Virginia-born William H. Kirkland's flag on an improvised flagpole in the Plaza de Armas next to the presidio. The Mexican garrison remained to keep the peace until United States troops took charge in 1856.[59]

Major Enoch Steen managed the transfer of power. He led four companies of First Dragoons across the desert wastes from New Mexico and set up camp near San Xavier on November 14, 1856. Leaving his weary men to refresh themselves as best they could, he rode on to Tucson. His orders obliged him to "establish a post there in relation to which he will receive special instructions." He took one hasty look around, however, and developed an unconquerable aversion to the whole Tucson area. Grain and pasture were in short supply, and housing inside and outside the decaying presidio was limited to "miserable huts, unfit for use taken in the best condition." In violation of his orders he led his men back upstream to a spot near Calabasas, ten miles north of the newly established boundary, and justified

his action in a long report to Santa Fe.

The report was not well received. Colonel Benjamin E. L. Bonneville indignantly wrote that a camp sixty miles from Tucson would not do and ordered him to move to a point closer to the original objective. Steen, described by one of his officers as "a miserable old 'setting hen,'" fussed and clucked, pointing out that the people in Tucson who were calling most loudly for American troops were peddlers of whiskey and flesh. Nevertheless he moved his camp to a spot on Sonoita Creek, twenty-five miles east of the Calabasas site and not much nearer Tucson. The new post was called Fort Buchanan.[60]

Tucsonans did not like Bonneville either. When the news reached California that Ignacio Pesqueira, governor of Sonora, had removed the twenty-six presidials and their families to Imuris, south of the border, the *San Francisco Weekly Chronicle* noted on November 14, 1856, that the retiring military force had "persuaded some of the native families to accompany them to avoid the brutal treatment and other numerous evils . . . inflicted by the Americans on the Spanish race wherever the former has the upper hand." The Mexicans had their prejudices too, but experience taught them that the American presence was not all bad. Seventy years later, in an interview with Mrs. George F. Kitt, of the Arizona Historical Society, Carmen R. Lucero recalled:

I have often heard my mother say that the coming of the Americans was a Godsend to Tucson, for the Indians had killed off many of the Mexicans and the poor were being ground down by the rich. The day the troops took possession there was lots of excitement. They raised the flag on the wall and the people welcomed them with a fiesta and they were all on good terms. We felt alive after the Americans took possession and times were more profitable.[61]

CHAPTER 4

The Great Transition

Tucson was still a Mexican village in the late 1850s. The municipal government, with its various alcaldes, functioned as usual, though by 1858, as a reporter for the *New York Herald* noted, Americans were being "elected to town office."[1] The community was still dependent on itself for most things, including food and fun. Occasionally a troupe from Sonora presented *títeres* (puppet shows) or *romerías* (shows with clowns and acrobats).[2] San Juan's Day and San Agustín's Day were the great occasions, celebrated with dances and gambling, cockfights and carousing.[3] There were no roads worthy of the name—until the Americans built them—but great changes were on the way. These transformations went forward on three fronts: transportation, trade, and politics.

As the most important town in the region, Tucson was bound to develop and expand when the wagons and the stagecoaches began to clank and clatter down the village streets, starting in 1857 with the inauguration of the San Antonio and San Diego Mail Line—commonly known as the Jackass Mail because passengers and mail traveled by muleback between Yuma and San Diego.[4] The government gave organizer

James E. Birch enough support to make possible eighty-seven stations, some of them no more than campsites, on a route covering 1,476 miles. An Ohioan named Phocion R. Way, an employee of Charles D. Poston's Santa Rita Mining Company of Tubac, arrived at Tucson by way of the Jackass Mail on June 11, 1858. He left a classic description of the village—still in American eyes a "miserable place," its population reduced to about 200, "about a dozen" of whom were Americans. The Anglos he found pleasant and entertaining; the Mexicans offered a complete contrast:

There is a small creek runs through the town. The water is alkaline and warm. The hogs wallow in the creek, the Mexicans water their asses and cattle and wash themselves and their clothes and drink water out of the same creek. The Americans have dug a well and procure tolerably good water, which they use. . . .

There is no tavern or other accommodation here for travelers, and I was obliged to roll myself in my blanket and sleep either in the street or in the corral, as the station house has no windows or floor and was too close and warm. The corral is where they keep the horses and mules, but I slept very comfortably as the ground was made soft by manure. I would rather have slept

41

The Butterfield Overland stage approaching Tucson from the north. From William H. Hilton, Sketches in the Southwest and Mexico, 1858–1877, William Hayes Hilton, artist (Los Angeles: Dawson's Book Shop, 1963).

in the street as a great many of the natives do, but it is hardly safe for a stranger. Someone might suppose that he had money about his person and quietly stick a knife into him, and no one would be the wiser—there is no law here, or if there is, it is not enforced. Might makes right.

Frontier Americans were already killing each other in conventional Wild West fashion, as Way duly noted. A man named Batch was shot dead by another named Fryer. The killer "is running at large and no particular notice is taken of it. . . . I guess King Alcohol was at the bottom of the trouble."

Like most other travelers, Way was inclined to generalize from isolated experiences, and as a result the women of Tucson suffered in his estimation:

Among the native women here I believe that chastity is a virtue unknown. Some of the young girls are pretty. They are remarkable for the ease and grace of their movements and their brilliant black eyes. Some of them are very bold. They have a great fancy for Americans and a greaser stands no chance with a white man. They are generally tender hearted and humane and in sickness are noted for being good and faithful nurses. Nearly every man in our mail party seems to have a lover here, and when the mail arrives they are always at the station to welcome them. One of our party named Beardsley seems to be a great favorite with the senorittas, and has a fine looking black-eyed girl for his especial favorite. He is laying on the ground within six feet of me at this moment fast asleep, while she is setting by his side keeping the flies from disturbing him.

"There is no place to board and not much

to eat in this d——d town," he concluded, and only the employees of the stage company had "a little bacon and coffee and bread so hard from age you could not bite it."[5]

The Jackass Mail was not a conspicuous success. Financial problems, the death at sea of the organizer before the first trip was made, the loud complaints of dissatisfied passengers, and, finally the competition of the Butterfield Overland Mail were too much to overcome. Only forty full-length trips were made. Then for a while the line operated between San Antonio and El Paso on the eastern end of the line and between Yuma and San Diego on the western end, leaving the middle portion to the Butterfield organization—better planned and superior in equipment and financing. Butterfield began service in September, 1858, after a year spent in preparation. Sixteen stations between Stein's Pass, on the western boundary of New Mexico, and Yuma, on the Colorado, were ready when the first coach left Missouri. The initial arrival at Tucson occurred on October 2, 1858.

Waterman L. Ormsby, a reporter for the *New York Herald*, went all the way through to San Francisco on that first run. Writing was his business, and he had much to say, but not about Tucson. "The inhabitants are mostly Mexican," he said. "There are but few Americans, though they keep the two or three stores and are elected to the town offices. The town has improved considerably since the acquisition of the territory by the United States."[6]

Ormsby may not have been aware of it, but Tucson was one of the important stops on the line, and one of the best. The El Paso facility included a comfortable hotel with bar and dining area. Tucson could offer nothing as fancy as that, but it came reasonably close. Superintendent William Buckley

came to town only two months before the first coach was scheduled to arrive and found what he was looking for—the house of Juan Santa Cruz just outside the old presidio, where his daughters, Atanacia and Petra, were born (they made important Tucson history a few years later). It was a big building, about sixty feet square, with a spacious courtyard in front and a large fenced area in back. Buckley appointed William S. Oury his local manager and started at once to arrange for meals and hotel accommodations for guests and corrals and storage buildings for the livestock and equipment.

The Buckley House, as the station was called, was on the corner of Pearl (now vanished) and Pennington streets, a hundred yards west of Main Street and near the gate of the old presidio. Pearl was then called Calle del Correo (Post Office Street) because Mark Aldrich, the first postmaster, had his office there, directly across from the station entrance. Behind the Aldrich establishment, facing on Main Street, was Solomon Warner's store. Oury and his brother owned the house adjoining the station on the north, making everything handy for him. Blacksmith Ramón Pacheco occupied the building south of the station. Calle de Correo was the business center of the community, and the biweekly arrival of the eastbound and westbound stages added a bit of drama to the life of the town.

Tucson was a "timetable" station, meaning that drivers made every effort to arrive on schedule. The westbound mail came in at 1:30 P.M. on Tuesdays and Fridays; the eastbound at three in the morning—a ghastly hour for the bruised and sleepless passengers—on Wednesdays and Saturdays.[7] The drivers were serious about the schedule. Charles H. Meyer, druggist and justice of the peace, remembered in later

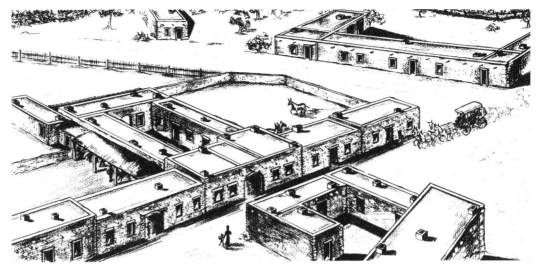

The Buckley House (formerly the Santa Cruz residence), local headquarters for the Overland Stage Company. Drawing by Dianne Vaughn. Courtesy Tom Peterson and Journal of Arizona History.

years that "the stage minded not God or man; its only aim was to get through on time. It never failed but once, and that was when the driver tried to ford the Rillito at flood height and was washed down stream."[8]

The pause at the station was brief—just long enough for a change of horses or mules and a few mouthfuls of whatever there was to eat, probably beans. When the shakedown period was over, five-minute stops were scheduled at intermediate points and twenty minutes at meal stops. Any passenger who wanted twenty-one minutes, according to Charley Meyer, was out of luck:

Several times I saw men who would go off to get a new hat or a cigar or something, when the stage was due to start. The next would be the toot of the horn as the stage started out and the man would rush out and request that the stage tarry. "Wait two days for the next stage," was the only consolation he got, and there was nothing else for it.[9]

Under the circumstances it was not surprising that some travelers remembered

their Tucson experience with anything but pleasure. Raphael Pumpelly, an engineer with headquarters at Tubac, tells how he arrived exhausted, threw himself on the floor "of the first room I could enter" (a saloon), and slept for twelve hours. Awakened by a pistol shot, he went in search of food:

I have no remembrance of having eaten for a week. So when I saw some men hurrying to a house where a man with a revolver stood ringing a bell, I turned to enter. The man stopped me. "Fifty cents first!" he said, holding out his hand. There were jerked beef, and beans, and some things they called bread and coffee. You ate what was pushed to you; the memory of that pistol acted as a persuasion.[10]

When Pumpelly's book was published, the editor of the *Arizonian* denied that any of this happened. Pumpelly, the editor said, actually went to bed at the Buckley House, and when the dinner bell rang, he "combed his silken hair and dined."[11] Men sometimes exaggerated the discomforts of the frontier.

"The Overland Mail Company brought a

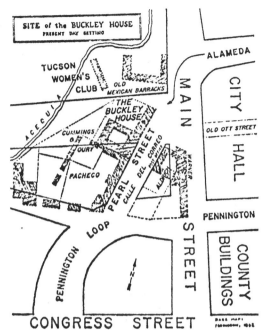

The heart of Tucson in the 1850s. Courtesy Donald H. Bufkin and Journal of Arizona History.

Raphael Pumpelly, the engineer who saw Tucson at its worst. From Raphael Pumpelly, My Reminiscences (1918).

new prosperity to Tucson merchants," says historian Bernice Cosulich.[12] Wagon trains followed the coaches, and the village became an increasingly important commercial center. The Anglo storekeepers and freighters prospered. The mining industry began to be important. Indian agencies and military posts had to be supplied. A rising tide of immigrants, California bound, took the southern route through Tucson. All were good for business.

It must be admitted also that the opening of this frontier attracted a good many undesirables—bandits, con men, lawless riffraff from both sides of the border. The San Francisco Vigilance Committee and the Texas Rangers are said to have encouraged this migration. The ne'er-do-wells sought their recreation and sometimes their living in public places and were therefore highly visible to people passing through. As a result Tucson, like other western towns, became known as a cockpit of violence and a den of iniquity. It cannot be denied that a bad side existed, but it would be unfair to ignore the responsible citizens who kept the town and its business going. They were mostly brave, hardy people, moderately honest, loyal to each other, public-spirited, and mindful of the needs of others. A quick look at a few of these first-comers will give a good idea of what they were like.

Samuel Hughes was in many ways representative. At the time of his arrival in 1858 he was a slender, balding, black-eyed little Welshman, far gone with tuberculosis but undaunted by that and other problems. He could do almost anything and do it suc-

Samuel Hughes.

what they needed. Their faces were concealed by their rebozos, he noted, with only one eye showing, "and they all looked cunning as a fox," but that evening he had a chance to see what they looked like when he attended a community dance. Everybody came, young and old, Papagos and Apaches. One old lady brought her dogs and cats and led a pig. She explained that the dogs and cats were loose because they could take care of themselves, but the pig was on a leash because "Gringos are very fond of pork." [15]

Sam liked Tucson, and it was his home from the first day. In a matter of hours he was in business:

> I had a good harness, and I traded it for some grain and sold the grain. Then I went to butchering. I made money hand over fist. until War broke out, buying and selling grain and meat to the Overland Stage Company and supplying stations between Maricopa Wells and Apache Pass. . . . My partners gambled; but I never did except in horses, sheep and cattle, and land and *adobe* houses. [16]

cessfully, though his entire education consisted of three days in a Pennsylvania schoolroom, and he was barely literate. [13] He was only a small boy when he came with his family from Wales to the United States, but he went to work almost at once and learned a variety of skills. When he went to California with the forty-niners, he was a professional cook, and his services were much in demand. With his profits he bought a hotel and invested in mines and cattle. His lungs went bad, however, and he was heading for a warmer climate in Texas when he camped with a small party beside a Tucson irrigation ditch on March 12, 1858. It was said that he had been hemorrhaging so badly when he reached Gila Bend two days before that he could hardly go on. [14]

On the morning of the fourteenth he found that he had pitched his tent beside the town's water supply, and the local housewives began coming with their ollas for

The first man Hughes met in Tucson was a fiery southerner as opposite as he could be from Hughes but just as representative of the genus pioneer. He wore a plug hat and swung a cane and introduced himself as Palatine Robinson of Kentucky, owner of a store at Tubac [17] until recently—now a resident of Tucson. He had a good business, a beautiful young wife, a lovely blonde baby, a dashing appearance, and a strong sense of his own importance. He was also a good pistol shot and a persistent gambler. Phocion Way, who came through with the Jackass Mail, called him "a good-looking, generous, wholesome Kentuckian" and had good words for his wife. [18] John C. Reid, who traveled through the Southwest and northern Mexico in 1858, praised her amiability

Mark A. Aldrich.   *Solomon Warner.*

and called her husband "chivalrous, generous . . . the soul of honor." [19]

There was a dark side to Robinson's character, however. On September 10, 1859, he was playing cards in a Tucson gambling house when R. A. Johnson took offense because Robinson would not lend him any more money. The result was violent brawl which was broken up by other men present. Johnson followed Robinson home, however, and raved and threatened until a charge of buckshot silenced him for good. The next morning Justice J. W. Holt ruled that Robinson had fired in self-defense, but he had to face a charge of murder later on. [20]

When Hughes arrived, the little American colony included another nonstandard pioneer, Mark A. Aldrich, a stoop-shouldered, pale-faced serious, quiet man with a rattrap mouth and firm convictions. He had been a successful businessman in Illinois before the gold fever hit him, a friend of Abra-

ham Lincoln and Stephen A. Douglas, husband of a lady of distinguished family, and father of several children. His store was the first permanent mercantile establishment in Tucson, and he was the first American alcalde, or mayor, having replaced Juan Elías, who was not active enough to suit the Americans. Some private ghost must have haunted him, for he never went back to his wife and children. Instead he began living with a local girl named Teofila León, had a child by her, and provided for them as well as for his legitimate family when he died in 1873. Nobody condemned him for his informal domestic arrangement. [21]

So it was with the rest of them—no two alike but every man able to stand on his own feet. Solomon Warner arrived on March 2, 1856, eleven days after the Mexican troops left, and almost overnight became a figure in the community. He had a deep voice, a barrel chest, a generous nature, and a sense

William S. Oury.

Granville H. Oury.

of humor. He was a mason by trade but became a merchant and brought in the first stock of American goods. During the Civil War he lived in Mexico, where he is reported to have done very well. Back in Tucson after Lee's surrender, he dammed a branch of the river for waterpower and started a flour mill to replace the one destroyed during the Civil War.

Like many other pioneers, he loved to tell a tall tale, and he told one to a *Citizen* reporter in 1875. At the age of thirty, Warner said, keeping his face straight, he was operating a gristmill back in New York State and courting an attractive widow with two little boys who loved to play around the mill. One morning, he said,

I was startled by a frightful scream. Rushing to the hopper, from which the sound seemed to come, I was just in time to catch a passing glimpse of the four copper toes of the boots of the unfortunate twins. Before the mill could be

stopped, the widow's mites had passed between the upper and nether mill stones and had been ground into and irretrievably commingled with that day's grist.

Unwilling to face the mother, Solomon said nothing and allowed her to believe that the boys had been lost or kidnapped. "The day's grind of flour," he added, "attracted considerable attention from its superior excellence." The widow's grief and his own remorse drove him to a wandering life, and eventually he came to Tucson.

If Solomon told any more such tales, they have not survived. For a time he prospered, apparently loved and respected by all.[22]

Respected also but not always loved were the Oury brothers, William S. and Granville H., the latter usually called Grant. Born in Virginia and reared in Missouri, they reached Tucson in 1856 after an interval spent in California. Grant was a lawyer and politician. Bill was a soldier, farmer,

Peter R. Brady.

Fritz Contzen.

businessman, and local manager for the Butterfield stage company. He had had an incredible career in Texas before he was well out of his teens, barely escaping death in the Alamo and drawing a white bean at Salado when every tenth man captured by the Mexicans was shot. He was a Texas Ranger, a soldier in the Mexican War, a kind but hottempered southerner who was always prepared to do battle—especially with Indians. "He was always ready to go when there was any Indian fighting to do," Atanacia Hughes remembered in later years, but he was willing to take on white men too, when they asked for it. He had killed two men in duels after he came to Tucson and soon became, as his grandson-biographer admits, a "controversial" character.[23] But he *was* respected.

Bill was a close friend of Peter R. Brady, who likewise was anything but the stereotype of the pioneer. Born in Washington, D.C., where his father was secretary to President Andrew Jackson, Peter began his career as a midshipman in the United States Navy, came to Texas during the Mexican War (in the course of which he met Oury), and first saw the Southwest as leader of Colonel Andrew B. Gray's railroad survey of the route from the Texas Gulf Coast to San Diego. In San Francisco he helped organize the Arizona Mining and Trading Company to develop the mines at Ajo, west of Tucson, the first American mining enterprise in the area. He was an Indian agent, an army interpreter, and even a librarian before the Civil War and was a loyal husband to Inez García, a woman of Spanish blood from Durango.[24]

Another friend of Oury's from Texas Ranger days was Fritz Contzen, the plump but adventurous son of a good German family who migrated to Texas in 1848 with his brother, who was a forester. He was with Major W. H. Emory's Boundary Commis-

Hiram S. Stevens.

Charles H. Meyer.

sion in 1854, and when that job was done, he acquired land and became a rancher in the Santa Cruz Valley. In 1862 he married into an old Spanish-Mexican clan and started a family which is still represented among the public-spirited citizens of Tucson. Fritz was not a likely candidate for the role of heroic adventurer, but he undertook the most hazardous enterprises, like carrying the mail through the heart of the Apache country, always coming through safe. At the same time he liked a good joke, even if it was on him. He was a brave man with a great sense of humor.[25]

Then there was Hiram S. Stevens, a Vermont boy who enlisted in the army at nineteen, served in the Mexican War, and was discharged in New Mexico. He reached Arizona in 1854 and acquired a small ranch near Sentinel Peak. Ranching, however, was only one of his multiple interests. He had done some gambling before he settled down, and he liked to take chances. He had his finger in almost every moneymaking enterprise that came along. He was post trader at Camp Crittenden, a miner, a Tucson storekeeper, a delegate in Congress for two terms, and a responsible member of his community. Sometime before 1860 he married Petra Santa Cruz, whose father and grandfather had been born inside the old presidio. Hiram and Petra lived in a big house on Main Street, which became a focus for the social life of the town and an oasis for visiting dignitaries. Stevens became wealthy, but he shared his wealth.[26]

Charles H. ("Charley") Meyer was another who shared, but in a different way. Born in Germany and speaking English with a thick accent, he came to Arizona with the United States Army, serving in the supply department of the Hospital Corps. He liked Tucson and settled there in 1858 as the town druggist. Like many others in his business, he was glad to prescribe informally for his friends, and was often called Dr. Meyer. As a perennial justice of the peace he was widely known also as Judge Meyer. His exploits in this capacity started a run of stories which were told with chuckles by several generations of Tucsonans. He introduced the concept of the chain gang, new to the community, and the streets were cleared of the offal of two centuries, becoming almost embarrassingly clean. Legends grew up around his courtroom. Usually his verdicts involved a fine amounting to the sum in the accused man's pocket. Although he had very little law, if any, his sense of justice was strong, he had profound common sense, and he made his rulings stick. He was so conscientious that he once fined himself in his own court for speeding in his buggy. Sometimes he sentenced a criminal to a certain number of lashes at the whipping post in the Military Plaza. He would order half the stripes administered and tell the accused to come back the next day for the rest. Thus he rid the town of many undesirable characters. In his own day, says Frank Lockwood, "he was trusted, honored, respected, and thoroughly enjoyed."[27]

Although his base of operations was at Tubac, Charles Debrille Poston, "Father of Arizona," was at home in Tucson and well known to everyone there. A Kentuckian and a lawyer by profession, he was a man of great charm and talent, a conceiver of monumental enterprises who intended to be rich and famous but never quite made it. The gold rush took him to San Francisco, where he worked in the customhouse and incubated a scheme to exploit the mines of southern Arizona. It was he who organized the Sonora Exploration and Mining Company. With

Charles Debrille Poston, the "father of Arizona."

Herman Ehrenberg, a German engineer, he prospected the mountains south of Tucson in the summer of 1854, organized his company in partnership with Major Samuel Heintzelman, of Fort Yuma, and went to Ohio to look for investors. He and his staff appeared in Tucson on the feast day of San Agustín in 1856. Pausing only to let his men enjoy the festivities, he moved on to Tubac, set up his offices in the old fortifications there, and for a few years conducted his operations in something like baronial style. He was a proud and sensitive person, talented as a writer, good at making friends—and enemies—a great raconteur who sometimes, but not always, told the truth—a curiously flawed but always interesting figure who never failed to make news wherever he went.[28]

The list could be extended almost indefinitely, for men of character, good and bad, kept coming as the fifties progressed. Paddy

Charles Trumbell Hayden, Tucson merchant.

Father Joseph Machebeuf, an important Tucson visitor in the 1860s. From the Reverend W. J. Howlett's Life of the Right Reverend Joseph P. Machebeuf, D.D. *(Pueblo, Colo.: N.p., 1908).*

Burke, of Boston, who helped raise the American flag over the Tucson presidio in 1856, was one. Nelson Van Alstyne, of New York State, Texas Ranger, wagonmaster, and peace officer, settled on the Tanque Verde Ranch eighteen miles east of downtown Tucson. Well known in later years was Charles Trumbull Hayden, father of perennial Congressman Carl Hayden, a Connecticut schoolteacher who came to town on the first Butterfield stage. He became a merchant and freighter, was Tucson's first probate judge, and was a prominent citizen until he moved to Tempe in 1871.[29]

A pioneer for a few weeks was Father Joseph Machebeuf, vicar-general of the Catholic Diocese of Santa Fe, who visited the neglected Tucson flock in 1858. Francisco Solano León lent him a two-room house for

a headquarters. He helped bring religion back to the people on the Santa Cruz, who immediately began to talk about building a new church. After two months he went back to Santa Fe and to immortality as Father Joseph, Archbishop Lamy's right hand, in Willa Cather's *Death Comes for the Archbishop.*[30]

These are the founding fathers of the American city of Tucson, but they did not stand alone. They worked with Mexican men and women of old families, of property, and sometimes of education—men and women with names like León, Carrillo, Otero, Elías, Samaniego, Pacheco, Romero, Velasco, Sais, Ortiz, and Amado. Intermarriage over the decades had made every member of this aristocracy kin to everybody else, and when new families like Pedro Aguirre's

52

Pedro Aguirre, pioneer trader and rancher.

A splendid couple, Estevan and Altagracia Ochoa.

arrived from New Mexico after the Civil War, they quickly joined the universal cousinship. These people were not the poor, ignorant, indolent Mexicans of the Anglo stereotype.[31]

Estevan Ochoa, for example, though small in stature, was a great gentleman, a successful businessman, and a credit to his adopted country. His ancestors came to Mexico with Cortés. He himself was born in Chihuahua into a rich mining and ranching family. As a youth he was restless, journeying to Independence, Missouri, to learn English and get ready to become a freighter on the Santa Fe Trail. He settled in Mesilla, New Mexico, opened stores in several places

in partnership with Pedro Aguirre, already mentioned, and was one of the earliest to raise his voice for separate territorial status for Arizona. Probably in 1860 he settled permanently in Tucson. With P. R. Tully, he later organized the famous firm of Tully and Ochoa and became a supporter of all good causes in his community. Hughes, Stevens and Ochoa, with their families, were on close and friendly terms.[32]

As old and proud was the family of Ramón Pacheco, whose forbears had migrated to the Santa Cruz Valley well before the turn of the eighteenth century. The first child was born in Tubac in 1775. Miguel Pacheco, a grandson of this child, was an acting judge at Tucson in 1846. He owned land, operated a dairy, and managed a distillery which produced 300 gallons of mes-

First ladies of Tucson: the Santa Cruz sisters Atanacia (left) and Petra (Mrs. Sam Hughes and Mrs. Hiram S. Stevens) and their aunt Guadalupe Santa Cruz (center).

cal a year. His son Ramón owned farm- and ranchland and operated the blacksmith shop. He tried storekeeping without much success, but whatever his fortunes he was proud of his heritage and became an "encyclopedia" of local and family history.[33]

The women of the old Mexican families left few records of their lives and experiences, but several lived to tell how it was before Tucson became an American town. Ana María Comaduran Coenen, for example, was interviewed in 1927, when she was eighty-five. Her grandfather was the presidial captain who had dealt diplomatically with Colonel Cooke in 1846. "Life was

simple and pleasant before the Civil War, she recalled, "but it was also hard."[34]

The best record of all was left by Atanacia Santa Cruz, born on August 4, 1850, in a house just outside the walls of the fort. She played inside the enclosure and remembered the soldiers marching out on March 10, 1856, on their way to Imuris, in Sonora. First her father and then her mother died, and she grew up in the house of Hiram Stevens and her sister, Petra. Eight-year-old Atanacia was probably at the *baile* which introduced Sam Hughes to the social life of Tucson in 1858, and in 1863, just before she was fourteen, she married him in the old church at San Xavier. It was a happy marriage and produced fifteen children. Hughes and Stevens became business partners and occupied houses near each other on Main Street, and the sisters were not separated. They were attractive, lively women, hospitable and gregarious.[35] Had Phocion Way known them, he might have thought better of the Mexican ladies of the village.

The pioneer men and women of Tucson were in most ways a credit to their community, but in the second half of the twentieth century it is the fashion to downgrade them. John Upton Terrell speaks for a good many serious and thoughtful people of this era:

It should be understood that almost every Spanish and Mexican *colono* and ordinary American who sought his or her fortune in the Apache country stood low on the social scale, a great many of them the dregs of their respective societies. There were among them few persons of education, and an even smaller number with any type of professional training, and not very many possessed social amenities acceptable any place that ranked above a bawdy-house waiting room. The vast majority . . . were uncouth, ignorant, bigoted, and looking for something for nothing.[36]

54

The fact is, they were a remarkably varied and diversified group, and it is almost impossible to generalize about them, except that they were thoroughly grounded in the fine art of survival or they would not have been there. They all hoped to do well—perhaps get rich—but it is not safe to say that they were all trying to get something for nothing.

The word they liked to use about themselves was "enterprising," meaning that they had drive and ambition and could see how money might be made when other people could see nothing at all. Pete Kitchen, who lived in the Santa Cruz Valley near Nogales, raised hogs in spite of the Apaches and was famous for his hams all the way to Santa Fe.[37] Solomon Warner, as already noted, saw the need for a flour mill.[38] John B. Allen heard the boys in the California Column wishing in 1862 that they had a piece of pie, so he went into the pie business and made money. He became adjutant general of the territory in due time and was addressed as "General" on ceremonial occasions, but his friends usually called him "Pie" Allen.[39]

There was nothing permanent about anyone's good fortune. These men lost money—sometimes more than they made—and they often had to borrow. Sam Hughes was in business as a moneylender, at high monthly interest rates. Newspaper stories mentioned their enterprises with respect, as if they were great capitalists, but the facts were often depressing.

On July 3, 1886, the *Arizona Mining Index* (Tucson) headed a front-page story "The Dead Broke Rich Men of Tucson." Only sixteen men or firms in the town, said the writer, were "sufficiently secure in their affairs to be sure of the future." Sam Hughes, the shrewdest of all the Tucson traders, was "just about able to live and that is all."[40]

Surveyor General John B. ("Pie") Allen.

This dim view seems to have some justification if one looks at the last days of those old pioneers. Solomon Warner came to his finale as a frail old man, crippled by encounters with the Apaches, with very little to show for his years of hard work.[41] Hiram Stevens, discouraged by business reverses and fearful of the future, put a bullet through his head and tried unsuccessfully to take Petra with him.[42] Estevan Ochoa, when he died in 1888, was "a victim of the railroad which caused his firm as well as many others, to go by the board."[43] Even the great Charles Poston died a poor pensioner with only his memories left.[44] There were some rich men in Tucson when the twentieth century opened, but they did not include many of the first-comers. If the pioneers were looking for "something for nothing," they did not succeed—at least not for long.

With transportation established and trade under way, the great need in the Gadsden Purchase (including, of course, Arizona) was for protection, legal and military—the kind of protection that only an organized government could provide. True, Arizona after 1850 was part of the newly organized Territory of New Mexico, but the territorial capital was far away at Mesilla on the Rio Grande, and Tucson was not even in a working judicial district. There were no courts within reach, no real law and order, no elective or appointed officials the citizens could call on without risking their lives in a journey across Apachería. From the beginning of this unsatisfactory arrangement Arizonans dreamed of having their own government and attempted to get action as early as 1856. It was clear to them that all good things—settlers, the railroad, development of the mines, control of the Apaches—began with territorial status. The first bill presented to Congress, on December 22, 1857, asked for protection for the Overland Mail, about to begin service. The company could not maintain operations without help from the military, and Arizona had to be organized before it could ask for troops. Fifteen times between 1858 and 1861, says Ben Sacks, the best historian of the movement, the citizens drew up petitions and sent them to Washington, and fifteen times they were rejected.[45]

The leaders and organizers were Anglos, mostly living in Tucson, but their friends and neighbors of Mexican ancestry, now American citizens, were also eager for a new day. Leading all the rest were the names Charles D. Poston and Sylvester Mowry. Poston needed troops to protect his mining interests south of Tucson, and he hoped for

Sylvester Mowry, soldier, miner, lover, and tireless worker for an independent Arizona. Courtesy California State Library and Arizona Historical Foundation.

high office in the new territory. Mowry had a mine of his own in the same general locality but he seemed to be more interested in promoting Arizona than in bettering his own situation.[46]

Mowry was as interesting, in a different way, as Poston. He was a Rhode Islander, a graduate of West Point, an army lieutenant when he came west. He served in Utah, California, and the Pacific Northwest and in 1855 was in command of the post at Fort Yuma, where he developed a severe case of Arizona fever. So sure was he that his destiny was in the new country that he resigned his commission in 1858. In 1860 he bought the Patagonia Mine, not far from Tubac. In appearance, education, dress, and instincts he was an eastern gentleman. He was an excellent speaker and writer, and he knew im-

Fred Ronstadt, carriage maker, musician, and ancestor of important people.

portant people. His friends in Arizona remembered him as "a good fellow. He liked a good toddy, and he was a great story teller." His enemies pictured him as obsessed by mineral riches and loyal to nothing but the pursuit of wealth. They noted also that he was usually in the company of charming and accommodating women.[47]

The New Mexicans were willing and eager to divide the country and give Arizona independent status. At first the idea was to run the dividing line east and west. The present north–south division was first proposed in 1860.[48] Meetings were held at Mesilla and Tucson. Memorials went off to Congress signed by such people as Mark Aldrich, Solomon Warner, Peter Brady, Fritz Contzen, Granville Oury, Juan Elías and Teodoro Ramírez.[49] Another who signed

was Frederick A. Ronstadt, German born, who came to Arizona from Mexico in 1854 and joined the Arizona Mining and Trading Company to work the mines at Ajo. He had married in Mexico, had risen to high rank in the armed forces of Sonora, and had become a first citizen of his adopted Mexican state. His son Fred, born in Mexico in 1868, came to Tucson in 1882, learned the carriage maker's trade, figured prominently in the community's musical history as performer and bandmaster, and became the progenitor of a large and active clan, some of whom have become nationally known.[50]

Washington turned a deaf ear to all applications. Nathan P. Cook, an engineer and surveyor, was sent to the national capital as delegate from Arizona, but he was not seated.[51] The only sign of interest in the affairs of Arizona was approval of the construction of wagon roads to the West Coast, particularly an El Paso–Fort Yuma route. Such a road was actually surveyed and approved in 1858, but it went up the San Pedro to the Gila and missed Tucson entirely.[52] Meanwhile Poston and Mowry were toiling in Washington to win friends for a separate Arizona.

Mowry's most significant contribution was a pamphlet entitled *Memoir of the Proposed Territory of Arizona*, published in Washington in 1857. It was brief—only thirty pages—but it was written with considerable power and pride and with the gloomiest feelings about conditions in the area. Mowry painted a rosy picture of its mineral resources and foresaw the emergence of "an immense agricultural state" but declared that it was in a "state of anarchy" with "no law and no self-respect or morality among people." To make matters worse, Sonora was up in arms about the disastrous filibustering expedition of Henry Crabbe,[53] and Ameri-

Ronstadt's wagon-and-carriage shop about 1894.

cans dared not cross the border. "Justice and humanity imperatively demand," Mowry insisted, that Congress erect "a separate Territory under the name of Arizona."[54]

He refused an appointment as delegate in Congress in 1857,[55] but the campaigning went on. By February, 1860, ten petitions had failed to have the least apparent effect. Five elections for delegate had been held, and Congress had refused to admit the candidates.[56] In April, 1860, a convention at Tucson actually formed a territorial government, drew up a provisional constitution, and elected officials, including a governor. Some Tucsonans were tapped. Palatine Robinson was adjutant general. Granville H. Oury was a justice. The marshall was Samuel G. Bean, of Mesilla, brother of the notorious Roy Bean, "Law West of the Pe-

cos." Congress never recognized the existence of this de facto government. Its organizers were mostly convinced secessionists, however, and it was a sort of precursor of the Confederate organization which functioned in the Southwest in 1861.[57]

More bills bombarded Congress in 1860, but pro- and antislavery legislators could not come to an agreement about anything, and in 1861, when Congress was in a mood to create new territories, Poston and Mowry were back in Arizona, and nobody was left in Washington to carry the banner.[58]

Besides, it was too late. The nation was on the verge of civil war, and such matters as the territorial aspirations of a few men in a remote part of the continent were lost among larger issues.

CHAPTER 5

The Tides of War

Business was good in Tucson in 1860, and the town was growing. Bartlett had guessed that 350 people lived there in 1852.[1] The 1860 census counted 623.[2] In 1858, according to Sam Hughes, the business community consisted of three stores, two butcher shops, and two blacksmith shops. There was no saloon, though tequila was sold in the stores. Very shortly, however, Palatine Robinson was advertising fine wines and liquors in his new emporium,[3] and the demands of the traveling public no doubt called into being other drinking establishments, like the one Raphael Pumpelly says he used for sleeping purposes when he arrived on the stage, exhausted, in 1859. In that same year William and Alfred Rowlett dammed the Santa Cruz above town and installed a gristmill.[4]

The newcomers were a cosmopolitan lot, coming from all sections of the United States and from twelve foreign countries, according to the 1860 census. In moral character they ranged all the way from solid citizens to desperadoes. Travelers always took particular note of the bad ones. "Probably never before in the history of any country," remarked Samuel W. Cozzens, who visited Tucson in 1859, "were gathered within the walls of a city such a complete assortment of horse-thieves, gamblers, murderers, vagrants, and villains."[5]

It seemed that there was no effective way of controlling the criminal element. Mark Aldrich came close in 1860 when he became the first American alcalde. He set up a whipping post in the military plaza and was making effective use of it when the murder of an unarmed man convinced him that his fellow townsmen were letting him down. A number of them saw the killing, but not one reported it or offered to testify. Aldrich waited one day for something to happen. Then he resigned. His letter minced no words:

If the time has arrived when the law abiding portion of this community, either through fear of giving offense or for want of moral courage, fail to make the necessary complaint for the arrest and trial of those who commit a breach of the peace, I think they have no use for a Judge or Court, and as Judge of the Criminal Court of Tucson, I resign the same.[6]

Business improved in spite of the lawless element. Big ranches were still in operation, though their time was short; mining activity was increasing; freighters were hauling

William S. Grant, the unfortunate Yankee. Courtesy State Historical Society of Maine, Portland, and Journal of Arizona History.

built. In May, 1860, he arrived at Fort Buchanan and within a week was delivering supplies.

He was able to underbid his rivals because he was a good idea man. His "secret weapon," as his biographer, Gilbert Pederson, calls it, was a scheme to produce most of his own supplies. He bought the Rowlett Mill on the Santa Cruz, rebuilt it, and was soon producing ten bushels of flour an hour. At the millsite he erected a store, a warehouse, and a blacksmith shop. He opened two logging enterprises in the Santa Rita Mountains, leased the Canoa and Kitchen ranches in the Santa Cruz Valley for his beef herd, and started a stage and hotel business for travelers to and from Fort Buchanan. He spent money as if he owned it all, and he had every reason to believe that he would soon be a rich man in spite of the army quartermasters and the secretary of war in Washington.[7] The times, however, were against him.

South Carolina seceded from the Union in December, 1860. Texas did the same three months later, and Congress moved the Butterfield stage operation north to the central route, effectively isolating Tucson. In April, one month later, Grant lost a wagon train worth $140,000, heading west from the Gulf Coast, to the Texas rebels. Confederate forces were already on the move. In July, Colonel John R. Baylor and his Texans reached El Paso, and the Union commanders in New Mexico Territory prepared to abandon their posts. Grant's warehouse in Tucson was used at first to store their military supplies, but just when Lieutenant Richard S. C. Lord, in command of the First Dragoons at Buchanan, had all the barrels and boxes neatly stacked, orders came to destroy everything, supplies, buildings, and all. The people of Tucson, Lord was told, were

from the West Coast and from Guaymas on the Gulf of California; and new revenue was coming in from military posts in the Gadsden Purchase. The merchants and liquor dealers were disappointed when Major Steen turned up his nose at the "miserable huts" of Tucson and took his men elsewhere, but Sam Hughes and Hiram Stevens had contracts for beef and hay and other commodities, and William S. Grant, a newcomer from Maine, was rapidly becoming the biggest contractor in the region.

Grant was a sharp-eyed, energetic, resourceful Yankee who sold his father's shipbuilding business in 1859 for $100,000 and bid successfully for government contracts to supply the forts in New Mexico and Arizona—two in existence and two soon to be

"traitors of the deepest dye" who had "openly talked secession."[8] No part of the government stores should fall into their hands. On July 15, Lord gave Grant half an hour to remove his records and personal possessions—then took a live coal from the stove and set the buildings afire. According to Benjamin Sprague, one of Grant's employees, about 20 Anglos and 250 Mexicans watched the funeral pyre of Grant's hopes and ambitions. Lord reported that they were "very hostile." Although they expected to be attacked,[9] the soldiers and civilians made it back to the Rio Grande, and Grant began a thirty-five-year campaign to get his money back from the United States government.[10]

Meanwhile, back in Tucson, the secessionists, urged on by Colonel Palatine Robinson, were preparing for action. Robinson actually led a group of men to Tubac and took possession, in the name of the Confederacy, of Poston's abandoned mining enterprise headquartered there, though he had not a shadow of legal authority for so doing.[11]

In Tucson secessionists were more determined and possibly more numerous than the Union men. On March 18, 1861, two days after a bigger mass meeting in Mesilla, sixty-eight of them assembled, declared themselves on the side of the South, and elected Granville Oury their delegate to the Confederate Congress. He was not seated, but for a while everything else seemed to be going for the southerners. John W. Baylor set up New Mexico and Arizona as a Confederate territory, with himself as governor, and the southern Congress approved his action.[12] There was hope for better days.

Any improvement had to start with control of the Indians, and some of the delegates to the Tucson convention did not care which side provided it. With the departure of the Union troops the whole country had begun going up in smoke. Cochise and other Apache leaders attacked everywhere, and Mexican bandits hurried in from Sonora to assist in the work. The fate of Tubac was typical. On August 2 a band of raiders killed two of the inhabitants and ran off all the livestock. A messenger went off to Tucson to ask for help, and the entire village moved to the larger town. A correspondent for the *Alta California* concluded his account in the issue of September 2, 1861: "General desolation: Our prosperity has departed. . . . We think no man ever before saw desolation so widespread. From end to end of the Territory, except alone in Tucson and its immediate vicinity, there is not a human habitation."[13]

What the town and its environs needed and petitioned the Confederate Congress for was an Indian-fighting army. Please send troops! In due time the troops arrived, but not because Tucson needed them. Tucson was just a way station on the road to California, where there were gold and food and a large body of secessionists. On his arrival at Mesilla in December, 1861, General Henry Hopkins Sibley began planning immediately to expand westward, and early in January, 1862, he ordered two detachments to cross the desert to Tucson. One party, led by Colonel James Reily, was charged with a mission to Governor Pesqueira of Sonora, who was in a position to provide friendship and support for the cause. The other, commanded by Captain Sherod Hunter, would occupy Tucson and keep a watch on the Gila River Trail, where Colonel James H. Carleton's California Column would sooner or later appear. The two commands would travel together as far as Tucson.[14]

Hunter was a man about whom not much is known but much can be deduced. He was a native of Tennessee, thirty-seven years old in 1861, who had settled, probably in 1859, on a plot of land beside the Mimbres River twenty-five miles north of today's Deming, New Mexico, near a community (now vanished) called Mowry City. His business was farming. He was a man of courage and decisiveness (he had taken out a marriage license when he was only seventeen). A tintype likeness has survived which shows him in a neat Confederate uniform, his hand jauntily on his hip and a heavy saber at his side. A mist of dark whiskers surrounds a thin, handsome face, and a little mustache outlines his grimly downturned mouth. He won good opinions from his superior officers after he joined a militia unit on August 1, 1861, and was almost immediately made a first lieutenant, probably by vote of the men in his company, and when the Tucson expedition was decided on, General Sibley handpicked him to lead it. Of his approximately sixty-five volunteers, over a third were old frontier hands from Arizona, and the group was considered a crack outfit. It was not, however, a company of spit-and-polish regulars. Boyd Finch, their historian, calls them "the frontiersmen of the Confederacy." Observers in Tucson noted that they never drilled and that they "slept where they pleased."[15] Early in February they set out on what was to prove a difficult mission.

The weather was terrible. Rain and snow plagued the West from December to February in that winter of 1861–62. Without tents or warm clothing Hunter's men slogged through the downpours, arriving at Tucson, battered and weary, on February 28.

One civilian traveled with the company—none other than Hiram Stevens, of Tucson. What he was doing in Mesilla, why he was allowed to travel with a military company, whether or not he took the oath of allegiance (as Hunter expected everybody in Tucson to

do) are questions which must remain in doubt. Similar questions could be asked about Mark Aldrich and other leading citizens who seem to have got along with Hunter, and with Carleton too, later on. Aldrich witnessed an affidavit which Stevens made for Carleton about the size of Hunter's force. Some of his neighbors left town. Charles T. Hayden is said to have "shouted for the Union," but he was far away when Hunter marched in.[16]

Hunter's first act on arrival was to requisition clothes for his men. His next concern was to call in Union supporters and advise them to take the loyalty oath or get out. Bill Oury brought a stronger message to Sam Hughes: "Take the oath or be shot." Sam did not back down. "I was here before you were," he replied, "and I won't go!" On mature consideration, however, Hughes decided to save his skin and his property. He turned everything over to his partners, Hiram Stevens and Alphonse Lazard, who promised to look out for his interests. They did it effectively, and Sam managed to stay busy in California until he could come back with the Union troops.[17]

Estevan Ochoa came to Hunter's quarters by invitation and was given the ultimatum. Dean Lockwood quotes his answer: "Captain Hunter, it is out of the question for me to swear allegiance to any party or power hostile to the United States Government; for to that government I owe all my prosperity and happiness. When, Sir, do you wish me to go?"

The language seems a bit ornate for the occasion, but there can be no doubt that Ochoa's answer was negative. He left at once. Hunter allowed him to take a horse and a few personal possessions, and the Confederate sentries passed him as he headed out into the Apache-infested wilderness. Nobody expected him to get through to Mesilla, but he made it, and a few months later he was back in Tucson rebuilding his business.[18]

Solomon Warner also refused to take the oath. Leaving his store and his goods in Hunter's hands, he rode south into Mexico, settling in the border hamlet of Santa Cruz. There he started another store, married a Mexican widow who possessed some helpful resources, including a beautiful daughter, and lived, for that time and place, like an aristocrat until it was safe to return to Tucson.[19]

Another Union man who headed for Mexico was Peter Brady, who went to live with his wife's people at Altar, in northern Sonora. When the California Column arrived, he sent back useful dispatches to Carleton and his officers, writing under the name George Peters.[20]

Hunter himself did not linger long in the shadow of the presidio. On March 3, having seen Colonel Reily off to Sonora, he marched his command down the Santa Cruz to the Gila, where Ammi White—miller, storekeeper, Down East Yankee and Union man—was accumulating supplies for Carleton. Supposedly also he was relaying information about the Confederates to advance agents of the California troops. White was a busy man—too busy buying and selling and making money to keep an eye out for the enemy—and he was completely surprised by Hunter's arrival. Everything he had gathered fell into the captain's hands, including 1,500 sacks of wheat. Hunter hated to destroy all this good grain, so he gave it back to the Pimas from whom White had bought it.[21]

He had a second unexpected bit of luck. Within hours of his arrival Captain William McCleave of the First California Dragoons rode in, unaware of the enemy's presence. Carleton had sent him ahead to arrange for purchase and storage of hay and to seek information about J. W. Jones, a Union messenger who had failed to return from his mission (the Confederates had captured him). McCleave was a seasoned soldier, but he had no reason to suspect a trap. He knocked on Ammi's door, was admitted, and was received by Hunter himself, who impersonated White until his men could get the drop on the Union detachment. Two days later captors and captives returned to Tucson, while a small patrol rode off down the Gila to probe for the Union advance guard. They ran into a force of 272 men under Captain William P. Calloway eighty miles east of Yuma at a Butterfield stage stop called Stanwix Station. After a brief skirmish the Confederates withdrew and outran pursuit.[22] They carried the news that Carleton was on his way, and Hunter realized that he was in no position to contend with Carleton's 2,000 men. As a first step in the evacuation of Tucson he paroled his enlisted prisoners and sent McCleave and White off to the Rio Grande under guard.[23]

Calloway's force occupied the Pima villages without incident and began a cautious move toward Tucson. On April 15 they made contact with one of Hunter's patrols near Picacho, a volcanic peak forty miles north of town. Lieutenant James Barrett was sent with a small squad to flank the enemy on the east, and Lieutenant Ephraim C. Baldwin was ordered to move straight ahead.

The Confederates might have surrendered, but Barrett could not wait to negotiate. He ordered a charge through the brush and was killed, along with two of his men. Saddler George Brandes remembered many years after the event that "when we came upon Lieutenant Barrett's body, we saw that he had been shot through the neck and he still had the first finger of each hand over the bullet hole, trying to stop the flow of blood." Three of the pickets were captured. The Battle of Picacho Pass is sometimes called the westernmost engagement of the Civil War. There were, however, several other skirmishes, including the one at Stanwix Station.[24]

Stung by his losses and probably overestimating Hunter's strength, Calloway beat a hasty retreat, not stopping until he had put a hundred miles between himself and danger. The California papers got word that Hunter had 1,500 men in Tucson.[25] Calloway waited for Colonel Joseph R. West's larger force before returning to the Pima villages. From there the Union troops took a roundabout way to Tucson—up the Gila to abandoned Fort Breckinridge and thence to the Santa Cruz from the northeast.

Accompanying Colonel West on this circuitous march was the energetic and resourceful Sam Hughes, coming home from California. At the Pima villages West called him in to ask about local conditions without getting much satisfaction from the wary Hughes and finally told him he would have to help drive the livestock if he wanted to stay with the group. West added a warning related to a band of natives camped nearby: "The Apaches are at peace and friends with the Union men, and if you should shoot and kill one, you will be tried and shot." Unabashed, Sam predicted that if the troops did not move on at once the Indians would get their horses. He bet West a pair of boots that they would. His prophecy proved to be correct. Many years later he recorded what happened next: "When I got off gard in the morning the Gen was Settin in front of the tent I Sed good mornin Gen he Respond sur-

ley I won my boots if you had bet no responce."

Hughes did not get his boots, but the colonel did move the remains of the horse herd.[26]

When West's cavalry came charging into Tucson, Hunter had been gone for two weeks. He had left Lieutenant James H. Tevis behind, however, to watch for the head of Carleton's column. Tevis expected the enemy to come in by the river road from the Pima villages. He barely made it out of town as the Union horsemen galloped in.[27]

It should have been a triumphant entry, but few of the citizens were on hand to watch.[28] It took some time for them to filter back, and the turnout was still small when Carleton rode in on June 7 to a salute from his two fieldpieces. Some said that he delayed his entrance until the cannons were in place and ready to fire,[29] but Carleton always provoked criticism.

A soldier named George O. Hand kept a diary which indicates that the behavior of the troops was about what the townspeople should have expected. Someone shot Mark Aldrich's cow, and Mark's complaints were at first ignored. A volunteer complained of being bitten by one of the local pigs. The animal was tried by a kangaroo court and "sent to the oven." A lieutenant moved in with a local girl and threw out an ambitious rival who tried to muscle in. The men revealed their prejudices. When "Carleton's nigger" came on the floor with a "señorita," the affair was broken up with "stones and bricks from outside."[30]

It was now the turn of the southerners to swear allegiance or take the consequences. General Carleton (he was promoted while his expedition was on the road) was an arbitrary ruler and went after every secessionist he could catch. One man he wanted—

and caught—was Sylvester Mowry, living at his silver mine in the Patagonia Mountains and keeping 100 employees busy. One of them was a German metallurgist named T. Scheuner, who in a letter to Carleton accused his employer of disloyal conduct—making pro-Confederate statements and selling percussion caps to Hunter. The general sent Colonel Edward E. Eyre with a large detachment of troops to make the arrest. Mowry was routed out of bed before daybreak, and Carleton picked up an unexpected windfall in the person of Palatine Robinson, who happened to be visiting Mowry.

Since there was no civil law in Arizona, Carleton had set up military courts, and at his order West convened a board of officers to try the supposed rebels. The court ruled that Mowry had shown himself to be "an enemy of the Government of the United States" and that he had been "in treasonable correspondence and collusion with well-known secessionists." On June 17 they sent him to prison at Yuma.[31]

He insisted, and continued to insist, that he was not on either side—that all he wanted was protection from the Indians and that he had petitioned both factions for help without committing himself to either. From Yuma he flooded the newspapers and powerful people with appeals for help. After his unconditional release in early November, 1862, he sued Carleton and others in the California courts for more than a million dollars. In 1868 the government finally paid him $40,000, but he declared that that was nothing compared with what he had lost, and he continued to accuse Carleton of confiscating his mine illegally and selling it at auction. Later investigation has shown that Mowry was at the very least careless of the truth. Nevertheless he was able to stir up a hot and highly rhetorical feud with Carle-

ton, and his friends in the Arizona legislature were able to push through a resolution condemning the general.

Mowry made nothing more out of his mine, but he continued to live like a rich man, prompting one good historian to judge that he was, "to put it bluntly, a confidence man." Wherever his money came from, he did not enjoy it long. In October, 1871, he died of Bright's disease in his London lodgings with only his friend Poston at his bedside. In our time he has had a spirited defender in Bert M. Fireman and a no-less-convincing critic in Constance Wynn Altshuler.[32]

About Palatine Robinson and some twenty others there could be little doubt. They were all sent to the Yuma prison in the summer of 1862. Robinson, crippled by Apache bullets and in feeble health, was hardly a ghost of his former aggressive self, but he was still regarded as a dangerous desperado. The only good thing about him was his loyal wife.[33]

Meanwhile, back in Tucson, Carleton was making things almost as hard for his friends as for his enemies. For the benefit of his hospital fund he taxed every business in town except food and clothing stores—five dollars a month if the gross was less than $500—more if it was more. Gambling houses were assessed $100 a month a table; saloonkeepers, $100 a month to stay open.[34]

Having thus, as he boasted, brought law and order to Tucson, Carleton prepared to move on to the Rio Grande. To maintain stability after he left, he created by proclamation a "Territory of Arizona" with himself as governor, having an eastern boundary which moved forward with him and his troops. He also set up a "District of Western Arizona," including all the land between Apache Pass on the east and the Colorado

River on the west, with headquarters at Tucson. Major David Fergusson, his chief commissary officer, was to be in command.[35]

The troops, moving in three sections, ran into trouble at Apache Pass, convincing Carleton that a permanent military post was needed at this strategic point. Fort Bowie was established as a result.[36]

Major Fergusson, left in charge at Tucson, busied himself trying to determine who owned what. There had been confusion in this matter since 1856, when the Mexican troops left, carrying with them the presidial records, such as they were. Some undoubtedly dealt with the transfer and ownership of land. From 1856 to 1862 possession was the only proof of ownership. One of Fergusson's first orders obliged everyone within three miles of the center of the village to register his property.

The registrar was William S. Oury. His appointment must have been something of a surprise, for everything belonging to him and his brother Granville had been confiscated and sold by Carleton's order. He must have made his peace effectively to be entrusted with this special appointment—or perhaps he was the only man in town willing and able to handle it. In a second order Fergusson commissioned J. B. Mills, Jr., to produce an official map of Tucson and the fields surrounding it. The Oury property book and the Mills map are the first records of land ownership in Tucson and are basic to every discussion of land use, municipal growth, and population distribution. Unfortunately Oury's key numbers do not fit the locations on the Mills map. Recently, however, serious attempts have been made to reconcile the two, and the pieces may someday fall into place.[37]

The year 1863 marked a great divide in the history of Tucson and of Arizona. After years of futile effort, the citizens suddenly found independence within reach. In February, Jefferson Davis created the Confederate Territory of Arizona. In March the Congress in Washington moved in the same direction. A bill dividing Arizona from New Mexico on the present north–south line was introduced and hotly debated. The tide turned, however, when John Watts, delegate in Congress from Tucson, displayed a choice specimen of silver ore, worth $5,000 a ton, from Poston and Heintzelman's mine. Congressman James Ashley of Ohio told how men from Cincinnati had not only "sacrificed all their wealth invested there, but many of them have lost their lives."[38] Congressman John A. Gurley of Ohio argued that "millions in silver" would be lost if action was not taken. Benjamin F. Wade, another Ohioan, carried the banner in the Senate, and on February 20, 1863, the measure passed. Abraham Lincoln signed the bill into law on February 24, and the Territory of Arizona was born. It had no capital, no legislative body, no code of laws. But it existed.[39]

The birth had been prepared for by much work behind the scenes. Poston and Heintzelman were in Washington calling on senators and congressmen, arguing and persuading. Poston claimed to have been the key figure. In 1884 he recalled that Ben Wade had given him good advice:

He said there were a number of members of the expiring Congress who wanted to go West, and offer their political services to the "galoots," and if they could be grouped, and a satisfactory slate made, they would have influence enough to carry the bill through Congress. Consequently an "oyster supper" was organized to which the "lame ducks" were invited, and there and then the slate was made and the territory virtually organized.[40]

The first territorial officials were thus named, with Gurley of Ohio as governor. When all was settled, Poston recalled, he realized that no provision had been made for him and asked, "What is to become of me?" Gurley replied, "O! We will make you Indian agent."

That was how Poston came to be known as the "Father of Arizona." Ben Sacks, who reports these proceedings, thinks that General Heintzelman really deserved the title. He provided the oysters and gave the party.[41]

It took the lame ducks eleven months to get organized and cross the country to their assignments. In the meantime Arizonans were working on their own to improve conditions. In Tucson the townspeople were about to build a new church—dedicated, naturally, to San Agustín. Nothing had been done after Father Machebeuf's visit in 1858, but with the arrival of Father Donato Rogieri in 1862 enthusiasm was born again. Rogieri was an energetic and dedicated priest, and he was determined that Tucson should have a Catholic house of worship.

All we know about this early builder comes from a journal kept by W. W. H. Davis in 1853 when he was on his way from Independence, Missouri, to New Mexico to become United States district attorney. Father Donato was a member of the party. An Italian by birth, he had spent five years in the Holy Land and could speak Arabic. Nothing in his past had prepared him for life in the American West, but he was cheerful and eager to learn. Davis remarks that "as a traveling companion he was more agreeable than many who understand our languages and manners better." He "greatly improved upon acquaintance, and his good qualities more than balanced his eccentricities." He leaped into the breach when the

cook proved to be ignorant of the refinements of making flapjacks, and he revealed, on the occasion of an Indian scare, that he had a pair of pistols concealed in his extra shoes.[42] His heart must have sunk very low when he reached his new parish, but in no time at all he was busy building. He knew it would have to be done a little at a time, but in 1863, a year after his arrival, the concrete foundation of his new church was ready, and it was time to start work on the walls. Ana María Coenen, four years old in 1863, tells what happened that summer:

The adobes were made on the property of Solano Leon, where the Manning house is now located. When services were over every morning, Father Donato would tell the congregation not to leave until he had changed his robes. Then he would instruct them to follow him and they would go to the place of Solano Leon and each woman would return with one brick in her arms. Father Donato would carry one brick also. The entire church was built by the people of the parish.[43]

The walls were just beginning to rise when Father Donato left. He was a restless soul and never stayed long in one place. In 1863 he was back in New Mexico, and in 1864 he was killed by Apaches on the road between El Paso and Chihuahua.[44] Through the mid-sixties the church stood still. Most of the time the sheep were without a shepherd. Fathers Charles Messea and Aloysius Bosco were assigned to San Xavier and Tucson in 1864, and Archbishop Lamy made the long trip from Santa Fe to install them, but in less than a year they were back in California.[45] In 1866, however, the archbishop sent John Baptist Salpointe, a Frenchman who had been a missionary in New Mexico for six years, to take charge. He arrived with a letter of introduction to William S. Oury, and Oury passed him on to Juan Elías. The best Elías could do was

Bishop John Baptist Salpointe.

to find a house for Salpointe and his fellow priest Francis Boucard.[46] San Agustín's church was just as Father Donato had left it. Salpointe wasted no time in useless regrets, however. In 1868 a roof was finally installed, and a school building was erected next door. In the same year Tucson became a vicariate apostolic, with Salpointe as vicar apostolic and Francis Jouvenceau of Yuma as vicar-general. The Protestants were far behind. In 1865, Arizona, with Nevada, Utah, and New Mexico, became part of an Episcopal missionary district, but a church organization in Tucson was some years in the future.[47]

The year 1863 was the year of the prospector as well as the year of the politician and the priest. There was gold in the hills. Pauline Weaver found it on the Colorado just north of Ehrenberg in 1862.[48] In a few weeks 1,500 people were scrambling for sudden wealth. A short time later the bubble had burst, but more exciting discoveries were made farther east near present-day Prescott and Wickenburg, on the Hassa-yampa River, and in the Harquahala Mountains. Camps sprang up on Big Bug, Lynx, and Weaver creeks. Carleton heard about the "vast gold fields" and sent troops to protect the prospectors.[49]

All this was of great interest to Tucson, the focal community of Arizona Territory. The mines opened by Poston and Heintzelman and Mowry's venture in the Patagonia Mountains pointed to a time when Tucson would be the mining capital of the region. The strikes in central Arizona in 1863 revived these hopes, and some of them were realized as the century moved forward. Long before the Apaches were subdued, prospectors were investigating every rocky ridge in the territory, taking their chances and sometimes losing their scalps. Tucson was the supply point for many of these ventures.[50]

The fact that the country was still divided and still at war seemed not to have any meaning to the scrambling prospectors and sweating miners. It had little bearing, either, on the progress of the newly appointed territorial officials toward their Arizona destiny. There were eleven of them, headed by John N. Goodwin, who was promoted from chief justice to governor when John A. Gurley died on August 18. Not the least important member of the group was Richard C. McCormick, territorial secretary, who had a background in journalism and carried with him a printing press which he planned to use for government business and for turning out an official, or semiofficial, newspaper.[51] The party crossed the Arizona line on December 27, and two days later, beside a waterhole called Navajo Springs, they took the oath of office and were officially in business. Goodwin fixed the capital at Fort Whipple, recently established in the Chino Valley, where there was a concentration of miners.[52]

Not all the officers were present. United States Marshal Milton B. Duffield and Indian Agent Poston journeyed by separate routes to San Francisco and Los Angeles and from there to Tucson. Poston arrived on January 17, 1864.[53]

Goodwin was a hard-working governor and began his administration with a tour of his territory, accompanied by a military escort. He reached Tucson in May and on the eleventh proclaimed and provided that the town should thenceforward be an incorporated municipality and the seat of one of the three district courts in the territory. Judge William T. Howell held the first term of court there at the end of the month.[54]

Tucson, as the most important town in the territory, should have been the capital. General Carleton, however, was against it because of the predominance of southern sympathizers living there. Goodwin settled on a point twenty miles south of his first capital as the site of a permanent Territorial headquarters, and Prescott began rising on the banks of Granite Creek.

Goodwin's administration was of two minds about the southerners in Arizona, particularly in Tucson, viewing them with suspicion on the one hand and trying to win their support on the other. The appointment of William S. Oury as the first mayor was undoubtedly an attempt at conciliation.[55]

To get on with the election of a legislature, a census had to be taken, and Marshal Duffield was charged with taking it. He completed the assignment within the year (1864), and his figures are of interest. He counted 1,568 residents in Tucson. La Paz on the Colorado was next with 352. Tucson

United States Marshal Milton B. Duffield.

had the wealth too. Mark Aldrich was worth $52,000. Charles T. Hayden claimed $20,000.

Elections for the first legislative assembly were announced on May 26, and ballots were cast in July.[56] A few of the old-timers were successful candidates. Poston was chosen territorial delegate in Congress and went off to Washington; Francisco S. Leon and Mark Aldrich were elected to the upper house, or council. Five Tucson members of the house were comparative newcomers: W. Claude Jones, John G. Capron, Gregory P. Harte, and Henry D. Jackson. Apparently Arizona was attracting new citizens of superior quality.

A particularly interesting immigrant was Coles Bashford, a highly competent New York State lawyer who had been governor of Wisconsin. He was living in Washington when the Territory of Arizona was orga-

John C. Capron, businessman in a hurry.

Coles Bashford, former governor of Wisconsin, a founding father of Arizona.

nized, had traveled west with the governor's party, and was the first lawyer to practice in the Arizona courts. A plump man with a bulldog face, he was ambitious, energetic, and successful in making a place for himself in the new territory. He was president of the council in the first legislature, and three months before the first roll call he went to work with Associate Justice William T. Howell to produce a 400-page legal code. The work was done by the clip-and-paste method, with provisions borrowed from the statute books of a number of other common-wealths. The two men knew that such a compilation would be badly needed, and needed at once, and theirs was ready for re-vision when the first lawmaking body con-vened.[57]

Of the Tucson representatives Jesus M. Elías, W. Claude Jones, and John G. Capron were the best known. Elías belonged to a family long prominent in Sonora and Ari-zona. Jones was a newcomer who had prac-ticed law and held public office at Mesilla and El Paso. He had dallied with the Con-federates, but he was a capable leader and served as speaker of the house in the First Legislature.[58] Capron was perhaps the most interesting of the three. A Vermonter, born in 1828, he is said to have arrived in 1857 on the first stagecoach—possibly as a driver. He is listed in the 1864 census as a merchant with a stock of goods worth $10,000. In 1869 he moved to San Diego, where he achieved distinction as a businessman and banker. He was a "kindly, sensible man" but a "whirlwind" in business, always on the move, and "very much of a man." His Ari-zona experiences meant a good deal to him, and he kept in touch with his old friends in later years through membership in the Ari-zona Pioneers Historical Society.[59]

The governor and the legislators confronted a number of serious problems. The most pressing was the Indian threat. The United States Congress paid no attention to a request for funds, and it was obvious that Arizona would have to fight its own Indian battles. A volunteer militia was therefore organized and did good service in 1865–66, though lack of funds kept the men practically barefoot and close to starvation.[60] Communication was another great need. Urged on by the legislature, Poston labored in Washington to get something done, and Arizona was given a dozen postal routes. Two of them—to the Patagonia and Cerro Colorado mines—originated in Tucson.[61]

The legislative body also recognized the need for an educational system. The governor recommended that public schools and a university be provided for, and a grant of $500 was allocated to each of the four county-seat towns, providing the towns raised an equal amount. Only one qualified—Prescott, the capital. A board of regents was appointed to govern the territorial university, but no location was chosen, and no steps were taken toward organization. Useful laws were passed, however, to regulate the mining industry and establish toll roads. Historian Gilbert Pedersen thinks that the "Founding First," meeting in a room without a floor or adequate furniture for a month and a half, "accomplished more for Arizona than any legislature since then."[62]

There were seeds of difficulty in the fact that the first territorial officials were "carpetbaggers." They were men of background and experience, and they served Arizona well—as long as they were able to put up with her. Most of them went home as soon as they could. William Thompson Howell, for example, the father of the Arizona legal

Judge William Thompson Howell, who stayed in Arizona only long enough to write down the laws.

system, was in Arizona less than six months. He told Governor Goodwin that "he would not act as a judge in a district where two out of three people were barefooted, where a court was held in an adobe shack with an earthen floor, and a dry goods box was used as a rostrum."[63] Even the governor, who did his best for the territory while he was in charge, stayed only a year. As soon as he could get himself elected as a delegate in Congress, he left for Washington, never to return. He continued to collect his salary from September, 1864, to April, 1865—illegally—but he was governor in name only. Secretary Richard C. McCormick was, in fact, the chief executive.[64]

The people tolerated this carpetbag rule for a while because unity was important at the start and because the new government was trying to be nonpartisan. In a couple of years, however, they turned on the interlopers and campaigned bitterly against them.

The love of money was, as usual, the root of evil and touched off the explosion. The carpetbaggers were inevitably involved in contracts and government business. They were even called the "Government Ring." They are said to have worked with a group of powerful Tucson merchants known as the "Tucson Ring," suppliers of military posts and Indian reservations. With or without evidence many historians believe today that the two groups were in collusion, and the myth of the Tucson Ring is so commonly accepted that many a popular novelist would have trouble plotting his stories if he were deprived of the wicked ring as a whipping boy.[65]

By 1870 the citizens were calling for a government of Arizonans, by Arizonans, and for Arizonans. "It is time," trumpeted the *Tucson Weekly Arizonan*, "the people of Arizona choose for officers men from among themselves. There is no just reason why we must be represented by starved-out politicians . . . who would not remain a single hour in Arizona if divested of official patronage. It remains for the Democrats to explode the carpetbag system of representation."[66] The carpetbaggers were replaced by native sons in time, but the Washington Ring functioned through the 1880s.

Among the laws passed by the First Legislature was an ordinance empowering the board of supervisors in each county to establish a school district wherever one hundred people occupied an area four miles square. Public School District No. 1 was organized in Tucson under this law on November 18, 1867. Appointed to the school board were Pie Allen, William S. Leon, and William S. Oury. An adobe building, formerly a saloon, was rented as a schoolroom, and Augustus Brichta became the first teacher paid out of

Schoolmaster and saloonkeeper Augustus Brichta.

the public funds. Brichta was a native of New York State, a Mexican War veteran, a forty-niner, and a graduate of Saint Louis University. He introduced fifty-five Mexican boys to the mysteries of book learning for six months in 1868.[67] Instruction ceased when money ran out.

More successful was the Sisters Convent and Academy for Females, established by the Sisters of Saint Joseph next door to San Agustín Church in 1870. At Bishop Salpointe's invitation Sister Monica of the Sacred Heart convoyed six cloistered women from their home convent in Saint Louis by way of San Francisco to their new assignment. The trip was almost too much for them. They were seasick on the steamer to

The seven sisters of Saint Joseph who braved the wilds of Arizona in 1870. From left: top, Sister Ambrosia, Sister Hyacinth, Sister Monica, Sister Emerentia; bottom, Sister Maxima, Sister Martha, Sister Euphrasia.

San Agustín's Church in 1870, the sisters' school and convent adjoining.

San Agustín's final abasement—the church as a garage and service station, early 1930s.

San Diego, uncomfortable in the carriage that took them to Yuma, terrified by the "wolves" (coyotes) at night on the desert, and uneasy about the proposals made to them by lonely pioneers. They almost drowned crossing the Colorado River, and were scorched, frozen, buffeted by high winds, and punctured by thorns. "It is beyond description, what we suffered in riding 200 miles in country like this," Sister Monica recalled, but she was delighted at the end of the journey by the *"grand celebration"* (italics hers) at Tucson, with fireworks, a torchlight parade, and a fine supper. She named her establishment the Villa Carondelet after her mother convent and was happy.[68]

Thus the seeds of education took root, encouraged by the new government, and began to grow. One provision of the legislature took effect immediately: Tucson became the capital of the territory.

CHAPTER 6

Roads to Civilization

By 1870 the way was open to better days for town and territory, but progress was slow toward civilization, as the term was then understood. Survival had to come first, and sometimes survival was so close to impossible that nothing else mattered. Education, refinement, creativity had to wait for a better day, and the pioneers, through their own acts and attitudes, gave the impression that they were headed back to the Dark Ages. To understand them, one must understand the difference between their idea of civilization and the notions which prevail a century after these beginnings.

In the first place, their descendants have their doubts about the whole business of being civilized. They note that the bringers of enlightenment in the 1870s were often unscrupulous materialists who cheated the government and the Indians and that many of them were easterners who had no intention of, in Poston's phrase, "building a state in Apacheland." Some believe that the Indians, a threat to the pioneers, had a better program for living than the whites; others, that the Mexicans, downgraded by the gringos, were really the masters of the art of living.[1] What, then, did "civilization" mean to the pioneers?

The best of them, like the Jesuits of two centuries before, were "trying to make things better." Improvement would come, they thought, if more people would come to settle, if farming and mining could be encouraged, if sheep and cattle could multiply on Arizona's hills, if outside investors could be induced to help develop Arizona's resources, if roads could be built and railroads subsidized. These goals achieved, there would be money for education, recreation, and the arts and letters. Isolation would be ended, and the remote corners of Arizona Territory would be accessible. There would be churches, libraries, theaters, hospitals, newspapers, museums—all the amenities "civilized" communities take for granted. At the end of the Civil War, Tucson had none of these things, and it seemed for a while that they would never come, though "good" people were immigrating in increasing numbers. Even when the capital was moved, after bitter battles in the state legislature and charges of massive bribery and corruption, the town remained a frontier village, raucous, crude, and often violent.

Newcomers were horrified at what they saw. With the departure of the Union troops and the achievement of civil government,

J. Ross Browne's sketch of Tucson, 1864. From J. Ross Browne, Adventures in the Apache Country *(1869).*

there was a period when no one seemed to be in charge, and the wicked flourished. Murder went unpunished, and there was actually a feeling, at least in some circles, that nobody in Tucson was anybody unless he had killed somebody. According to Sam Hughes, General Carleton was incredulous when he learned that Sam had not committed a single murder. J. Ross Browne, who traveled from San Francisco with Poston in 1864, called Tucson "literally a paradise of devils":

Murderers, thieves, cutthroats and gamblers formed the mass of the population. Every man went armed to the teeth, and scenes of bloodshed were of everyday occurrence in the public streets. There was neither government, law, nor military protection. The garrison at Tucson confined itself to its legitimate business of getting drunk or doing nothing. Arizona was perhaps the only part of the world under the protecting aegis of a civilized government in which every man administered justice to suit himself, and where all assumed the right to gratify the basest passions of their nature without restraint.[2]

It must be remembered that Browne was a journalist who never hesitated to make a bad story worse, and he gave his readers back East, perhaps unconsciously, what they wanted to hear. Murderers, thieves, and cutthroats hardly formed "the mass of the population," though there were too many of them, but it was true that Tucson's municipal housekeeping was casual in the extreme, both in peacekeeping and in street keeping. Sam Hughes noted in 1871 that the streets at the southern edge of town were so cut up by "ravines" that wagons could not get through and that open wells in nearly every lot were "in such condition as to endanger life daily." There was no department of sanitation, and dead animals sometimes lay in the streets for days. John G. Bourke, serving with General Crook, reported facetiously on local methods of giving directions:

"You want to find the Governor's? Wa'al, podner, jest keep right down this yere street past the Palace s'loon, till yer gets to the second manure pile on yer right, then keep to yer left pas the post-office, 'n' yer'll see a dead burro in the middle of th' road . . . 'n' jes' beyond that's the Gov.'s outfit. Can't miss it."[3]

Bourke's picture needs some correction. Tucson was not dirty all the time. In 1870, John H. Marion, of the *Arizona Miner* (Prescott), no friend to Tucson, remarked that the streets might once have been "filthy in the extreme" but that a "strong, well-organized chain gang"[4] had brought about a change for the better.

Bourke and Browne served up standard pictures of frontier manners. Bourke indeed knew the town well and introduced actual people and places—the Shoo Fly Restaurant, Don Estevan Ochoa, Bishop Salpointe, the chile-flavored food—but he also introduced or invented such eccentrics as Jack Long, a human chestnut whose "roughest part was on the outside." Addressing the waiter at the Shoo Fly, Jack says, "See yar, muchacho, move roun' lively now, 'n' git me a Jinny Lin' steak. . . . A Jinny Lin' steak, mee son, 's a steak cut from a hoss's upper lip." And so on, in the manner of Bret Harte, Horatio Darby, and others of their school. Tucson was bad enough, but these humorists made it worse.

Perhaps it was necessary to laugh to survive. Serious people found Tucson a very discouraging place. Mina Oury, Granville Oury's wife, arrived in 1866 after a weary,

These adobe buildings on Ochoa Street were the seat of government when Tucson was the capital of Arizona Territory. The structure on the right is said to have served as the capitol.

Congress Hall saloon, Charles O. Brown, owner, at right, his son William at left. The establishment was a meeting place for legislators.

roundabout trip through Mexico and found the town "the most forlorn, dreary, desolate, God-forsaken spot on earth,"[5] and others reacted in the same way. By 1869, however, conditions had changed for the better. Even J. Ross Browne admitted that at the end of the sixties, when his book was published, Tucson had "greatly improved."

Some improvement was certainly due to the shifting of the capital from Prescott, but the added prestige and a little extra business did very little to civilize the village or change its character and appearance. The state capitol, for one thing, was not even a separate building. It was a series of adobe rooms with dirt floors and mud roofs on Ochoa Street, just off Stone Avenue near the center of the downtown district. Several small cubicles were used for committee meetings, and two larger ones served as assembly rooms for the upper and lower

houses. The whole complex was rented from Hiram S. Stevens.[6] Ashamed of its inglorious quarters, the legislature petitioned the United States Congress for $100,000 to build a suitable statehouse in Tucson, but of course nothing came of that.[7] The members were sometimes obliged to caucus in San Agustín Church (technically a cathedral after Bishop Salpointe's elevation in 1869),[8] and informal meetings were held in the popular Congress Hall saloon, built in 1868 and operated by a well-known pioneer named Charles O. Brown—occasionally in Mrs. Wallen's Shoo Fly, so effectively celebrated by Captain Bourke.

Primitive or not, the adobe rooms of the capitol were a welcome sight to some of the legislators. Andrew S. Gibbons and Octavious S. Glass, for example, had to travel in 1868 from Thomas and Callville, in the far northwestern corner of the territory, reaching Yuma after a terrifying trip down the Colorado River in a fourteen-foot boat. Stage service from there, they learned, had been suspended after an Indian attack which cost the lives of one set of passengers. They arrived six days late at Tucson and were thankful just to be there, partaking of Mrs. Wallen's bacon and beans.[9]

They missed Governor McCormick's opening speech covering the problems of the territory, but his main concern would have been familiar to them. The Apaches were always the most pressing issue, the chief obstacle to "civilization," and there was no help in sight. The government never seemed to be able or willing to help, and the troops stationed at Tucson impressed the citizens as being close to useless. The effectiveness or ineffectiveness of these troops had an important bearing on events of the early seventies and gave great concern to the legislature and the people. Tucson was at the heart of the situation.

United States forces had been based there since 1862, when General Carleton established a military plaza near the center of town. Its focal point was the Tucson Depot, erected to house military supplies near the future site of the Santa Rita Hotel. Regular army troops replaced the California volunteers in 1866, and the post was reestablished as Camp Lowell in memory of a young officer killed in the Civil War. At first it was a tiny encampment occupied by one fifty-eight-man company of the Thirty-second Infantry, and the men had all they could do to escort army supply trains and maintain a couple of outposts on the Mesilla road. By 1869 troop strength had risen to 100. A year later the army expanded the post area, claiming 367 acres of land east and south of the depot and the village. Armory Park is a relic of those days.

This Camp Lowell never became a permanent installation. A few buildings—a guardhouse, an adjutant's office, and an arsenal—were erected on the military reservation. Shops and storehouses were rented in town, but the men continued to live in tents and drown their sorrows and frustrations in the local bars. This continued until 1872, when General George Crook decided that Camp Lowell was "unfit for the occupation of animals, much less the troops of a civilized nation" and ordered construction of a new post northeast of town, too far away to be a civil nuisance but close enough to stimulate business.

The citizens were glad to see the soldiers go. Tensions between the two groups were sometimes severe when the soldiers, bored and unhappy or out for a good time, made trouble. A particularly outrageous episode was reported by the *Arizonan* on March 12, 1870. A few days before, twenty men, drunk and belligerent, had shot up the town, killed Mr. Pennington's dog because he barked at them, and wounded two citizens. Editor Pierton W. Dooner indignantly recommended that the officers "devote a little less time to *fandangos* and billiards and turn their attention to the necessity of instituting discipline among the mob which they claim the honor (?) to *control*. It is enough that the people are constantly harrassed by Indians without being subjected to the outrages of a depraved and drunken soldiery." It should be added that the officer corps continued to contribute greatly to the social life of the town after the move was made.[10]

Had the soldiers been a little more effective in containing the Apaches, the townspeople might have felt better about them, but it seemed that the raiding and killing and burning increased in the early seventies.

The new Fort Lowell, watercolor painted in 1908 from a sketch made by Colonel J. B. Girard in 1875.

Departmental commander General George Stoneman was the object of blistering editorials in the Tucson and Prescott papers. It was useless for him to point out that his orders obliged him to try to conciliate the tribesmen, get them to settle on reservations, and live by farming and hunting. This to the people of Arizona seemed like utter nonsense. In their opinion the Apaches respected only force. If civilization in any form were to come to Arizona, they would have to be beaten and crushed. Many—perhaps most—of the Anglos thought that they would have to be exterminated. With this view the Papagos and the Mexicans were in sympathy by custom and inheritance. [11]

These people were desperate. Their neighbors and sometimes their own people had been killed and mutilated. In 1869, Larcena Pennington, for example, had been captured, abused, stripped, and left for dead. She had survived miraculously and crawled back to her family, living for days on roots and berries. [12] Few of the victims survived. It was an utter impossibility for a white person living in Arizona to see the Apache as an abused and deprived human being, robbed of his lands and his liberty, defending his home and his way of life. White people of a later generation are in no danger. Conditions in 1870, from the white point of view, were insupportable.

Arizona's third governor, who opened legislative proceedings in an improvised capitol at Tucson in 1870, tried to bring some order out of this chaos. Anson Peacely-Killen Safford was a man of little education but of great administrative talent, a farm boy from Vermont and Illinois who, like so many other Arizona pioneers, came west with the forty-niners. He was a small, dark man—only five feet five and known as "the little governor"—but brave, conscientious, and good at handling public affairs. [13] He had had some political experience in California and Nevada before President Grant

"The little governor," Anson Peacely-Killen Safford, father of Arizona education.

company in the field; they were mostly Mexicans by birth and not mounted. I took command of the company, and acted a part of the time in conjunction with Captain E. Miles and his command of the regular army; and also, for a time, with Lieutenant Cushing. We were in the field twenty-seven days. . . . I believe that a few companies of this class of our citizens would be found invaluable in subduing the hostile Indians.[14]

There was no disagreement about the seriousness of the situation. Every newspaper editor in the state was up in arms. Local groups were outraged. The legislature memorialized Congress, asking for help and citing more than eighty affidavits sworn to by victims of Apache attacks. The *Arizona Miner* printed three pages of accounts of murders and robberies. Mexican outlaws, preying on traffic between Gila Bend and Yuma, added to the seriousness of the situation. To many people, humane in their ordinary relations and probably Christians, the only solution seemed to lie, in the words of *Citizen* editor John Wasson, in "the slaying of every Apache man, woman and child."[15]

An object of strong suspicion was a group of Arivaipa Apaches who, instead of living on the San Carlos Reservation near Globe, as they were supposed to, had settled in their old home, the beautiful Arivaipa Canyon, near Camp Grant. They were issued rations, kept under surveillance, encouraged to farm, and paid for gathering hay for the soldiers. The arrangements for taking care of them were made in February, 1871. In March there were frequent attacks on military supply trains, ranchers in the Santa Cruz Valley, and travelers on the highways. Tucsonans were convinced that Indians from Camp Grant were using their settlement near the post as a base of operations and were being sheltered and fed by the army between

made him governor in 1869, and he went at his job like a professional. He began by traveling through the territory at great personal risk, camping where night overtook him and seeing for himself how desperate the situation was. Then he went to Washington and made a strong appeal to Congress for help. Appearing before the Sixth Legislature in Tucson in 1871, he talked about depredations on the southern overland road. In the preceding month of August, he said, the raiding was severe:

Two stage drivers were killed, one stage captured and all with it killed, and a stage station twenty-two miles east of Tucson was taken, and but one of the inmates escaped alive. Several others were killed about that time. The condition of affairs became so alarming that the citizens of Tucson contributed a sum sufficient to place a small

Juan Elías, Apache nemesis.

The leaders were well fitted for their roles. Oury had attacked an Indian camp in 1863 and knew how it was done. Elías had lost two brothers in Apache attacks and asked only for a chance to even the score. Every white man, every Papago, and every Mexican in southern Arizona stood with them.

They rendezvoused at Sam Hughes's house that night. Food, ammunition, and guns were loaded into a wagon, and they set off under cover of darkness. Hiram Stevens did not go along, but he posted a guard where the road crossed the Cañada del Oro north of town to keep any messengers from carrying a warning to Camp Grant. At the crack of dawn on April 30, a Sunday, the men had the camp surrounded and moved to attack. In a matter of minutes over a hundred Indians were dead, some, it was said later, the victims of mutilation and rape. Only eight of the dead were males. The rest were women and children. The men were said to be out hunting. Perhaps they were, but no white man believed it. Between twenty-five and thirty Indian children were carried away as captives by the Papagos in the group. In 1977, Don Schellie, of Tucson, published a novel focusing on two of the these children.[17]

This terrible deed aroused great indignation in the East and complicated the problems of Indian management immeasurably. There was a great hue and cry, demanding that the perpetrators be brought to trial. Eventually they were taken to court, and a jury of their peers acquitted them all.[18]

Only one of the attackers ever publicly repented. Sidney R. DeLong, prominent businessman and first elected mayor of Tucson, confessed in later years that that this chapter in his career was the only thing he regretted,[19] but William S. Oury called it

depredations. They said that parties had been sent out to track the raiders and had traced them from the scene of their atrocities to Camp Grant.[16]

William S. Oury and other civic leaders organized a committee of safety and decided that total elimination of the Indian encampment was the only answer. Before they acted, however, they tried once more to persuade General Stoneman to take action. Oury carried the message and brought back the answer, not unexpected, that the general had merely repeated his instructions from General William T. Sherman—to use "moral suasion and kindness." No hope there. So plans were laid, and on April 28, 1871, Oury and Juan Elías placed themselves at the head of a force of 148 men—94 Papagos, 48 Mexicans, and 6 Americans—and prepared to take violent action.

Sidney R. DeLong, merchant, Indian trader, first mayor of Tucson.

"a glorious and memorable event" and read a paper about it before the Arizona Pioneers Historical Society after the group was organized in the mid-eighties.[20] It would have been hard to find one citizen of Tucson who doubted that the slaughter was necessary, and the years did not change them. Mrs. Sam Hughes was one who never wavered. She commented in her old age on the stealing and killing which happened "almost every night"—on the trackers who followed the raiders to Camp Grant and established their guilt:

No, Mr. Hughes did not go to Camp Grant but he furnished the means to go; he approved of the plan and gave the ammunition and the arms; yes, they were given out from this very room we are sitting in. . . . Well, we finally got peace, but not till after the citizens took things into their own hands. I don't think we gave much

credit to the troops. . . . But ah! The citizens. They were different. They were always ready.[21]

After such a lawless act, civilization for Tucson seemed an impossibility to people outside Arizona, but to the pioneer mind the Camp Grant Massacre was an execution, quasi-legal because it was an act of the people, had been prepared for by assembly and agreement, and was decided on as a measure of last resort when all appeals to higher authority had failed. These considerations do not make the slaughter any less brutal, but they do make it more understandable.

Three years later the same belief in the right of the people to make their own law led to a notorious lynching on the plaza in front of the old presidio. Vincente Hernández and his wife were former citizens of Albuquerque and friends of merchant William Zeckendorf, who had allowed them credit and set them up in a store and pawnshop on South Meyer Street. They were apparently charming, lively people and made friends at once. The whole community was shocked to learn, on the morning of August 3, 1873, that their place had been entered the night before by thieves and the couple murdered with the utmost brutality. Responding in a familiar pattern, twenty of the best trackers began looking for sign, and thirty of the rest organized a "Committee of Safety." The chairman was none other than William Zeckendorf, an educated, civilized, humane European who had accepted the values and procedures of the frontier. It was understood that if the murderers were caught they would be put to death at once.

They were caught, three of them—traced to their homes and brought before the committee. A young Mexican named Sahuaripa confessed all after being forced to look at the dead faces of the victims and implicated one Córdoba, a more hardened criminal. A third man named Fichi had stood guard during the murders. The three were prepared for execution, along with a twice-convicted Anglo killer, who was awaiting death in the county jail, and escorted to an improvised gallows in the plaza.

By the time these arrangements were complete, the townspeople had returned from the funeral of the murdered couple. Zeckendorf addressed them—told what had happened, assured them of the killers' guilt, noted the condition of the jail and the proximity of Mexico should the men escape. "I now ask you," he concluded, "what punishment they deserve."

"*Que mueran!*" came the chorus. "Let them die!"

Only former Marshal Duffield dissented. Arizona's Angry Man, as historian B. Sacks calls him, was on the prod as usual. "You can hang a Mexican," he objected, "you can hang a Jew, you can hang a nigger, but you can't hang an American citizen." Big and tough as he was, they overpowered him, tied him up, and left him in the courthouse under guard while the condemned men were placed in a wagon under the gallows. The nooses were adjusted and the horses were driven off, leaving the men dangling.

The legal authorities—deputies, sheriff, judge, and district attorney—had taken pains to be absent, but a coroner's jury sat upon the case and ruled that "the criminals came to their deaths by hanging at the hands of the population of Tucson, and that said hanging was justifiable."[22]

The lynching became something of a cause célèbre. John G. Bourke gave the world a highly fictionalized version in 1880, John Spring published an eyewitness account in 1903, and H. H. Bancroft used it

as an example of folk justice in his *Popular Tribunals*.[23]

Such examples of extralegal violence notwithstanding, Tucson was taking steps, admittedly short and slow, toward better times in the years just before and just after 1870. General Crook had quieted the Apaches for the moment. Stage and mail lines competed for business and brought the outside world closer. A jail and a courthouse were built in 1868, and the first black businessman in the community, a barber named Samuel Bostwick, opened a shop in 1869.[24] Bishop Salpointe and the Sisters of Saint Joseph arrived in 1870, and John Wasson's *Citizen* made its appearance on October 15 of that year to urge the reelection of Richard C. McCormick to Congress and to give battle to the *Arizonan*. The result was a spectacular journalistic feud which crackled and flashed for several months. Editor Pierton W. Dooner called Wasson "a servile, self-asserting, stupid upstart . . . but yesterday dragged from the gutters of political and social corruption." Wasson, whose fuse was equally short, called Dooner "the malicious booby of the *Arizonan*" and inquired, "Whenever was this shameless editor honest?" The name-calling continued until Dooner gave up in 1871 and his paper went out of business.[25]

The year 1870 was a year of beginnings. A first for Tucson was the founding of Carrillo Gardens on South Main—a place where the townspeople could find shade, water, company, and amusement outside the saloons. This was progress! Even more important was the opening of a public school for boys in April. This was a dream come true for many of the first citizens, with Governor A. P. K. Safford in the lead.[26] The school building was an elongated adobe on the corner of Meyer and McCormick streets. It was

Carrillo's Gardens, 1887. Helene Goldschmidt (left), Marianne Wittelshofer, and Hannah Mansfeld. Photo by Leo Goldschmidt.

furnished with desks and a blackboard, and a supply of textbooks was on hand for sale to those students who could afford to buy them. Poor boys got theirs free. The teacher was an educated, personable, highly talented young Swiss immigrant named John (originally Johann) Spring. On the first day he faced almost 100 boys of all ages. On the third day they numbered 138.

Spring was equal to his task, though few of his boys had a word of English, and even fewer were accustomed to discipline. For three months he kept them quiet, kept them clean, and taught them penmanship, arithmetic, geography, drawing, and English. It was, as Spring remarked thirty-two years later, "a perfect chaos of boys," and he recalled "that dirt floor, those two rows of uncouth, unpainted, and unvarnished desks

and the many bare feet of the youngsters dangling from the benches"—all suggesting to him that "mighty oaks from little acorns grow."[27]

When Spring asked for an assistant for the next term and was refused, he gave up the effort, but the seed had been planted. The first permanent public school opened in Tucson on March 4, 1872.

A few months earlier, Mrs. L. C. Hughes, wife and chief assistant to the owner and publisher of the *Star*, had started a girls' school. This redoubtable woman, often called the "Mother of Arizona" because of her unremitting campaigns to bring enlightenment and decency to an uncurried territory, battled for "temperance," for women's rights, for higher education, for good works of all varieties, as did her hus-

Schoolmaster John Spring in uniform.

Editor John Wasson.

band—lawyer, newspaperman, and future governor. Mrs. Hughes's academy was not the first school for girls in Tucson, but it was a step forward.

The Tucson public-school system really began to flourish in 1873, when the civic leaders made a vigorous and successful effort to set up a creditable education program. John Wasson was the leader. In his view the way to start was to find capable and dedicated teachers, preferably women (John Spring said that the town could get two ladies "for the amount of my salary"), and his search led him to Stockton, California, where Maria Wakefield, a native of Minnesota, was beginning a successful teaching career. Her descendants say that Governor Safford acted as intermediary. He met Miss Wakefield by chance, learned that she was planning to go back to Minnesota, and encouraged her to apply for the vacant post in Tucson. She turned out to be exactly what John Wasson was looking for. Maria was a

vigorous young woman, twenty-five years old, experienced, capable, and indomitable. She was handsome and patrician, with a firm mouth, a commanding eye, and a fine head of hair piled high on her head. Wasson warned her of the perils of traveling through the Indian country, but she never hesitated. Bringing with her as her assistant Harriet Bolton, another unshakable young woman, she booked passage by stagecoach for Tucson and took charge on arrival. Tucson and Arizona owe her a great deal. When she retired thirty-five years later, the *Citizen* of September 23, 1909, paid her tribute:

These two women not only inaugurated the public school system in this city but encouraged the building of public schools in other parts of the Territory. In this city they personally raised $3,500 among the business men to build the first public school. The great educational system of Arizona is the direct outgrowth of the work they commenced.

Miss Wakefield and Miss Bolton may

Maria Wakefield, pioneer teacher.

Harriet Bolton, who came to teach but stayed to become Wasson's wife.

have been the first unmarried Anglo women to take up residence in Tucson, and they were objects of great interest to the young bachelors of the city. Only four months after her arrival Miss Wakefield married merchant Edward N. Fish after what must have been a whirlwind courtship, and shortly thereafter Wasson married Miss Bolton. A new era in education had begun. George C. Hall and his wife opened the Congress Street School in February, 1881, with 280 students.[28]

The new dispensation, doing things the Anglo way, carried over into the social relations of Tucson. First-family Mexicans and

Edward Nye Fish, pioneer merchant, whom Maria Wakefield married.

Alexander Levin, Tucson's hospitable merchant of joy.

top-ranking Anglos still met, mingled, and intermarried on terms of perfect equality and mutual esteem, but as more and more young women from the States appeared on the scene, some separation of the two groups was inevitable. Depression times during the eighties, resulting in competition for jobs and business, brought changes also. James Officer writes: "We note throughout the 1880's that fewer and fewer Spanish names are included in the newspaper accounts of social affairs sponsored by ranking Anglo families. Even such men of prestige as Mariano G. Samaniego and newspaper publisher Carlos Velasco were beginning to feel the sting of Anglo prejudice."

Even so the two groups got along, and still get along, better than elsewhere. "Upward mobility and social acceptance," Officer concludes, "seem more possible for Span-

ish speakers in Tucson than in neighboring Phoenix, El Paso, Los Angeles, or Albuquerque." Richard Griswold del Castillo, in a study of the Tucson and Los Angeles barrios, agrees.[29]

A symbol of community cohesiveness all through the seventies was an enterprise conducted by Alexander Levin, a fat, jolly, outgoing German, to please himself and his friends with good food and drink. He came to Tucson in the summer of 1869 and started the Pioneer Brewery in partnership with J. Goldtree. Soon after, he bought Wheat's saloon, fitted it up "very prettily," and within a month was giving "very agreeable entertainments with music and dancing." Before the year was out, he had built a hall for dancing and dining at the brewery, and early in 1870 he took over the Hodges Hotel on Main Street, opening it officially with a "grand supper." He next turned to a long-range project for making a three-acre park out of his brewery grounds. In 1878 he added a large building suitable for all sorts of entertainments, and in 1879 he built a bowling alley and shooting gallery. The Sixth Cavalry band sometimes supplied music, and there was nothing to rival "Boss" Levin's Opera House anywhere in Arizona Territory. It was a major calamity for the town when the roof fell in with a resounding crash in 1879, but Levin replaced the old dirt roof with a magnificent new tin one, and all was better than before.[30] It was easy for the citizens to love Tucson and each other at Levin's pleasure palace.

Men also enjoyed themselves, it must be admitted, outside Levin's Park. The town had its tenderloin district, where less-refined diversions were available. Most of the saloons were concentrated near the corner of Meyer Street and Congress, a long block south of the old presidio, but the real good-

The Calhoun Opera Company at Levin's pleasure palace.

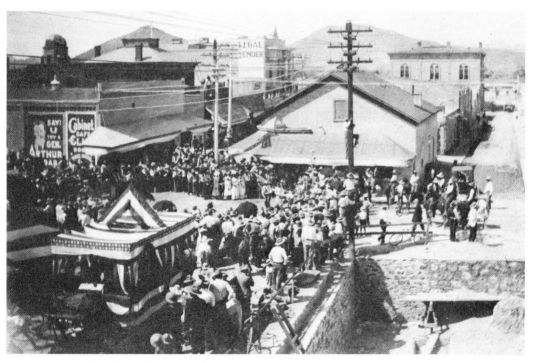

The Wedge in its final days.

George O. Hand, soldier, saloonkeeper, and diarist.

time district occupied an area three blocks long just north of Congress on Maiden Lane—originally known as Calle de la India Triste (Street of the Sad Indian Girl). It was supposedly named for an Indian maiden who went to live with a Mexican officer in the presidio and was cast out by both her people and his when he died. On the north side of Maiden Lane was the "sporting district." Between Maiden Lane and Congress was a narrow segment of land called The Wedge because it came to a point at Stone Avenue. Mostly residential, it was guilty by association.[31]

Not much has been written about the Tucson tenderloin, but it was a reality, and a lively place for many years. Like all other such districts in frontier towns, it filled a need, and its right to existence was not much questioned until the turn of the century. It took some time for Tucson to become a family-oriented community. In 1882 the proportion of unmarried men was still high,

and most of them were comparatively young. They were happy to spend their money for the real or fancied benefits offered along Maiden Lane.[32]

Few if any of the girls who worked there were Anglos until after 1880. They did not keep diaries or write letters to the newspapers, and their patrons revealed as little as possible about any connection with them, but some scraps of information are available. George O. Hand, whose impressions of Tucson have been quoted, operated a saloon in partnership with George F. Foster during the seventies, and his daily records are revealing:

January 3, 1875. Pleasant morning. Several drunken men in town. Tom Gardner and J. B. Brown are on the war path. Bullfight tonight at Smith's corral. Best of the season. One Mexican nearly killed. Lotteries in the evening. House full. Streets full of drunken men all night. Closed at 11 o'clock. Preaching at the courthouse today.

March 7, 1875 (Sunday). Very dull. Stores are all closed. My 45th birthday. Took a hot bath. Pat O'Meara got drunk, fell down, and someone stepped on his nose. Puppet show in the evening. Overstreet hit a Mexican and the Mexican hit Harrison with a stone, cutting his head. Took a walk after closing and got home at three in the morning (Cruz).

March 9 (Cruz—$1.25).

March 16. Windy. Sober all day.

April 10 (Big Refugia—$2.00).

The women's names are those of prostitutes whom George visited. In justice to Hand it should be noted that he became the night watchman at the courthouse in the 1880s, attended church services when they were available, and apparently ordered his life considerably before he died in 1887.

In spite of everything the leading citizens of Tucson continued to try to make things better. One prerequisite for improvement was village incorporation. Until that was achieved, nobody could be sure he had title to his property. Major Ferguson with his map in 1862 and William Oury with his list of landholders had made a beginning, but legal titles under United States statutes were still not available. As the community expanded, this lack created a major problem. It was amazing how fast the town grew. By 1877 it had two hotels, a county courthouse, a United States depository, two breweries, two flour mills, four feed and livery stables, and ten saloons. There was some residential expansion along Main Street north of the center, but growth was mostly southward between Camp Lowell and the river channel, even after the military post was moved beyond the town limits, and the land on the reservation remained undeveloped for some time.[33]

Businessmen did the best they could to establish a clear line from the vendor who sold them their property back to an original Spanish owner, but some of the land was government-owned and could be possessed only if proper arrangements were made. "Needed ingredients," says historian Gilbert Pedersen, "were a workable congressional act for granting townsites to proper local authority, territorial legislation giving details of the division of town sites, and completion of United States surveys so that public lands conveyed by the United States to a municipal corporation would be properly described."[34]

Congress acted in 1867; the territorial legislature in 1871. The survey was the hardest thing to arrange because surveyors did not like risking their lives in Apache country. John Wasson became surveyor general in 1870, however, and completed the work in the following year. The next step was a public meeting to petition the county

supervisors to incorporate the village, and when all necessary steps had been taken, Tucson became a municipality with a mayor (Sidney R. DeLong) and four councilmen. Lots went on sale for five to ten dollars, titles of landowners were confirmed, and many parcels were distributed by lottery.

It was at this stage that Tucson ceased to be a Mexican town and became an Anglo community. Ownership of land had been passing steadily into Anglo hands since the earliest days of American occupation, and even in population Tucson was changing. In 1864 the first territorial census counted 1,526 people, most of them of Mexican ancestry. The count in 1870 was 8,007, and many of them were from the States. Most were engaged in some form of commerce. Tucson was growing in importance as a center of trade and transportation. It was a way station on the road to California, for freighters as well as for travelers, and on the routes into Mexico. It supplied the military posts in southern Arizona and provisioned the mines and the ranches when they went back into operation after the war. Several large mercantile firms kept caravans of wagons on the road, some with as many as thirty men in a crew. They could be months on the road—four months from Santa Fe was the rule—and as a result the owners had to keep three stocks of goods in circulation—one in the store, one in the hands of buyers who did not always pay promptly, and one on the road.[35] A wagon train could be worth anywhere from $25,000 to $50,000. The risks were great, and a trader had to be shrewd, resourceful, and prepared to stand heavy losses.

Some of those early-day merchants were remarkable people. Edward Nye Fish, of Barnstable, Massachusetts, for example, joined the rush to California in 1849, started

William Zeckendorf.

Louis Zeckendorf.

a store in San Francisco, and came to Tubac in 1864 as post trader. In partnership with Simon Silverberg, of San Francisco, he organized E. N. Fish & Co. on Main Street in Tucson; freighted supplies to forts, mines, and ranches; built the first steam-operated flour mill in Arizona; and invested in the Silverbell mines northwest of Tucson. He served his community as a county official and school trustee. His orderly New England soul was offended by Tucson's disorderly ways, and he urged the property owners "to cause the public streets in the town of Tucson to be repaired" in front of their businesses.[36] Fish's descendants are still trying to make things better.

Then there were the three Zeckendorf brothers, William, Louis and Aaron, German-born but at home in the West. Aaron died in 1862, but "Bill" and "Louie" were long-time partners. William arrived in New York in 1856 at the age of fourteen, already

well grounded in German, French, and Hebrew. He joined his brothers, already in business, in Santa Fe and in 1869 arrived in Tucson, where the firm had connections, as manager of their new store. Ten years later he opened a store of his own. Albert Steinfeld came over from Santa Fe to join his uncle Louis when William left. In time he took over the business, renamed it, and built its foundations so securely that it was still going strong a century later.[37]

Business rivals of E. N. Fish and the Zeckendorfs included Charles T. Hayden, who soon moved to Tempe, and the Jacobs brothers, Lionel and Barron, from San Bernardino, California. They arrived in 1869 with a wagonload of merchandise, mostly canned goods which sold for a dollar a can. They opened a store in 1871 and later organized the Pima County Bank, Tucson's first.[38]

Another big firm was Lord and Williams.

Albert Steinfeld.

Lionel Jacobs.

The guiding hand belonged to Charles H. Lord, a medical doctor who came out of the Civil War a major and appeared in Arizona as a contract surgeon at the Cerro Colorado Mine south of Tucson in 1866. By 1869, in partnership with Postmaster W. W. Williams, he had become involved in various mercantile ventures, including banking, mining, and government contracts. A heavyset man with a full face partly concealed by a heavy crop of dark whiskers and a mop of black hair, he had the look of one who knew he was in charge of important matters. He liked to live expensively and had the means to do it. The *Arizonan* reported on January 2, 1870, that Lord and Williams's sales "last week amounted to more than $12,000." A year later, however, the editor informed the public that Dr. Lord "has not our confidence and we know but few whose confidence he possesses."[39] The rich have bitter enemies.

Barron Jacobs.

Business as usual at Zeckendorf and Staab's store, 1874.

man with flowing whiskers, a serious face, and melancholy eyes, P. R. became a familiar sight on Tucson's streets. He was always present when something needed to be done. He was twice mayor of his village, served for four years as territorial treasurer, and worked for all good things but particularly for public education and causes supported by the Catholic church.[41] When he died in 1903, Sidney R. DeLong, his partner and fellow member of the Pioneer Society,[42] wrote that

As important in the life of growing Tucson as Lord and Williams was the firm of Tully and Ochoa. Estevan Ochoa has been introduced already. Pinckney Randolph Tully was his equal in personality and ability—a typical frontiersman in that he had been everywhere and done everything in the West before he came to Tucson. His family moved from Mississippi first to Arkansas and then to western Missouri, and P. R. followed the Santa Fe Trail to Santa Fe in his young manhood, arriving two years ahead of General Kearny. In 1849 he drove a herd of sheep to California and on his return became Don Estevan's partner with headquarters in Las Cruces, New Mexico.[40] He brought a caravan to Tucson in 1858 and sold the entire cargo to Solomon Warner a few hours after his arrival. The company opened a store at Tubac in 1864 and kept it open until the town was abandoned. In 1868, P. R. settled permanently in Tucson and took charge of a big building at the corner of Main and what is now Broadway with a huge corral and ample storehouses nearby. A tall, wiry

Pickney Randolph Tully.

Dr. Charles H. Lord.

"he was always a great friend of the poor, and will be long remembered by many for his unostentatious acts of charity. . . . It was said of him that he was more the friend of others than of himself."[43]

P. R. undoubtedly deserved good opinions, but he and his firm have suffered in the general condemnation that has been visited on merchants of the "Tucson Ring."[44] Top-ranking army officers accused them. General August V. Kautz, departmental commander, charged the ring with high crimes and misdemeanors in 1876, and General Crook declared that at the bottom of the Indian troubles was "greed and avarice on the part of the whites." As early as 1871 General George Stoneman accused the merchants of "fleecing the government" in large-scale corruption.[45] Modern historians, for instance, Jay J. Wagoner, state that "the firm of Tully and Ochoa profited immensely from its po-

litical alliance with the 'federal ring.'"[46] These charges are easy to make, difficult to prove. P. R. Tully was certainly above petty theft, and he did take enormous risks. The *Citizen* for December 24, 1870, reported a savage attack on a Tully and Ochoa wagon train and concluded, "We have not the figures but presume they have lost within the past few years not far from $100,000."

Tully and Ochoa went out of business after the railroad reached Tucson, but in 1890 P. R. petitioned the court of claims for reimbursement of losses sustained in four Indian attacks on company trains in 1867, 1868, 1869, and 1870. He was awarded $12,065 in 1897 in satisfaction of all four claims.[47] Since one wagon train was worth from $25,000 up, the award does not seem excessive.

The bad reputation of the traders was closely tied in with a general loathing of the Indian agents, who, in the words of John BretHarte, "suffered a pervasive and undeserved obloquy." The case of Joseph C. Tiffany was a classic example. Tiffany was a fat, pious, slow-witted, well-intentioned man, in charge of the San Carlos Agency from 1880 to 1882, who made some mistakes but did everything he could for his Indians. His malodorous reputation was almost entirely the creation of L. C. Hughes, editor of the *Arizona Star*. His assaults on the unfortunate agent were quoted by John G. Bourke in *On the Border with Crook*, and, says John Bret-Harte, "all subsequent generations of Arizona historians have learned to damn him as an article of faith."[48]

Tiffany twice returned to Arizona to stand trial for his alleged crimes, but his case was never called. With General Crook and Captain Bourke against him he had to wait until 1975 for a defender to arise, and his reputation as a crooked Indian agent is probably

Philip Drachman.

Jacob S. Mansfeld.

fastened on him forever.[49] The Tully and Tiffany stories serve warning that sweeping generalizations about these pioneer types are dangerous.

Among the enterprising businessmen who came to Tucson in the early days of the territory were a few Jews who came to grow up with the country. Philip Drachman, for example, came in 1854, worked for the Zeckendorfs during his boyhood, started his own shoe store, and achieved solid prosperity.[50] His descendants are still among Tucson's first citizens. Jacob Mansfeld, born in Germany, arrived in Arizona in 1870 at the age of thirty-eight and founded the Pioneer News Depot and Bookstore, "having learned that no such business existed at the time in the Territory." Jacob's evaluation of Tucson at the time of his arrival provides a useful corrective to the caricatures of J. Ross Browne and John G. Bourke. He wrote in 1884:

The American population numbered about Two hundred Souls. They were a good Set of People and no Lines were drawn in Society. . . . The Citizens of Tucson of the present time may learn a lesson from former times. Unity and good feeling among the Citizens of this Town made Tucson in the Early Days as good a place as could be found any weres on this Coast.

It is interesting to note that in 1884 Jacob was thinking of the early 1870s as the "Old Days."

Mansfeld started the first public library in Arizona Territory in 1871, the year after his arrival, but the difficulties he faced were tremendous. The mail came twice a week by buckboard from Yuma, and goods imported from San Francisco were eight days on the road, if they arrived at all. In 1870, Tucson was three weeks without mail. His "Christmas goods" appeared in the middle of January, 1871. "People here were used to such things," he said, "and took it good naturedly."[51]

96

Mansfeld's news depot and bookstore, 1890s.

New faces and new businesses came every year, but their efforts and resources failed to bring the growth and prosperity that the leaders constantly envisioned. Everybody knew that Arizona's potential was enormous. All that was needed was vision—and money, especially money. The seventies saw the mounting of a vigorous campaign to attract outside capital, and the tone of communications during this period changed from the negativism of Brown, Bourke, Cremony, and Cozzens to rosy-hued pictures of a wonderful land of opportunity.

Poston may be said to have begun it. Mowry carried it on. Richard C. McCormick—secretary, governor, and delegate in Congress—did his share with letters in eastern newspapers, speeches in Congress, and a book called *Arizona: Its Resources and Prospects*, published in 1865. He recommended among other things that Congress appropriate $5 million to bring Civil War veterans to the western states as settlers.[52] Another pamphlet, subsidized by the territorial government in 1871, was titled *Resources of Arizona Territory*. It was put together by three commissioners—Governor Safford, John G. Campbell, and Charles H. Brinsley—to "sell" Arizona.[53] As newspapers were founded, they carried on the campaign. The *Arizonian* was established at Tubac in 1859 by capitalists who had "large interests in the Gadsden Purchase."[54] After six months it was moved to Tucson and renamed the *Arizonan*. It was followed by the *Arizona Miner* at Prescott in 1864, the *Arizona Citizen* at Tucson in 1871, the *Sentinel* at Yuma in 1872, and the *Star* at Tucson in

1877.[55] The editors needed local support, but they appealed also to the nation at large, which could be reached through the "exchange" system. Eastern and California newspapers regularly printed news from Arizona until the exchange list was cut back in the later seventies.[56]

Travelers and writers of handbooks helped by reporting what they saw to a nation eager for information about the West. An early example was Hiram C. Hodge's *Arizona as It Is: The Coming Country Compiled from Notes of Travel During the Years 1874, 1875, and 1876*. Hodge recommended the development of artesian wells to bring into cultivation fifteen to twenty million acres of "as rich land . . . as can be found on the continent." Several similar works appeared in the 1880s and 1890s.[57]

They all helped, but more was always needed. Arizona was slow to emerge from its "almost continuous economic depression."[58] Nothing seemed to prosper for very long. Stock raising, for example, boomed in the 1870s in spite of the Apaches, but drought and overgrazing brought problems in the 1880s.[59] The government was always parsimonious. It did lay out two wagon roads, as has been noted, but it refused to subsidize railroad construction until the end of the seventies, and it responded to no urgings in finding artesian water, clearing the Colorado River, or subsidizing silver. Its most important contribution was the construction in 1873 of a military telegraph line, available for civilian use, from San Diego to Tucson and Prescott.[60]

Mining, which was to become Arizona's most profitable industry, was slow to develop, contrary to what one would think. The newspapers were always full of mining news, and prospectors were always trumpeting the immense promise of this or that dis-

trict. At the same time really important discoveries—the Bradshaws, the Harquahalas, the Globe area, Tombstone—kept hope alive. Capital was needed for development, however, and eastern moneymen were slow to see a future in this rugged, arid, dangerous land so far from their bank vaults and so hard to reach. This attitude was an exasperation to Arizonans, who were convinced that under their feet were untold riches. "There is no question about the gold here," wrote Territorial Secretary Richard C. McCormick to a friend in New York. "The only question agitating my mind is how much of it I shall get. I am hoping to have my full share, but the country is so new, inaccessible and undeveloped that the future is much in the clouds."[61]

Only the rich could hope to make a real killing in the mines, but even the humblest citizen could have a share of the action. The key word was "feet." The owner of a promising prospect would sell so many feet of his claim, and observers reported that everybody in Tucson had "'feet' on the brain." Even the holders of many feet, however, were "patiently waiting for currency affairs at the East to become settled so that capital can be transferred here without the ruinous loss of half or two-thirds."[62] When capital did become seriously interested in Arizona, it was not silver and gold that brought the big money. It was copper.

Production statistics reveal the truth. Major metal production in 1870 was valued at $800,000. In 1875 it was valued at $954,300. In 1882, five years after the Tombstone strike, it was valued $11,113,023, but the shafts were already flooded, and the boom was over. In 1895, after the panic of 1893, the figure had dropped to $9,126,000. By 1900 the big companies had moved in, and in 1902 the

Saint Mary's Hospital, 1880.

value of metals had jumped to over $20 million. Real, vigorous development was impossible without the underpinning of investment capital from the outside.[63]

All the while, slowly but surely, Tucson was approaching a state of civilization. The capital was returned to Prescott in 1877, but the town continued to be the largest and most important community in Arizona Territory. Richard Hinton's *Handbook to Arizona* spelled it out in some detail. He noted that 276 children were now learning in three schools and that Carrillo's Gardens boasted "500 peaches, 2,000 grape vines, 200 quinces, 60 pomegranates, and 9 apricots, all in bearing," along with "a profusion of lovely flowers."[64]

Hinton might have added many other encouraging signs. The first Presbyterian church was organized in 1876; the Methodists followed in 1879; the Episcopalians in 1880. Saint Mary's Hospital was completed and opened in 1880. An ice plant, "very near the automatic," went into operation in 1879, and a public bathhouse with showers added its cleansing influence in the same year. The approach of the railroad triggered a real-estate boom. Block 100 on

Military Plaza was sold by the city for the breathtaking sum of $20,000. These were new times indeed![65]

To a young telegraph operator on his way to the military post at Fort Grant in 1880, however, Tucson was still a rough-and-ready place. Will C. Barnes, later to become one of Arizona's best-known chroniclers, arrived in a cloud of dust on the stagecoach "with brakes shrieking and long whiplash cracking," dismounting in front of a one-story white-adobe building called the Cosmopolitan Hotel. He was assigned a cot in a small room where nearly a dozen others were occupied by men "in various grades of intoxication," fully dressed. That was bad enough, but not the worst:

The lavatory, or "wash room," consisted of a long wooden sink in the dark hall that led to the back of the bar-room. This sink was about ten feet long, and was equipped with six or eight tin basins. A barrel of water, fitted with a wooden faucet, stood on a shelf over the sink. The waste water drained off at one end through a pipe which led to the street. The thing fairly reeked with microbes, bacilli, and germs. Happily no one knew much about such things in those early days. A number of coarse, common-use towels, a cracked mirror, to which was chained a dilap-

The Cosmopolitan Hotel in 1874, as Will C. Barnes saw it.

idated hair-brush that had been used for many years and had shed a lot of its bristles, and a brass-backed comb minus many teeth, completed the toilet facilities.

It seemed to Barnes that every other building was a saloon, and in many of them gambling went on at a furious pace, day and night. The buildings between the saloons were occupied by *nymphes du pave* "of every race and color." The gamblers and saloon-keepers were "the most elegant males in town." It was a busy, colorful place as huge freight wagons rolled through the narrow streets, army ambulances dashed past filled with officers, and the stagecoach careened recklessly around corners.[66]

It would seem from Barnes' account that Tucson in 1880 was primitive enough to suit anybody, but at least one man yearned for earlier times. John G. Bourke grew sad and sentimental as he contemplated the decline of the old and the advance of the new. What he missed was the leisurely pace of life. In earlier times "nothing was done energetically" except riding and dancing, and "nothing disturbed the monotonous routine of daily life but an occasional 'carrera" (horse race) or a 'pelea de gallos' (cock fight or perhaps Don Carlos Velasco was about to christen another olive branch." Now the Americans are making all the money and whipping up the pace. "I know it is heresy to say so," he confessed, "but I am just a trifle sorry to hear that Tucson is being so rapidly Americanized." He liked it better as it was, "dirty, dusty and vermin-infested," but a more gracious place for all that.[67]

The Orndorff Hotel, once the Cosmopolitan, with second story added.

CHAPTER 7

Chariot of Fire

March 20, 1880, was a high point in the life of R. N. (Bob) Leatherwood, mayor of Tucson. The biggest party in the town's history was about to take place, and he was in charge. The railroad tracks had reached the outskirts. The new water tank was almost finished. The first train would usher in a new era for what had once been the post farthest out, and the village had reached a point emotionally just a little below frenzy.

The thought of what was coming had sent the newspaper editors into ecstasies. L. C. Hughes of the *Star* wrote on May 1, 1879: "The first sound of the locomotive's whistle will be the notice of a new life for our city and its vicinity, and we look forward to the time when the last spike is driven that connects Tucson with the outside world by a band of iron with a degree of pleasure that we cannot describe."

Leatherwood was as excited as anyone else—perhaps more so since he was in charge—but he had handled important assignments before, and this one did not terrify him. He had done everything possible to prepare for the arrival of the official party of Southern Pacific officials, scheduled for 11:45 A.M. He had involved almost every

man and woman in the village in the preparations, and on that March morning they were all poised for action.

In 1880, Leatherwood was a thirty-six-year-old Confederate veteran, a native of North Carolina, who had saved his military cap and uniform and wore them on great occasions. He had been a resident since 1869 and was the proprietor of Leatherwood's Stables, at the corner of Church and Pennington, where the southeast corner of the old presidio had stood. Although he was anything but impressive physically—a small, thin man, almost emaciated, with a goatee and moustache—he was proud and tough and efficient, and people knew that Bob Leatherwood was a man they could count on. His record of public service was impressive—city councilman, member of the state legislature, Pima County sheriff, county treasurer, captain of the Arizona Rangers who went out after Geronimo in 1876—and he was colorful enough to start a run of stories. Robert H. Forbes, of the University of Arizona, used to tell about the time Leatherwood came in from working his mining claims in the Catalina Mountains and sat in on a poker game at the Fashion Saloon. The

Mayor R. N. Leatherwood.

conversation turned to religion, and Bob bet a man across the table that he could not recite the Lord's Prayer.

"Hell, yes, I can!" the man declared, slapped his double-eagle gold piece down beside Bob's and began, "Now I lay me down to sleep. I pray the Lord my soul to keep."

"You win, you win," Bob interrupted, and shoved the stakes at him.[1]

In 1879, Leatherwood helped dispose of the $10,000 in bonds issued by the city to pay for the depot and yards demanded by the Southern Pacific. He took office as mayor on January 1, 1880, and was immediately caught up in the preparations for welcoming the iron horse.

At first it seemed that his main respon-

sibility was waiting. There was no end to the delays and difficulties the construction people had to overcome. The tracks reached Yuma in September, 1877, but further progress was often interrupted—by bad weather, lack of steel rails, New Year's Eve celebrations by the Chinese track workers. The railhead reached Casa Grande, sixty-five miles north of Tucson, and all work ceased. In January, 1880, however, activity was resumed, inducing the *Citizen* to run an editorial headed "Toot, T-o-ot, T-o-o-o-t," which prophesied that the rails would arrive in sixty days.[2] Three hundred Chinese laborers appeared at Casa Grande. Construction superintendent J. H. Strobridge rolled in from California in his special car, and on January 14 the great machine swung into operation. The track layers went forward at the rate of a mile a day, with sixty-five miles to cover. By February 10 the railhead was only eighteen miles from Tucson, and work trains were almost in sight.[3]

It was time for some serious thinking about several subjects. One was the Excursion. With the inception of regular rail service the SP was offering a round trip to San Francisco at special rates. Everyone with the money to buy a ticket wanted to be included when the special train departed on March 24.[4]

The other matter on everyone's mind was the welcoming celebration which was being actively promoted by Bob Leatherwood. "Every public-spirited citizen must assuredly recognize the importance of having a grand jollification," the *Citizen* declared.[5] And that was where the mayor came in. He appointed eight committees and chaired both the Committee of Reception and the Committee on Toasts and Speeches. He saw to it that everybody who was anybody in Tucson was involved. His committee lists sound like a who's who of the community in 1880, and they all worked.[6]

The excitement mounted as work trains became visible far to the north. A cheering crowd gathered at the edge of town on March 17 to watch the track layers and stare at Locomotive No. 41 with sixty-five cars behind. Passengers and freight were already arriving by courtesy of the construction trains. Superintendent Strobridge's private car was included, and some of the Tucson ladies called on Mrs. Strobridge in her rolling domicile. Telegrams went off on the seventeenth to invite the mayors of Yuma, Los Angeles, and San Francisco to the impending "jollification."[7] Folklore says that one was sent to the pope, and that his holiness, or somebody speaking for him in Tucson, acknowledged the invitation, sent a blessing, and inquired at the end, "Where in hell is Tucson, anyhow?"[8]

In due course the twentieth arrived. Committee members were getting ready to put on their dress-up clothes when word came that the special train was already in, more than an hour early. Caught by surprise, the mayor hastily assembled his reception committee and hurried to the scene of action. They arrived about the time the Sixth Cavalry band struck up a lively tune and a small battery of cannons began delivering a thunderous salute, creating some auditory problems as first greetings were exchanged.

Charles Crocker, vice-president of the Central Pacific and a top man in the Southern Pacific organization, had brought with him his son Charles, president of the Southern Pacific of Arizona; James Gamble, head of Western Union; and a number of other notables. The official party mounted a bunting-draped platform to face the welcoming committee. Committee members Charles R. Drake and William S. Oury made

speeches. Estevan Ochoa made a speech and presented to Crocker an engraved silver spike made from the first bullion produced by the Tough Nut Mine, in Tombstone. Then came a procession to Levin's banquet hall on Pennington Street, where the staff, surprised like everybody else by the early arrival, was frantically active. By two o'clock the banquet was ready.

When the meal was over, Leatherwood turned the meeting over to Charles D. Poston, who proposed the toasts and introduced the speakers, who responded. Following established custom, Poston called for the first toast to the president of the United States, following it with one to the railroad. "The Chariot of Fire has arrived in Tucson," Poston intoned, "on its way across this continent. We welcome the Railroad as the Messiah of civilization, and we welcome the road builders as the benefactors of mankind." It was Crocker's place to respond. He knew he was no match for Poston in spread-eagle oratory. He spoke briefly and simply, mentioning the prospector with his pick and his burro as the "true pioneer," and sat down.

It went on and on after that, and some of the speakers were carried away by the emotions of the moment. One of them was Benjamin Morgan, who responded to a toast to the City of Tucson:

It is no vain eulogy which I speak in her behalf, when in this presence I assert that no city of her size can boast of a higher state of morals or perfect protection to property and life . . . at no distant day do I prophesy that Tucson, the mud town on the banks of the Santa Cruz, will be Tucson the magnificent. . . . Today she greets these, her honored guests, who speak by their presence the happy prologue to the swelling act of the imperial theme.

Rollin Squire, of San Francisco, rose to remark, with fine irony, that he was "spellbound" by Morgan's vision of the future. "I have been negligent in my search after the splendors of this pueblo," he confessed. "I will diligently seek to know them."

When the last silver tongue was silent, the hall was cleared, and a "grand soiree" began. The *Star* reported that 1,200 people were on the floor, dancing until midnight, when, "in respect to the time-honored custom of Sabbath observance," the party broke up.[9]

The Excursion got off the following Wednesday at 3:00 A.M. Ninety-six people paid fifty dollars apiece for the round trip to San Francisco.[10]

Now that the railroad was a reality, not one Tucsonan doubted that wealth and prosperity were inevitable, and it was true that life thenceforward was, for many people, simpler, easier—and cheaper. Orders to the West Coast, and later to Kansas City or Saint Louis or New York, could be transmitted in minutes by telegraph and received in days by train. Prices on practically everything were revised rapidly downward. Ordinary people rejoiced in the new dispensation, but the signs were ominous for the merchant princes of yesterday. Weeks before the great celebration the *Citizen*, under the heading "Increasing Trade," reported with gruesome triumph:

The near approach of the iron horse has already begun to produce a demoralizing effect upon high prices in this city. The enterprising firm of L. Zeckendorf & Co. are among the first to adapt themselves to the system, and are selling goods at prices unheard of before in this Territory. Their business tact will not go unrewarded, and their increased sales will no doubt more than counterbalance profits at high prices.[11]

Many of the old firms were already in trouble. Stock on hand had to be sold at a loss to compete with cheap new goods brought in by rail. Old customers failed to pay promptly when money was desperately needed, and some did not pay at all. Catastrophe followed. Tully and Ochoa sold off everything, distributed the proceeds among their creditors, and went out of business. William Zeckendorf went into bankruptcy in 1883. Safford, Hudson & Company failed in 1884.[12] Solomon Warner closed the doors of his mill, never a money-maker, in 1881 and spent the rest of his life in less-than-genteel poverty working on a perpetual-motion machine. Trouble began for Hiram S. Stevens and led to his suicide in 1893.[13]

The most spectacular of these failures was that of the great house of Lord and Williams a year after the arrival of the rails. Dr. Lord kept up appearances as long as he could, living and entertaining in high style, sending his daughter off on a tour of Italy, doing business as usual. When he saw the end approaching, however, he fled to Mexico and tried to convince the companies holding his life-insurance policies that he was dead. These companies got on his trail and found that he was alive and practicing medicine in Mexico City, where he died in 1884. He was not universally condemned, however, when the news got back to Tucson. "He may have had many enemies," said the *Star* editorial writer, "who in the hour of his misfortunes assailed him, but they were far outnumbered by his host of friends, who judged his heart aright."[14]

A particularly sad failure was the decline of Alex Levin, the generous and cheerful host of the seventies whose pleasure garden was one of the assets of Tucson, whose entertainments were a welcome break in the monotony of frontier village life, and whose food and drink were said to equal the best in San Francisco or New York. Something happened to the rotund "Boss" after 1880. The greater attraction of Carrillo's Gardens (Carrillo had eight acres to Levin's three) may have contributed. At any rate, by 1884 there was talk about Levin's entertainments, and in June of that year the *Star* sent a reporter to look into it. The conclusion was that "'The Park' under its management has outlived its usefulness. . . . the nightly consorting of the vile and the vicious within its precincts, has made its name the synonym of iniquity." [15] Since Levin was a city councilman at the time, this blast may have been political, but it would seem that Levin's Garden was not what it used to be.

The changeover from pioneer times to "civilization" seems to entail misfortunes of this kind. What was respectable or at least tolerable to the first comers is insupportable to those who arrive later. The Arizona pioneers themselves were conscious that times were changing, and they were alarmed by it. When Bill Oury rose from his seat on the platform beside the tracks at the great celebration in 1880, he revealed his concern:

The pioneers of Arizona have spent the best years of their life in preparing the way for that progress which we now see consummated; our life and death struggle with the ruthless Apache to retain a foothold upon the land of our adoption running through many dark years is now a thing of the past, our mission is ended today. Here, then, arises the question: What are you to do with us? The enterprise of such men as now surround me has penetrated every nook and corner of our broad land, and we have no frontier to which the pioneer may flee to avoid the tramp of civilized progress. Moreover the weight of years has fallen upon us; consequently the few remaining years that the Divine Master has in store for us must be spent amongst you. Therefore, in the whirl of excitement, incident to the race after the precious treasure imbedded in our mountain ranges, our last request is that you kindly avoid trampling in the dust the few remaining monuments of the first American settlements in Arizona. [16]

Oury could not have foreseen that posterity would condemn him and his generation as selfish materialists and exploiters, but he must have had some inkling of what was to come as he and his friends began to feel more and more outdated. It was this feeling, or something like it, which led to the foundation of the Society of Arizona Pioneers in 1884.

Preliminary consultations of interested persons were held at the home of Jacob Mansfeld. It was Charles D. Poston, however, who issued the call for the first meeting, which convened at the Palace Hotel in Tucson on January 31, 1884. The potential members present numbered 145, but more than 100 sent regrets. The first session was comparatively peaceful, but the second, which assembled on February 9, was explosive. The burning question was who should be allowed in. Poston wanted everybody who came before 1876, the centennial year. Jacob Mansfeld proposed that the cutoff date should be April 30, 1871, the date of the Camp Grant Massacre, "when the people of Arizona protected themselves from the Indians." Others preferred March 20, 1880, when the railroad arrived. The date finally chosen was January 1, 1870. That left many in attendance outside the pale, and 100 of them walked out. Charles Poston withdrew also, highly indignant, and asked that his name be removed from the membership list. His request was granted, but his fellow pioneers made him an honorary member, and his name appears as founder on a plaque at the society's Tucson headquarters. [17]

The society, said their declaration of purpose, was to serve "historical and humanitarian purposes" and to "perpetuate the memory of those whose sagacity, energy and enterprise induced them to settle in the wilderness and become the founders of a new state."[18] They thought of themselves as a fraternity, united by the memory of past perils and hardships. On occasion they called each other brother. When one of them died (and by 1884 they were beginning to drop off with some regularity), the others felt his passing as a personal loss, turned out for the funeral, and comforted the family. They set up a Widow and Orphan Fund and an Indian Depredation Fund for victims of Apache raids. They started a library and urged every member to write down and contribute his life story. They had monthly meetings and occasional social functions and tried to avoid internal dissensions. The members were serious in calling their organization "a moral, benevolent, literary and scientific association."[19]

Their sense of mission was strong. Hiram Stevens compressed it all into a few sentences when he retired from the presidency on December 29, 1885:

My Fellow Pioneers: . . . my remarks must be few, but believe me, they express the cherished sentiments of a pioneer's heart, one, my Brother Pioneers, who like you rejoices in the knowledge that the members of our Society were the first to bring American civilization to the savages of this country, and with those who arrived since the Pioneer days, have freely and fearlessly sustained it by their means and their best efforts.[20]

The idea, expressed only thirteen years after the Camp Grant Massacre, that these people were "bringing American civilization to the savages of this country" may seem almost comically ironic a hundred years later, but those pioneers were just as serious about Pax Americana as the Romans were about the Pax Romana and as the British were about their mission to the "lesser breeds without the law," in Kipling's phrase. They must be judged by the light that was given to them.

Bill Oury's fears were justified. The whistle of the first locomotive brought to the Old Pueblo an era of rapid growth and change. The population increased explosively. The commercial district expanded southward, and new residences rose on the fringes. Along the tracks, three-quarters of a mile northeast of the business district, warehouses and shops appeared, and Congress Street began to develop as a connecting link with downtown, the first east–west thoroughfare to break the old north–south pattern.[21] As the business district expanded, the Mexican families who lived on or near Main Street and Meyer were bought out or forced out and concentrated farther south, around Church Square, the old Plaza de Mesilla, where the freight wagons from the east used to end their journeys. The district was still occupied mostly by Hispanic families in 1981.[22]

With the growing Anglo influence came a change in building styles. Brick and lumber were in; adobe was out. Newcomers preferred to freeze in winter and stew in summer rather than live in one of those "ugly mud houses." The idea of stepping through one's front door into the street was equally repugnant, and in the new residential districts a front yard interposed a decent interval between residence and road.[23] With all the other baggage they brought from farther east, the new residents imported the green lawn, as noted by the *Citizen* in 1882.[24] Grass was not easy to grow in Tucson, but some conservative families regarded it as a proof of superior status. A few still do.

The place to live in the post-railroad era was on north Main Street—the old Camino Real. Fourth, Fifth, and Sixth avenues farther east were favored also, as time went on, but the "Mansions of Main Street," as historian Janet Ann Stewart calls them, were

Tucson in 1880, seen from Sentinel Peak. Photo by Henry Watkins.

the showplaces of Tucson until well into the twentieth century. One by one new houses appeared on the east side of the street, their character changing as "gables, wood trim, and other High Victorian paste-on forms" were added to the traditional adobe basics, creating "a compatible blend of Mexican and American building traditions" with "a special charm of their own."[25] The impact of these new developments was somewhat lessened, however, by long delay in installing a sewer system. The Sanborn fire maps, the earliest appearing in 1883, show an outdoor toilet tucked away in an obscure corner behind even the most elegant residence.

The dominance of the Anglo life-style was reinforced by American technology. The telephone came first. A small exchange was installed on April 1, 1881, and the *Star* reported on May 26 that "the latest improvement in our growing city is the establishment of the telephone headquarters adjoining the postoffice, where our citizens and visitors can now communicate with all parts of the city, and by telegraph connections with the remotest parts of Europe, Asia and Africa." Gaslights were first turned on in the evening of March 20, 1882. Zeckendorf's new store was ablaze, and the *Star* composing room had "half a dozen jets throwing light upon the busy fingers of the compositors."[26] In the same year a public benefactor named Al Johnson attempted to provide the town with electricity. Al owned one of the city's ice plants and thus had a base of operations. He installed a "steam-driven, direct-current

Two mansions on Main Street: the Frank Hereford house and the Owls Club.

The young aristocrats. Owls Club members, left to right: above, W. T. Gibbon, A. M. Butler, Frank Hereford, H. B. Tenney, Selim Franklin, and Leo Goldschmidt; below, Charles Howe, Charles Roche, and Levi Manning.

Edison bipolar unit" and went into business—prematurely, it turned out, for he went broke after two years, and a successful electric company was not organized until 1895.[27]

Another ambitious project which failed to catch on was a streetcar proposal, drafted in 1881 by P. R. Tully, J. S. Wood, and James Buell. They filed articles of incorporation with the city recorder on July 6. The object was to build a line out to Buell's new addition for the purpose of selling lots. The project never got beyond the paper stage, and Tucson waited until 1898 for mule-drawn streetcars.[28]

More successful was the attempt in 1882 to bring well water to the homes and businesses of the city and provide fire protection for the brick-and-lumber structures which were replacing the old fire-resistant adobes. In 1881, Sylvester Watts, of Kansas City, set up a "water farm" and pumping system on the west bank of the Santa Cruz four and a half miles from town. Several wells were sunk on a 720-acre tract, and a redwood flume in the bed of the river carried the water to the village. A total of seven wells at Eighteenth Street and Osborne Avenue supplemented this supply, and a standpipe was erected to provide for a gravity flow. On September 6, 1882, the first water passed through the Tucson Water Company's mains and appeared at the hydrant at Congress and Main, one of thirty-five in the city. This system served the community until 1890, when the city took control from the private company.[29]

September, 1882, marked the end of the era when water for all purposes was obtained from private wells (thought by the Anglos to be polluted) or from water carriers who filled their vessels at the springs south of the business district and sold it for five cents a bucket. After 1882 the public baths at Carrillo's Gardens were gradually replaced by tin tubs in Tucson's homes, and the faucet gradually eliminated the olla of drinking water swinging and sweating in the patio.

Even before an adequate supply of water became available, the men of Tucson were preparing to organize a volunteer fire department. The *Star* of July 7, 1881, noted that "the members of the incipient Tucson Hook and Ladder Company had a meeting last night at the club-rooms of the Gem saloon, about 20 of those who signed the roll being present." In a short time the company was no longer "incipient." It owned twenty-two rubber buckets, six axes, six picks, and nine shovels. In October it acquired a 1,400-pound bell from a Boston firm at a cost of $495. By December this facility had been installed in a community tower, ready for use when water was turned on in the new mains. The city council cooperated by authorizing the installation of twenty alarm boxes. When the city charter was adopted in 1883, a fire department was created, fire regulations were approved, and money was set aside for purchasing equipment. Two hose carts with a thousand feet of hose arrived, and a hand-drawn hook-and-ladder truck was acquired in 1886. Tucson could now say proudly that it was as well equipped to fight fires as any town in the Southwest.[30]

There was still enough water for everybody, but the situation was becoming precarious, and in 1885 there was serious trouble, ending in a lawsuit which threatened to split the Anglo community and caused bad feeling among the Mexicans.

The difficulty went back a long way. For centuries the Santa Cruz had flowed almost perennially, but as more and more people settled in the valley, this happy situation changed. They cut down the mesquite tim-

Silver Lake about 1890.

ber and overgrazed the bottomlands, thus bringing on quick runoffs and floods which lowered the bed of the river and eliminated the storage function of the swampy areas along its banks. The settlers had to build more and more dams to ensure a water supply. The Papagos built one just above San Xavier. Maish and Driscoll put in another to form Silver Lake, which supplied water for Lee's mill and formed a pleasant resort area.[31] Solomon Warner built another for his mill in 1883. When Sylvester Watts dug his wells at the foot of Sentinel Peak, he reduced the supply of available water still further, and rumblings of discontent began to be heard. There was talk of suing Warner because water leaked through his gates and was lost, and W. O. Dalton, the *zanero*, or water overseer, quit his job because he did not think Warner should be sued.[32]

More serious trouble came because of the activities of a group of Chinese gardeners. Chinese had been in Tucson since the sixties, and more came when the completion of the railroad freed the track workers to find places for themselves. A group of them came to Tucson in the early eighties, intending to go into business as truck farmers. They started a major gardening project on land leased from Sam Hughes, Leopoldo Carrillo, and W. C. Davis just across the Santa Cruz from downtown. Hughes and Carrillo were familiar figures. Davis was a hardware merchant who had come from Pennsylvania in 1869. He was known as "Tin" Davis because he was a metal worker by trade and as "Dry Wash" Davis because of his habit of rubbing his hands together as he talked.[33] These three men seldom let a dollar slip through their fingers, and they were glad to rent their land near Sentinel Peak to these industrious and ambitious farmers. Others who had gardens in the area were Bishop Salpointe and the Sisters of Saint Joseph, who needed vegetables for their convent and hospital.

Truck gardens, unfortunately, need twice as much water as small grain, and the Chinese farmers wanted to water their plants "every day"—not just on weekends. They were accused of "stealing" water out of the community ditch, carrying it off in pottery jars. Their singlemindedness and determination might have seemed admirable had it been on a smaller scale, but by 1884 they were cultivating 100 acres and were expecting to expand to 150 in 1885. This meant more money for them, and for the owners of the land, but it also meant more water consumption, and the proprietors began to worry about it. Carrillo used a tremendous amount in his gardens, and he was the object of the bitterest attacks in the water feud which followed. Hughes and Davis were involved, however, and took a beating also.

In the spring of 1885, after the first irrigation in April, the three men moved to preempt the major share of the water for themselves and their friends. They were appointed by a group of landowners—or appointed themselves—as "commissioners" to control the water supply, and they issued several edicts intended to place the reins firmly in their own hands. First, they set up a system of water tickets which farmers could buy and exchange for delivery. Under the old system the landowner had paid the *zanero* when his allotment was in the field. The new system made it easier to refuse an applicant, who had to come in and apply. Next they revived the idea of the "Fence." This was a stone-and-brush barrier which had once existed along Mission (or Hospital) Lane. Some old residents remembered the Fence, but it had not existed for many years. In earlier times most of the cultivated land was south of the lane, and the Fence had been erected to keep out invasion—animal or human—from the north. The commissioners claimed that the new, or recently cleared, land north of the Fence had less claim to water than the previously developed fields. In the late spring Lorenzo Renteria, the new *zanero*, began notifying owners north of the long-vanished Fence that there would be no more water for them.

Their crops dying and their tempers rising, the owners north of the line organized and went to court. Plaintiffs included E. N. Fish, Cirilo Leon, Francisco Romero, and others. The trial began on May 8 and lasted for several days. The testimony made it clear that the defendants had a technicality to stand on—the right of older fields to first water—but it appeared that the rule was never enforced. By tradition and custom water went to the fields which needed it most.[34] The complete legal records of the case are not available, but it would appear that the three gringos lost.

The Chinese gardeners, however, stayed in business. Clara Ferrin in 1897 described them as "industrious and persevering." They lived in small huts at the foot of Sentinel Peak, sold their produce from house to house every morning, and kept accounts by "marking down on the casement of the door the amount bought each day."[35]

The Chinese Gardens affair was typical of the internal difficulties faced by Tucson during these years. The big troubles, however, were happening outside the city limits as outlaws and Indians paralyzed the territory.

CHAPTER 8

Renegades and Desperadoes

Peace and prosperity, said the Tucson prophets, would come with the railroad, but peace failed to arrive on schedule. The old lawless West had its final day in Arizona in the years after the arrival of the rails, and the first decade of the new century was well under way before some of the old offenses were brought under control.

On the one hand, the Apaches made their last stand in the mid-eighties, and Tucson was a focal point in the final chapter of the Indian wars. Fort Lowell was an important military base, with soldiers and officers coming and going; the town was important as a supply center for troops in the field; and its two newspapers reflected and shaped public opinion during a time when "the hostiles" were a matter of concern to everybody in Arizona Territory.

People hoped that the worst was over when Victorio was hunted down in Mexico in 1880. The Chiricahuas, quiet for the moment, were settled on the San Carlos Reservation, near Globe. Geronimo the troublemaker was with them, thinking about going back to the wilds but not quite ready for the warpath. On August 30 in that year of 1880, however, long-simmering hatreds

came to the surface when trouble broke out at Cibecue Creek,[1] and a month later Geronimo fled to Mexico, beginning a campaign of terror which lasted two and a half years. It was like the early seventies all over again, and once more the Tucson leaders decided to take action. A force of fifty "hard-riding frontiersmen," with Captain William J. Ross as leader, left for Mexico on May 10, 1882, resolved to wipe out the renegades. On their return, a little over a month later, they reported killing thirty-seven Indians, mostly women and children. Later they encountered a company of seventy Mexican soldiers, who considered for two days what to do with these irregulars, came near shooting them, and finally sent them home, minus their arms, dirty, exhausted, and embarrassed.[2]

Meanwhile new outbreaks were taking place, and Washington sent General George Crook back to Arizona, where he had dealt so effectively and honestly with the Apaches ten years before. He arrived in September, 1882, and went to work at once to bring peace and order to the reservations.[3]

At first the citizens thought that he was wasting his time, and when Chatto began

William J. Ross, leader of the frustrated company of Indian fighters.

Mayor Charles M. Straus.

his famous raid through Arizona and New Mexico, just as Crook was preparing to go into Mexico after the renegades, they were sure of it.[4] Sidney DeLong, the former mayor, wrote from Hermosillo, Sonora, to Mayor Charles M. Straus, that the whole country south of the border was "panic stricken," and when his letter was published in the *Citizen* on April 1, 1883, faith in the efficacy of the army reached a new low. Editor Wasson commented sarcastically, when Chatto evaded pursuit, that Crook was now in southeastern Arizona, "where he should have been two weeks ago."

By now, however, Crook was ready to pursue the Indians into Mexico. Relying on his Indian scouts and half a dozen dedicated officers, he disappeared into the wilderness of the Sierra Madre and came out in June with 325 Apaches and Geronimo's word that the rest would arrive within a few months.[5]

Several small bands did filter in, but Geronimo delayed his own appearance for eight months. One reason was his desire to put together a sizable herd of stolen cattle to use for his own advantage north of the border. When he finally came in, he had 350 head of livestock to drive across the line. Lieutenant Britton Davis, sent to escort him, knew that to separate Geronimo from his booty would be to lose him again. An attempt was made by a collector of customs from Nogales and a deputy sheriff from Tucson to seize the livestock and arrest the Apaches, but a bottle of Scotch whiskey solved the problem. The civilian officers partook liberally of the offered refreshment, and while they were sleeping it off, Geronimo, his cows, and his escort moved off through the night toward San Carlos. When morning came, they were out of sight.[6] Geronimo was back on the reservation once more, and there was joy in Tucson.

Crook's popularity leaped at once to a new high, and on June 19, Mayor Straus and his friends and allies staged one of the great receptions of those times for the general and his officers. These gentlemen got off the Southern Pacific train in the evening, not expecting their arrival to be noticed, but Straus had been tipped off by someone at Fort Huachuca that the party was coming, and a welcoming committee was waiting at the station. Crook was a quiet, modest fellow who would no doubt have welcomed a chance to avoid the celebration, but he submitted gracefully to "a delightful moonlight ride" through the streets to Levin's Garden, where a theatrical company put on a show for him. A public reception at Porter's Hotel followed, and the finale was a banquet at Levin's establishment, where the repast was followed by toasts proposed by Mayor Straus and responses by selected guests. Crook responded to a toast to "the Army of the United States," but he did not waste many words or many minutes doing it.

A high point, or a low in the minds of some listeners, was the reading of an original poem by Charles D. Poston, concluding with this stanza:

All hail to the chief, who accepts this ovation
To honor the grandest achievement of arms.
Ere long he may be the chief of the nation,
The people will then be free of all harms.[7]

For two years Crook's standing remained high. There were no outbreaks in Arizona in 1884 or in the first months of 1885. On the San Carlos Reservation, however, the pot was boiling again, and on May 18, Geronimo was off for a last fling at the old raiding life. His band numbered only forty-two warriors and about ninety women and children, but in the minds of the Anglos and Mexicans of the region those forty-two mobile, ruthless riders seemed like an army of a thousand. The newspapers screamed for more troops and blasted the ones already on the scene.[8]

Crook did not share in the fear and excitement. He was prepared for what had happened and soon had his forces deployed to intercept the fugitives if they should break back across the international boundary. About 2,000 troops were involved.

At first their luck was not good. Chihuahua, Geronimo's second-in-command, slipped across the border and raided through Arizona and New Mexico. The press raised a great outcry, mostly directed at Crook, but the general ignored the attacks, while Captain Emmet Crawford and his Apache scouts pursued the renegades in Mexico. When they returned, exhausted and unsuccessful, Crook sent Crawford and Lieutenant Charles B. Gatewood to take up the pursuit.[9] The Apaches countered as Josanie (also known as Ulzana) mounted another daring raid through Arizona and New Mexico.[10] The outcry against Crook grew louder and caused so much consternation in Washington that Lieutenant General Philip Sheridan, in command of the United States Army, came to Fort Bowie to look into the situation. The result was a command decision to use every available means to run Geronimo to earth in Mexico.[11]

Meanwhile the people of Tucson were preparing once more to take action on their own. The Society of Arizona Pioneers, officially known as the Arizona Pioneers Historical Society, refused to join in the hyster-

The figure in the center (below, standing on the ground) is said to be Robert Tribolet, Geronimo's bootlegger.

ical attacks on Crook and the army. They drew up a document declaring their confidence in him, recommending removal of the Indians, peaceful or warlike, from the Territory, and appealing to President Chester A. Arthur for support. Granville Oury was commissioned to carry the message to Washington, and while he was arranging a meeting with the president, the directors applied to the army in Arizona for weapons which they proposed to use in protecting settlers between Tucson and the Mexican border.

They were actually issued "fifteen stand of arms and two thousand round of ammunition," but when the transaction came to the attention of Adjutant General R. C. Drum, he ordered the rifles returned, and they were.[12] Whether the valiant pioneers would have made a difference cannot now

be known, but Josanie had his own way, spreading destruction through New Mexico before making a successful dash for safety in the mountains of Mexico. Emmet Crawford and his scouts were off in pursuit at once. The finale is the best-known chapter in the history of the Apache wars. Crawford was killed by Mexican irregular troops, but Geronimo agreed to come in at the end of two months, and he did come in, meeting Crook just south of the border to talk terms.[13]

The conference was almost a public function. Mayor Straus of Tucson was one of several civilians in Crook's party, and C. S. Fly, the Tombstone photographer, was there, lugging his heavy camera. In the neighborhood also, just out of sight, was another civilian who ought not to have been there. His name was Robert Tribolet. He was a bootlegger who had a small ranch or camp south of the border, where he would be safe from interference by American authorities. He broke up the conference.

Tribolet remains a mysterious figure. A large clan of Tribolets was in Arizona, with a base at Tombstone. Siegfried, Manfred, and Godfrey were in business there in 1882. Siegfried, a brewer and butcher born in Switzerland, was head of the clan. In Phoenix, where he moved after the Tombstone mines flooded, he was a successful businessman. [14] Bob's connection with this family is not clear, but he was a black sheep, wherever he belonged. He is said to have been the first businessman in Sierra Vista, near Fort Huachuca, but he kept a saloon in Tombstone and specialized in selling liquor to the Indians. Local tradition says that he lost his life when he held up the Nacozari stage in Mexico and was shot by Colonel Emilio Kosterlitzky's *rurales*. [15]

This was the man who appeared just outside Crook's camp at Cañon de los Embudos on March 30, 1886, with a supply of liquor which he began dispensing to the Apaches, scouts and renegades alike. He is said to have sold thirty dollars' worth of whiskey in one hour and could have done a hundred dollars' worth of business if his stock had been larger. When Geronimo and his lieutenants were well lubricated, Tribolet is said to have told them that the troops planned to shoot them the minute they crossed the border. [16] Alarmed and excited, Geronimo and Naiche headed back into the wilds with a party of warriors, women, and children.

With their disappearance the Tucson Ring was back in the picture. The big merchants who were suspect in the seventies were mostly gone by now, and if they had successors in this nefarious business, nobody has wanted to name them, but the old suspicions were reborn. It is "not likely to have been an accident," says Dan Thrapp, the most careful of historians, "that he was there with his whiskey. . . . It is more likely that he was well acquainted with the hostiles and that he was a man on a mission. If this is true, he was most likely motivated by the infamous 'Tucson Ring' of contractors and others who counted on large profits from dealings with Army camps or in other ways benefited from continuation of hostilities." [17]

No evidence has yet been uncovered connecting Tribolet with any "infamous" Tucson firm. He did not need to be. Crook himself commented to Charles F. Lummis, when he heard about Tribolet, "Oh, no, there's no way of dealing with Tribolet. He has been tried before but bought his way out. If we had shot him down like a coyote, as he deserved, it would have raised a terrible row. Why, that man has a beef contract for our army!"

"The government," Lummis explained, "is obliged to advertise and let contracts to the lowest bidder. Tribolet got one."

He also managed to get Crook out of his job. General Sheridan and President Arthur were unhappy when they heard that the general had promised the Apaches that they could come back to Arizona after two years in the East. They expected unconditional surrender. When Crook reported that Geronimo had decamped, they let him know that they were seriously displeased, and he resigned, as they hoped he would. General Nelson A. Miles succeeded him, sent the Apache scouts home, established a heliograph system for signaling (which never did any real good), and ordered two officers— Captain Henry W. Lawton and Lieutenant Charles B. Gatewood—to go after the fugitives. These officers brought them back early in September, 1886. On September 8

117

Lieutenant and Mrs. Charles B. Gatewood.

memorating the surrender and removal of the Apaches.

Crook was now forgotten, and Miles was the hero of the hour. It would be appropriate to honor him, and Miles was willing to be honored. There was one drawback, however. Tucson wanted to honor Gatewood too. Though Tucsonans did not suspect it then, we know now that Miles took steps to get Gatewood out of the way. Gatewood said nothing, but his wife recorded her opinions about the situation:

A fete was given in Tucson, the guest of honor being Lieut. Gatewood. In the arrangements, so much was said of him that Gen. Miles got enraged at playing second fiddle, and at the last minute, after we had accepted invitations of all sorts & had clothes made for the occasion, he ordered Lt. Gatewood to stay behind and look after the office during his absence—a clerk's work & unnecessary. . . . Such a storm of comment and inquiry met him when Lt. Gatewood—the man for whom the Tucson fete was arranged—did not appear that he found himself cornered, and made the mistake of publishing in a San Francisco newspaper, that he "was sick of the adulation of Lt. Gatewood, who only did his duty."[20]

Mrs. Gatewood may have misjudged the role of the lieutenant and exaggerated the "storm of comment," but there can be no doubt that she and her husband were not present at the ceremonies and that Miles had the party all to himself.

There can be no doubt either that the Tucson citizens and their wives arranged a really sumptuous celebration. The town was decorated and illuminated. A *Star* reporter wrote that, on the day preceding, one could look up from the corner of Main and Congress toward the railroad station and see "only a mass of evergreens and a bright array of flags and bunting." Distinguished visitors arrived—Captain Adna R. Chaffee of the

they were placed on a train, under guard, and began an exile which started in Florida and ended in Oklahoma.[18]

A bitter controversy followed between groups of interested soldiers and civilians over who deserved credit for bringing Geronimo in—General Miles or Lieutenant Gatewood. It can still strike a spark today. Gatewood, a quiet, modest man, never claimed any credit for himself, and Miles, who was neither quiet nor modest, did everything he could to keep Gatewood from getting any.[19] The basic elements of the Miles-Gatewood situation appeared clearly at the great celebration in Tucson com-

Gatewood and his Indian scouts.

Sixth Cavalry, General Stoneman's daughter, and Mrs. Miles (who came with her husband). The parade through town included 400 Papagos under Chief Huilz, the Tucson schoolchildren, and the clubs and societies of the town. Miles was waiting at the San Xavier Hotel to review them. Cannon boomed a salute. The regimental band from Fort Lowell concertized briefly. Then came the presentation ceremonies at Levin's Park.[21]

They adhered closely to a standard pattern. General Royal A. Johnson, the master of ceremonies, read telegrams of congratulation from the great and the famous. Then Judge William H. Barnes rose to make the speech of the day. It was a full-dress perform-

ance. He began with the migrations from Europe two centuries before and outlined the events which had made the United States "the strongest, the freest, the happiest and best of all the nations of the earth." Approaching the present, he examined the crimes of the bloodthirsty Apaches and came at last to the achievement of General Miles, who had given them their quietus. The final act was the presentation of a ceremonial sword to "the captain who gave peace and security to the people of Arizona, New Mexico, Chihuahua, and Sonora." "You shall not draw it at the command of any despot," Judge Barnes admonished. "In your hand it shall flash in defense of liberty and to main-

Parade in honor of General Nelson A. Miles, November 8, 1887, passing the courthouse on Pennington Avenue. Guests in carriages are accompanied by a guard of honor composed of members of the Arizona Pioneers Historical Society.

Tucson citizens assembled for presentation of the gold sword to General Miles at Levin's Park.

Pioneer Hose Company No. 1 assembled on Church Street for the Miles parade.

tain upon earth government 'of the people, by the people and for the people.'"

Miles, a handsome man with an elegant manner and a formidable mustache, responded at some length. "To serve one's country," he began, "is a duty that affords the patriot more happiness than aught else." He paid tribute to the soldiers and officers who had fought in the Apache campaigns, but the name of Charles Gatewood was not mentioned.

It is not mentioned in Miles's *Personal Recollections*, published ten years later. "On the 8th of November, 1887," he writes, "I was presented by the citizens of Arizona with a very beautiful ornamented sword in token of their appreciation of my services in ridding their country of the Apaches." In conclusion he pays "special tribute" to the officers who "so zealously, courageously and persistently pursued the hostiles to the end" [22] and names seven of them, pointedly omitting Gatewood.

Historian James H. McClintock, writing in 1916, added to his brief account of the Tucson celebration the information that Miles was the one who elaborated the uniform" and made himself in consequence "a gorgeous vision." [23] Miles had his supporters, and has them now, but Crook and Gatewood are the soldiers whom later generations have delighted to honor.

The Apaches were not the only troublemakers in Arizona in the 1880s. White men contributed their share. The early part of the decade could be accurately described as the "Time of the Desperado."

Tucson was not completely wide-open, but the peace officers and the justices always had more than they could handle. The first village marshal was William Morgan, a Civil War veteran who had settled near Sonoita, where he lost his possessions and al-

most lost his life in several hard fights with the Apaches. By 1871, when Tucson was incorporated, he had become a resident. At an election held on May 17 he was named marshal by a majority of the sixty-six citizens who made it to the polls. He served less than three months, however, leaving town in July and yielding the office to John Miller. [24]

Morgan was described as "a fearless fighter and a true friend," but Miller was as tough as they came—and needed to be. Born in Missouri, he served in the Mexican War, migrated to California in 1850, and appeared in Arizona in the 1860s, working as a miner for a while and locating in 1869 at the Cienega Station, east of Tucson, in the middle of Apache country. Attacks were so frequent and so severe that Miller and his partner, "Shotgun" Smith, abandoned the place in 1870 and moved to Tucson just in time for Miller to be elected marshal. As William Hogan, Tucson's police historian puts it, this was "a sizable chore for one man." As an example of what Miller's official life was like, Hogan tells of an episode in 1871 which occurred as the marshal was taking a prisoner named Estrada to the lockup. The man was allowed to stop at a house near the plaza to pick up his blankets:

The request was granted. Estrada stepped inside while Miller stood at the door. Instead of picking up the blankets, Estrada got hold of a Spencer carbine and snapped the gun at Miller's chest, but the weapon failed to discharge. When Estrada saw this, he sprang upon the officer and a desperate struggle ensued. Miller thought the man had a knife, and as soon as he could, he drew his pistol and began shooting. The first shot just missed Miller's head as Estrada knocked the weapon in that direction. The powder burned Miller's face. In the struggle four shots were fired, the fatal ball piercing Estrada's heart. After Justice Meyer's inquest on the body, an examination of constable Miller was held, which ended the affair, since his action was held to be justifiable.[25]

Miller seems to have been contentious as well as brave, and he instituted legal action against Sheriff Isaac Q. Dickason and Justice Charley Meyer when he considered that they were acting contrary to the public interest. He did not run for reelection in 1873, but he continued to be heard from in matters of law enforcement, even after he moved to Florence, Arizona, in 1878.

The best known of Miller's successors was Adolph George Buttner, a German immigrant who enlisted in the Union Army, stayed in after the Civil War ended, and came to Arizona from California in 1866 with the two companies of the Fourteenth Infantry who relieved the units of the California Volunteers left to keep order in the Territory. In 1868 he was court-martialed for desertion, found guilty, and confined for a time, but received an honorable discharge at Fort Lowell in 1870. Elected village marshal in 1876, he became the target of criticism—and bullets—from men whom he had offended in line of duty. After his reelection in 1878 a would-be assassin almost shot him to death in his own house, and the *Star* noted that his life hung "by a slender cord." The article revealed, not surprisingly, that Tucson was home base for a large population of thieves and murderers and credited Buttner with holding them in check.

Defeated in 1879, he was elected again in 1881. By that time the arrival of the railroad had increased the problems of law enforcement, more officers were needed, and the marshal became Tucson's first chief of police. He headed a force of six men, and the value of his services was recognized by a grateful citizenry at Levin's Park on February 25, 1881, in the ceremonial presentation of a

"Royal Highness" Adolph George Buttner.

gold badge and an address which credited him with "efficiency and integrity." His tenure was not, however, particularly happy. He tended to be high-handed and peremptory (George Hand called him "Royal Highness Buttner"). His health was bad, and economy-minded officials chipped away at his salary. It was probably with some relief that he took to his bed in 1885 and died. Because of Buttner and his like, however (says William Hogan), Tucson "in the 1870s and '80s was a fit place in which to live."[26]

Opinions varied about Tucson's fitness for civilized living in the eighties. It was still pretty much a frontier village in spite of the changes already noted. Maiden Lane flourished until the late nineties, when the girls were moved away from the center of town to a short passageway between Convent and

Mose Drachman.

Naturally there were "tin horns" and "short-bit sports" who cheated and scrounged for a living. A group called "boosters" were given money to sit at the tables "to create an atmosphere of interest and sociability in the gambling room." They called themselves the "Sons of Rest" because they were constitutionally opposed to work. "They were a worthless lot," Mose concluded, "but not vicious men, just lazy and willing to accept things as they came." Their leader was Charles Alzamorra, known as "Frying Pan Charley." Once when he was frying eggs in a restaurant, he heard that a game was in progress next door and walked over, frying pan still in hand, to participate in the action. His nickname was the result.

Drachman liked the gamblers, but he helped put them out of business. He supported General L. H. Manning when he closed the Tucson houses in 1893, and he voted as a member of the lower house to purify the state when the legislature ran them out in 1907.[27]

Meyer streets called officially Sabino Alley and unofficially Gay Alley. The saloons were open all night—at least some of them were—and gambling was unregulated until after the turn of the century. Mose Drachman, born in 1870, spent a good deal of time in his Uncle Sam's cigar store on Congress Street in the middle of the saloon district, saw it all, and many years later recorded his memories. The leading gamblers, according to him, came from "good families in the East" and were "men of character and honor, never dealing a crooked card." Mose's optimism may have resulted from the fact that they gave him good advice, including admonitions to stay away from the gaming tables. They were, he said, influential in civic affairs. "The saloons and the gamblers combined to control the politics in Tucson."

Charles Alzamorra, "Frying Pan Charlie," leader of the Sons of Rest.

Jim Brazelton at the end of the trail.

No one could foresee such purification in the early eighties, when conditions in Arizona were at their worst. The railroad brought all sorts of men and women to the Territory, and some of them were hard cases looking for something to steal or somebody to kill. Ranchers were back in business, and rustlers plied their trade on both sides of the border. Miners followed veins of gold and silver; claim jumpers, hijackers, and stage robbers followed in their wake. Life and property were often in peril all over the Territory, but especially in the south, and Tucson was a focal point for illegal as well as legal activity. Governor Safford thundered in his message to the Ninth Legislature in 1877 that robbers and highwaymen were "a scourge to humanity and should be swept

from the earth as remorselessly as the most ferocious wild beast."[28] He recommended capital punishment for offenders.

The men of Tucson agreed with the governor and were willing to take the punishment of highwaymen into their own hands, as Jim Brazelton learned to his cost when he began robbing in New Mexico, and when that territory became too hot for him, he drifted west and found employment in Leatherwood's stable in Tucson. There he became friendly with another employee named David Nimitz, and when he resumed operations as a holdup man, he used Dave's place on the south side near Lee's mill as his headquarters, bullying Dave into supplying him with food and ammunition. Jim was big and tough, boasted that he was not afraid to die, carried a Spencer carbine and a pistol twenty-four hours a day, and was a hard man to say no to. David did not say no.

Jim picked the Tucson–Florence stage as his first target and held it up at Point of Mountain Ranch, seventeen or eighteen miles north of Tucson. Arthur Hill was the driver, and one of the passengers was John P. Clum, editor of the *Citizen*, published at that time in Florence. Some of the passengers were armed, including Clum, but they did not think they had a chance when Brazelton bellowed and waved his firearms. Clum wrote about his experience in the next issue of his paper.

One week later, on August 8, as Arthur Hill was driving the same route, a passenger named John Miller asked him to point out the place of the holdup.

"There." said Hill. "The robber hid right behind that bush—and there he is again!"

Sure enough, Brazelton was back, and the little drama was repeated. On both occasions Pima County Sheriff Charles Shibell tried to pick up the robber's trail but lost him. In his editorial column Clum reproved him for his failure. One of the possemen, however, was Juan Elías, an expert tracker who noticed that Jim's horse had one crooked hoof. In Tucson he saw that track again and traced it to Dave Nimitz's door. They put Dave in jail and persuaded him without too much trouble to tell what he knew. All he asked in return was that they should kill Brazelton out of hand and thus prevent him from seeking revenge. The result was a confrontation in August, 1888, with Shibell and Deputies Bob Leatherwood, Charles O. Brown, Charles T. Etchells, and I. O. Brokaw. The dead outlaw's body was propped up against an adobe wall, cartridge belts, carbine, and all, as a warning to other evildoers, and photographer Henry Buehman took his picture.[29]

As an example to other wicked men, Brazelton's fate did little good. John Clum noted in the *Citizen* on August 16, 1878, that "three stages of the Southern Pacific were robbed last week" and that other depredations had taken place. The citizens of Tucson offered a $1,000 reward for the apprehension of "land pirates," and General O. B. Willcox declared that he was prevented by an act of Congress from assisting with his troops. By 1881 conditions were so bad that Governor John J. Gosper wrote to the secretary of the interior about the "cowboys"—gangs of desperadoes in the Tombstone vicinity—said to be protected by merchants and peace officers who took payoffs and bought stolen goods. Gosper's successor, Governor Frederick A. Tritle, complained to President Chester A. Arthur, and the president, on May 3, 1882, issued his famous proclamation threatening to use the army to force the gang members to "retire peaceably to their respective abodes."[30] The editor of the *Tombstone Epitaph* was outraged

by this assault on the character of his town, but to outsiders the message seemed appropriate.[31] The editor himself had reported four robberies, five shootings, and eight killings in the preceding three months.[32]

Robbery seemed to be Arizona's favorite outdoor diversion. The Black Canyon stage, running from Phoenix to Prescott, was a favorite target. In 1884 it was robbed on January 13, April 21, June 1, and October 18.[33] Other stage lines fared almost as badly. There was so much pilfering and rustling that the citizens of frontier towns felt obliged to take matters into their own hands and dispose of the thieves permanently. Two murderers were lynched at Globe on August 3, 1882. A Bisbee robber and killer was suspended at Tombstone on December 9. On March 28, 1884, five more Bisbee bandits were hanged simultaneously in the same town. Two killers were extinguished at Holbrook on April 4, 1885, and there was a double lynching at Flagstaff on January 19, 1887.

Nothing seemed to discourage the troublemakers. The first train holdup took place seventeen miles east of Tucson on April 27, 1887,[34] and Arizona's only real feud, the Graham-Tewksbury vendetta known as the Pleasant Valley War, broke out in 1887 and ended in 1892, when only one survivor of the two families was left.[35]

Tucson was often involved in these matters. Wyatt Earp, on his way to California with the body of his brother Morgan, eliminated Frank Stilwell, supposedly one of the killers, with a double charge of buckshot in the railroad yards at Tucson on March 22, 1882.[36] Edwin Tewksbury, the sole survivor of the Pleasant Valley trouble, spent months in the Tucson jail, was tried twice in Tucson courts, and was finally acquitted and freed on March 12, 1896. And Pearl Hart, the lady stage robber, escaped from a Tucson cell on October 12, 1899.[37]

The general climate of lawlessness was reflected in the daily life of the community. George Hand, who went to work as a janitor at the courthouse in 1882, recorded in his diary the activities of his volatile fellow citizens. Typical of his entries are these notes from 1882 and 1883:

Oct. 9, 1882. Fine morning. Two men dead. One natural death, the other named Hewitt, supposed to have been beat till he died.

Oct. 18. A Mexican named Torres, who was during the last term of court acquitted of stealing a lot of clothing was last night arrested for stealing a trunk of clothing from Jack Ennis. He is now in jail.

Nov. 1. Man killed last night.

Nov. 2. Chinaman got a bad beating this morning.

Nov. 7. Day passed off quiet until night—a row occurred at the Park Theater. Alex Levin in trying to stop it got 2 bad cuts on his head. John Dobbs got knocked under a table. Several others beaten by the railroaders. No one killed.

Jan. 1. White, jailor, opened cell door. Two prisoners jumped out and gave him a terrible beating and escaped. Paul [Bob Paul, the sheriff] is red hot.

Jan. 17. Paul took a prisoner to the hospital today. He was shot in the act of robbing a man 5 days ago. Both bones and elbow broken and shattered badly. He will not steal with that hand in a long time.

March 3. Some son of a gun came in my room and appropriated a pound of fine cut tobacco, leaving me without a chew. That was very unkind.[38]

Even the first citizens sometimes brawled in those violent times. On March 21, 1883, Hand reported an encounter between Judge F. M. Smith and L. C. Hughes, editor of the *Star* and governor-to-be:

Judge Smith met L. C. Hughes today and interviewed him in regard to some things in this

Missionaries to darkest Arizona. Governor L. C. Hughes and Mrs. Hughes.

morning's paper. Hughes said he knew nothing of it. Then Smith called him a liar, an unconvicted thief and repeated it and many other pet names besides telling him if he ever used his "Smith's" name in his dirty paper he would cowhide him if it was his last act. There were many others who would like a chance to tell him what they think of him. He is in a bad hole to win.

Hughes's wife Josephine was as intent on remodeling her fellow men as her husband was and irritated some of the citizens just as much. On March 21, 1883, less than three weeks after the encounter with Judge Smith, she shepherded into the Methodist Church none other than Frances E. Willard, founder of the WCTU, come to battle in the Territory of Arizona for "temperance"— which meant prohibition and the death from thirst of every barfly in Tucson. In the weeks that followed, Mrs. Hughes accompanied her on a tour of the territory.[39]

Violence and crime continued to be facts of life in Tucson as the century progressed toward its close, and men paid for their crimes with their lives. The first legal hanging in Pima County occurred at Tombstone on July 4, 1881,[40] and others followed.

Not all the malefactors were punished. The perpetrators of the notorious Wham payroll robbery escaped punishment in 1889. On May 11, Paymaster Major J. W. Wham was carrying more than $28,000 in cash for disbursement to the soldiers at Fort Thomas, near the Apache reservation. He was ambushed by a band of robbers in a narrow defile, and there was a battle in which eight troopers were wounded, none fatally. Wham was commended for his resistance by a jury later on, but he lost his payroll.

After considerable undercover work by United States Marshal W. K. Meade and others, eight men were arrested and charged. They were all Mormon ranchers and farmers

from the Safford area. The case was called in Tucson on November 11, 1889, and for thirty-three days spectators and participants were treated to a great display of legal fireworks. The best lawyers in the territory were employed on both sides. The prosecution was headed by United States Attorney Harry Jeffords, assisted by William Herring, a brilliant easterner. Appearing with him were Herring's son-in-law Selim M. Franklin and Ben Goodrich—both extremely capable. On the other side were Frank Hereford, in the front rank of local attorneys, and Marcus Smith, perennial delegate in Congress and a trial lawyer who had made a circus out of many a courtroom. The mainstay of the defense was the presence in the area of a dozen or so unidentified drifters, presumably members of a gang of outlaws who had escaped to Mexico with their loot. The jury concluded that there was a reasonable doubt that the accused were guilty and on December 14 returned a verdict of acquittal.

The public was indignant and incredulous. "What," they wanted to know, "happened to the jury?" One witness was actually indicted and tried for perjury, but the verdict stood up, and down through the years some people, especially in the Safford region, have argued stoutly that the defendants were innocent. Privately, however, Safford sages will talk about how bad times were for those country people in 1889 and how all that government money provided a way out of their difficulties for some of them. The case is still one of the most celebrated episodes of Gila Valley history, and there have been several reenactments of the holdup in which descendants of the participants are said to have played leading roles.[41]

At the end of the eighties Tucson was by no means a calm and peaceful place, but most of the shootings and killings were done

Defendants (back row) and counsel in the Wham robbery trial. From left: defendants M. E. Cunningham (seated at left), Lyman Follett, Ed. Follett, Dan Rogers, Gilbert Webb (seated, with cane), Thomas Lamb, Walt Follett, and W. T. Webb; counsel (seated) Mark Smith, Ben Goodrich, B. F. Hereford, Frank Hereford.

by peace officers in the legitimate exercise of their responsibilities or by criminals, real or suspected, in the illegitimate pursuit of their own ends. Ordinary people were comparatively safe, as they had always been, in their homes and on the streets. It would be another ten years, however, before it could be said with any certainty that Tucson had purged itself of frontier attitudes and patterns of conduct.

CHAPTER 9

Growing Pains

Times were bad in Tucson and in Arizona in the early 1890s. The economic depression which began in the eighties lasted for ten years. All major industries were depressed, beginning with mining. The Sherman Silver Purchase Act of 1889 was intended to stabilize prices through government purchase of fixed amounts of the metal, but the act was repealed on November 1, 1893, and the results were disastrous. "The shrinkage in the value of silver," said Governor L. C. Hughes in his report for that year, "has resulted in the closing of almost all our silver mines." The loss, which he estimated at almost $6 million, was offset by the growing importance of copper, but it was deeply felt nonetheless.[1]

The cattle industry was also hard hit. When the rains came in the late eighties, the ranges had been overstocked. When they refused to come in the early nineties, the ranchers suffered severe losses. In 1890 the railroads contributed to the disaster by raising rates. The cost of shipping to eastern markets threatened to bankrupt the shipper. Cattlemen Walter and Ed Vail, of the Empire Ranch, southeast of Tucson, stayed solvent by reviving the practice of trail driving

and walked their herds to California at a considerable saving. Ed Vail and Tom Turner, Ed's foreman, with eight Mexican cowboys and a Chinese cook, made the drive in spite of multiplied hazards and obstacles.[2] On their return they reported to a meeting of area ranchers at the Palace Hotel in Tucson, and the result was a decision by all of them to "ship by hoof." The railroad read the signs correctly and restored the old rates.[3]

Business was so bad in Arizona that the population of Tucson, its largest city, declined in 1890 to a little over 5,000—down 2,000 from the number recorded in 1880. Tucson was actually, for the moment, shrinking.

A sign of the difficult times was a continuation and expansion of the lawlessness that had characterized the eighties. Stagecoach and highway robberies were common, and train robberies, beginning in May, 1887, attracted many practitioners, professional and amateur. The Southern Pacific passenger train was stopped at Pantano Station, eighteen miles east of Tucson, on August 10, 1887. Larry Sheehan, a cocky outlaw who had just moved into Arizona Territory from New Mexico, was picked up at Stein's

Pass near the state line by Sheriff John Slaughter of Cochise County and charged with the crime. A Tucson judge released him and several of his henchmen on bail, and they busied themselves at once planning another robbery. On February 22, 1888, they stopped a train near Stein's, made a break for Mexico with their loot, and crossed the border just ahead of a posse headed by United States Marshal W. K. Meade. Unwarily and unwisely Meade rushed on into Chihuahua and was arrested by the commandant of the Mexican garrison at Janos. When the marshal and his posse crossed the border two weeks later, minus their arms and horses and considerably ruffled, an international incident seemed to be in the making. It did not materialize, however, since Meade was clearly in the wrong.[4]

Sheehan and his men were tracked down and killed, with the help of a properly propitiated detachment of Mexican troops, on March 16, 1888, but they had given notice that express cars could be robbed successfully, and as a result trains were stopped somewhere in the West every few months. Usually they were stopped for profit, but sometimes they were wrecked for fun. General Superintendent J. A. Fillmore of the Southern Pacific, outraged by one such case, offered a $1,000 reward for conviction of "the person or persons who wrecked our west bound passenger train, number twenty, about two miles west of Benson, Arizona, at about 11:30 o'clock, on the evening of August 12, 1889."[5] The federal government was already offering another $1,000 for the arrest and conviction of anyone robbing a train or stagecoach carrying United States mail, but mail and express robbery continued to attract practitioners. By 1933, when the last attempt was made on the Southern Pacific, the company had survived fifty-nine

robberies, according to historian Eugene B. Block.[6] One famous holdup took place on January 29, 1895, near Willcox, east of Tucson. Grant Wheeler and Joe George placed an ambitious charge of dynamite on top of the express-car safe and weighted it down with eighteen sacks of Mexican dobe dollars. The explosion scattered coins all over the landscape, and for the next few days "the whole of Willcox" was out gathering them up.[7]

The most celebrated episode happened at Fairbank, in the San Pedro Valley near Tombstone, on February 15, 1900. Jeff Milton, already well known as a lawman, was guarding the express car for Wells, Fargo. He stood off five robbers, ending the career of one of them, known as "Three-Fingered Jack" Dunlap.[8] Jeff was left with a permanently crippled arm but continued to accumulate credits as a peace officer.[9] His exploits, however, had little effect on the urge to stick up trains.

Lawlessness in the cities was just as hard to bring under control, and some of the leading citizens contributed to the problem. Gentlemen still carried pistols in the early nineties and used them when occasion demanded. The most notorious shooting in Tucson's history occurred on September 24, 1891, when two of its most prominent professional men engaged in a gun duel at the corner of Pennington and Church streets in the heart of the business district. The principals were lawyer Francis J. Heney and Dr. John C. Handy, a highly regarded physician who had been named chancellor of the yet-unborn University of Arizona in 1885 and was chief surgeon for the Southern Pacific. He was loved by many, especially by poor people, for his willingness to go anywhere, any time, to help a patient, but he had a hair-trigger temper and could be a for-

Dr. John C. Handy, who lost the gun battle.

midable, unforgiving enemy. At the time he was having domestic problems. His wife was suing for divorce, and he is said to have threatened to kill any lawyer who had the courage to represent her. Heney took the case.

Both men were tough and fearless, but Handy was bigger and more belligerent. Heney, slighter in build, had come to Arizona to cure his tuberculosis, but he had shown himself willing to challenge anyone, in or out of the courts. He may have felt sorry for Mrs. Handy. He may have wondered just how dangerous a man Handy was.

Supposedly the doctor renewed his threats when he heard of Heney's action. Jeff Milton remembered that he tried on one occasion to run the lawyer down with his team and buggy. Finally the two met face to face on the street at noon of that September day.

A few bitter words were exchanged, and Handy moved to attack. There was a wild melee, and different spectators told different stories about what happened. It seems clear that the angry physician struck his enemy in

Lawyer Francis J. Heney, who won the fight.

131

Mrs. John C. Handy, the cause of the difficulty.

Goodfellow was the best gunshot-wound doctor in Arizona, having had almost unlimited opportunities to gain experience in that violent mining town, which was said to "have a man for breakfast every morning." A railroad engine and caboose picked up Goodfellow at Benson, and he himself took the throttle to begin one of the wildest rides in railroad history. He lost his patient but continued to build his own career. He moved to Tucson, bought the Orndorff Hotel, transformed it into a hospital, and did important work in surgery before leaving for service in the Spanish-American War. When that was over, he moved to San Francisco and spent the rest of his life far from his triumphs in the Arizona desert.[11]

the face and grappled with him for his pistol. Insiders said that he meant to kill Heney with his own weapon. Struggling, they fell to the ground and somehow the smaller man pulled the trigger and sent a bullet through Handy's intestines. There was small hope of surviving such a wound, but Handy told his friends as they carried him away to try to get Dr. George Goodfellow in from Tombstone. It was his only chance.[10]

Dr. George Goodfellow, who lost his patient.

GROWING PAINS

In the years that followed the Handy shooting, murder, rape, and robbery continued to get newspaper headlines. The police themselves were sometimes featured. On July 19, 1893, for example, two policemen engaged in a duel with knives on Congress Street just before nine P.M.[12] The frontier tradition of personal journalism also refused to die. Editors slashed at each other and at prominent personalities, just as they had done since the first printing press came to Tubac. In the 1890s, however, they sued more often than they shot at each other. A famous episode involved the brothers R. C. and G. W. Brown, editors of the *Florence Enterprise*. In a long article published on July 21, 1892, they accused Brewster Cameron, chief clerk of the Territorial Department of Justice, of "getting juries that bend the supple hinges of the knee at his will." The editors were sentenced to one day in the Yuma penitentiary. The newly organized Arizona Editorial Association brought such pressure to bear, however, that Governor L. C. Hughes issued a pardon on April 22, 1893, just before the sentence was to be carried out.[13]

A year later J. O. Dunbar, the pugnacious editor of the *Arizona Gazette* in Phoenix, branded the governor, the territorial secretary, the attorney general, and the United States marshal as "a gang of hoodoos, . . . patronage peddlers, land grant sharks, assassins and looters." He was convicted and fined $1,000, to the great indignation of his fellow Democratic editors, who protested that "any utterance of the press may be considered as libel" according to this precedent.[14]

Violence in the streets and in the press helped convince supercilious easterners of Tucson's backwardness and provincialism. They noted also that the streets were still

Henry Buehman, mayor and photographer.

unpaved, the old adobe houses primitive and run down, the saloons, gambling houses, and good-time girls still doing a rush business. The citizens themselves were often discouraged. Mayor Henry Buehman, on January 5, 1897, complained that the thoroughfares were filthy and that a general cleanup was needed. Two years later he remarked mournfully that Tucson was not a safe place for children to grow up in. Its moral atmosphere was "far from bracing."[15]

Much, however, depended on who was talking. Governor John N. Irwin, for example, told an eastern audience in 1891 that life could be beautiful in Arizona. "It is the simple truth," he declared, that life in that territory "is safer today than life in New York, . . . just as pure, just as sweet as is the life of any American family living in New York or New England."[16]

Lawyer J. George Hilzinger backed him

Sabino Alley (Gay Alley) in 1955. Merrille L. Sutton photo (Wong-Sutton Photographers).

up in 1897. "In 1885," he assured his readers, "there were twelve policemen and a marshal required to restrain the lawless element, while today there is but a slight occupation for three policemen and himself. . . . The number of arrests for carrying concealed weapons is comparatively small, and . . . murder and arson are comparatively unknown." Hilzinger noted that arrests for assault and battery in 1890 totaled thirty-one; in 1896, zero.[17]

Undoubtedly Tucson was progressing, but before peace, prosperity, and stability could be attained, three mainstays of frontier living had to go: the crib, the gambling room, and the all-night saloon. They had to go, but their going was contingent on some other important and far-reaching changes. Reform was next to impossible, for instance, while the percentage of young unmarried men remained high. When the balance shifted to family-oriented men, as it did in the 1890s, a change was possible. The reformers consolidated their forces and began to chip away at the tenderloin, the bars that never closed, and the gambling fraternity.[18]

At the beginning of the decade the nightlife district was in the heart of town along Meyer Street and on both sides of the Wedge, but in 1891 the sporting district was moved to Gay Alley, as already noted, and in 1902 the Wedge itself, with all its memories, was razed to allow for a much-needed widening of Congress Street.

The gamblers were less vulnerable—for a while. In the early days they enjoyed a measure of respectability, and carried weight in civic affairs.[19] With the saloonkeepers, they claimed to be the cornerstone of Tucson business, and practical men of affairs argued that closing them down would be civic suicide. "Grass will grow in your streets," they said, "if you run them out."[20] The police department in Tucson, as in other western cities, was partly supported by the fines and fees collected from the girls and the gamblers. How would these funds be replaced?

It took years for the reformers to make much progress, and their first successes were small. The *Star* announced on January 29, 1906, that "wine rooms admitting women and children will no longer be permitted in Tucson. The city council passed an ordinance yesterday prohibiting any saloon from having private rooms or booths. The object of the ordinance, it was stated, is to reduce the number of saloons in Tucson to 30." The following year another ordinance prohibited women singers from "loitering" in bars.[21] These entertainers had long been a part of the barroom furniture in the better places. Their disappearance may have reduced business—but not by much.

The campaign against gambling moved by slow stages also. In western towns regulation usually consisted in charging high license fees and moving the gambling establishments off the main streets or to the upper floors of the saloons. In 1906 the legislature passed an edict, aimed solely at Tucson, forbidding a gambling establishment or any other business inimical to public morals to locate within 4,000 feet of the center of the university campus.[22]

For all practical purposes gambling in Tucson was closed down in 1905, when General L. H. Manning was elected mayor. He had been known to turn a card himself, but he announced that if he was elected he would close up the dealers. He was, and he did. He raised the license fees, shut down the games from 10:00 A.M. to 6:00 P.M. and limited permits to thirty days. The load was too heavy for the gamblers, and most of them left town or quit the cards.[23] In 1907

the legislature outlawed gambling throughout Arizona. It did not cease to exist, of course, on that account.

Manning, the son of a Confederate colonel, grew up in Mississippi and came to Arizona in 1884. His beginnings were modest, but by 1905 he was a rich man, active in merchandising, mining, and real estate. He and Epes Randolph, a high official of the Southern Pacific, built the Santa Rita Hotel in 1904. When he took charge of Tucson, things naturally began to move. He put the police force into uniform, recommended oiling Tucson's dusty streets, and took care of the vagrant problem—which had been troublesome for twenty years—by putting tramps and hoboes to work on the streets.[24] In 1908 his council passed an edict closing all saloons at 12:00 midnight, thus eliminating all-night bars and a considerable portion of Tucson's night life.[25]

Gambling was a harder nut to crack. Manning and his councilmen could discourage but not eliminate it. It simply went underground. In 1936 gambling was still a "burning question" in city hall, mostly because it was going on outside the city limits. The profits were going to interests from California.[26] In 1951, County Attorney Robert Morrison began a campaign to eliminate "gambling and vice." Sixteen slot machines were seized from the El Rio Country Club, the Old Pueblo Club, and the Tucson Press Club.[27] Morrison estimated that the yearly take of gamblers in Arizona was $10 million.[28] And so it went, and so it will probably continue to go.

The reform effort did not stop with campaigns against booze and vice. Woman suffrage was a vital part, proposed in the eighties and perennially reproposed thereafter. Editor L. C. Hughes of the *Star* crusaded for it, and so did his formidable wife.

135

With that cause Josephine Brawley Hughes joined the battle against booze,[29] driving the saloon men to conclude that if women were given the vote the days of liquor would be numbered, and that was one good reason why the women's movement in Arizona was so slow in getting off the ground.

Pressure from the drys intensified, however. The Anti-Saloon League became active in Arizona in 1906, along with several other reform organizations. Tucsonan Eugene W. Chafin, twice a candidate of the Prohibition party for the United States presidency, was one of the leaders, along with L. C. Hughes and enthusiasts from the Ministerial Alliance, the YMCA, the YWCA, the Good Templars, and even the IWW. The children of WCTU members were organized into the Loyal Temperance League and did their share of marching, singing, and placard carrying. With the attainment of statehood in 1912, women at last could vote on these matters, and the result in 1914 was a successful drive to initiate a prohibition amendment to the state constitution. The long drought of the twenties had begun.[30]

Tucson's growing pains resulted in the elimination of open prostitution, liquor, and gambling, but positive as well as negative action was needed, and positive action came. Sometimes it came in spite of vigorous resistance from the community. A case in point involved the founding of the University of Arizona—unwelcome, undervalued, and resented in Tucson.

The First Legislature in 1864 created a territorial university on paper and even wrote a constitution for it. A board of regents was provided for, and an income from the sale of public lands was set aside. No attempt, however, was made to implement these provisions. There was, in fact, for some time strong opposition to spending

money for any educational program. The country was so sparsely settled and the immigrants were in such constant danger that mere survival was about all they could hope for. Regent Gilbert W. Hopkins was killed by Apaches less than a year after his appointment, and a similar fate could be expected for any resident of the territory. The first schoolroom in Arizona, according to Robert H. Forbes, was built on the Sopori Ranch, south of Tucson, before 1860, when Apache raids were so frequent that the main house was provided with portholes for defense.[31]

Higher education in this environment was almost unthinkable, and until 1885 nothing was done, or even proposed, to carry out the wishes and dreams of the first idealistic legislators. In that year the Thirteenth Legislature—the "Thieving Thirteenth"—convened at Prescott. The time had come for the placing of territorial institutions, and the larger communities were eager for the spoils. First prize was the state capital. Tucson wanted it back. Second prize was the insane asylum (with an appropriation of $1,000). Third prize was the state prison. The university and a teachers college were to be located, but they seemed superfluous, and nobody wanted them. The university was considered to be particularly undesirable, though an appropriation of $25,000 went with it. According to Mose Drachman, the sentiment of the Tucson community was expressed by a local bartender: "What do we want with a university? What good will it do us? Who in hell ever heard of a University Professor buying a drink?"[32]

Tucson wanted the capital and wanted it so badly that the merchants raised $5,000 and sent Fred Maish to Prescott to see how much he could accomplish with it. They also instructed lawyer C. C. Stephens, a member of the upper house and a very capable man, to bring the capital back or suffer the consequences. On account of wintry weather, however, the Tucson delegation had to go to Prescott by a roundabout way, and when at last they arrived at journey's end, the spoils had already been divided. Prescott retained the capital. Yuma had the prison. Phoenix was about to get the asylum. Realizing that he was beaten before he started and hoping to salvage something for his hometown, Stephens supported Phoenix in its bid for the mental hospital and voted to give Tempe the normal school. He felt that he had done the best he could when the university went to Tucson.

On his return, however, he was subjected to all sorts of insult and humiliation for his "disloyalty." Threats of violence made it necessary for him to hire a bodyguard. The *Citizen* informed him that his fellow townsmen looked on him with "loathing and contempt" and suggested that it was hard to imagine what he was made for "unless to make a horse thief feel respectable by comparison." When Stephens called a meeting at the Opera House to explain his actions, he was subjected to such a torrent of profane and personal abuse and such a barrage of rotten eggs, spoiled vegetables—and even a dead cat—that he had to retire from the platform. He did remind the hecklers before he left that someday they would thank him for what he had done, but at the time no one listened or believed.[33]

Having disdained the university, Tucson next tried to forget it. One farseeing citizen, however, refused to join in the general revulsion. He was Jacob Mansfeld, the European-educated newsstand proprietor. One of the four appointed university regents, he alone bothered to qualify for the position, and when the other three refused to listen to

his pleas for action, he persuaded the governor to appoint new ones. The $25,000 appropriation which went with the institution carried a proviso that a site had to be located within a year or the money would be lost. Mansfeld and his new colleagues searched long and unsuccessfully for a suitable—and cheap—location. Finally Jacob found one out on the mesa three miles east of the downtown section and began a campaign to get it. He badgered the owners so successfully that they agreed to donate forty acres for the new institution. Their names were E. C. Gifford, W. S. Reid, and B. C. Parker. Gifford was a Tucson saloonkeeper. The other two were Tucson gamblers.[34] When the deed was filed on May 3, 1886, the university was in business—without a classroom, a faculty, or a student,[35] though Dr. J. C. Handy had been invested with the title chancellor.

The next step was to hire an architect and erect a building. Ground was broken on October 27, 1887, with appropriate ceremonies, including the firing of a ceremonial howitzer. The principal speaker was C. C. Stephens, no longer in danger of a vegetable barrage. He looked forward with enthusiasm to the day when the university would display "its cool verandas, its broad porches, its silvery fountains, its shaded walks, its academic groves, its crowded halls of thoughtful students, . . . quaffing with sparkling eyes and eager delight of the ever-living fountain of learning of all ages, their countenances illumined with the clear light of ever-living truth, their souls hungering for that knowledge which is more precious than rubies and above all price."[36]

Stephens's pleasing dream was somewhat deflated when cash ran out before the building was completed, and the regents had to petition the legislature for more money.

When it was granted, after four years' delay, they added the roof and the windows. Their enthusiasm was further eroded when Chancellor Handy, after a year of service, refused to attend board meetings. He had quarreled with board secretary Charles M. Straus and was angry because he wanted a one-story building while the majority favored something higher which would show up well from downtown. The board voted to replace him, and J. S. Wood became the new presiding officer.[37]

The original idea was to provide assistance for the mining industry, and the university was often referred to as the School of Mines. The shift to agronomy could be attributed to the United States government. Under the terms of the Hatch Act (1887) any school of agriculture at a land-grant institution was eligible for an annual $15,000 grant for an experiment station. The second Morril Act (1890) added another $15,000 with an annual increment of $1,000 for ten years. With an eye on all this largesse, the regents in July, 1889, created on paper a school of agriculture with one professor, who was also to direct an experiment station. The only member of the board with a college degree was Selim M. Franklin, a young lawyer who had made the final appeal in the legislature for the university to come to Tucson. Automatically he became the first professor of agriculture. He knew nothing of the subject and accepted the appointment on a temporary basis (he hoped), because somebody had to. These arrangements looked impressive enough to justify an application for federal funds, and to the astonishment of almost everybody a grant of $10,000 was forthcoming. In 1890 the two acts produced $30,000.

The first fruits of these miracles was the appointment in 1890 of the first paid faculty member, Frank A. Gulley, a product of the Michigan State Agricultural College who had spent the last five years working and teaching in Mississippi and Texas.[38] With the faculty Gulley had selected, including Theodore B. Comstock as dean of the mining school, the University of Arizona officially opened on October 1, 1891, with six faculty members and thirty-two students. Six were college freshmen; the rest were enrolled in "preparatory courses." There was not a single high school in Arizona in 1891, and for the next thirty-five years the university offered secondary-school courses along with the regular college curriculum.[39] The work was divided between a school of agriculture and a school of mines with some liberal-arts courses included to satisfy requirements for degrees. Gulley also started an agricultural experiment station.

Everything was concentrated in the building now known as Old Main, which housed classrooms, laboratories, library, assembly hall, living quarters for faculty members, and a second-floor dormitory for students. Noah and his animals in the ark could not have experienced closer relationships than those students and professors, along with their Chinese cook.[40] The results appeared on May 29, 1895, when the first graduating class, three members strong, received their diplomas from President Comstock. By then there was no doubt that Tucson was proud of its school. In spite of inclement weather the assembly hall was full, and the audience listened appreciatively to the essays read by the graduates and to the speaker of the evening, the Reverend Howard A. Billman, a Presbyterian minister, as he assured them that "universal learning" would not bring about "an age of mediocrity."[41]

Sadly one must admit, however, that,

The University of Arizona, completed and in business, July, 1891.

The University of Arizona, forty years later.

Thomas Fitch. Courtesy Library of Congress.

without adequate facilities, library, or faculty salaries and with very few well-prepared students, the University of Arizona was that in name only for many years. It did attract some dedicated teachers, and they built, almost brick by brick, something like the university that C. C. Stephens had visualized in 1887.

Its presence did have a profound effect on the development of Tucson. It opened the minds of young people, prepared them for a variety of careers, and added a cultured element to the population. It even influenced the growth of the city.

Students of land use in Tucson point out that early development of the community was on a north–south axis along the Santa Cruz River and Main Street. East–west growth was contained by the arable lands west of the river and by the Camp Lowell Reservation on the southeast and the cemetery on the northeast.[42] This pattern was hard to break, as Thomas Fitch found when he came to town in 1882.

Born in New York State, Fitch drifted westward while still in his teens, became a shrewd lawyer with important connections, and cherished a burning ambition to be a United States senator. Following his dream, he lived in California, Nevada, Utah, and Arizona, always busy, always ambitious, always disappointed. He was a dynamic man, darkly handsome, with a great reputation as an orator and considerable talent as an actor, and wherever he lived, he joined or organized theatrical companies. When he moved to Tucson, he did more than that. He built a theater.[43]

Fitch's opera house rose on the southwest corner of Sixth and Congress. The location is now close to the heart of downtown, but at the time the townspeople complained that it was too far out. Only the Lexington Stables, the waterworks, and the Old Adobe Schoolhouse were anywhere near it. Nevertheless Fitch went ahead with his plans, and his opera house opened on October 30, 1882, with a performance of *Old Shipmates*, carried off in fine comic style by the Frank Mordaunt company of traveling actors. In November the Tucson Dramatic Club filled the stage with a performance of T. W. Robertson's *Caste* with Fitch in the role of Captain Hawtree. There were other performances, but the times were out of joint for Fitch. A serious depression was beginning. His theater was not a model for provincial opera houses, and the location was against it. Tom left town in 1883, and his temple of the muses became a skating rink. In 1884 it burned down—"fortunately," said the *Star*. "It was inconveniently situated and unprofitable to its owners."[44]

Fitch was ahead of his time in more ways than one, but the railroad accomplished what he conceived. Service facilities and warehouses were erected along the tracks, resulting in the development of Congress Street as an east–west artery. The opening of the university, connected with downtown by Third (now University) Street, made a new area available for residential development, and when the first mule-drawn streetcars began operations in 1898 (replaced by electric cars in 1906), the east–west expansion of the town was well under way. Tom Fitch's palatial mansion, built on Military Plaza in 1882 with the first air-conditioning system in the Southwest (cool air circulating within the walls), no longer seemed suburban.[45] Several platted additions were already in existence on the mesa when the university opened, and by the end of the century new residential neighborhoods had come into being northeast and southeast of the original village site, with lands set aside for parks and schools. Everything followed an Anglo pattern, marking a complete break with the original Spanish-Mexican formula. Don Bufkin comments on the grid concept of expansion with houses set back from the street on ample lots and adds:

Absent also were the mixture of small-neighborhood commercial uses that were so typical of the Mexican village areas. Entire blocks, averaging generally four acres, were allotted to schools and parks and interspersed in the residential neighborhoods. Basically the land-use arrangements that evolved in the first easterly growth surge to a large extent are those that are the goal of present-day city planning efforts.[46]

That "first surge" seemed miraculous to long-time Tucsonans. It was nearly impossible in 1900 for even the most romantic imagination to foresee what was coming half a century later. Anyone who predicted metropolitan status for Tucson was hooted at. Mose Drachman tells of a far-sighted citizen named Charles Hoff who would sometimes say, "I may not live to see it, but some day

Tucson will be a big city. You will see skyscrapers against the skyline."

"Great was the good-natured laughter that such a statement produced."[47]

In 1900 the only significant movement of population for most observers was the shift of the business community eastward along Congress toward the railroad. This caused distress and forebodings among the merchants west of Stone. As banks and grocery stores and saloons sprang up in the developing area, these merchants decided that they would have to make a decisive move, and it was then that the Wedge was removed, making Congress a broad avenue instead of a street so narrow that two big wagons could not pass. They had waited too long, however, according to Mose Drachman. "It was too late."

Even then a hard core of conservative citizens hated to see these changes and resisted them as long as they could. The new water system was welcomed, but when agitation began for a sewer network, the response was negative. One individual said that he did not want a sewer—he had just installed a good cesspool. The line went in on Congress anyway, but when plans were made to turn the corner on Stone, the businessmen on that corner were opposed. A line on Congress was enough. Mose Drachman told his friends that what the town needed was a few first-class funerals. "If some of the old fossils would die off, we could make a good town of it." He admitted later that "some of these men saw the light and came over to our side and helped to bring about a great many of the improvements."[48]

Men like Drachman wanted their city to become better as well as bigger—better for all its inhabitants including their neighbors, the Indians. They proved it by supporting the Tucson Indian Training School, which

The Reverend Howard A. Billman, who directed the Indian School and became president of the university.

for over seventy years offered the rudiments of an American-style education to hundreds of young native Americans and helped change the course of history for the Papagos.

The school was a Presbyterian missionary enterprise, an offshoot of President Ulysses S. Grant's policy of putting church groups in charge of Indian welfare. The Bureau of Indian Affairs constructed a school building at San Xavier del Bac in 1873. In 1888 it was the Presbyterians' turn. They established the first "contract school" in the Territory, the Tucson Indian Training School, agreeing to teach a student body of Indian children for $31.25 a quarter for each child. The government provided money for cur-

rent expenses and temporary quarters in an old adobe school building at Sixth and Congress on the outskirts of downtown Tucson. Eleven boys and girls from the Pima Reservation arrived on January 4, 1888, to begin their studies under supervision of an acting superintendent and three teachers. Nine months later, on October 21, the Reverend Howard A. Billman arrived from Cincinnati to take charge. A slender, bearded, high-voltage young clergyman, he went at his job with great energy and high resolve. Although he was new to the area, he had a surprisingly clear mental picture of what needed to be done and how to do it. He wrote to Mrs. C. E. Walker on December 10 that "the standing danger is that we shall give them such a home here and feed and clothe them in such a way that we shall send them home simply unfitted for the condition of life where Providence has assigned their earthly lot." He knew that lecturing an Indian was not the way to reach him. "He cannot be told from a platform. You must serve by his side at the expense of blistered hands and aching limbs."[49] Through the sixty years of its existence that was the way the school was run.

Billman's first task was the completion of a two-story building on four square blocks near the site of the university. The Presbyterian Women's Board of Home Missions had leased the land from the city for ninety-nine years at a dollar a year. In November, 1888, the move to the new campus was made, and fifty-four young Indians were on hand. Three months later eighty-four were enrolled, and Billman was having to turn away applicants since he was equipped to handle only seventy-five. A year after his arrival the school was moved again, to a more ample acreage at what would later be Twenty-second Street and Tenth Avenue,

The Indian School, 1895.

and there it remained until 1907. By then the eastward movement of the city had engulfed it completely, and the establishment was shifted for the last time to a site far south on Ajo Road. It lasted there until 1960, when financial difficulties and changing conditions forced it to close.[50]

Billman was a product of his times in most ways, but in some of his attitudes he was ahead of his generation. His views were recorded in the course of an interview conducted by the editor of the *Galveston Daily News* in April, 1893 (reprinted in the *Star*). The Indian has had "the worst possible treatment," he said. "Of course we could not civilize them while we were fighting and killing them and when the government decided that it was cheaper to feed than to fight the Indians it was just as far off from any civilizing influence." The tribesmen have been "pauperized," and have become "more lazy and worthless than before,"[51] he said.

Billman limited his goals and hoped only to make life better for his charges when they returned—as he knew they must—to their native villages. He kept his boys busy on the school farm and in the bakery, the woodworking shop, the blacksmith shop, and all the maintenance activities of the school. Half their time was spent in the classroom and half in manual labor. The girls were taught homemaking and household arts and were kept on a schedule as rigid as that of the boys. If they showed any talent or interest, however, they were given a taste of music and literature. In a *Historical Circular of the Indian Training School*, issued in 1905, Superintendent Haddington C. Brown described a typical day at the school, work and study mingled, and concluded:

Tea comes at five, after which we have prayers, and the evening study hour from six until seven, when workers and pupils end the labors of the day, and the children retire at eight, tired but happy.

We are not only a school but a home. We bring in just as much of the home as is possible with so large a number.[52]

Billman left the school in 1894 to head the University of Arizona. His successor was a remarkable man who liked Indians and liked working with them. He was the Reverend Frazier S. Herndon, a native of Missouri who directed the school from 1895 to 1903. At the time of his arrival government support had been withdrawn, and new ways had to be found for raising money. Herndon found them. One of his devices was to contract with the City of Tucson to grade and maintain the streets. The energetic young clergyman brought in more students, expanded the curriculum, added new buildings, and made friends with the reservation Papagos. When he left the school, it was to work as a missionary in the outlying villages and in the Papago community on the south side. Under his administration the first Papago boy was graduated in 1903. He was José Xavier Pablo, a leading man of the tribe later on.[53]

During Herndon's administration the Indian boys and girls found relief from loneliness and boredom in two extracurricular activities: music and athletics. They liked to sing, and they learned to sing in parts, making boys' and girls' choruses possible. They took piano lessons, and there was a twelve-piece band which tooted heartily to the great enjoyment of all. American games were a delight to the boys. When a football team was organized, everybody wanted to be on it, leaving the track team undermanned. The coach, with great resourcefulness, immediately set up a rule: football players had to be on the track team. In a very short time the pendulum swung, and everybody wanted to run.[54]

The superintendent who stayed longest—twenty-six years—took charge in 1915. Martin L. Girton did almost as much as Herndon to develop the school. He visited the Papago fathers and mothers to persuade them to turn their children over to him, hoarded his funds, developed programs he thought would benefit his charges, and kept the institution on course.

Commencement programs tell something about the experience of the boys and girls at Escuela, as the school was familiarly known. On May 22, 1921, for example, thirteen eighth-graders and one high-school candidate were graduated. The exercises

opened with an operetta presented by the first four grades, assisted by the junior choir. It was called *Fairies Are Really Truly*. A group of boys followed with a choral number entitled "Dream Brownies." The only concession to the Indianness of the students was the reading of an essay by Mida Chiago: "Pima Life, Ancient and Modern." On May 12, 1935, Dorothy Lewis read a composition entitled "The Future of the Indian Girl." It would be interesting to know what sort of future she saw for herself and her classmates.[55]

Most friends of the Indian at that time had no notion of preserving, or even respecting, native cultures. The idea was to inoculate the Indian boys and girls with American ideas and ways. It seemed right then to feature piano selections entitled "Snowshoeing" and "Happy the Hop Toad." It is necessary now, however, to remind ourselves that the Presbyterians, like their Jesuit predecessors, were "trying to make things better."

For a few of the graduates, it must be admitted, their white education may have been a hindrance rather than a help. A *Star* reporter noted casually in 1950 that "one graduate of the school who returned to his tribe and built a modern home was almost run off the reservation."[56] Thanks to the conservative policies of Superintendent Billman and his successors, however, this sort of thing probably did not happen often, and there can be little doubt that Escuela did much good for a wide variety of tribesmen from many reservations. In 1950 twenty tribal divisions were represented, students coming from as far away as South Dakota.[57]

The greatest benefits were reaped by the Papagos. That they have a homeland today, says historian Mary Huntington Abbott, is due in part, at least, to the school. Only two of their communities, Bac and Gila Bend, had solid legal titles to their land. The desert Papagos outside these communities, roaming, unorganized, and suspicious, owned nothing. Never having been at war with the United States, they had no treaty to protect them. White ranchers and Mexican immigrants were gradually taking over the land that had always been theirs, and there was nobody to fight their battles—that is, there was nobody until the Good Government League was organized.

The league was an informal association of Papago men, most of whom had been trained at Escuela. They began assembling sometime between 1908 and 1911 at one or another of the villages to discuss tribal problems. With the help of missionaries, the Indian Rights Association, Indian Commissioner Cato Sells, and Arizona Governor G. W. P. Hunt, they persuaded President Woodrow Wilson to issue an executive order giving the Papagos title to their homeland. On January 1, 1916, Tucson newspapers announced: "Papagos Regain Inheritance: 4000 Square Miles Set Aside For Tribe."[58] Cattlemen, businessmen, and the Tucson Chamber of Commerce protested furiously, but to no avail. The Papagos owned their reservation—the largest in the United States.

The site of Escuela is occupied now by a highway interchange on I-19, but its impact is still felt. It grew up with the city.

For Indians there were bright spots like Escuela. For the Mexican residents of Tucson the picture seemed to darken steadily. The little Spanish town was rapidly becoming a big Anglo town, and the Mexican half of the community inevitably lost status and influence. Business and professional men of Latin background, like Carlos Jacome and Mariano G. Samaniego, were still important in

Carlos I. Velasco, founder of the Alianza Hispano-Americana.

the life of the city, but even they were beginning to feel excluded, and less-well-to-do Mexicans were having to move to the south side as their homes and properties were absorbed by the waves of Anglo expansion. Tucson's Spanish Americans never suffered as much from Anglo discrimination as did their brothers and cousins in other southwestern cities,[59] but the barriers were going up, and their leaders were unhappy about it. Leadership and organization were needed, and in 1894 they found a way to provide them.

The idea man was Carlos I. Velasco, editor from 1878 of the Spanish-language Tucson newspaper *El Fronterizo*. In 1894 he was fifty-seven years old, a round-faced, in-

Mariano G. Samaniego, Mexican-American leader.

At first it was just a group of friends who wanted a club of their own. About fifty charter members responded to the call of the founders, and a committee was appointed to draw up an *acta de fundación* and set forth the objectives of the society. These were based on the Christian virtues of brotherly love and charity, but several categories of human beings were expressly excluded: nonworkers, former convicts, and "members of the African and yellow races." The society "was founded by Hispanoamericans and it exists solely for them."[61]

The need for such an organization was widely felt, not just in Tucson but throughout the borderlands, and as fast as the word spread, new "lodges" began springing up. In 1895 a *logia* was organized in Florence, and in 1896 others were born in Clifton, Bisbee, and Globe. In 1897 a supreme lodge was created in Tucson, and by 1927, there were 127 lodges in existence. By 1929 there were 240 with a combined membership of 14,125.[62] On the Alianza's fiftieth birthday,

tensely earnest man with a bushy mustache and burning eyes whose devotion to *la causa* was already legendary. "He was all heart," says his biographer. "He sacrificed himself always . . . to the extent that he suffered enmity, poverty and insult in defending the people of his race."[60] On the evening of January 14, 1894, he asked Pedro C. Pello and Mariano G. Samaniego to meet with him in his office, and of that meeting was born the Alianza Hispano-Americana, which became an important influence in the affairs of the Southwest and Mexico—the first such specialized organization in the United States. It was the ancestor of LULAC (League of United Latin American Citizens), MECHA (Movimiento Estudiantil Chicano de Aztlan), and all the other multifarious Chicano groups that raised their voices in the 1960s and are still being heard from.

The Alianza headquarters on West Congress Street.

The Alianza membership in early days.

January 14, 1944, the membership enrolled in nearly 300 lodges was almost 20,000 in six southwestern states and Mexico.[63]

The objective, besides the promotion of brotherly love, was frankly political. In union there would be strength, and in union there *was* strength. The Aliancistas, says James Officer, "were able to restore a generally healthy inter-ethnic condition to the community."[64] Early in its history, however, Alianza became a mutual protection society, organizing as an insurance company in 1918, and therein lay seeds of trouble.

Those were proud and prosperous times, especially after the construction in 1916 of a fine two-story headquarters building at 129½ Congress Street in downtown Tucson. Older Tucsonans cherish happy memories of the dances, dinners, and anniversary celebrations which packed the second-story hall with cheerful company. There was even a newspaper, an *órgano oficial*, which had ac-

cumulated twenty-five volumes by 1932, when it was reorganized, with features especially appealing to its Latin readers. There was news of members and of the Alianza's *mesa directiva*, comments and reports on the state of the insurance program, and tributes to the recently dead. Even a few snatches of passionate poetry were included.

The membership was proud of the insurance program and the good things it did for widows and orphans. It was this program, however, which undermined the health of the society. With a million dollars in assets to be managed, some trouble was to be expected. Edward C. Jacobs recalled in 1966 that the first setback occurred in 1917, not long after the headquarters building was completed, "when an official of the organization helped himself to $15,000 and left for Mexico, never to return."[65]

Other problems had to be met after 1926, when the insurance program was extended to the fifteen lodges in Mexico. New regulations had to be followed, and money had to be deposited with the Mexican government before the Mexican *hermanos* could be covered, and more problems arose in 1930.[66] By 1932 a serious split had developed between factions in the society, and the temperature rose so high that the Arizona Corporation Commission felt obliged to take a hand.[67] With the decay of confidence in the management, membership began to decline, and by 1966 only about 2,000 of the crew were still with the ship. In that year the headquarters building was razed to make way for the new city-county government complex, and the society, for all practical purposes, was dead.[68] It had played a tremendous part, however, in making Tucson a more tolerant and civilized town.

Part of the growing-up process for Tucson was the adjustment it had to make, over the years, to the hordes of sick and frightened people who invaded the desert country from the eighties onward in search of healing. Mostly victims of tuberculosis, they were known variously as health-seekers, consumptives, and lungers. Every city in the West had its share of them. For a while Denver was the TB capital. Then California had its turn, followed by New Mexico, Texas, and Arizona.[69] Tucson, in particular, with its warm, dry climate and its good railroad connections, attracted thousands of them.

Arizona Territory was eager for new settlers, and even sick people were theoretically welcome. The leaders boasted of Arizona's climate, stressing its therapeutic advantage and downplaying its heat and aridity, and newspapers extolled it as a paradise for invalids. Every immigrant brought statehood a little closer, for one thing, and his small hoard of dollars swelled the wealth of the commonwealth. Tucson's weather, the

Star declared, was its "great resource" and would bring in large returns.[70] The town "will soon be known as the sanitarium of the Southwest," the editor commented on March 2, 1888.

By 1890 the rush of health-seekers was well under way. Modern methods of controlling tuberculosis had not yet been accepted, and doctors in the East, Middle West, and South usually told their patients that their only hope was to move to a warm, dry climate and let nature heal them. Some of them made their recommendations in print. A typical comment was made by C. L. G. Anderson, a former army doctor, in the course of a medical meeting held at Hagerstown, Maryland, on April 9, 1890. Titled "Arizona as a Health Resort," it was published in a medical journal and circulated in pamphlet form. Every part of the Territory, Anderson declared, could provide a hope and a haven for a sick man, but he particularly recommended the desert country of southern Arizona. Even the air, he said, "is a real asceptic with antimicrobic fluid freely invading and preserving every accessible part of the person. . . . I never met a case of phthisis in an old settler, and it is well known that tuberculosis is very rare among Indians and Mexicans."[71]

It was this sort of advertising which started the familiar saying that in Arizona the general health was so good that when a town wanted to start a cemetery it was necessary to shoot somebody to provide a body for burial.

Small towns near Tucson competed for the patronage of the lungers. A typical advertisement appeared in the *Star* in 1895:

Arizona health seekers should remember that the greatest benefits are derived during the summer months, and in the foothills of the Santa Catalina Mountains among the live oaks at Ar-

Typical shelter in Tent City about 1908. Courtesy Arizona Historical Society and Journal of Arizona History.

cadia, Oracle. It is cool and pleasant and free from dust. Altitude 4500 feet. For further particulars address S. E. Dodge, Oracle, Arizona.[72]

There was money in caring for invalids, and many people made a living at it, but as the flood of immigrants increased, the demand for living space outran the supply. By 1892 the Tucson Board of Trade had to be reminded by a prominent Tucson doctor that many arrivals "could not find desirable accommodations; hence the desirability of a good hotel."[73] Those who came with cash in hand found the doors open, but, sad to relate, many sick and desperate people arrived with almost none, hoping to camp out in the desert or find a hole to crawl into and get well or die. These unfortunates for a long time had no place to turn, and their plight was made worse by the terrible fear of the disease which made even good people send them away.

The *Star* ran an editorial in 1890 warning its readers that consumption was contagious through "germs transmitted by saliva." Do not let a consumptive person spit on the floor; do not sleep in the same room with one. A suspected mother should not nurse her child.[74] A well person should stay at least four feet from an infected one.[75] As a result of such warnings the lunger's chances for human contact, and even for survival, were severely reduced.

By the beginning of the new century the poorest invalids were concentrated in several tent towns, the largest on then-vacant land north of the university. When Dick Hall arrived from Saint Louis in 1910 with his stricken mother, a brother, and a sister, they

149

The Desert Sanitarium for tubercular patients (now the Tucson Medical Center) in 1935.

settled in a tent "of the better sort" on Park Avenue three blocks north of Speedway. It had "a wood floor, wooden sides, a steel roof three feet above the canvas and two cotton-wood trees which gave us some shade":

The interior, about thirty feet long, was divided into a bedroom for Mother and a kitchen-bed-room-living room for the rest of us. Thirty-five feet to the rear was a one-hole toilet. An outside faucet supplied water from a shallow well. . . . The streets were unpaved and consequently it was very dusty. There were no street lights. . . . It was "a place of squalor shunned by most citizens."[76]

The area was isolated—a mile from the streetcar stop at the entrance to the university—and most of the invalids were too weak to walk that far. It was a sad and lonely place:

The nights were heartbreaking, and as one walked along the dark streets, he heard coughing from every tent. It was truly a place of lost souls and lingering death. Sometimes life was too much to bear and a victim would end it. He

was soon replaced, however, by others who hoped for a cure.[77]

Substantial help for the lungers came with time, especially for the ones who could pay. The Whitwell Hospital, on North First Avenue (later the Southern Methodist Hospital), rose in white-painted majesty on the fringes of Tent City in 1906. Much farther out, the imposing and well-endowed Desert Sanitarium was built in 1907. Some of its buildings are still part of the Tucson Medical Center. As the years passed, hospitals, sanitariums, clinics, and boarding houses for invalids multiplied—the Wyatt Clinic, the Barfield Sanatarium, Clark's Rest Home, and many more. The city directory for 1935 carried the names of twenty-one of them. The Right Reverend J. W. Atwood, Bishop of the Episcopal Church in Arizona, founded Saint Luke's-in-the-Desert in 1917 for young men who needed help but lacked the means to pay for hospital care,[78] but the service offered free to people who had nothing was limited to the Adams Street Mission,

Oliver E. Comstock, minister to the sick and desperate.

opened by the Reverend Oliver E. Comstock in 1909.

Comstock was a combination printer and Baptist preacher who arrived in Arizona in 1907 with a daughter who had contracted tuberculosis in Georgia. He built a house at 727 North Second Avenue in the developing residential area near the university, only a short ride on his bicycle from Tent City. The invalids soon became his major interest. He bought land in 1910 and set up three tents, which he called the Mercy Emergency Hospital, operating it in conjunction with his mission and depending for funds on his own small resources and any money he could wheedle from his friends and the Tucson organizations he belonged to. He was remembered as "arriving on his bicycle on a Sunday morning—a small, lean man with white eyebrows to go with his white sideburn whiskers, an almost bald head and a ruddy face. He wore round, shell-rimmed glasses through which he peered with sharp but kindly eyes."[79]

He had some volunteer help, but he went from tent to tent himself to visit with the sick, taking them gifts and seeing to it that they had soup, a few groceries, and simple furnishings for their tents. Not until 1916 did the Organized Charities of Tucson begin to take an interest in him and his work.

An important event in Brother Comstock's life was the arrival in 1915 of novelist Harold Bell Wright, himself a victim of tuberculosis. Planning to rest, write, and recuperate, he set up a rather elaborate camp high above the town on the lower slopes of the Catalinas, but just before Christmas a bad cold sent him to Saint Mary's Hospital. There he received such fine and friendly treatment that he wanted to do something in return and decided to stage a benefit performance of *The Shepherd of the Hills*, dramatized from one of his most successful novels. A professional actor took the leading role, but local amateurs played the other parts, and Tucson society gave enthusiastic support. The performance was a tremendous success.[80]

Somehow Comstock managed to meet Wright and enlist him as a patron of the Adams Street Mission. In all the world there was probably no better beggar than Comstock. He was accustomed to wringing the last possible dollar out of Tucson clubs and individuals, and if Wright made any resistance, it was ineffectual. Comstock emerged from the encounter with a new facilty on Adams Street—a four-room masonry building where once his tents had stood. The next year Wright staged *Salt of the Earth*, and Comstock added a new wing to his hospital.[81]

His task now became easier. Interested men and women gave labor and supplies.

Harold Bell Wright at work at his camp in the Catalina Mountains.

The DAR built and equipped an operating room. The name was changed in 1928 to Comstock Hospital, in recognition of the founder's efforts, and in 1929 the Organized Charities assumed responsibility for the entire operation. In 1930 a children's wing was added, and in 1934 the plight of crippled and undernourished victims of the Great Depression induced the directors to convert it into Comstock Children's Hospital.[82]

More of the load was taken from Comstock's shoulders by the government. Several hundred veterans of World War I were among the 7,000 health seekers living in Tucson in 1920, many of them existing in

hovels and shacks for want of funds. Only the Red Cross felt any obligation to look after them, and the job was too big for the Red Cross to handle. The local veterans' organization and the Tucson Chamber of Commerce came to the rescue.

"We had to do something," said Orville McPherson, secretary of the chamber and a veteran himself. With the help of $4,000 contributed by the Red Cross, the veterans leased Pastime Park, just off Oracle Road on the north side, originally a beer garden and later a skating rink and dance hall. The old wooden buildings could house forty or fifty patients, only a fraction of the number who needed care. McPherson went to Washington and, as he said, "pounded on a few desks." Congressman Carl Hayden supported him and sponsored an appropriation of $25,000 for remodeling and adding to the Pastime facility. When the word got out, however, that there would be room for 275 veterans in the new cottages, applications came in from a thousand. The long-term result was the building of the big pink-stucco veterans' hospital on South Sixth Avenue, opened in 1928.[83]

The health-seekers' invasion produced some interesting by-products. One was "Happy Days in the Old Pueblo"—a department in the *Star* by and for the shut-ins. It began when Emma Perry, a concerned citizen, asked Editor Ralph Ellinwood to let her see what she could do. Calling herself Theodosia, she invited contributions. A few

invalids responded; them more came in, and for seventeen years the column provided an outlet for a group of people who otherwise would have had none. Ellinwood hosted an annual Happy Days party, and in 1926, Amy Brinegar, sister of *Star* staff member David Brinegar, edited the first of a series of Happy Days yearbooks.[84]

Tent City passed out of existence, a tent at a time, in the 1920s as the city expanded eastward, and when Comstock died in 1937, it was only a memory.[85] The work of his hands and heart remained, however, in the Children's Hospital and in the memories of those who had known and worked with him. It was such people as he who brought Tucson through its growing-up period and made it a mature and responsible American community.

CHAPTER 10

Great Events

In 1898, Arizona moved closer to the rest of the United States. Whatever else may be said of the significance of the Spanish-American War, it did continue the slow process of integration begun in 1863 with the achievement of territorial status and continued in 1880 when the chariot of fire arrived. It was part of a pattern of events—some large, some small but significant—which brought Arizona territory closer to maturity, broadened its horizons, and linked it to the rest of the country. Tucson was still the largest community—would remain so until 1920 when Phoenix surged ahead—and it stayed close to the center of the stage.[1]

The war with Spain, with all its hyperactivity, its impassioned rhetoric, its eager volunteers, and its mismanagement and melodrama (with Colonel Theodore Roosevelt making sure that he had an extra pair of glasses as he led his troops to glory) is hard to take seriously now. We had small reason for being in it, and our valorous resolve was partly the product of supercharged journalism, but the West, Arizona, and Tucson played significant roles in America's "splendid little war"—a sort of togetherness none of the three had experienced before.[2]

The Cubans wanted to be free, and the United States had always been on the side of freedom fighters. For thirty years and more the Cuban rebels had been fighting and dying for the cause, and their leaders had been going into exile in the United States between uprisings. In 1893, José Julián Martí crossed from the mainland to try again and was killed at once. Máximo Gómez and Calixto García caught the torch as it fell and put it to use, literally, in a campaign of destruction and terror in the summer of 1895. In the spring of 1896, Spanish General Valeriano Weyler countered by destroying country haciendas and putting the entire population into towns and villages in a *reconcentrado* program and cutting off supplies to the *insurrectos*. In 1897 he was approaching his objective—wiping out the rebels—but in the process he was coming close to wiping out everybody else, and the whole country was close to starvation.

The revolutionaries had only one hope—to gain support in the United States—and their propagandists were active on the mainland. Two of their officers lectured to a sympathetic audience at Prescott in 1898.[3] Their accounts were backed by horror stories

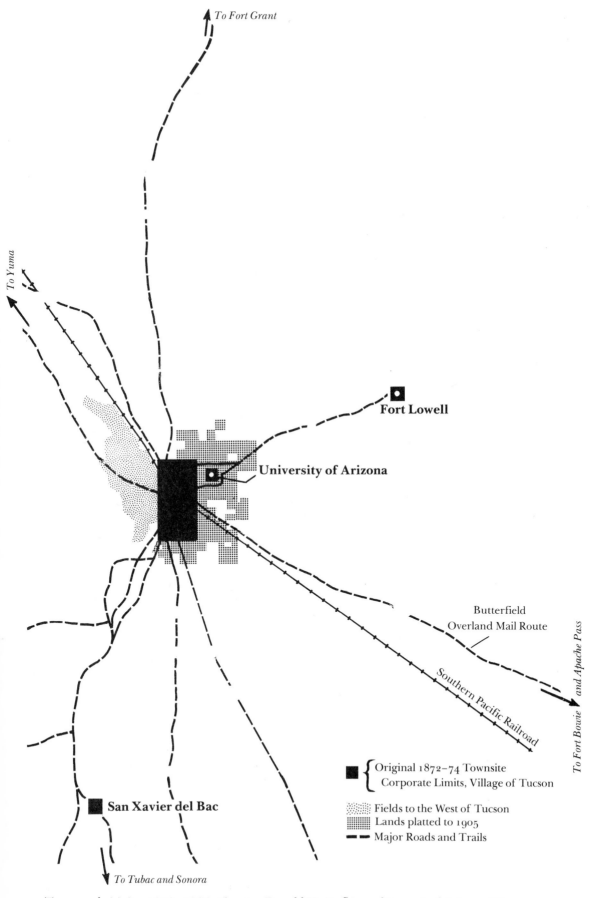

To Fort Grant

To Yuma

Fort Lowell

University of Arizona

Butterfield
Overland Mail Route

To Fort Bowie and Apache Pass

Southern Pacific Railroad

■ { Original 1872–74 Townsite
Corporate Limits, Village of Tucson

Fields to the West of Tucson
Lands platted to 1905
Major Roads and Trails

San Xavier del Bac

To Tubac and Sonora

Tucson and vicinity, 1872–1905. Courtesy Donald H. Bufkin and Journal of Arizona History.

sent home from Cuba by correspondents of the Hearst and Pulitzer papers, and before the end of 1897 Americans were convinced that General Weyler was a butcher and that his campaign was a succession of atrocities.[4] There was a universal outcry for his recall to Spain, and extremists shouted for armed intervention, though Washington rejected any such course of action.

Madrid was disturbed by the hue and cry in the United States—offered autonomy (but not independence) to the *revoltosos*, and even relieved Weyler of command. These measures, however, were too little and too late. All over the United States funds were being raised to aid the "starving Cubans," and the president sent the cruiser *Maine* to the Caribbean to show the flag. Toward the end of January, the ship visited Havana, where mobs were said to be threatening American life and property. The Spaniards regarded this gesture as a threat, and on February 10, Spain recalled its minister to Washington.[5]

The fuse of war was lit on February 15, 1898, at a quarter to ten in the evening, when the Maine was blown up as it lay at anchor with all hands aboard. The explosion shook the whole city of Havana and sent reverberations to every corner of the United States.[6] All agreed that Spain was guilty. The *Maine* was "surrounded by torpedoes" and could not leave the harbor without permission.[7] It made no difference that the Spanish cruiser *Alfonso XIII*, at anchor near the *Maine*, sent all its boats to help with the rescue. It made no difference that the United States naval commission charged with investigating the calamity filed a report which carefully avoided fixing the responsibility. The country sneered when the Spanish minister denied that his government was to blame. On March 8 a bill was introduced in Congress to appropriate $50 million for increasing the armed forces and providing for "defense."

On that same day 700 aroused Tucson citizens attended a mass meeting at the Opera House to let the world know where they stood on the Spanish question. Mayor Henry Buehman presided, and Mose Drachman acted as secretary. "Stirring speeches" were made by Colonel H. H. Herring, Judge William Barnes, and others, and two United States naval officers told of what they had seen in Cuba. At the end contributions to a help-Cuba fund were called for, and the assembly resolved that "the citizens of Tucson, in mass meeting assembled, declare their sympathy with the Cuban insurgents and urge that the government of the United States recognize the independence of the Cuban republic."[8]

The war fever rose swiftly. Early in the year Governor Myron H. McCord began besieging Washington for permission to organize a volunteer regiment, and recruiters were actually at work in early April. McCord hoped to enlist 1,000 men from Arizona as a separate regiment of volunteers, and he could easily have done it, but after the declaration of war on April 25 he was informed that only 170 men from Arizona would be accepted for a special regiment of cavalry to be raised in Arizona, New Mexico, Oklahoma, and the Indian Territory. The number was later raised to 200, but the whole arrangement was a great disappointment to McCord. Nevertheless his preparations enabled his Arizona Territory to be first in filling its quota "and fifteen percent more," as he announced on May 5.[9]

Every able-bodied man wanted to enlist. There were no cries in 1898 of "Hell, no, we won't go!" Women were not immune. The *Citizen* quoted "the editor of a paper in Missouri" who wished she could participate:

Onward, roll onward, Oh, Time in your flight,
Make me a woman that's clear out of sight.
. . . .
Onward, roll onward, Oh Time, quickly fly,
Make me a man, or else let me die.
This world as it is fairly fills me with pain,
Oh, make me a man so I can lick Spain. [10]

The volunteers never considered that war is made up of gore as well as glory. The Spanish dragon was old and feeble and incapable of breathing very much fire. The Cuban people would welcome them as saviors. They would return as heroes after a few weeks in the field. They had no inkling of the malaria, the dysentery, the yellow fever, the long delays, the heat, the bad food, and the Spanish bullets awaiting them.

In Tucson it was generally believed that the Spaniards were terrified at the thought of a regiment of Arizona cowboys: "The Spaniards have heard of them as the flying cavalry who shoot on the wing and have their pockets full of dynamite." [11] As it turned out, only a few of the Pima County boys who went off the Whipple Barracks on April 30 were bona fide cowboys. Hal Drachman, for example—a city boy—persuaded his cousin Mose to pull wires to get him in. [12] The Pima County contingent, second-largest in the territory, included miners, peace officers, gamblers, and journalists. There was even "one college instructor" (an English teacher from Tempe Normal School) among the volunteers assembled. [13] Theodore Roosevelt, their lieutenant colonel and leader (though General Leonard Wood was the titular commander), was more romantic than accurate when he wrote:

In all the world there could be no better material for soldiers than that afforded by these grim hunters of the mountains, these wild, rough riders of the plains. They were accustomed to handling wild and savage horses; they were accustomed to following the chase with the rifle. . . . almost all had at one time or another herded cattle and hunted big game. . . . Most were from the wilderness. [14]

Roosevelt himself, who has been described as a "plunging, rearing, restless, winged creature," [15] liked to think of his men in similar terms. A more balanced view is offered by their historian, Charles Herner: "Although untrained, the Arizonans were outdoor men, with some experience with arms and horses. Moreoever, they were willing to learn and morale remained high. In a short period of time, the men were uniformed, mounted and drilled. In short, they were becoming soldiers." [16]

They were fortunate in their leaders. Colonel Wood was an experienced soldier and a fine organizer. Roosevelt, who resigned his position as undersecretary of the navy to take the second position, had all the necessary political contacts and the drive and enthusiasm of a young rhinoceros. Major (later Governor) Alexander O. Brodie was a professional soldier and knew his business. The two captains, William O. ("Buckey") O'Neill and James B. McClintock, were extraordinary men and excellent leaders. Naturally the Rough Riders, as they came to be called, were the best-known unit in the little army, "the first to go forth as an organized unit for military service outside the territory." [17]

Several of the men became well known later on. Tom Rynning, once a Regular Army sergeant, continued his career as a noncom in the Rough Riders and served later as head of the Arizona Rangers. John C. Greenway, born in Alabama and an athlete at Yale, transferred to A Troop of the Rough Riders as a first lieutenant when

157

Left to right: General Leonard Wood, Lieutenant John C. Greenway, Charles Sipes (orderly), and Colonel Theodore Roosevelt training for Cuba, 1898. Courtesy Post Museum, Fort Huachuca, Arizona.

Captain Buckey O'Neill was killed in action. After distinguished service in World War I, he became a top man in Arizona mining. His bronze likeness stands in Statuary Hall in Washington, D.C., and a replica in front of the Arizona Historical Society in Tucson stares commandingly across Second Street.

Of special interest in Tucson was Sergeant David Hughes, son of pioneers Sam and Atanacia Hughes, who was working in the Copper Queen Mine at Bisbee when Major Brodie asked him to assemble fifteen suitable men and take them to Prescott. A husky, athletic, likable young fellow, Hughes developed into a fine soldier and an aggressive leader. One of his buddies reported in a letter home dated July 15, 1898, that "Hughes was pretty near scalped by a bullet" during

the assault on Kettle Hill. "He regained consciousness in 10 or 15 minutes and went to fighting again."[18] Later he came down with tropical fever but survived and wrote a good account of his experiences.

Tucson had to take a back seat to Phoenix and Prescott as war preparations got under way. Phoenix ladies hand-sewed the regimental flag, and the men were sworn in and shipped out from Prescott. On May 4 the volunteers boarded a special train for San Antonio, and Arizona saw them no more until October. In Texas they mingled with a still more heterogeneous set of recruits, including many "dudes" from the East, most of whom fitted in surprisingly well with the hardy westerners.[19] They all sailed together from Tampa, leaving their horses behind— a fact which prompted one wag to remark

David Hughes, Sam's son, in his Spanish-American War uniform.

longer to the sick and miserable men, but they behaved well and had much to be proud of. The first returning contingent landed at Montauk Point, on Long Island, on August 15, 1898, most of them in wretched condition. David Hughes telegraphed his father in Tucson: "Have just landed and am feeling fairly well. Am ready to go again." [21] Not many of the returning heroes could say the same.

Since there was danger of spreading yellow fever, the men were kept in quarantine for a time, and they came back to Arizona almost one by one, asking only to rest for a while. Sergeant C. E. McGarr provided a more or less typical case. He arrived on the evening of September 23, "little more than a skeleton, from Cuban climatic fever." His uniform was "held together with pins. He is now at the home of his mother on California Avenue, uncertain whether he will live or die." McGarr reported that "the sufferings of the Rough Riders were terrible." The medical service was "entirely inadequate"; the food was "insufficient and abominable." [22] He would have agreed entirely with Ed Andrews, who wrote from Cuba on July 15, 1898, "My curiosity in regard to warfare is fully satisfied." [23]

Dave Hughes had a better homecoming. There was a big reception for him at the San Agustín Hotel, and "every man, woman and child who could possibly be there came to shake the hand of this modest but great hero." He was thirty pounds underweight, however, and never completely regained his health. [24]

The end of the war was in many ways an anticlimax. Governor McCord resigned his office to head a regiment of volunteers, but he had got his men only as far as Albuquerque when the war ended. Even the Great Cause lost much of its luster. The *Citizen*

that Roosevelt's Rough Riders were now Woods' Weary Walkers. [20]

It was all over in a few months—113 days, to be exact. The time seemed much

Volunteer troops leaving Tucson, 1898.

remarked sourly that the *insurrecto* leader General Calixto García had "revealed clearly to our people the untrustworthy and despicable character of a portion of the insurgent forces."[25] There could be no doubt, however, that Arizonans had acquitted themselves well and had called the world's attention to their existence.

Events like the war with Spain did not happen often, but in the years after 1898 many smaller events occurred which had far-reaching consequences and turned out to be great events indeed. One of these was the appearance on Tucson's sandy streets of the first locally owned automobile.

It may not have been the first car in town, or in Arizona. Barnum and Bailey's circus is said to have exhibited one as a curiosity in Tucson and Phoenix in 1898 or early 1899. After that it was inevitable that somebody would feel an irresistible urge to own one. Seemingly the urge was first felt in Phoenix. The *Herald* commented in May, 1899, that a motor car was about to appear on the streets:

It will, we understand, be the property of two or three of our citizens who will put it in for their personal pleasure and possibly as a money-making proposition. A fine single seated gasoline automobile can be had for $1000. . . . The auto-

Dr. H. W. Fenner and his 1900 Locomobile steamer, the first automobile in Tucson. Buehman photo.

mobile will find an elegant field here with our level country and fine roads over which to operate.[26]

Whether Phoenix actually scored an automotive first is debatable, for at some time in that year of 1899, Dr. H. W. Fenner, of Tucson, imported a Locomobile. Years later old timers recalled that a huge crowd assembled at the Southern Pacific station to see it unloaded and watch as Dr. Fenner tried to get it going. The car was a steamer, and a complicated ritual was needed to set it in motion, but "at last the owner was successful and with cheers from the audience it started down the street in a mist of steam and 'bangs.'"[27]

Fenner, an Ohioan who had come to Tucson in the eighties, continued in the forefront of automotive affairs. When city licenses were first issued in 1905, he was

awarded License No. 1. Undoubtedly he was a member of the first automobile club, organized in 1904, bought his gasoline at George Martin's drug store at Congress and Church, and took his business to W. E. Felix's drive-in station, the first in Tucson, opened at North Sixth and East 10th Street before 1915.[28]

The new contraptions moved at what seemed, to men and women emerging from the horse-and-buggy era, fantastic speed, and spectators viewed them with a fascination amounting to passion. Young men known as "scorchers" pushed them to the limit, set records, and raced each other on level streets outside the business district where there was little or no traffic. One of these streets was used so frequently that it was called Speedway. Young Harold Steinfeld, of the mercantile family, owned several cars, including a Stutz Bearcat, and out-

A scorcher and his machine: Harold Steinfeld at the wheel of his Buick.

scorched everybody. When Barney Oldfield was in town, probably in 1914 or 1915, they scorched together.[29]

It took years for city officials and conservative citizens to adjust to all this blinding speed. Only five years before the arrival of Dr. Fenner's machine, bicycle riders were traveling too fast for safety and causing trouble thereby. Two of them collided on the university campus in June, 1894, and "one cycle was demolished." About the same time two boys were brought before the city recorder "charged with riding the tandem at too great speed and so knocking down a little child."[30] Naturally the automobile was considered extremely dangerous, and its use in settled areas was severely restricted. In 1903 the city council decreed a speed limit of seven miles an hour. In 1913 it was still fearful and refused to go higher than ten.[31] Who could have foreseen in 1904 that trans-

continental automobile races would soon be familiar news items, that "touring" would become a national pastime, and that the development of every town in America would be affected? Urban sprawl, shopping centers, inner-city decay, and five-o'clock traffic jams were just over the horizon. By 1918 the number of cars owned in Arizona exceeded 1,800, and the automotive age was under way.

There was less magic in a streetcar, but it had its own importance. Tucson was served after 1898 by mule cars which operated on two lines, one from the Southern Pacific depot to the university, the other, opened in 1900, from downtown to Carrillo's Gardens on the south side. The mule cars were slow and unreliable, more to be endured than to be enjoyed; they were subject to pranks by university students and mischievous boys; and they fastened a sort of rural image on

Mule car off the track at Congress and Stone, 1901.

the town. By 1902 the newspapers were calling for electric cars, and in 1906 they arrived. The Tucson Rapid Transit Company purchased five double-truck, two-man, California-style cars from the Los Angeles Street Railway Company in 1905 and took delivery in May and June, 1906. Portions of the line, on newly laid heavy rails, were opened for business on May 31 with great rejoicing and fanfare. The whole town turned out to watch as company and city officials boarded the cars for a first run to the university and on to Elysian Grove (owner Emanuel Drachman's new name for Carrillo's Gardens), where a banquet and speeches offered refreshment to one and all. The cars continued to roll, over routes which varied and with equipment which underwent some improvement, until 1930, when buses replaced them.[32]

Tucson's railway connections with the world outside were improved also in the first decade of the new century. Rail linkage with Mexico was in special need of upgrading. Commerce was possible only by using the Santa Fe line from Benson to Guaymas, and in 1909, Tucson businessmen, urged on by the indefatigable Mose Drachman, persuaded Epes Randolph, of the Southern Pacific, to connect Tucson with Nogales. Tucson raised money; the county approved a $150,000 bond issue; the SP contributed $600,000. On Sunday, June 19, 1910, the first train went into service. Unfortunately the Mexican Revolution broke out a few months later, disrupting business, and the United States Congress failed to approve the bonds. For once the Southern Pacific came out a loser, but the road was an asset to Tucson and southern Arizona.[33]

In 1912 a bigger railroad came to town. The El Paso and Southwestern, belonging to Phelps Dodge, had already developed a system reaching far up into northern New Mexico, at the same time serving the mines at Bisbee and the smelter at Douglas through a branch line beginning at Deming and skirting the southern tip of the Chiricahua Mountains. By 1910 the management was considering the possibility of extending service all the way to the Pacific Coast. The route proposed would cross the Southern Pacific at Benson and proceed north up the San Pedro and Gila valleys to Phoenix, bypassing Tucson entirely. Again Tucson business leaders united and went to work. This time they focused their efforts on Walter Douglas, of Phelps Dodge, determined to persuade, browbeat, or cajole him into bringing his railway to Tucson. Three bankers—John Mets, N. E. Plumer and John Ormsby—joined forces with Hugo J. Donau, manager of Steinfeld's, to organize the Railway Holding Company for the purpose of acquiring a right-of-way through town. This meant money, and on February 21, 1911, the holding company issued a general call for subscriptions. Tucson responded with enthusiasm, and Walter Douglas saw the light. On October 31, 1912, the last spike was driven, and the sixty-six-mile extension of the line through Benson to Tucson was completed. The first train arrived on November 20. The station was still to be built, but it was in use by December, 1913. It was considered to be an architectural gem—a beautiful building with classic lines—and its charm was enhanced by the addition in front of a lush green park, complete with marble fountain. The cost to the community was $75,000, but some of the money went toward construction of a new YMCA, a gift of Phelps Dodge to the city.

In 1924 the Southern Pacific bought the E.P.&W. line to end competition, and eventually the route was abandoned. During its lifetime, however, it was a real asset to the town.[34]

The arrival of the first airplane on February 17, 1910, opened the door to the Air Age. It was a great event from any point of view. Cross-country flights were still a few years away, and the machine was disassembled and brought to Tucson by train from Phoenix, where the enthusiasts of the Aero Club had raised $15,000 to bring Charles E. Hamilton and Glenn H. Curtiss, two famous fliers, to an "Aviation Meet." Tucson refused to be outdone. Led by Chamber of Commerce President George F. Kitt and park owner Emanuel Drachman, airminded men in the Old Pueblo scheduled a meet of their own.

Five days after the Phoenix affair Hamilton himself arrived, lured by a $2,000 guarantee. Aided by two mechanics, he began putting his machine together. Excitement mounted. The whole town, including reporters, came to watch. The great man talked freely, revealing that he had set a record at Fresno—a mile in one minute twelve seconds—which he hoped to break.[35]

The "big eight-cylinder Curtiss biplane," with pusher propeller, was to fly from the ball park at Elysian Grove on Saturday and Sunday. A "thrilling spectacle" was anticipated. On Saturday, with an excited crowd watching, Hamilton took off to the south and made a "spendid flight" at "terrific speed." On Sunday he did it again, reaching a height of 900 feet. This time, however, the machine refused to stop on landing and ran into a post at the end of the field, scaring the spectators and damaging the elevator plane sufficiently to put Hamilton out of business. The next day he left for Douglas and El Paso, where he crashed and died.[36] The Tucson sponsors of his appearance,

Charles K. Hamilton in flight at Elysian Grove, February 20, 1910.

through lack of paid admissions, had lost $1,500, but they had made history.

The leap from the stagecoach to the airplane had been made in an unbelievably short time, and progress continued with giant steps. In November, 1911, only a year and a half after Hamilton's exhibition, the two pilots who had survived in a transcontinental air race met at Tucson. William Randolph Hearst had offered $50,000 to the first aviator to span the continent in a fixed time. Robert C. Fowler had started from California and had surmounted many difficulties before reaching Tucson. Calbraith Perry Rodgers, coming from the East, had covered more ground, thanks in part to a three-car "hangar train" which followed him, providing a buffet-sleeper for his convenience and a chauffeur for the automobile which met him when he "came down." The manufacturers of Vin Fiz, a popular soft drink, paid for these creature comforts, and the plane was known as the Vin Fiz Flyer. Fowler landed on the university campus and waited for Rodgers, who "stunned thousands of watchers" with his daring maneuvers before landing. To avoid the great crowd assembled at the university, he came

down on a vacant lot several blocks to the south. The men met and compared notes before leaving.

Rodgers got through California, and Fowler reached Florida, but both exceeded the prescribed time, and no prize money changed hands.

From then on airplanes and "bird men" came more and more often to the Southwest. Equipment improved, and aviators learned new skills. Women were occasionally involved. In 1915 pixie-faced teenager Kathy Stinson provided special attractions at the Southern Arizona State Fair in Tucson— stunt flying, racing an automobile, and carrying the first airmail in Arizona. Several times she picked up a mailbag at the fairgrounds and dropped it on a vacant lot near the city post office.[37]

It was war, and the threat of war, however, which made Tucson a real center of air activity. From 1910 for nearly twenty years Mexican revolutionary forces fought the *federales* in northern Mexico, sometimes raiding across the line. The worst outrage was committed at Columbus, New Mexico, in 1916. Army airplanes patrolled the border from then on, and a formally organized Air

The second Tucson airport, on South Sixth Avenue, in 1929.

The irresistible Kathy Stinson, ready to fly. Buehman photo.

The Desert Botanical Laboratory on Tumamoc Hill.

Patrol was on duty in 1919.[38] With America's entry into World War I the pace picked up as military aircraft flew back and forth between California and Texas. Always eager to do their part, the members of the Tucson Chamber of Commerce leased and graded an airstrip between Oracle and Stone where Amphitheater High School was later built and saw to it that fliers were met and welcomed and that lodging and gasoline were available to those who needed it. The army's Flying Circus used this field as part of a Liberty Bond rally in 1919, and not long afterward Mayor O. C. Parker was advised that Tucson had been chosen as the site of one of the thirty-two official army landing fields in the United States. After an exchange of letters terms were agreed upon, and in July, 1919, land was acquired on South Sixth Avenue for the first real Tucson aviation field. The cost of land and improvements was estimated at $5,000. The field was 2,000 feet square with paving on two sides and was surrounded by a barbed-wire fence. An eight-inch well provided water, and the government paid for machine shops and a hangar which would accommodate ten planes. "The work of clearing and leveling will start at once," said the *Citizen*, and estimated that all would be finished in two weeks. It was not until November, however, that Mayor O. C. Parker, an undertaker-turned-politician, was able to open the first municipally owned airport in the United States. On November 20, Councilman Randolph E. Fishburn, an engineer who had supervised construction, flew in from Phoenix with the Barr Flying Circus and made the first landing at the new field off North Oracle. This was another great event which brought the outside world a little closer.

A different set of events, beginning some years before, had brought the outside world to Tucson in a different way. In 1903 the

Godfrey Sykes.

Andrew Ellicott Douglass.

Carnegie Institution of Washington chose the town as the site for a "Desert Botanical Laboratory." The object was to ascertain "the methods by which plants perform their functions under the extraordinary conditions existing in deserts." The founders were Daniel T. MacDougal, assistant director of the New York Botanical Gardens, and Frederick V. Coville, chief botanist for the United States Department of Agriculture. An important addition to the staff in 1906, when activities were expanded, was a many-talented Englishman named Godfrey Sykes, who could do anything mechanical and was a thoughtful human being as well. Under his supervision the Desert Laboratory, built of native volcanic rock, rose on Tumamoc Hill, near the city, and scientific work began. As a result some very distinguished and interesting people made Tucson their home,

or came visiting, until money problems forced a transfer of the laboratory to the United States Forest Service and, finally, to the university.[39]

The Desert Laboratory was manna from heaven, secured without any effort by Tucson or its citizens. Another scientific enterprise, the Steward Observatory, took sixteen years of unremitting struggle and bitter disappointments before it became a reality. Andrew Ellicott Douglass, of the university faculty, was a prime mover. A native of Vermont, he came to Arizona in 1894 to work for astronomer Percival Lowell at the new Flagstaff Observatory and became an assistant professor of physics in the University of Arizona in 1906. He began campaigning for an astronomical facility in 1907 and labored fruitlessly for years to persuade Arizona's practical politicans that a telescope was just as important as a new building to house the School of Agriculture. He never did convince the legislature, but in 1916, Mrs. Lavinia Steward solved his problem by giving the money needed to build the observatory, which was named for her. War production got in the way of the manufacture of the mirror for the telescope, and it was not until April 23, 1923, that Douglass had the satisfaction of dedicating his dream facility. It was the ancestor of the great installation at Kitt Peak, sixty miles west of town.

Meanwhile his interest in cycles of climate had diverted Douglass into what became his most important contribution to science—the study of tree rings and the establishment of a 2,000-year chronology which proved to be of inestimable value in dating the relics of vanished cultures in the Southwest. After the university acquired the Desert Laboratory, some tree-ring research was carried on there, bringing together under one roof two great pioneer thrusts.[40]

While all these important events were taking place—small acorns growing into mighty oaks—the face of the town was changing slowly but steadily, new house following house as streets and subdivisions opened up in the eastward expansion of the community. The area between downtown and the university was filling in, and a fine residential district was opening southeast of the business section, while Main Street and nearby Paseo Redondo continued to attract the well heeled. East Congress continued to develop as a commercial street.

All this expansion was accomplished without much fanfare, but the first decade of the century produced one great building event, the opening of the Santa Rita Hotel

The pride of Tucson: the Santa Rita Hotel.

Epes Randolph.

at Broadway and Scott on what was once the Camp Lowell Military Reservation. General L. H. Manning, then mayor, and railroad magnate Epes Randolph had been pushing construction for a year, and their hour of triumph came on the evening of February 4, 1904. A large and distinguished company of invited guests inspected the 200 rooms, visited the bridal chamber—a "dream in mahogany"—and rode the elevator to the rustic roof garden, six stories above the street. They danced the night away to the music of two orchestras, and next day the editor of the *Citizen* was hardly able to contain his enthusiasm. The new hotel, he said, not only was "the largest and finest in Arizona" but "could not be excelled any-

where in the whole world."[41] It was the pride of the city and continued to be for the next half century.

It must be conceded that for eight years after the opening of the Santa Rita visitors noted a certain incongruity between the big-city distinction of the new hotel and the small-town character of its surroundings. The electric streetcars helped, but they ran down the middle of the old sandy streets. Great clouds of dust rose when automobiles moved from intersection to intersection unless the city moved to send in water wagons with sprinkling equipment—and they were used only in the business district. It was not until 1911 that paving began on Stone Avenue,[42] and for a long time only the main downtown thoroughfares were surfaced.

Tucson was not only dusty; it was also hot. Air conditioning was many years in the future, and people who could afford it went to California, or some other cool place, during the hot months. Rich families often maintained homes in two places. Businessmen who had to mind the store sent their wives and children away, doing their best to withstand the heat and the separation cheerfully. As in other southwestern towns with similar problems, bachelors' and grass-widowers' groups tended to spring up and offer solace to the male lonely hearts. *Star* editor William R. Mathews used to tell about one such group with a love for practical joking who would pick a likely victim and tell him about a party going on at the house of a girl named Agnes where he would be welcome if he presented himself at the door. When the door opened, Agnes's "husband" would accuse him of meddling with a married woman and start shooting. The play would end at the police station (the officers were cooperating), where the victim went through a final humiliation. "When he appeared to be on the point of breaking down, his friends would walk in on him and give him the laugh."[43]

Some of the superheated citizens realized that a solution to their summer problem was only a few miles away, if they could just get to it. This was the high, cool, pine-clad top of the Santa Catalinas, the slopes and canyons of Mount Lemmon, no more than thirty miles away but difficult of access. A man named Weber built a log cabin at the summit sometime before 1900, but he was almost alone until 1909, when Jim Westfall moved in with his wife, Lita Camacho, and erected a 40-by-40-foot log establishment known as Maricopa Lodge, where guests were entertained. Mrs. Westfall cooked the meals, and the boarders relaxed on a balcony which circled the building. Inside, the partitions did not reach the ceiling, and a curious inmate could see what went on in the next room. The only link with the outside world was a burro train which snaked periodically up the Old Indian trail in Sabino Canyon. John Knagge, plumber and sheet-metal worker, owned the burros. The trail he followed, first used by the Indians in the remote past, was improved in 1906, when a campaign was begun to make the mountain more accessible. Supervisor Thomas H. Meagher of the Forest Service started the work, then called for a subscription to help with the expense. He got what he asked for "in less than twelve hours." From then on Knagge's burros could get to the top, loaded with whatever the mountain dwellers needed or desired (Knagge once transported a cookstove). It was said that "the Knagge pack

Upper end of the Mount Lemmon control road.

171

string was the corner grocery store" up on top.[44]

The burros passed out of the picture in 1920, when the upper slopes became accessible, with some difficulty, to motor vehicles. The Forest Service and the United States Bureau of Public Roads undertook to construct a road from Oracle, at the north end of the mountain, along the east side as far as the Stratton Mine and the old Gold Camp, following trails already in use by the miners. At Stratton Camp new construction began, following a difficult seven-mile route to the top. Those last seven miles were hair-raising for nonmountaineers, and the way was so narrow that a control system was set up, with a gateway at Stratton. Beginning in the morning, cars went up at 8:00, 11:00, 2:00, and 5:00. They came down at 9:30, 12:30, 3:30, and 6:30. Stratton provided free water for overheated radiators, and it was often needed. When conditions were right, one could make the seventy-five miles from Tucson to the summit in three and a half hours. When conditions were bad, the trip could last eight hours—or more.

In spite of difficulties, however, the new road opened the mountain area to settlement, and rustic cabins began going up under the pines as many Tucsonans flocked to this cool retreat. Elmer Staggs, who owned a Reo Speedwagon, organized the Mount Lemmon Stage and Freight Line and made two round trips a week, delivering passengers and supplies. He was not a careful man, and his packing habits were a trial to Mrs. Westfall, who did not suffer unwary deliverymen gladly. On one occasion Staggs packed a can of kerosene on top of the groceries, which included a sack of flour for her. When he arrived, she reached down for it over the balcony railing and took it inside,

"General" Frank Hitchcock. Courtesy Don Schellie and Tucson Daily Citizen.

sniffing suspiciously. Almost immediately she reappeared, still holding the sack, and dumped the contents on Elmer's head.[45]

The difficult Tucson–Oracle–Stratton–Gold Camp road was not the final answer to the Mount Lemmon problem. What was needed was a good mountain highway following the shortest possible route from Tucson to the top. From time to time abortive attempts were made to get something started. In November, 1915, a bond election was held to raise money for surveying the road. It passed by a narrow margin, and in December at least part of the proposed route was surveyed. Nothing happened after that until 1928, when George W. Chambers, president of the Tucson Lions Club, with the assistance of a group of determined citizens, circulated another petition urging the board of supervisors to take action. The dream might never have come true, how-

The Catalina Highway, 1941.

ever, had it not been for "General" Frank Hitchcock, former postmaster general, editor and publisher of the *Tucson Citizen*, and an important force in Tucson's public and political life until his early death in 1935. Born in Ohio, he was a Harvard-educated lawyer who became a power in the Republican party organization and was sometimes described as a "maker of presidents." He was eccentric in some ways—he never married and kept aloof from the social circles in which he might have been expected to move—and was the subject of many interesting anecdotes about his personal and private life, but he got things done. As postmaster general, for example, he was

responsible for introducing postal savings, parcel post, and the airmail service. He had enough clout to secure government funds for building the mountain road, which cost in hard money a million and a quarter dollars.[46]

Tucson gave him all the support he could ask for. A Santa Catalina Highway headquarters was opened at 48 East Congress Street in November, 1930. In 1931 the Forest Service, the State Highway Commission, and the United States Bureau of Roads began working together to sponsor an official survey of the route, and crews started operations in October. Hitchcock went to work at once to tap the federal treasury, and in February, 1933, he succeeded. Governor

W. B. Moeur announced that the chief of the Federal Bureau of Public Roads had advised him of the good news. The work would be done by federal prisoners and the government, "without cost to the state." He gave Hitchcock full credit.[47]

The key to the situation, in its early stages, was the federal prison camp at Molino Basin, on the eastern slope of the range, a few miles above and beyond the foothills. Here was an available supply of labor, and Hitchcock used it. The road to Molino Basin is officially designated and marked today as the Hitchcock Highway. Later the Civilian Conservation Corps pushed the work forward, and by 1940 the task had been completed as far as the prison camp. Picnickers were driving out in large numbers and using the spots marked for recreation. Day by day the clearing, blasting, and grading went on at the rate of about two miles a year. Thirteen years after the general's death in 1935 the entire route was open for traffic, and the way was clear to the high country. The Mount Lemmon Realty Company was selling lots at Summerhaven in 1948 in response to "tremendous public demand."[48] In due time the road was paved and improved, ready for the hundreds of overheated Tucsonans who would travel it every weekend in summer and for the snow enthusiasts who would take their skis to the ski lift in winter. With swamp coolers and refrigeration it is no longer necessary to leave town to get relief from the heat, but Mount Lemmon is there for anyone with a car he can trust and an hour for the mountain road.

Physical changes—roads and buildings—multiplied in those early years, but cultural changes were not far behind. In many cases the beginnings seemed small, but these seedlings developed into full-grown trees later on. The Woman's Club, for example, started with fifteen members in 1900, moved into its own clubhouse in 1915, and went on to a career of unrivaled public service. Trailbreakers in the arts were often immigrants to Arizona who brought special talents and energies to their new home. The relaxed atmosphere of the place and the informal friendliness of those already on the ground warmed their hearts and stimulated their efforts. Harold Bell Wright was one nationally known author who made a home in the Old Pueblo, and many more of his tribe—poets, novelists, historians—came later. Painters and sculptors found friendship and support among the local citizens. Judge Samuel Kingan, an ambitious watercolorist, helped found the Fine Arts Association in 1924. His large house on Franklin Street, left to the university, became the Fine Arts Center, ancestor of the Tucson Museum of Art.[49]

In the field of music, developments were particularly interesting. Tucson had always been musical in its own way. Mexican *típica* (strings and brass) groups had existed from the earliest times, and small orchestras had dispensed waltzes and polkas at dances and parties. Perhaps the first American-type brass band was organized by Anton V. Grossetta at the Southern Pacific shops in the early eighties. Grossetta played the clarinet and was joined by Fred Ronstadt with his flute and piccolo when he came to Tucson to learn the carriage maker's trade in 1882. About 1889 they started the Philharmonic Club (Club Filarmónico Tucsonense), which became a superior group of about forty members. It gave free weekly concerts and once performed in California. The musically gifted Ronstadt played several instruments, conducted, arranged, and composed, and his group added a great deal to the life of the town.[50] The major credit for elevating Tuc-

The Club Filarmónico, Fred Ronstadt conducting, 1896.

son music to a high plane, however, goes to Madeline Dreyfus Heineman, a talented immigrant who made things happen.

Madeline Dreyfus, Mattie to her friends, was born in Virginia City, Nevada, where her German-French parents owned a mercantile business. Later the family moved to California, where she was trained in piano and voice and displayed unusual musical talent. About the turn of the century she married Simon Heineman and moved to Tucson, where he had lived for four years, first as an employee of the Zeckendorfs and later as a partner in a firm dealing in wholesale liquor and cigars.[51] Mattie at once began taking an active part in the budding cultural life of the town as a member of the small, recently founded Sorosis Club. In 1906 she initiated the real musical progress of the community by organizing the Saturday Morning Music Club.

This was another small beginning which turned out to be a great event. Only twelve women were involved, and since they met at each other's homes and made music only for themselves, they had no impact on the community. Great achievements, however, were just ahead. The first important break in the club's routine came on January 26, 1910, when Mattie and her friends presented Mme Frieda Langendorff, a "world famous singer," in concert at the Opera House. The newspapers were not quite sure how to handle this departure from the familiar patterns. The *Citizen* remarked, with some foreboding, that the concert was probably "the forerunner of very high-class music in Tucson" but called the performance "delightful"—the "musical treat of the year"—and noted that a good house gave the singer "unstinted applause."[52]

The list of sponsors included the most prominent women in the city and reflected Mrs. Heineman's talents as an organizer.

They included Mrs. Robert H. Forbes, Mrs. A. E. Douglas, Miss Frances Babcock, Mrs. Selim M. Franklin, Mrs. J. J. Ivancovich, Mrs. B. M. Jacobs, Mrs. Frank H. Hereford, Mrs. A. Steinfeld, Mrs. Epes Randolph, and Mrs. George Kitt. The husbands of these women were prominent professors, lawyers, and businessmen, and they themselves were exceptional people.

It was the first of many triumphs for Mrs. Heineman. She was a charming, gracious person who exercised complete authority in her little world without causing the least resentment—a really miraculous achievement in any human situation but particularly so in Mattie's special circumstances. She had tremendous energy—never stopped—and nobody questioned her or debated her ideas. The respect she commanded and the cooperation she got were almost unbelievable.[53]

After the Langendorff concert she went on to become a successful impresaria, bringing many of the great names in music to her postfrontier town. The Sam J. Mansfelds had the finest house in town, perhaps in the Territory, and Mattie always took her artists there for dinner. Mrs. Mansfeld's brother Leo Goldschmidt, who was himself a good organist, always took care of them and saw that they were well entertained. All the great ones came: Schumann-Heink, Paderewski, Pavlova, the Russian Ballet, and many more.

But Madeline Heineman was more than an importer of talent. She was equally interested in fostering talent at home, and an important offshoot of the Saturday Morning Club was the Junior Branch, in which the musical education of the children of Tucson's first families was attended to. Once a year the children assembled at Mrs. Heineman's house and waited their turn to play on the grand piano in her living room before a panel of judges, who graded each performance. Mattie herself was a vigorous teacher of both piano and voice.[54]

Her great legacy to her town, however, was the Temple of Music and Art which in due time arose on South Scott Street beyond the Santa Rita Hotel—a magnificent endowment for a small desert city. It was her dream for many years, and at times it must have seemed an unattainable dream. When her husband, Simon, died in 1924, she must have felt that hope was dormant if not dead. She had many friends, however, and they included the Berger brothers, Harry and Alexander, who had money and were patrons of the arts. Harry was a Tucson businessman; Alexander grew peonies and played the cello in Fredericksburg, Virginia, but spent the winters on a ranch he owned at Vail, some distance east of Tucson. In 1926 he offered $100,000 toward the building of the temple. A loan from the Juilliard Foundation opened the doors still wider,[55] and on November 11, 1926, Madeline Heineman, soon to be Mrs. Harry Berger, presided over the ceremonies which began changing her dream to reality. Her friend Amelita Galli-Curci, of the Metropolitan Opera Company, was there, elegant in black, to take part in the celebration, and was photographed, looking somewhat ill at ease, holding the shovel with which she turned the first bit of earth for the excavation.[56]

Madeline intended the temple to be the artistic center of the city, and for a good many decades it was. It was big enough. Architect Arthur Hawes drew up plans to include an auditorium which would seat 1,000 people. Special features included a salon for the display of paintings—a real boon to the growing colony of local artists—a stage large enough to hold a full symphony

Groundbreaking for the Temple of Music and Art, Amelita Galli-Curci with fingers on spade, Madeline Berger on her left.

orchestra, five sets of scenery for future dramatic companies, a small recital hall, a green room, eight dressing rooms in the basement, and a number of studios and practice rooms. As a last refinement there was to be a tearoom. The price tag on the whole enterprise was $180,000.[57]

Some rough times were ahead when money was short and it seemed that nothing could save Tucson's cultural monument but an intervention from on high. Depression times came, and bankruptcy seemed inevitable, but the worst never happened. A few life memberships were sold at $250 each. The auditorium was rented out as a movie theater. Every little bit helped, and the temple survived, thanks in no small part to the support of Madeline's fellow townsmen. In 1929 she counted 700 members in the various branches of the Music Club. When she

retired from the presidency in 1940, after thirty years of service, the number was closer to 1,000. She died in La Jolla, California, in 1943, but her ideas went marching on.[58]

The little plants which took root in the early years of the century and flourished through the teens and twenties were overshadowed by the great event of 1912—statehood for Arizona. Thirty years of unremitting effort were behind this triumph. Delegate Marcus A. Smith (who maintained a residence in Tucson) began beating the drum in Washington in 1882, and during his long service (1882 to 1908, with interruptions), he never stopped beating. Sometimes Washington listened. In 1888 the Fiftieth Congress admitted that Arizona "was fitted for statehood" in a report on "Admission of Arizona, Idaho, and Wyoming into the Union."[59] This encouraged Governor

Mrs. Berger's Temple of Music and Art. Buehman photo.

C. M. Zulick, in his message to the state legislature in 1889, to declare: "The time has now arrived when Arizona should be relieved from this state of tutelage and be endowed with the duties and responsibilities of statehood. The rapid increase in wealth and population, the energy and patriotism of her people are sure guarantees that she would wear the robes of state sovereignty with dignity and honor."[60] Admission, however, was twenty-four years away, and one wonders why.

One reason for the delay was prejudice. The rest of the country regarded Arizona as a remote and backward region where English was seldom heard and the population was a mixture of Indians, Mexicans, and second-class Anglos, hardly fit for self-government. Another reason was politics. Three times Delegate Smith got a statehood bill through the Democratic House, only to have it turned down or ignored by the Republican Senate, to which the prospect of two additional Democratic senators was painful in the extreme. Twice—in 1891 and 1893—constitutional conventions were held in Arizona to put together a document which would be a basis for self-government, in case it came. The labor was lost. In 1896

the Nineteenth Arizona Legislature had better luck when it authorized the building of a capitol which would be a credit to a newborn state. The structure was completed and is the one in use today. Meanwhile a succession of lobbyists (including Governor Louis C. Hughes in 1894) traveled to Washington to reason with the legislators and the presidents. Still nothing happened.[61]

When Theodore Roosevelt became president in 1901, he added another difficulty to the statehood problem. He was convinced that New Mexico and Arizona ought to be admitted as a single state. The New Mexicans were willing to put up with this arrangement, since the capital would be in Santa Fe. A few Arizonans thought joint statehood would be better than no statehood at all, but most of the citizens were outraged at the thought, and loud cries of protest arose—cries so loud, in fact, that in his last message to Congress on December 8, 1908, Roosevelt recommended separation of the two territories. President William Howard Taft, who had enjoyed a visit to Phoenix and the Grand Canyon in October, 1909,[62] lined up with the Arizonans (though he had some reservations). A statehood bill passed

178

the house in January, 1910, and six months later, on June 20, the president signed an enabling act—the first step toward formal acceptance. Immediately Governor Richard Sloan, a Taft appointee, called a special election to choose delegates to a constitutional convention.

The convention assembled in Phoenix, worked diligently, and finished its labors on December 9, 1910. A coalition of labor representatives and Democratic liberals dominated the sessions and produced a constitution featuring many controversial provisions. They added up to what was called "direct democracy," expressed in the initiative, referendum, and recall. The people could pass laws independently of the legislature, could reject measures passed by the legislature, and could turn public officials out of office by popular vote.[63]

President Taft was opposed to these provisions, particularly the recall, which would endanger the inviolate status of the judiciary. As everyone knew he would, Taft vetoed the statehood bill, but Arizona circumvented him by voting on December 12, 1911, to leave out the offensive propositions. Taft signed on February 12, 1912, and nine months later, on November 9, the voters restored them.[64]

Tucson sent five of its first citizens as delegates to the convention—William P. Cooper and Samuel L. Kingan, lawyers; Carlos C. Jacome, merchant; George Pusch, rancher; and James C. White, railroad man. Every one was a Republican, and every one was out of step with the men who dominated the convention. The liberal Democrats, led by George W. P. Hunt, had their way, and when the document was completed, the Tucson Republicans refused to sign it, as did all the other party members who took part in the convention.[65]

Carlos C. Jacome, a member of Tucson's rebellious delegation to the constitutional convention.

All this may explain why the great event of Valentine's Day, 1912, aroused no particular enthusiasm in Tucson. There was a big celebration in Tombstone, including "an enthusiastic fusillade of pistol shots in the old-fashioned manner," but nothing like that happened in the Old Pueblo. The *Citizen* noted the event—and pointed out that Admission Day was the fiftieth anniversary of Arizona's admission to the Confederate States of America.[66]

Two measures dear to the hearts of many Arizonans, particularly women, were omitted from the constitution: woman suffrage and prohibition. A serious attempt had been made to include an antiliquor clause, and the women brought heavy pressure to bear on the delegates, through petitions and per-

James C. White.

months of the struggle, in 1914, as historian Nancy Tisdale Clark points out, "are unmatched in the history of Arizona for sheer drama and emotional impact."[69]

"Temperance" had been a national issue since 1910, when the Anti-Saloon League sent its propaganda machine into action and the WCTU dispatched its emissaries into every corner of the land. The attainment of suffrage for women in Arizona gave the reformers renewed hope. They organized the Temperance Federation of Arizona in March, 1914, and called for a convention to meet at the end of the month to draft a prohibition amendment to be submitted to the voters under provisions of the initiative. Four hundred delegates attended, representing the Prohibition party, the Anti-Saloon League, the WCTU, the YMCA, the YWCA, the Good Templars, and the Min-

sonal pleas. A proposition to submit the issue to the voters was defeated two to one.

Workers for women's rights were likewise spurred to convulsive activity, and again prayers and petitions inundated the assembly. One list of signatures from Gila County alone was ten feet long, but when the votes were in, the verdict was against suffrage, thirty to nineteen.[67]

With regard to these questions, however, the voters of the state proved to be more hospitable to change than did the convention delegates. At this point the constitutional provision for referendum was put to use for the first time. The suffrage issue was submitted to the people in the elections of 1912. They approved it two to one, and Arizona became the first state permitting women to vote.[68]

Prohibition took a little longer. The drys had been working and waiting for thirty years, however, and a few months more did not diminish their drive and energy. The wets were just as determined, and the final

William P. Cooper.

George Pusch.

named Alfred Donau helped organize the Arizona Local Self Government League to oppose the amendment. The members wanted local option—the right of each community to have or reject liquor—and they proposed, as an alternative to the prohibition amendment, an eight-year provision which would prevent the question from coming up again for eight years after the local group had declared its will one way or the other.

The issue was the dominant one in the elections. Chafin opposed Mark Smith for the senate. Smith was wet, and Chafin was ultradry. Most of the campaign oratory was devoted to the liquor question. As opposition crystallized, the drys had to give ground. The Pharmaceutical Association declared itself against Prohibition. The Catholic church did the same. So did promi-

isterial Union. Even the IWW and several labor unions sent representatives.[70]

Immediately a civil war erupted. The issue was how far the prohibitions should go. Two mighty voices from Tucson belonging to Louis C. Hughes (former governor and editor of the *Star*) and Eugene Chafin (twice candidate for the presidency on the Prohibition ticket) shouted that the state should be bone dry—no exceptions. The other wing argued that doctors and druggists should have access to a supply of alochol for medicinal purposes and that churches should have a right to use sacramental wine. The convention voted with Hughes and Chafin, but the doubters had given the wets their main argument. When the drys circulated their petitions and got the issue on the ballot for the November election, the wets went into furious action. A Tucson businessman

Samuel L. Kingan.

nent Episcopal clergymen and the American Federation of Labor. By the end of October the drys were running scared and redoubled their efforts for the cause. A Flying Squadron of professional workers, famous nationally, came to Yuma, Tucson, and Phoenix, shooting off volleys of speeches and songs. On November 3 the Drys won, but by a very slim margin. The vote was 25,887 for the amendment, 22,743 against.[71]

December 31, 1914, was the last day liquor could legally be sold in Arizona. It was hard to believe that such a thing could happen to Prescott and Phoenix and Yuma and Tucson, so recently wild frontier communities, but the peace officers said that they meant to uphold the law, and the saloonkeepers said that they meant to obey it. And so the last night arrived—a night of bright moonlight and sheer pandemonium. The church people gathered at the Methodist church for a vigil of thanksgiving. Everyone else gathered along Meyer Street and the intersection of Congress and Stone for a farewell to John Barleycorn.

Saloonkeepers and policemen were worried as the crowd gathered and began the last rites. Some pool halls closed early to avoid trouble. The bartender at the Santa Rita, when asked how business was, replied, "Too good." As the evening wore on, the noise and confusion mounted. "The intersection of Congress Street and Stone Avenue," the *Citizen* reported next day, "was a phantasmagoria":

The drinkers came out on the sidewalks. Automobiles with horns shrieking waggled along the streets, tipsy drivers dodging groups of drunken men. Revolvers cracked, whistles blew, the dust rose, and drunken yells helped the din.

But nobody got badly hurt, there were no serious fights, and the police had only five men in jail for being drunk.

The reporter admitted that "at one time there were two free-for-all fights milling on Church Street, to say nothing of a scrap between two dogs," but when midnight came, every saloon door was tightly closed, and they stayed that way. At the Santa Rita the bartender served "prohibition highballs" concocted of grape juice and seltzer.[72]

Not everybody believed that Prohibition was there to stay. On January 1, the day after those noisy last rites, saloonkeeper Louis Gherno took steps to find out. To his Pullman Saloon, opposite the Southern Pacific station, came Charles J. Cunningham to ask for a pint of Cane Spring whiskey. With him appeared Attorney General Wiley Jones; Leslie Hardy, Jones's assistant; County Attorney George O. Hilzinger; John B. Wright, Gherno's attorney; and Sheriff A. B. Forbes. When the stage was set, Cunningham made his request, Gherno handed him his pint, and Forbes arrested both of them. The little drama was carefully staged and was intended to test the "self-executing" phase of the new amendment to the constitution. The test was positive. Gherno stayed closed.[73]

The *Citizen* was full of news that cold January day. The party at the Old Pueblo Club the night before had been a big one. The commission plan of government would be up for trial in Tucson during the year. Rufus B. von KleinSmid, the new president of the University of Arizona, was planning his inauguration. And the battleship *Formidable*, an old English war vessel, had been sent to the bottom of the English Channel by a German mine or submarine. The last item was really the biggest news of all. In a few months American ships would be in danger, and American lives would be lost at sea. World War I was in the wings, waiting to come on stage.

CHAPTER 11

Tucson at War

World War I made Tucson over. For two years it focused the town's energies and tested its civic resolve as nothing had ever done before. It called for sacrifice, it imposed hardship, and it exacted its toll in young men's lives. Tucson emerged from it matured, seasoned, war-weary, and accustomed to regimentation.

The country had three years to take sides. After the assassination of Archduke Ferdinand in 1914 and the resulting explosion in Europe, America watched the developing drama from the sidelines, determined to stay neutral and uninvolved. When the *Lusitania* was torpedoed on May 7, 1915, with the loss of 128 American lives, the mood of the country started to change, and Americans began to believe that sooner or later they would have to join the British and the French, struggling to contain the German armies. It was imperative that they be ready when the time came, and "Preparedness" became the national watchword. As early as the fall of 1916, people began to assemble, marching and cheering and listening to emotional oratory. The country was ready to fight when, on January 1, 1917, Germany announced that it was resuming unre-

stricted submarine warfare as a means of cutting off supplies and munitions intended for its enemies. After February 1, all ships, hostile or neutral, in certain zones would be sunk without warning. In effect this was a declaration of war against the United States, and was so understood. The nation's formal declaration was not made until April 6, but as American ships continued to go down— the *Lyman M. Law* on February 14; the *Algonquin* on March 12—it was obvious that the United States was already involved.[1] On March 19, President Woodrow Wilson announced that the declaration would come soon and that mobilization was taking place.[2]

In Tucson, it must be admitted, the war was not yet the all-absorbing preoccupation that it was soon to become. In March life went on pretty much as usual. The new automobiles were getting a good deal of attention, and a huge auto show was scheduled for March 17 with a "Ten Thousand Tire Parade" through town.[3] Even counting five tires (including spare) a car, the *Citizen*'s figure was optimistic, since only 300 automobiles lined up.

Other interesting peacetime items ap-

Luisa Ronstadt Espinel in 1915.

Through March and April there were parties. Mr. and Mrs. George H. Smalley entertained at dinner for the Harold Bell Wrights on April 20. Miss Yndia Smalley, their young daughter (later a Tucson historian), was there. On Tuesday, April 18, the Saturday Morning Music Club, raising funds for the hoped-for Temple of Music and Art, staged Verdi's *Il Trovatore* at the Scottish Rite auditorium. The role of Azucena, the gypsy mother, was sustained magnificently by Tuscon-born Louise Ronstadt, who "came home" from California for the performance. She delighted 700 people, and the occasion was "a triumph." Using the name Luisa Espinel, she was gaining fame as a singer and actress on the West Coast, and the Saturday Music Club was delighted to feature her tremendous contralto at the year's final meeting on April 29.[5]

For those with simpler musical tastes *September Morn*, "a great tangoesque carnival," was playing at the Opera House—the best seats $1.50—and for ten cents one could see *The Purple Mask* at the Theatre De Luxe, followed by Charlie Chaplin in *Charlie's First Vacation*. Many summer pilgrims had already fled to the coast, and the *Star* began offering a regular column of news on their activities called "Arizona Exiles in California."

War was in the air, however, and the war fever was already rising. The university offered early graduation to seniors who wished to volunteer for service in the National Guard, which was then mobilizing. April 1 was designated as America Day, and everybody in Tucson turned out for a discharge of patriotic emotion. The mayor invited "every labor, fraternal, social and benevolent organization" to line up and march, and they all responded. The files disbanded at the Armory, and an overflow crowd of 2,000 as-

peared in the news. The firm of Bryant and Hartley, for example, advertised the "Snowball Iceless Cooler," made of porous material and cooled by evaporation. It was intended to replace the refrigerator for preserving food. "They are already in use in a number of Tucson homes," said the advertisement, "and are proving to be a success." It is probable that the Snowball was preceded by homemade models. Dick Hall, who arrived in Tucson with an invalid mother in 1908, tells how his brother Harry rigged up an apple box with a wet gunnysack outside and an electric fan inside to provide some comfort for the sick woman. Yuma and Phoenix are usually credited with inventing and developing the evaporative cooler, but Tucson might claim a share of the credit if justice were done.[4]

sembled. The Civil War veterans were there in what was left of their uniforms. Hardly anyone was without a flag, including the Boy Scouts and the Red Cross girls—all present en masse. Governor Thomas E. Campbell had been invited to review the parade and address the multitude, and loyalty overflowed.[6]

It would have been difficult to resist this emotional assault, but some people did. Tucson had its share of pacifists and conscientious objectors, as did the country at large. Even then young men saw no point in fighting to make the munitions manufacturers rich. Mrs. A. A. Worsley, described as the "spokeswoman" for the Tucson pacifists, told a reporter that she thought the United States ought to stay out of the conflict. "England started the war," she declared, "and Germany has been fighting on the defensive." She argued that the British had disregarded American rights as much as the German's had, and she made no secret of her feelings.[7] She may have wished later that she had. For the first time in history ruggedly individualistic Tucsonans were being propagandized and browbeaten into conformity. It was not healthy in the months which followed to be a maverick.

The great majority of Tucsonans were ready to march, as they demonstrated when the wheels of the military machine began turning on April 10. On Governor Campbell's orders the county assessor issued a call summoning every Pima County male between eighteen and forty-five to report at the courthouse and register for possible enrollment in the state militia. When his office opened that morning, Assessor L. R. Smith was "beseiged by 100 patriots," and more kept coming. One eighty-seven-year-old man tried to enroll. "I can shoot a lot straighter than some of these kids,"[8] he said.

Unfortunately his age outweighed his marksmanship.

Not all potential soldiers, it turned out, were eager to fight the Germans. Nogales became a concentration point for these "slackers," since it provided an avenue of escape to Mexico. Vigorous attempts were made, in Arizona as elsewhere, to bring them in and make them enlist or go to jail. Red-hot patriots recommended that they be shot. Equally vigorous attempts were launched, in the sacred name of Liberty, to defend them and assure them of their rights as conscientious objectors. In the East a "Committee on American Liberties" was active by the end of May,[9] but it spoke for a small minority.

In the southwestern states the reaction of the citizens was influenced substantially by events in Mexico. Pancho Villa and his troops had raided Columbus, New Mexico, on March 9, 1916, and the Punitive Expedition crossed the border not long afterward. Revolutionary bands kept the area stirred up until 1920. Fear of invasion during those years was uncomfortably real—so deeply ingrained that after 1916 the border was guarded and patrolled. For some time a detachment of the state guard was stationed at Naco, near Bisbee, but the area remained boringly peaceful, and the militiamen became more and more dissatisfied with their lot. When their emotions could no longer be contained, the men of Company M were said to have marched up and down the main street of Naco shouting that they wanted to go home. Six months later the unit had lost ninety-nine men through desertion.[10] This was undoubtedly the all-time low point for the Arizona National Guard, which became the 158th U.S. Infantry and made its mark in France as a crack outfit.

It was commonly believed that the Ger-

Mayor O. C. Parker. Courtesy Orville S. McPherson.

mans had infiltrated the Mexican *insurrectos* and were planning to attack border communities, and these fears were not without foundation. The "Plan of San Diego" came to light in 1915 after its proponents had devastated several ranches and towns in Texas and made a start at restoring the Southwest to Mexico. In 1917 the "Zimmerman Telegram" revealed that Germany was prepared to return the border states to Mexico in exchange for a military alliance. This revelation of Germany's machinations south of the border, officially revealed on March 1, 1917, propelled the American people, and their president, closer to a declaration of war.[11] On April 6, the very day the declaration was made, the *Star* headlined a story: "Villa Soldiers Moving Toward Boundary but German Leadership Is Denied." The denial proved that the fear existed.

Uneasiness about a possible invasion was reinforced by a dread of spies and saboteurs. German agents might be expected to interfere wherever possible with supply lines and communications. Ridiculous as it may seem to us in retrospect, the idea that Tucson itself might be in danger alarmed the mayor and the city council, and they reacted in the tradition of their frontier heritage. The *Star* carried another headline on April 6: "Auto Shotgun Squad to Guard City."

Mayor O. C. Parker fathered the idea. A muscular, tough, aggressive fellow with a bulldog chin, the mayor was the kind who took action where another would have appointed a committee. As the town's leading undertaker he was surprisingly gentle and sympathetic, but as a civic leader he was fast-moving and decisive. It was in character for him to assemble a posse of volunteers in twenty-four automobiles prepared to repel all invaders:

Ninety fighting men in 24 autos with a driver and four armed men with sawed-off shotguns in each car, will dash about the roads leading into the city to be the first to fight off any attack from without or to warn the city of approaching danger. . . . A big supply of buckshot was purchased by the safety committee for the arming of the shotgun brigade. The Red Cross, all ambulances in town, motorcycles and wagons have all been put into commission for an emergency at a moment's notice.

Guards have been established on all public works and at certain points where trouble may be expected.

A system of communications has been worked out in detail by which a few words spoken into a telephone or clicked over a telegraph wire will set the entire system of home guard protection into instantaneous operation.

The mayor even went so far as to acquire from automobile dealer Monte Mansfield a Ford chassis on which he proposed to mount two machine guns, "provided they can be found." [12]

In sober fact Tucson in the spring of 1917 had more defenders than it knew what to do with. Two home-guard companies were already in existence: the Arizona Eastern Drill Corps and the Tucson Rifle Club. "When the hour arrives for them to defend the city," observed the *Citizen*, wryly, "they may be found shooting at each other by mistake." To widen the breach between them, the mayor had earmarked $1,000 in municipal funds for arms and equipment for the home guard, and each group claimed it. His honor solved the problem by denying on May 1 that he planned to subsidize either one. [13]

Naturally all these warlike preparations, combined with reports that German submarines had been seen off New York and in the Gulf of Mexico, stimulated the human imagination, and reports began coming in of strange sights and sounds in nearby towns and in the sky over Tucson. On April 8 the *Star* reported:

More than a score of Tucson residents, all of whom swear they are total abstainers, have, for the past four nights, been seeing a mysterious airplane flying across the city at 1000 to 1300 feet. It makes its appearance each night at 8 to 10 p.m.

Though those who have seen this monster of the night believe it is a warplane, the bootlegging detail of the police are investigating the possibility that it may be furnishing a new means of transport succor to Tucson's thirst brigade in violation of the bone dry law.

The people of Tucson and Arizona were certainly not in the grip of "war hysteria" at that time, but they were indeed disturbed by the multiplying rumors that eddied around them and by the scare headlines in the papers. Both the *Star* and the *Citizen* were reaching for big type as the war news

came in. The air was full of worry and concern.

At the same time there was a universal resolve to support the great effort with every resource and to make short work of anyone who interfered with it. It was this resolve that opened the door to the labor confrontations of that spring and summer in Arizona. To most of those anxious Arizonans, the chief enemy was the Industrial Workers of the World.

What the IWW wanted was a better deal for the men in the mines and factories, and those men needed a better deal. It was the wrong time, however, for anyone to foment rebellion. The organization was openly and avowedly pacifist, which was enough to enrage the average citizen, and it was bent on stopping production at a time when every ounce of copper was needed. The leaders knew that they were in for trouble, but they did not know how much.

The first IWW chapter in the state was founded at Phoenix in January, 1917, just before the kaiser commenced torpedoing everyone. After an unsuccessful attempt to organize a walkout in the Goodyear plant near Phoenix, operatives moved into the mining camps to prepare for a statewide strike for better pay and working conditions. Trouble at Globe [14] began in April, just when Mayor Parker was organizing his shotgun patrol and Assessor Smith was registering Tucson's young men for service in the state militia. The Verde mines were closed down on May 23. Union members were slow to sign up for military service, and miners were prominently represented among the "slackers" at Nogales. Naturally most Arizonans were convinced that Germany was behind the strikes, considered hanging too good for the organizers, and approved of the violent measures taken to suppress the strikers during the summer months that were to follow.

Everyone felt the pressure of time. Preparations had to be made to train a million— two million—men in the shortest possible time. Industry had to be readied for war production. Food resources had to be mobilized. Profiteering and hoarding had to be curbed. Money had to be raised—for the Red Cross, for the YMCA, for the government. Housewives had to be educated in the techniques of conservation. Problems and uncertainties were everywhere.

The most pressing of the decisions that had to be made in the spring of 1917 was about the kind of army the nation was going to have. The first thought was for a traditional American military system with prominent citizens volunteering to enlist a company or a regiment, or (in the case of Theodore Roosevelt) a division.[15] The *Citizen* noted that it looked as if the new army would have more officers than men. Governor Campbell wanted to head a regiment.[16] Even Mayor Parker, that sympathetic but tough undertaker, went to Phoenix to negotiate for the rank of major in a regiment of "border cavalry," to be raised by him.[17]

The question had to be fought out in Washington. Speaker Champ Clark of the House was against conscription. "I am for letting the flower and youth of this country volunteer before we fasten the disgrace of a draft upon them," he said.[18] Others disagreed, some because they knew it was not going to be the old-fashioned kind of war, others because not enough volunteers were coming in. Epes Randolph, of Tucson, was for conscription because "our brave boys" ought not to have to go while "worthless slackers" remained behind.[19] In the end conscription won. The War Army Bill was passed by Congress on May 10.[20] Socialist

George Herbert Smalley.

leader Norman Thomas said the draft was "worse than the imposition of chattel slavery,"[21] but he had few listeners.

To Governor Campbell it was obvious that he needed help in a situation where everything had to be done at once, and he attacked the problem by appointing an Arizona Defense Council to take charge. Thirty-five men answered his call and met in the senate chamber in the Capitol at ten in the morning on April 19. George Herbert Smalley, former editor of the *Tucson Citizen*, acted as secretary. Other Tucsonans who took their places included D. T. MacDougal, of the university; university president Rufus B. von KleinSmid; General L. H. Manning, capitalist and former mayor; Albert Steinfeld, merchant; and *Citizen* editor Allan S. Jaynes. Dwight Heard, of Phoenix, was named chairman.[22] In subsequent meetings John C. Greenway, of Warren (who had won his spurs with Roosevelt in Cuba), was named chairman of the Committee of Public Defense and Security. Colonel Leroy Brown, of Tucson, headed the Committee on Military Training. Other men chaired twelve other committees, and the first Defense Council functioned until June, 1918, when Governor George W. P. Hunt appointed a council of his own.[23]

Meanwhile, Tucsonans were already in France, on their way to France, or getting ready to go to France. Samuel P. Martin was famous locally for being first. He went to Canada and enlisted at "the first call for troops" and by 1917 was a seasoned veteran with three wound stripes.[24] Another early participant was Glenton Sykes, son of Englishman Godfrey Sykes, who built the Flagstaff Observatory and was a familiar figure at the Tucson Desert Laboratory on Tumamoc Hill. With his brother Gilbert, Glenton had traveled to England to go to school. One morning a man stopped him on London Bridge and asked him, "Why aren't you in uniform?"

"I'm an American," Sykes responded.

"That doesn't make any difference. Everybody gets in or goes to jail."

"All right, I'll go!"

So Glenton took the king's shilling, with a package of cigarettes thrown in, and joined the Corps of Engineers. Gilbert was too young to be in demand, but he was about to qualify as a wireless operator when the war ended.[25]

Back in Tucson a number of young men did not wait to be drafted. Some were officers in the drill company at the university; some were noncoms in the National Guard. Two were from out of town. They went to the recruiting office at 90 West Congress Street for enrollment, and early in May they were sent off to officers' training camp at the San Francisco Presidio. The first contingent

Allan B. Jaynes, editor of the Arizona Citizen.

included Louis C. Brichta, F. W. Fickett, Jr., Charles Arthur Meserve, Eric Monthan, Orville S. McPherson, Charles E. Pickrell, and Harry I. Chambers. With them went Sheriff Harry Wheeler, of Cochise County, and Lewis Douglas, of Douglas, son of the famous mine operator "Rawhide Jimmy."[26]

The very day these men left for the Great Unknown, the War Army Bill was passed, and the machinery was activated which would try to train a million or more soldiers and put them in France in 1918. It occurred to forward-looking men at various places throughout the country that these recruits would have to be trained, and where better could they be whipped into shape than in the Great Southwest? Sixteen "cantonments" were being set up, many of them in the Sun Country, and Tucson businessmen

Mrs. Allan B. Jaynes (Kathryn).

the citizens as disgraceful. The editor of the *Star* refused to join in any such carnival of greed, merely reporting that on May 20 the five officers, headed by Brigadier General Henry Green, had arrived at the E.P.&S.W. station, where they were met by Mayor Parker, taken to the Old Pueblo Club, and put up for the night. The mayor assured them that the city was willing to give "all that we have," and service to the nation would be "full compensation."[27]

The mayor's noble sentiments were wasted. The cantonment went to Deming, New Mexico, where there was no Gay Alley and the bootleggers were fewer and farther between. But that came later.

It became clear, as the June days went by, that the great concerns of those in charge at this juncture were men, money, food, and public opinion. The draft provided the men. The War Army Bill, passed by Congress on May 18, cleared the way for registration, and Governor Campbell proclaimed June 5 as Registration Day. Probably no one in Arizona was aware that President Wilson had decided that the draft was necessary even before war was declared and that Secretary of War Newton D. Baker, fearing opposition, had thoughtfully arranged for the draftees' friends and neighbors to handle the paperwork and had made every effort to make Registration Day "a festival and patriotic occasion." The Committee on Public Information, headed by the controversial George Creel, was already grinding out propaganda for home consumption. As a result, almost everybody was ready for whatever sacrifices were demanded, including conscription.[28]

The Arizona Defense Coundil made the arrangements. At the same time Captain M. G. Browne of the First Arizona Infantry opened a recruiting office in downtown Tuc-

thought their town ought to have one. There was great joy in Dustville when it was learned that five army officers were actually en route to look into the possibility. Allan S. Jaynes, editor of the *Citizen*, erupted with clouds of journalistic prose at the thought. He visualized "a greater, bigger, richer Tucson, grown overnight with a host of armed men tramping her streets, and a golden stream of commerce filling her life and spreading her fame throughout the nation." He estimated rapturously that $2 million a month would be spent in Tucson, and he reported with great satisfaction that a hundred prominent citizens had assembled in the council chambers, the mayor presiding, to consider ways and means, possible sites, and committee assignments. This public licking of civic chops struck some of

son and urged young men to volunteer. A good many did, but the great majority waited for national registration and the draft. On the day appointed, 3,285 signed up in Pima County, 1,258 of whom were aliens—mostly from Mexico. There would have been more had not a great many foreign-born men (and some born in the United States) headed for the border and sanctuary in Mexico. Many of them were miners, and their exodus, according to the *Star*, left the mines of southern Arizona "crippled." This was apparently an overstatement, since production figures for the year show an increase over 1916.[29]

Having registered, the young men of Tucson had to wait for the wheels in Washington to turn as the machinery for selection was set up. Secretary Baker drew the first number on July 20, 1917. In due time a white postcard notified the conscripts, who had a few weeks to bask in their feelings of satisfaction in doing the right thing and in the congratulations of the middle-aged and elderly who were in no danger of being drafted. The *Star* printed a poem called "The Kid Has Gone to the Colors," of which the following is a typical stanza:

> The Kid, not being a slacker,
>   Stood forth with patriot joy
> To add his name to the roster—
>   And God, we're proud of the boy![30]

Americans were already arriving in Europe. General Pershing with the first contingent of regulars landed in England on June 7 and was in France by June 16. On June 22, fifty American aviators reached French soil. The first Tucsonans to report an Atlantic crossing were James W. Hardie and Fred Kain, members of a Red Cross ambulance unit. An "American Armada"—many ships carrying many men—penetrated the U-boat

screen a little later, reached France, and began training for combat.[31]

Back home the training of the conscript army moved at first at a snail's pace—understandably, since sixteen cantonments and sixteen camps, each holding up to 40,000 men, had to be built in a few weeks to provide quarters for the draftees. Not until August 5 was the first Tucson contingent chosen, and not until August 15 were the men summoned to appear before a draft board. On the following day eighty-three were examined, and forty-three were accepted.[32] The draft machinery was working, and it continued to work, not briskly, perhaps, but as efficiently as could be expected.

A great crowd gathered at Armory Park on September 5 to honor the boys who were about to leave and "bid them Godspeed," as the *Star* phrased it. There were cheers and speeches, including a memorable one by the new president of the university, von KleinSmid, who was just getting his memorable career under way. To give the men something to take along as a reminder of home, Mrs. Allan B. Jaynes, wife of the editor of the *Citizen*, presented a wristwatch to each one of them. A party of a different kind took place on the ninth, when the first contingent boarded the train for Camp Funston, Kansas. There was no program, but the crowd was noisy and cheerful.

There were letters home telling about the Kansas climate (it was colder than Tucson), the dust, the endless rows of wooden buildings, the rigors of short-order training, the funny incidents that happened as the men learned about military courtesy and the routine of camp life. "Conditions are not the most enviable," said one Pima County boy, whose letter was reproduced in a column in the *Star* called "Our Boys in Camp" on October 31, "but I am willing to suffer a little to relieve those across the water who suffer daily more than we will in a year."

Most of the Tucson contingent reappeared in town on October 16, when they passed through on their way to Linda Vista, California. During a two-hour stopover that evening, Tucson girls "stormed the train" and overwhelmed the soldiers with ice cream and homemade delicacies. It was a great sentimental occasion. Later contingents came and went with less fanfare.[33]

For every man on the battle line many civilians had to work at backup jobs. The Red Cross nurses and canteen workers come first to mind as examples. Some of them went overseas with the men and endured as much hardship as did the boys in the trenches. Harriett Elizabeth De Vaughn, who made her home in Tucson after the war, was on the front line for three years working in field hospitals. Nurses had no quarters, she remembered later—"caught catnaps when they could by rolling up in blankets on the ground; lived on canned corned beef, black coffee and hardtack when they could get it; worked all night, but frequently had to cease operating in the middle of the night and put out the lights because the enemy planes were roaring overhead." Mrs. De Vaughn was awarded the Croix de Guerre, and she earned it.

Typical of the nonprofessionals was Helen Campbell, daughter of Judge John H. Campbell, of Tucson, a tiny, pretty, sheltered young woman of Scotch-Presbyterian background, who volunteered for nurse's training and was sent to the Debarkation Hospital on Staten Island. She arrived after the armistice but spent a year helping care for the wounded as they returned from France. One of her patients was so grateful that he showed up on crutches outside her classroom in a Nogales, Arizona, school a few months after she left the Red Cross. Was there a romance? "No," says Helen, now Mrs. Land, "he had to go back to the hospital."[34]

Tucson supported all the Red Cross programs enthusiastically. Louise Ronstadt's recital on April 29 was a benefit performance. The *Citizen* on May 29 featured a full-page advertisement urging the public to become involved. On the same day the Business Women's Club voted to enlist its entire membership in Red Cross "war work." With so many hands at work it was not surprising that "a record number of bandages" was turned out in May. The Red Cross rooms were open Monday evenings; Wednesday, Thursday, and Saturday afternoons; and all day Tuesday and Friday. Ladies came to knit, sew, and talk.[35]

Every citizen was under almost daily pressure to work and contribute. On May 26 the *Star* announced that "Red Cross Week" was coming up with a goal of $2,500. By September 26 citizens to the number of 1,761 had become members.

Next to the Red Cross in vigor of campaigning was the YMCA, which provided services of its own in the training centers and overseas. On November 3 a drive started in Tucson for a YMCA "War Fund." The quota for Arizona was $50,000. Both the Red Cross and the YMCA returned to the attack several times during the war years, and somehow the harried citizens, hard-pressed to find the money for Liberty Bonds, a dozen war-connected organizations, European relief funds, and their own physical survival, managed to meet their quotas.

The support organizations did indeed make life more endurable for the boys in training and at the front. The army had its own program of entertainment for the troops, but the YMCA huts and the Red

Cross canteens were a welcome supplement. The YMCA called attention to the number of letters home that were written on its stationery, and there was always hot coffee, something to read, and a chance to exchange a few words with a young man or a girl from back home. The Knights of Columbus, the Jewish Welfare Board, the Salvation Army, and the Travelers Aid Society all provided services of one kind or another, and the American Library Association collected magazines. They all needed money to carry on their work, and somehow they got it.

Men were the government's first worry; money was its second. It borrowed much of what it needed from its own citizens through Liberty Loans. By the end of May the first issue ($2 billion) was on the market. The *Citizen* announced on May 3 that "a million hourly pours in for Liberty Loans." The pace, however, could not be maintained, and on May 23 the editor warned his readers, "Buy Bonds or We Pay Indemnity to Berlin." A total of $25,000 had been subscribed in Tucson by June 2, but it was not enough, and a week later the editor began talking about the "shame and humiliation" which would result if the response continued to be weak. A whip of a different sort was applied with the publication of an "Honor Roll" of people who had bought bonds. Mr. and Mrs. E. G. Bush invested $10,000. Others went over $1,000. One hated to see his name on that page opposite a $25 contribution. A slogan, "Bonds or Bondage," exerted a little extra pressure, but still the money did not come in, and on June 14 a last-minute appeal warned that this was the final day of the campaign in Tucson with a deficit of $100,000 still to be removed.[36]

All was well that ended well. By June 18 the country had oversubscribed the first Liberty Loan by a billion dollars, and Tucson, with "a magnificent spurt," had met its quota. It was "the first great victory of the war," in the estimation of the *Star* editor. Later Liberty Loan drives raised more money,[37] and in September, Congress passed "the greatest tax bill in the history of the U.S."—$2.4 billion.[38] Tucson did its share through it all. The men of the city may have been a little slow at times to reach for their wallets—but eventually they reached.

After manpower and money the great concern of that summer of 1917 was food. The people had to feed themselves and their Allies, and it would take a mighty effort to keep people on both sides of the Atlantic from going hungry. Some were already near starvation. There was danger that the British, with food on hand in November for only two months, might have to surrender by the end of the year. One of the first acts of the Arizona Defense Council was to tell the people what was ahead:

The urgent need of the hour is Conservation. Let all cooperate in prudent economy in our house and in our social life and activities.

Every effort must be made to bring all available land under cultivation. Each member of the council pledges himself to plant, or cause to be planted, a plot of ground not hitherto under cultivation.

. . . war conditions today demand that the organization and maintenance of all essential industries be kept in a high state of efficiency.

Disregard of law is reprehensible at any time; today it is treasonable.[39]

Among the signers of this document was John C. Greenway, manager of the copper mines at Bisbee, and he was probably responsible for the last two paragraphs. The Bisbee Deportations of July 11, carried out under his direction, were less than a month away, and his defense was clearly stated, before the fact.

One inevitable result of the campaign was the creation of a fear of shortages, causing people everywhere, but especially those in the big cities, to begin stockpiling. Headlines across the nation said in April that "hoarding of food must stop in Chicago,"[40] but Chicago was not the only place where fearful citizens were accumulating supplies.

As bad as hoarding and just as hard to stop was the practice of gouging helpless people who had no choice but to pay. After long delay a Food Control Bill was passed by Congress in August, making profiteering a criminal offense.[41] Passing a law did not, of course, remove the abuse, but it helped. "Liberty gardens" also helped. But the greatest need, it seemed, was for conservation. Every official from Herbert Hoover down preached "the gospel of the clean plate."[42] In a nation accustomed to throwing out more than it used, nothing must be wasted. The Food Administration was so earnest about it that it asked housewives to sign a pledge—and they did. In Tucson they "rallied" to the cause and joined the other one million American women who took the oath in October and November. Over 2,300 of them signed in the first four days of the campaign.[43]

Vigorous efforts to increase production and promote conservation began early and continued until the end of the war. Talk about "mobilizing food" began in April 1917, and meatless days were proposed in May. Sugar was a specially critical item, and by December of that first year the country was said to be in the grip of a "sugar famine." Everyone was asked to consume less of it.[44]

Wheat flour was another staple needed for export. One way of conserving it was the addition to the calendar of wheatless days and meals, along with the meatless schedule. In Tucson in January, 1918, the rule was two wheatless and two porkless days and one meatless (beefless) day a week. People were so conscientious about the program that they created a bad situation for the Arizona cattlemen. When consumption declined, the stock of beef on the hoof increased, and the ranchers had to ask for a suspension of the meatless rule so that they could get rid of their surplus.[45]

Substitutes of various kinds were employed by ingenious housewives, the most common being replacements for the loaf of white bread. Cornmeal was mixed with other grains ground for the purpose to make "war bread," which the Royal Bakeries advertised as "victory bread." Peanut flour was one of the substances suggested as a substitute for the wheat product.[46]

Still the supply of breadstuffs in Europe remained critical, and in a council of desperation the grocers of Tucson met and agreed to issue "bread cards" to families— one card for each member—which would carry a record of all flour, bread, and sugar bought and consumed. Over 10,000 cards were issued in the city.[47]

One man who was deeply involved in the food program was none other than George H. Smalley, of Tucson, who moved his family to Phoenix when he became secretary to the Federal Food Administration for Arizona. His job sometimes took him to Washington, and he brought back tales of the strange and wonderful things that were being developed as part of the war effort. The wireless telephone, he reported to skeptical listeners, had been perfected to such a degree that it was now possible to talk to Paris or Hawaii. Airplanes were being built that would fly so high as to be entirely out of sight from the ground. If not factual, the stories were at least prophetic.[48]

During that winter of 1917–18 the country was not only sugarless and wheatless but also almost coalless, and this caused great hardship in the East as well as mass layoffs caused by coalless factories and coalless trains. In New York harbor, 111 coalless ships, loaded with supplies for the Allies, were unable to move for lack of fuel, and they lay there until late January, when someone gave the right orders to the right people. The country even went lightless at certain times, especially along the Atlantic seaboard, to conserve electricity. Everything except fresh air was in short supply. Even paper was hard to get, and the housing situation was three degrees below hopeless. The city government in Tucson estimated that 500 new units would be needed to get the population through the winter, and Postmaster J. M. Ronstadt complained that he was getting great numbers of inquiries from outsiders who wanted to come to Tucson, where they could not hope for accommodations.[49]

It must be conceded that the war brought no real hardship to Tucson. There was occasional discomfort; there was boredom and monotony. There was need to be careful about every mouthful of food, but there was bread to eat, even if it was hard and heavy and made of strange substances.[50]

It was the desire to make the most of the food supply that threw the country into the arms of the prohibitionists. Grain was used to make booze as well as bread, and the choice between the two was obvious to most people, though there were some holdouts. In June, over their protests, a "prohibitive tax"—$5 to $9 a gallon—was placed on whiskey, making its manufacture impossible." A bill giving federal Food Administrator Herbert Hoover the power to fix prices, commandeer supplies, and impose penalties was before the Congress, but it was held up in the Senate.[51] The stumbling block was a prohibition clause which would make the whole country permanently dry. Wartime drought was one thing, but this went too far, and the Senate marked time until the pressure became too strong to resist. A constitutional amendment, to be submitted to the states for final vote, was approved on August 1, and the Food bill became law on August 8. No foodstuffs were to be used for the manufacture of beer or liquor. The distilling of whiskey stopped officially at midnight, September 9. A vote on the Eighteenth Amendment would not be long in coming.[52]

Everyone but the most impassioned drys knew that absolute, airtight prohibition was impossible—Arizona had known it ever since the state abolished liquor in 1914. On the day Tucson laid John Barleycorn to rest, the sheriff and his deputies began preparing for massive violation of the law, and the violators kept them busy. The year 1917 was just what they expected. A concerted campaign was mounted against bootleggers and prostitutes in February—the first of many. Three squads of officers, headed by the mayor and the sheriff, brought in thirty-two suspects. The focal point of activity was the San Agustín Hotel, once a convent of the Sisters of Saint Joseph—now a house of ill fame. Twenty men and women faced the judge on April 9. They were fined and turned loose to sin again. The law needed a better set of teeth, and for the moment liquor and prostitution were out of control.[53]

Bootlegging was so prevalent that the officers could not keep up with it. Since the Mexican border was only seventy-five miles away, considerable quantities of smuggled liquor crossed the line every day, headed for Tucson. The lawmen picked up an occasional small-time rumrunner, but they always hoped for bigger game, and on June 12, 1917, a really big fish came into their net—none other than Jeff Cole, proprietor of Cole's Auto Services, described as the "King of the Bootleggers." The title seems to have been earned, for the officers confiscated forty cases of whiskey at his base of business operations and picked up 1,080 pints at his home. They even arrested a female bootlegger named Cruz Carrillo. Business was so good that the smugglers sometimes grew careless. Ignacio de la Vega, for example, was picked up when he tried to make a customer out of Deputy Sheriff Sid Simpson. In October a seventy-three-year-old pioneer went to jail for peddling potables. Tucson, during those years, was dry in name only. A law passed in July, 1918, permitting confiscation of a smuggler's automobile was no more than a stone in the path of the torrent.[54]

The government made one concession to the thirsty. Beer with a 3 percent alcohol content was approved in November, 1917, on the theory that the nation's stock of bonded whiskey would last longer if the brewers were not cut off entirely and that the evils of bootlegging might be reduced. Near beer, in the minds of many survivors of those times, was one of the horrors of war.[55]

Prostitution was another problem without a real solution. The city administration admitted in July, 1917, that Tucson was "without laws to deal with Gay Alley." The girls could be picked up and fined, as they had been since the eighties, but they could not be run out of town. Army officers, concerned for the welfare of their young men, had raised the question. Soldiers were always passing through, and there was always a possibility that some sort of government installation would be set up near or in the city. In August, 1917, for instance, the town was

"surveyed for an aviation camp," but did not qualify. The mayor and council knew well enough that Gay Alley was one of the reasons.[56]

It took them another six months to forge a weapon that might end the fight. Still making "an effort to get an additional troop camp," they passed an ordinance forbidding "loitering," which meant that a woman living in Tucson had to have a visible means of support. Anyone, but especially a gambler or prostitute without a job or a bank account, could be ordered out of town. In February, 1918, the armies of the law were ready to march. On the very day the new ordinance became effective, policemen went from house to house telling the girls that they would have to get out. Most of them did, though some settled in other parts of town, to the considerable surprise of their new neighbors.[57] Before long, of course, they were all back in Gay Alley.

At the same time concerned citizens were meeting at the YMCA to listen to Lieutenant Paul Popenoe's report on the situation, made for the army. He described a "shocking state of affairs" in Tucson. Two hundred prostitutes were working in the city, he said, and 90 per cent of them were infected. Mayor Parker assured the assembly that the city was aware of the need for a cleanup and that "we are going to do it." The campaign which followed was not enough, however, to bring the hoped-for military base to Tucson. The closest thing to it was an army school for radio operators, set up at the fairgrounds in June, 1918. The university campus had been used to train "mechanicians" since the beginning of the war, and in August, 1918, it was designated as a military base, the center of a circle with a five-mile radius inside which prostitutes were not tolerated. The sheriff and his deputies breathed sighs of relief when the United States Army shouldered some of their burdens.[58]

Men, money, food, and faith—these were the things the government most needed, and in some ways the greatest of these was faith. George Creel and his crew in Washington set out at the beginning to convince the American people that the war effort was necessary for self-preservation; that the cause was noble, and the sacrifices were worthwhile; that the enemy was vile and unspeakable—the epitome of evil; that the American soldier was invincible if he was supported by civilians at home; and that "food would win the war."

The American people needed very few reminders, it must be confessed, but the Committee on Public Information made sure by enlisting the services of 150,000 Americans to talk, write, paint, report, and organize all over the land. The "four-minute men" to the number of 75,000 made 7,555,190 speeches at all kinds of public assemblies. Creel organized the nation's artists for the "Battle of the Fences." They decorated barns, fences, walls, and billboards with pictorial propaganda. The result was an incredible concentration of the country's will and resources on the one objective—to win the war.[59]

This was fine and, under the circumstances, necessary, but not all the consequences were good. The intense pressure to conform, measure up, go along allowed for no individual differences, tolerated no dissent, and sent otherwise good people off on witch-hunts and vendettas. Anyone with a German name was under suspicion, and after the passage of the Espionage Act in June, 1917 (amended in May, 1918), the spy chase was on. Citizens were encouraged to report any suspicious word or activity, and it was said that there was not a town in the United States in which someone was not viewed with suspicion and reported to the authorities for investigation.

Tucson was no exception. It is easy to see from the vantage point of seventy-five years later which way the wind was blowing when on April 13, 1918, Al C. Bernard, the acting mayor, called a meeting at the Armory to organize a "One Hundred per Cent American Club." The object was to promote war financing and to "detect Hun sympathizers and give information to the government."[60] The spy hunt was on.

It reached into the highest levels of the state government. Governor Hunt felt its sting when Editor Allen Jaynes of the *Citizen* printed a story which practically accused him of pro–IWW sympathies and implied that he was disloyal to the United States. Hunt promptly sued him for libel.[61] Less important men had no such recourse. Four days later William Houston, "a well-known old timer," was arrested for obstructing the war activities by advising others not to buy Liberty Bonds. A federal grand jury indicted him, and he was actually convicted—with a recommendation for clemency. On May 18 the grand jury returned four indictments for similar offences and remarked that there was an "utter and deplorable lack of patriotism" abroad in the land.[62] The man they targeted for special treatment was Curt von Einem, foreman of the Holstein Dairy. He had called Liberty Bonds "scraps of paper," had said that he expected Germany to win the war, and had told a man named Leonard Williams that he was a fool for enlisting. His incautious remarks got him two years in Leavenworth and a fine of $500.[63]

Then there was Mrs. George Mullarkey, arrested on the train for saying she hoped that Germany would win.[64] What happened to her the record does not say.

The great campaigns, however, were reserved for the slackers, deserters, and draft dodgers, of whom there were many in Tucson—at least the One Hundred per Cent American Club was convinced that there were. In June they decided to do something about it. United States Marshal Joseph Dillon turned the whole show over to them. They made elaborate preparations for a drive to round up every suspicious character in town. The city was divided into fourteen districts, and a squad was assigned to each one. Every exit from town was blocked, and about 100 automobiles were on hand to transport the catch to city hall. When organization president Dr. C. A. Schrader gave the word, the manhunt began. "Mayor Parker landed eighteen at the first pool hall," the *Citizen* reported. "He picked up two on the lawn of the Southern Pacific depot of draft age but with no cards. A number of Papagoes and Yaquis were picked up but released as soon as their nationality was proven." In all, sixty-six boys were brought in. Two were deserters from the army and were held. The rest were released so that they could go home and get their draft cards. By 2:00 Sunday morning most had been cleared. It was a return to the old vigilante system, and the results could have been unfortunate, but Tucson was lucky.[65]

Most of the young men of Tucson, and even some of the older ones, were eager to serve. Frank C. Lockwood, for example, head of the university English Department, turned his job over to Sidney E. Pattison in March, 1918, and went off to London to work for the Red Cross.[66]

One who felt he had reason to postpone his military service was Harold Steinfeld, one of Tucson's brightest and best-liked young men. A sad and regrettable episode was the result. Trouble began when his

Frank C. Lockwood.

father fell from a horse in California, was seriously injured, underwent an unsuccessful operation, and believed that he might not survive. He was in New York under treatment when Harold's number was drawn in the draft. Urged by his parents, young Steinfeld asked for an eight-month discharge on account of his father's serious illness so that the family business (which included some war-related activities) could be placed in competent hands. Finding that his draft board would be opposed, he prepared to submit an appeal to General Enoch Crowder, who was in charge of the draft. Although Harold strongly denied the charge later, he was credited with hiring Francis J. Heney, of San Francisco, famous for his shootout described in an earlier chapter, with Dr. Handy, to handle the appeal.

This touched off a highly negative reaction in his home town. The *Star* led the outcry in an editorial on March 9, 1918. "I do not think," the writer declared, "that the presence of Harold Steinfeld is necessary to

Harold Steinfeld in uniform.

the people of Tucson," and he discussed the situation with insulting irony. He returned to the attack when the alleged involvement of Francis J. Heney was made public, and in a subsequent editorial he gave Steinfeld credit for injecting a "race issue" into the controversy.[67]

By this time the whole sticky situation had evolved into a contest between the local draft board and the authorities in Washington. The Tucson chairman announced that the Steinfeld case would be decided by the local draft machinery, which was authorized to handle all exceptions. Even when General Crowder instructed the Tucson body to "suspend" any action on the case, the board ignored the mandate, announced that Steinfeld had failed to report for roll call and entrainment, and was in violation of the law. The sheriff was instructed to bring him in. By this time the case had gone to the president of the United States for review, but on April 3 the board certified Harold as a deserter, reminded him that he was now in the

army, and warned him of the penalties he faced.[68]

Harold did not wait to hear more. He "enlisted" in the armed forces, reported for duty at Camp Meade, and sent an eloquent letter defending his conduct back to the hometown papers. "My patriotism has been challenged," he wrote, "and I shall not allow anyone to question or even intimate that the motives behind my claim are not honest and patriotic. . . . I trust the public will, upon reflection, remember my past standing in the community and I believe that I am made out of the right stuff and am not the kind to shirk my duty or obligation."[69]

His father was back by April 19, ready to resume management. After the war Harold regained his place in public esteem, though the American Legion would never admit him as a member. The city mourned when he and his wife died in their penthouse atop the Pioneer Hotel in a fire set by an arsonist on December 20, 1970.[70]

Through the summer and fall of 1918, Tucsonans endured a somewhat meager existence, but they were not without diversions. The Opera House burned down in May,[71] but the other theaters offered interesting theatrical fare, and there was always homegrown fun. Saturday night "jitney dances" at the Armory offered "a healthy outlet for youthful spirits" with Phyllis Mansfeld in charge. "In a particularly partyless and danceless winter," said a *Star* reporter, Tucson's youth were able to look forward to "prize dances, spotlight dances, moonlight dances," and a chance to contribute substantially to the Red Cross. "Patriots as we all are," he went on, "we may sew for the Red Cross, cut bandages for the Red Cross, knit for the Red Cross, save tin cans and tin foil, sell tickets to people who want them not and drink tea we want not ourselves," thus mak-

Tucsonans in front of the old Elks Club, ready for the first Armistice Day parade. Charles Gimbel is Uncle Sam.

ing these young people at play a welcome sight indeed.[72]

Such innocent enjoyments came to an abrupt end, however, in September, when the great influenza epidemic struck down thousands overnight. By the first of October, according to the newspapers, 20,000 cases of Spanish influenza had broken out in the army camps in forty-eight hours, and 277 men had died. Three days later the count was 100,000, and the disease was spreading among civilians. People in the East felt the full impact first, but the sickness moved westward with frightful speed. There were 200 cases at Winslow, Arizona, on October 4, and 60 at Flagstaff. The *Star* reported on October 8 that Camp Funston, where so many Tucson boys had been sent, counted 2,070 cases. There had been 4,000 deaths in the nation in three weeks. The epidemic had spread to Mexico, Australia, Africa, and the American Expeditionary Force in France.

And there was no known cure.[73]

Tucson saw it coming and took steps before it arrived. On October 4 the university went into quarantine. A few days later the plague struck, but its ravages were not nearly as severe as they were in other towns, particularly El Paso. By November 1 the worst was almost over, and the health officers were getting ready to lift the quarantine at the university.[74]

The war, too, was almost over. The country was expecting news of Germany's capitulation almost hourly. On November 10, Mayor Parker decided that it was high time to think about celebrating the event when it came, and he called in the town's most influential men, headed by General L. H. Manning, to make plans. They decided that speeches and a parade would not fit the occasion—that a "spontaneous" celebration would be better. And that was what they got, sooner than they expected.[75]

A final act of World War I. University of Arizona President Rufus B. von KleinSmid confers the LL.D. degree on General John J. Pershing (left) at the dedication of the memorial fountain in front of Old Main.

That very night whistles and bells got every able-bodied Tucsonan out of bed at 12:45 when the news arrived, and at daylight they were all back in the streets. The grocery stores filled restaurant orders and then honored Mayor Parker's proclamation calling for a general holiday. The banks closed at noon. Crowds gathered at the intersection of Congress and Stone, where Dooley Bookman's band was playing "Dixie" and "Over There." Someone set out cans of "red fire." Someone else had a supply of firecrackers. A third someone tied some tin tubs and buckets behind his car, creating pandemonium as he drove down the street. Fire whistles, train bells, and pistols went off. A bonfire on the pavement at Congress and Stone crackled and roared while the police tried to keep the cars moving and hold down

a celebration that "at times approached a riot."[76]

It was all over. The final group of draftees was dismissed. The 158th Infantry, Arizona's own, was chosen as President Wilson's honor guard at the peace conference in Paris. Surplus government food was put on the market, and meatless, wheatless, sweetless days were over. Harry Berger erected the memorial fountain in front of Old Main on the university campus to honor the school's war dead—twelve men, including Alexander T. Berger, his son. General John J. Pershing dedicated the fountain on January 20, 1920. English Department head and Arizona historian Frank C. Lockwood came back from his YMCA assignment in London. Materials for new housing began to be available. Reconstruction was beginning. It was time to look ahead.

Not everyone was pleased to have it so. When the first anniversary of the armistice arrived, the *Citizen*'s account of the ceremonies was headlined, "So Soon Forgotten":

Can anyone who witnessed the celebration of the signing of the armistice in Tucson forget that momentous occasion. The city went wild with joy. The fame of those who were fighting with the colors in France was at its height. Their deeds of valor were on every tongue and a grateful nation poured out its thanks for their victory.

What a contrast to the pitiful celebration held in Tucson yesterday.[77]

That was one way of looking at it. From another point of view it is possible to believe that those Tucsonans were not so much forgetful of their soldiers, dead or alive, as they were eager to forget what they had just been through themselves.

CHAPTER 12

The Gold-plated Decade

The 1920s, from some points of view, were the best years Tucson had ever had—perhaps the best she would ever have. Not every hour was crowned with roses; not every year was a triumph. But if the decade was not pure gold, it was at least gold-plated, and the men and women who remember it think back on those days with smiling nostalgia.[1] The town was big enough to be called a city, but not too big to keep its community spirit. It was prosperous enough, but not too prosperous. Its rich people were not too rich; its poor people were not hopelessly poor. It was growing and developing, but not too fast (some people thought it was not growing fast enough). Factories and assembly lines were slow to arrive; wealth was based on commerce rather than industry; the arrival of officials of the Union Fibre Company in May, 1919, with plans for building a binder-twine factory at a cost of $10,000 was a pleasant surprise to everyone.[2] The Red Scare and the nationwide strikes of the early postwar years disrupted the rest of the country, but they were mostly just news items to Tucson. It was never as bad in the desert community as it was elsewhere, and the mid-twenties were a time of great prom-

ise and real achievement. The evil days came not, and nobody foresaw the great ruin and depression waiting at the end of the decade.

Having said this much, one must confess that the golden years got off to a bad start, even in Tucson. The inevitable letdown followed the intense concentration and the enormous expenditure of energy demanded of everyone during the years of conflict, and nature itself seemed determined to defeat any prompt return to better days. A drought had parched the ranges and brought hard times to the farmers and ranchers, who not only had to sell their undernourished beef but were forced to compete with a horde of rustlers who marched in with branding irons at the ready to try for a portion of the orphan calf crop. The rains came in the summer, but the fall and winter had been dry, and the farmers were feeling the pinch.[3]

Everything was in short supply. Gasoline cost thirty-six cents a gallon when available and was so hard to come by that the newspapers talked about a "gasoline famine," while the automobile dealers feared for the future and predicted a return to the bicycle and the horse.[4] In the summer of 1920 there was even a "water famine." During the daytime no water at all was available to house-holders in the northern part of the city, and "health conditions were seriously endangered." The city council was forced to take drastic action, forbidding any watering between 6:00 A.M. and 7:00 P.M., sending policemen on daytime rounds to check for violations and imposing on the violators fines of fifty dollars minimum and in some cases thirty-day jail sentences.[5]

With the removal of the wartime bridle on food costs, and with everything hard to get, prices naturally started going up, and consequently the High Cost of Living became a major topic of conversation and commiseration (the word "inflation" had not yet come into common use). Housewives were used to squeezing the last penny out of a dollar as a result of wartime pressures and shortages, but the war was over now. Why should the ordeal go on and on? The answer, in the minds of most of these women, was price gouging or profiteering. Middlemen and merchants were hoarding foodstuffs—holding them off the market until prices soared out of sight. The public outcry grew so loud that Washington had to take notice. On August 9, 1919, Timothy A. Riordan, of Flagstaff, federal food administrator for Arizona, came to Tucson. He announced that George H. Smalley, who had helped hold prices down during the war, would take his place on the firing line and that "profiteering will be vigorously prosecuted by the government."[6]

The news was welcome, but everyone realized that something more was needed, and something more was proposed. The first suggestion came from R. H. Southgate, secretary of the Central Trades Council, who proposed to the city council that the municipality buy surplus government food and put it on the market. Dr. Ira A. Huffman,

who managed the National Guard Armory, went a step further, offering the building for use as a public market during the emergency. Mayor Parker promised that the city would spend $5,000 for stands and stalls. The *Star* carried an enthusiastic editorial praising the idea, and Guy Monthan, of Monthan Brothers Truck Farms, took the final step by establishing his own market in San Agustín Plaza. By the end of the month valley farmers were setting up shop on Saturday mornings, and everybody came. "There was a hot time in the Old Church Plaza," the *Star* reported on August 31. The farmers sold out "lock, stock and barrel" to purchasers, who were on hand by the hundreds.[7]

The market helped. The news that the government was seizing huge stocks of hoarded food (24 million eggs in three cities were one item) and raising the penalties for profiteering helped also. The most welcome step of all, however, was taken by the city itself when it went into the surplus-food business. Both the mayor and the postmaster received lists of supplies available from El Paso. "Uncle Sam bacon," its equivalent selling in Tucson for seventy cents a pound, would be available for thirty-six cents plus shipping. There was a line at the post office on August 17 as the sale began, and the city aldermen went on schedule at city hall to take orders for surplus government food. Canned goods worth $500 were distributed by Councilman A. C. Bernard the first day. By the end of the month prices had started down.[8]

A shortage that was harder to handle was a serious deficiency in public funds. In 1917, Tom Campbell and George Hunt kept the state in turmoil for months, each claiming to be the legitimate governor. Hunt was in possession of the office first, but a court ruling put Campbell in charge in the spring of 1917 (he lasted until December), and in February he notified the legislature that the treasury was empty. Hunt was responsible, he said, for "unbelievable extravagance and recklessness," and all money appropriated for state institutions had been spent by the preceding December 31. The state prison had been "bankrupt" for three months. Only the university at Tucson had a chance of getting through the fiscal year without specially approved state funds. Campbell asked for $400,000 to keep things going. He got $200,000. The university naturally did not share in this pittance and had to survive as best it could until more money was available.[9] Tucson felt the shortage.

At the root of all these problems was a slump in the state's basic industries. Copper mining, for example, was a shambles. Almost the minute the armistice was signed, the flow of war materials was cut off, and producers who had been busy filling government contracts one day found themselves idle the next, creating great hardships for owners and workmen alike. Copper producers were left with huge surpluses on hand. Estimates of the oversupply in the nation ran as high as a billion pounds. Sales fell to 5 percent of output. The market declined from the government-supported price level of twenty-five cents a pound to eighteen, and the owners were looking at a potential loss of $80 million if miraculously a buyer showed up with cash in hand to buy them out.[10] In May, 1919, four of them were obliged, reluctantly, to pass a dividend, and they continued to cut production and wages through the rest of 1919 and all of 1920. By then 30 percent of the miners were idle and were asking for relief legislation. The alternative was to go on strike, and this they did

everywhere in the country. The industrial workers went out too. By February 14 the works at Jerome were closed down, and there was trouble wherever men were idle and their families were facing hunger.[11]

For the average citizen the great villain was still the IWW, which was credited with organizing the strikes and was attacked by every newspaper editor in Arizona. Researchers in recent years have shown that the Wobblies were less of a menace than was popularly supposed, but nobody would have believed it in 1920.[12]

For a while in 1919–20 an object of even greater fear and detestation was the evil agent from Moscow, a bewhiskered menace (as portrayed in the newspaper cartoons) with a smoking bomb in his hand. A great many people believed that the labor unrest was being fomented by this character and that he just might take over the country.

The Great Red Scare was much more of a problem in the East than it was in the West, but it did come to Tucson in November, 1919. Organizers sent out by United Americans to Fight Reds recruited in Phoenix, where ninety concerned citizens joined. On the evening of November 22 the scene shifted to Tucson. Frederick Vining Fisher, assistant national director of United Americans, made a "stirring address" to a mass meeting assembled there, plucking vigorously on one string: the choice facing every American between democracy and the dictatorship of the proletariat. A committee was appointed to prepare for a state convention to be held in Tucson "within a fortnight." Members included Judge W. H. Sawtelle, Charles F. Solomon, Dr. H. W. Fenner, Andrew P. Martin, and George F. Kitt.[13]

Apparently very little happened as a result of this movement. People in the western states were much more interested in the IWW than in the Bolsheviki. Their minds were on the supposed dangers present in their own backyards, and they approved of stern measures to repress them. The vigilante spirit condoned in wartime, which should have gone growling back to its jungle when the armistice was signed, continued to play its part in postwar days. The spirit was exemplified in the June 1, 1918, issue of the *Arizona Service Bulletin*, published by the Arizona Defense Council:

More and more there is being awakened throughout Arizona an uncompromising spirit of one hundred percent Americanism. The recent wholesome convictions of the federal court for disloyalty and sedition have shown clearly that in Arizona there is no place for the man or woman who is not ready to do his or her full share in winning this war.[14]

In 1918 it seemed right and proper to deprive some Americans of their liberty in the name of freedom and Americanism. In 1919 the feeling was still present and still strong. The American Legion, founded in the spring of that year, was composed of men who had fought for their country and were prepared to use a firm hand in putting down its enemies. When the first state caucus opened in Tucson on July 11, with Tucson druggist Andrew P. Martin (top sergeant, Battery B, 340th Field Artillery, 89th Division, AEF) as first state commander, the assembly was addressed by Donald Blevins, of the national organization. He told the men that their peacetime responsibility was to counteract "the dangers that beset the country":

Some people would have you believe that there is no danger of the case of Russia being duplicated. In the meantime, however, murder is being preached in the streets of the nation's

Andrew P. Martin (center) receives a medal from Governor Sidney P. Osborn. Adjutant General Alexander Tuthill is at left. Arizona Citizen *photo.*

metropolis. . . . Agitators have been spreading their evil doctrines and must be silenced.[15]

Four Legionnaires were killed on Armistice Day in November, 1919, while attacking an IWW headquarters in Centralia, Washington.[16] Nothing like that, fortunately, happened in Tucson, but Arizona came out of the war uncompromisingly antilabor and ready to take strong action against any group whose ideas it disapproved of. The controversy over the right-to-work principle (a national issue for the next half century) brought the conservatives out in full cry[17] and caused a major disturbance in Tucson in the early summer of 1920. The electrical-workers union, operating the city lighting plant, threatened to go on strike for better pay and working conditions, and the *Citizen* predicted that the worst was about to happen: "Tucson may be without light and power tonight, practically closing up every industry in the city, including all irrigation service in the valley, the Southern Pacific shops, street lights, the newspapers, residence and commercial service." [18]

F. E. Russell, manager of the Tucson Gas and Electric Power Company, told a reporter that all demands of the workers had been met but that something more—"a principle"—was involved: "Whether the open shop, which has prevailed for the past twenty-eight years with our company, during its entire life since 1882, is at last to be surrendered to closed shop practice." [19]

His argument against the all-union closed shop—that university electrical-engineering students would be unable to get practical experience working for the company—was not a very cogent one, but the businessmen of the Old Pueblo did not stumble over that. They were already unhappy about the strikes breaking out all over the nation, which were making headlines every day, [20] and were convinced that the labor unions were out to ruin the country. The labor fuse in Tucson was hanging fire, however, and no one knew whether there would be a real explosion. The Trade and Labor Council met on June 24 and voted that the electric company was "unfair"—a verdict which "automatically calls out the union engineers of the company." Members of other unions thought about a sympathy strike, but no one, including the electricians, walked off the job. [21]

The open-shop people, however, were concerned enough to start a campaign of their own. On June 25 they organized an Open Shop Association. Mose Drachman re-ported that 250 businessmen signed a resolution supporting the open shop though they sympathized (he said) with the workmen. "I do not fear the rank and file," Mose declared. The "un-American doctrine" was coming from the union leaders and organizers.

The showdown came at a construction site on East Congress. Edgar L. ("Pop") Southworth was in charge. He hired a boy—nonunion—to carry lumber and drive nails. At noon his union construction workers walked out. "I guess I pushed the button," Southworth observed.

If the walkout at the Scores Building had been successful, the unions might have won, but Southworth assembled a nonunion crew, and the work went on. On July 2 the Chamber of Commerce endorsed the National Open Shop movement. The Young Men's Business Club had already done so. A proposed strike of the teamsters working for the city, called for July 8, fizzled out, and the men were back with their teams almost as soon as they had left them. Right-to-work employers began displaying white cards in their windows. Closed-shop employers displayed green cards. The white far outnumbered the green. The closed-shop issue was dead in Tucson, and it remained dead for the foreseeable future. Pop Southworth was able to report by the middle of June that union and nonunion men were working side by side without friction on the Scores Building. [22]

Tucson was conservative, but reasonably so. It was as unwilling to support extreme conservatives as it was opposed to left-wing agitators and "radicals." The point was made when the Ku Klux Klan entered the picture, probably in 1921. It enlisted a good many citizens—no one knows how many—who believed that the organization would help to put down corruption, disloyalty, and sin in all its manifold forms. The Klan, however, did not succeed in disrupting the life of the town as it did in so many other places, including Phoenix. In fact, no public notice was taken of its early cross burnings and parades. In June, 1922, however, renewed activity brought the *Star* down on it with fists flying. "Klan's First Appearance Signal for Speedy Action," said the headline:

For the first time in many months, the Ku Klux Klan, or some individual using that name, has again become active in Tucson. A threatening letter received last week by the proprietor of a local cafe, and purporting to come from this organization, has been turned over to the local police for investigation.

Although the Klan has never been as active in Tucson as in other cities in the state and the southwest, it is nevertheless said to enjoy a fairly large membership in this city. This condition is one which is intolerable to those who stand arraigned [sic] on the side of lawful as opposed to unlawful punishment of offenders.

In the case of mobs—in which classification the Klan must be included—there is only one course to pursue. Its members must be surprised at the outset and handled with all the severity proper to the offense. To wait until the movement gathers recruits and courage is to court a reign of terror.[23]

In 1923, says historian Sue Abbey, Klan activities in Tucson were expanded, and it was reported that teenage boys were targeted for a membership campaign. The movement "died rather quickly after the boys found out that part of their duties as junior klansmen would be to haul wood up A Mountain for the burning of crosses."[24]

The Klan in Tucson was never investigated. No membership list was ever published. The newspapers refrained from noticing its activities or even acknowledging its existence. The Phoenix Klan, which was responsible for some beatings and one tar-

and-feathering, got some public attention, especially after Governor Campbell announced on May 21, 1922, the results of an investigation revealing that some 900 Arizonans were citizens of the Invisible Empire. In his opinion they were "not worthy of their citizenship in the United States of America." A grand jury interested itself in Klan activities in September, but it did not touch off an anti-Klan campaign, perhaps because nobody knew how much future the organization had. It was showing tremendous power in other states (1,700 members in Oakland, California, for example), and might conceivably emerge as a dominant force in Arizona. The Klan was something of a hot potato for journalists, and the *Tombstone Prospector* was one of the few newspapers in the state which seemed inclined to give full coverage to its doings. There was also the undeniable fact that in the early stages the membership included many men in high places—doctors, lawyers, judges, policemen, prominent merchants. Some of them thought that they were joining a businessmen's organization, like a service club. They were responsible citizens, profoundly disturbed by what was going on in the society around them and eager to set things right. When they saw what the organization was doing, and was capable of doing, they withdrew. If someone ever locates the Klan membership roster for Tucson, he will undoubtedly be surprised by the prominence of its leaders.[25] Whoever they were, they were soon appalled by the Klan's bigotry and violence, and the fiery cross ceased to burn on A Mountain. By 1924 the danger was over.

In the United States bad times like these always uproot large segments of the population and put them on the road. Tucson had had problems with indigents migrating to and from California ever since the railroad arrived, and the depression years of the early twenties threatened to make matters worse. Early in 1919 the city council decided that a new wave of transients would come in the spring, and for that reason they passed a special ordinance on February 5 to prepare for "the new era of tramps which is felt to be impending. There are signs both of the coming of spring and of the coming of hoboes and Martin J. Duffy, past master of the chain gang, has been sorting over the old shackles that were in use before the war ukase of 'Work or Fight' chased the idle off the ties."[26] The mayor and council were also counting on the ordinance involving "visible means of support" to help in controlling the "immoral classes."

The problem, especially for the police, was the increasing difficulty of defining the "immoral classes." The best people were breaking one particular law right and left—the commandment (made official by the Eighteenth Amendment and the Volstead Act): "Thou Shalt Not Drink." In spite of the existence of a hard core of passionate drys and eager reformers, Tucson had long been a tolerant town—in fact, a town where almost anything went, within reason—and it was almost impossible to dry the place out. Prohibition had, indeed, helped moisten the community, just as it had liquefied the rest of the country. Men and women who had never done much drinking before now carried pocket flasks to nightclubs and served cocktails in their homes. For this they were not often blamed or molested, public opinion having ruled that this was private business. The might of the law was usually reserved for the producer and the distributor—the still operator, the alky cooker, the importer and disseminator of Mexican liquor, in short, the bootlegger. The police were active in picking up these people and

the judges were conscientious about fining them and confiscating their stock in trade, but an arrest was only an occupational hazard for the offenders, a temporary interruption of a lucrative business. Liquor came up from Sasabe, on the border, on the backs of burros and from Nogales in cabs of locomotives, and the tide was impossible to stem.[27]

Other vices flourished along with the liquor traffic. In 1919 the girls were back in Gay Alley and on Church Street. The case of Cornelius C. ("Kid") Lee was one of many. Lee was a black man whose official business was operating the Kid Restaurant at 126 West Ochoa Street, but he was known to deal in narcotics and booze, and he was arrested in April, and again in June, for operating a house of prostitution. He asked for and got a jury trial, and the jury, as might have been expected, disagreed. The police, however, mounted a flank attack and rearrested their man for trying to bribe Night Captain Roy Wharton. The judge avoided the jury pitfall when he set up the trial for bribery, and the Kid probably did not escape retribution, but the basic question was still to be answered: Why was he allowed to build up a business in the first place? The *Citizen* proposed a probable answer: "Too much friendliness between policemen and Lee." The editor hesitated to blame Mayor Parker and his council, who had always showed themselves ready and willing to back up the law-enforcement agencies, but, he said, previous administrations "had shown no disposition to clean up the town." In other words, the old comfortable relationship between the Tucson underworld and the Tucson police was still in effect, unchanged by temporary setbacks and ineffectual ordinances. The city administration, as has been noted, found a way to run the girls

Policeman Jesus Camacho, the "mayor of Meyer Street," Courtesy Arizona Historical Society and Journal of Arizona History.

were personified in policeman Jesus Camacho, the tall, tough Mexican-American who patrolled Gay Alley and the adjacent streets in the twenties. He got along with everybody, though he was hard on crooks when he caught them. He collected the girls' monthly "fines" and patrolled the district at night, sometimes riding his horse, Bebe, sometimes walking with Bebe following close behind. He had a good deal of ground to cover and needed the horse. When he went to work for the department in 1910, says biographer Dick Hall, he was assigned to the district where he grew up, "the area south of Congress Street between Church and Meyer south to 17th Street":

There were forty-eight saloons in downtown Tucson and fourteen of them were in the three-block area between Church and Meyer. Here also were gambling houses, Chinese markets, small hotels, and Sabino Street, the red-light district, also known as Gay Alley. In this area lived Mexican working people, many Mexican aliens, Chinese and Black families, small-time thieves and pimps.

out of town when there was a chance of getting an army installation for Tucson during World War I, but the officials continued to think as their predecessors had back in the eighties. Vice was inevitable, they believed, and it was better to control it and make it pay than to try fruitlessly to eradicate it.

When a group of women approached Mayor Parker with a petition to close up the red-light district, he told them: "There are more single men than married men in Tucson. There is no trouble there. As long as I am mayor, it will stay open." Turning to one of the women, he added: "There is a vacant house next to you on Fourth Street. If I close the Alley, the girls will be asking to rent it."[28]

Tucson's attitudes toward these matters

Camacho did his work so well that he came to be called the "Mayor of Meyer Street." When prohibition became the law of the land, he enforced it most of the time, but he was capable of warning friends with liquor on hand when he heard that the federal agents were planning a raid. He may have accepted favors from the girls he supervised. There were "many who loved him." But he was devoted to his family and may have resisted temptation. The important fact is the existence, side by side, of respectable Tucson and the nonrespectable tenderloin, each deriving some benefit from the other until the early thirties, when the reformers got the upper hand. During the final years a tall fence was erected across the entrance to the alley so that nobody could see what went on inside. Concealment was a step toward abolition.[29]

An idea of the status of law and order in Tucson in those years can be gained from the reports of the Police Department submitted to the mayor and council each January 1. The report for 1926 computed the total arrests at 3,582. Of these arrests, 1983 were for traffic violations, including drunk driving. Only 115 arrests were made for making or transporting liquor, and only 50 for prostitution, soliciting, or operating a disorderly house. Only one arrest was made for murder, but 137 men were picked up for fighting or disturbing the peace. Eighty-five stolen automobiles were returned to their owners, but only one man was arrested for car theft. There were two wife beaters, one shoplifter, and one case of indecent exposure. It would seem that Tucson was a lively town, more inclined to go in for good times than for serious crimes. One can only conjecture how much influence on these statistics was exerted by cozy relations between the police and the lawbreakers.[30]

With so many troubles and difficulties during the late teens and early twenties, Tucson might have seemed to an outsider a lost cause or at least a frozen asset, but such a judgment would have been far from accurate. Things were better in Tucson than in most of the rest of the country. They usually were. There was no police strike, as in Boston. There were no mob scenes and flag burnings, as in Chicago; no confrontations between strikers and the National Guard, as in Seattle. In the very midst of Tucson's difficulties the *Citizen* could assure its readers, with complete confidence, that they were about to see "the dawn of a new prosperity epoch" and that good times were at hand.[31]

And why not? There was justification for optimism. The town was growing, for one

thing. In 1910 the population was 13,193, in 1920 it was 20,292, and in 1927 the Police Department was looking out for a population of 35,000. Enrollment at the university passed 1,000 for the first time in February, 1920. In June the faculty inaugurated the first summer school.[32] And there was money to spend. Ryland and Zipf's clothing store at 640 North Stone advertised the latest styles for men. Steinfeld's and Jacome's did the same for women. Geraldine Farrar drew big crowds at the Opera House in May, and Nazimova played at the Lyric in June in *The Red Lantern*. It cost money to see them. The *Star* on April 4, 1919, ran a significant advertisement:

Are You Living the 20th Century Way?
Have You an Electric Iron?
Have You an Electric Toaster?
Have You an Electric Percolator?
The 20th Century Way Is the Electrical Way.

Happiness, obviously, was powered by electricity and could be purchased. It could also be purchased in the form of new housing. "Weekly building permits," the *Star* announced on June 20, 1919, "foot up nearly $20,000." Grady Gammage's new mansion at 630 North Tyndall would cost $6,500. The supreme proof that there was money in Tucson, however, was the oil boom of 1919. Yes, there was one, and the infection struck almost all the leading citizens, making them dream of sudden wealth, early retirement, and a baronial life style.

The germ originated in Texas, where wildcatters were bringing in new fields and the papers were reporting new gushers every day. The Texas oil companies were eager to share the wealth, and the Tucson papers were full of oil news and irresistible advertisements from companies who still had a few shares for lucky investors. It was no special wonder that someone should dream of a great untapped reservoir of petroleum much nearer home. It is possible that the dreamer was none other than H. W. Zipf, of Ryland and Zipf's clothing store, later postmaster. He was the one who leased 8,300 acres on the Canoa Ranch, north of Tubac—a tract five and a half miles long and less than a mile wide, supposedly sitting on top of a sea of oil. On May 15, 1919, he assigned this property to the Canoa Oil and Gas Company, formally organized with twenty-five members, including him. Mayor Parker was the president. Other officers included Fred Ronstadt, vice-president; H. S. Corbett, secretary; and Leo Goldschmidt, treasurer—all first citizens. The other twenty-one members were on the board of directors, and the list included such formidable figures as General L. H. Manning, Judge J. H. Campbell, editor A. R. Jaynes, merchant Mose Drachman, and attorney S. L. Kingan. The Arizona Corporation Commission approved the sale of 2,500 shares of stock at ten dollars a share, and the members of the board subscribed for 125 shares each to raise money to start drilling.[33]

The excitement spread like a scandalous rumor. Oil leases were taken out on acreage near Benson—at Bowie—at Pantano—all east of Tucson. The fever spread westward to Yuma, where a newly organized company promised to "start drilling soon." Word went round that the Texas oil companies were involved in Arizona and that one of them was leasing in southern Pima County. Three thousand claims from the Bowie field, the newspapers reported, were recorded at Safford in one four-day period in mid-May.[34] There were a few skeptics. Glenton Sykes, out with the geology professors from the university to look at the prospects, heard that somebody had poured a fifty-gallon bar-

rel of oil down the test hole on the Canoa project,[35] but the believers kept on believing. The *Star* assured them, "Tucson has excellent prospects for oil," and C. C. Magenheimer, former president of Tucson Farms, declared solemnly that on the Del Rio tract, just west of the Tucson city limits, he had struck gas at 400 feet while drilling a water well. Since Magenheimer was at the moment "one of the most successful oil producers of southern California," his words carried weight. "Success in the oil business," the *Citizen's* editor admonished, "requires experience, ability and . . . money," but the employees of the city engineer's office, heedless of warnings, "entered the oil company field with locations near Pantano." The gambling spirit in Tucson, the *Star* said, "is more rampant than it ever was."[36]

J. F. ("Pop") McKale, long-time university teacher and coach, caught the fever and talked about it to the Pioneer Society on November 14, 1964:

I . . . invested in an oil well in lower Sabino Canyon. Somebody found a little grease on top of the water and I became a millionaire. With two or three other friends who had invested in that oil well, probably to the extent of a hundred dollars, we hired a Packard car from Shad Bowyer, who ran an auto service. It was the only one in town, as I remember. We paid forty dollars to go out there and see our property. It was the most wonderful feeling to know that I was a millionaire. I got over it shortly. Mark Twain said that a mine is a hole in the ground owned by a liar. I'll go for that. I invested in a couple of mines with my savings and went back to Michigan for the summer, feeling wealthy, prosperous and important. When I came back to Tucson in the fall, I agreed with Mark Twain.[37]

The oil fever soon passed. It is not certain that any serious drilling was done. If there was, it was unproductive. Poorer but, one hopes, wiser, the citizens went back to their

211

Monte Mansfield, "Mr. Tucson" in the Gold-plated Decade.

former enthusiasms and spent their cash on less visionary projects.

Their great obsession was with automobiles. In February, 1920, Arizona was reported to be ninth in the nation in per capita ownership of cars. The annual auto show drew huge crowds, and the newspapers portrayed the newest models—Marmons, Kissels, Hupmobiles, Overlands, Hudsons, Essexes, Nashes—all shining and graceful and desirable. Tucson women were involved. "Ultra snappy new Apperson makes a strong appeal to the sportswomen of Arizona," said one advertisement.[38]

The final focus of all this motorphilia was the annual road race from El Paso to Phoenix, which started at 8:00 A.M. on November 2, 1919, from the Chamber of Com-

merce in El Paso. Forty-three dealers and owners had entered their carefully tuned machines in competition for a purse of $11,300, the winner of which would take 70 percent. The biggest and fastest car was a Pope-Hartford owned and driven by Hugh Miller. The smallest was a Ford belonging to dealer Monte Mansfield, of Tucson, driven by W. J. (Bill) Taber.[39] The Deming road was a dirt track along the railroad in those days. A few miles out, just east of Lanark station, the worst happened. A group of tipsy picnickers were shooting a rifle, and a bullet hit Johnny Hutchings, driving a Buick, in the back, fatally wounding him. Oliver Lee, of Alamogordo, New Mexico, involved in a famous feud situaiton, was riding along as mechanic, and many people in the region thought that the bullet was meant for him. Major William F. Scanland, a patient at the Fort Bliss Base Hospital, was later convicted of the murder and sentenced to a term in prison. While he was free on appeal, he was beaten to death by persons unknown near Arlington, Virginia.[40]

There was more trouble ahead. S. O. Bottorff and Floyd Brown, of El Paso, driving a Haynes Special, got as far as Vail, twenty miles east of Tucson, hit a curve at eighty-seven miles an hour, overturned, and were decapitated.

These accidents dampened but did not destroy the intense interest of everyone along the route. The Tucson police had turned out in force to ensure safe passage through town, where the cars would stop only long enough to take on gasoline and water. R. B. Armstrong, of Fort Worth, driving a Dodge, arrived first and was off in a flash. Close behind was Miller in the Pope-Hartford. Not many minutes later Monte Mansfield's Ford appeared, to the cheers of the crowd. Taber came in, "running like a jackrabbit. Seen down Stone Avenue, all that could plainly be discerned were four wheels and a light cloud of dust. Far above the cheers could be heard the staccato explosions of the little motor. Taber took on gas and left within a minute."

The crowd remained all day in front of the *Citizen's* bulletin board, eager for the latest news, and gave a rousing final cheer when they heard that five cars had finished the race. Miller had reached Phoenix first, Armstrong second, and Taber, in Monte's Ford, third. It had been a good day for Tucson in spite of the unfortunate accidents.[41]

The passion for auto shows and auto races brought on a subsidiary enthusiasm for better roads. Great improvement was obviously needed. A traveler from Tucson to Michigan brought back word that "most of the earth's surface is mud," and even in a dry state like Arizona rough, rocky, unimproved roads were a major problem for motorists. The papers were full of news about road conditions, organizations promoting better highways, and discussions in the state and national legislatures about appropriations for new and stronger linkage between American cities.[42] As early as June, 1920, Congress was talking about improving highways as an aid to military operations, and plans were being made to send out a fleet of army trucks on a transcontinental tour to study the possibilities.[43]

In Arizona the most impressive effort was mounted by the Arizona Highway Association, organized by Phoenix capitalist Dwight B. Heard. Its object was to initiate a proposal (through the initiative provided for in the state constitution) to raise the limit of the bonded indebtedness to provide funds for highway improvement. The procedure was to get enough signatures on a petition to make action by the legislature mandatory

and bring the measure to popular vote. On instructions from Heard and his group, Tucson members F. W. Ronstadt and R. B. von KleinSmid called together members of the Pima County Board of Supervisors, the Tucson Chamber of Commerce, the Community Council, and the Good Roads Association. The proposal was "coldly turned down" by the assembly. The Tucson and Pima County citizens thought that they were being deceived and used to pay for roads that would chiefly benefit Phoenix and Maricopa County. When a similar meeting was held in Maricopa County, the people were unreceptive because they thought that *they* were being deceived and used to pay for roads that would chiefly benefit Tucson and Pima County.[44]

In spite of such setbacks, road building and road propaganda went forward at a steady pace. Enthusiasts were always holding meetings, like the great convention of the United States Good Roads Association at Phoenix in 1922, and never stopped petitioning the legislature for funds. The new road from Douglas to Rodeo, New Mexico (a very small hamlet in the exact middle of nowhere), was hailed as a link in the first transcontinental highway.[45] A news item in June, 1920, was devoted to A. L. Westgard, who had worn out eighteen automobiles in seventeen years as a pathfinder for the American Automobile Association and was currently engaged in mapping a system of highways to connect the national parks.[46]

It would not be correct to assume that every Arizonan was road-minded. Historian Rufus K. Wyllys points out that "in 1929 Arizona had no more than a mere 281 miles of hard-surfaced highways. That fact was something of an indication of the bitter opposition which old-timers among the taxpayers had theretofore shown toward highway construction."[47] In Tucson, however, civic leaders were aware from the early twenties that climate was what they had to sell, that tourists and winter visitors offered an important solution to their problems, that automobiles would bring the tourists, and that roads would bring the automobiles. They knew which side their bread was buttered on: the road side. In the summer of 1920 they were looking for a way to finance an "auto camp ground."[48] In August they were ready to launch "a big program of building for the tourist trade."[49] It was not until the fall of 1922, however, that the big push for visitors began with the organization of the Tucson Sunshine Climate Club.

This extraordinarily successful enterprise, conceived and financed by Tucsonans, helped fix the direction of future development in the desert community. Every year a campaign was mounted to raise funds. The goal was $75,000 in 1924. It was a more realistic $35,000 in 1931. The money was spent on advertising in metropolitan newspapers and in national magazines and on an attractive illustrated booklet touting Tucson's climate and scenic attractions. In 1924 the club was seeking permission to reprint Harold Bell Wright's *Why I Did Not Die*—an account of his recovery from tuberculosis, thanks to the city's clean air and continuous sunshine—as a feature of the brochure. In the two years since its founding, the directors noted, the club's advertising had been worth $2 million to Tucson. New arrivals in 1924 had averaged more than two a day, at a cost of $19.12 per arrival.[50] On just one day, October 18, 1923, seventeen winter visitors had arrived.[51]. Manager William H. McGovern was tireless in getting out the message and making sure that those who heard it were given proper attention. Newcomers were met on arrival, if at all possible, and

helped to find lodgings and any comforts they needed. According to the club's figures for the fiscal year 1936–37, its advertising program had brought in 18,325 inquiries, which generated 19,000 replies. Visitors arriving after March, 1936, bought property valued at $937,000. And so on.[52]

Not one single person in those days questioned the wisdom of attracting new residents—at least not one single member of the Tucson Chamber of Commerce. Old residents have always liked the town as it was when they came and have hated to see it grow—a feeling probably shared by the Piman farmers living in the valley in 1754 when the first Spaniard (Father Middendorff) tried to make Tucson his permanent home. The managers and directors, however, have always wanted growth and expansion, and they will no doubt continue to do so until the water fails and the country goes back to the desert from which it came.

It should be noted that the motorcar brought more than tourists to Tucson. It also brought problems. More cars meant more traffic. One day, before the rush started, Yndia Smalley drove her new Ford through town, and as she reached the intersection of Stone and Congress, she passed the friendly policeman on duty there and remarked, as she drifted by, that she did not know how to stop. The officer left his post, ran to catch up, and told her how it was done.[53] In 1920 the police were ticketing citizens for speeding. In May, Dr. von KleinSmid was among the victims and had to pay a ten-dollar fine.[54] By August, 1921, drunk drivers were becoming a menace.[55] Such things were part of the price that had to be paid for increased population and prosperity.

An even more pressing problem caused by the rising tide of tourists was the need for more and better accommodations. Boardinghouses and modest hotels took care of people of moderate means, and in the twenties there were still some tent colonies for tuberculars, but people with money demanded first-class quarters, and if Tucson wanted their dollars, Tucson had to give them what they wanted. The answer was El Conquistador Hotel, bigger and finer than anything Tucson had seen before or has seen since.

At the time the Tucson Sunshine Climate Club was being born, the movers and shakers were talking about a luxury hotel, but it was not until March, 1925, that they took action.[56] At that time the Chamber of Commerce hired the Hockenbury System of San Francisco to make a survey and present recommendations. Within ten days the recommendations were ready: build a first-class hotel, with cottages attached, on the outskirts of the city. Since this was what the members already had in mind, they approved the report and organized a stock company to raise money. An executive committee, with General Manning at the head, set out to sell $300,000 worth of shares. Half the issue was picked up the day it was offered, and within a short time it was oversubscribed by $40,000. Jubilant, the committee organized itself into the Tucson Tourist Hotel Company, celebrated with a sumptuous banquet at the Santa Rita, and set about choosing a site. Half a dozen tracts were offered, but the one chosen was far out in the desert, on Broadway just east of Country Club. Ben B. Matthews and Mr. and Mrs. J. M. Roberts donated 120 acres. The tract was outside the range of the city water system, and in July preparations were made to sink a well. In the meantime the public was invited to submit suggestions for a name—a contest which Ralph Ellinwood,

editor of the *Star*, won with the stately title El Conquistador. Henry Jaastad, Norwegian-born and later a perennial mayor of Tucson, was selected as the architect, and by the end of September he had submitted sketches for the main building. Drawings for the cottages, garage, and outbuildings were to come later. The style was "Arizona Mission," with reminiscences of California and Spanish Mexico. The main building was as large and magnificent as a European monastery—280 feet across the front—and was surmounted by a sixty-five-foot bell tower with copper dome. There would be forty-six guest rooms. Eight of them were on the ground floor, along with a solarium, a tea terrace, a curio shop, a dining room, a kitchen, a lobby, storerooms, and a servants' dormitory. Suites would have tiled baths and sunporches. In front a palm-lined driveway would sweep past a great lawn. In the rear another lawn would surround a swimming pool. A thousand flowering plants, including a rose garden with 350 varieties, would feast the eye with greenery and blossoms. There would be horses at the hotel stables and golf at the Tucson Golf and Country Club a few blocks west or at the new municipal course west of Alvernon, in what became Reid Park.

Unfortunately the great hostelry cost more money than the builders had planned, and in spite of its dimensions it contained too few rooms to meet expenses. In fact, the funds were all gone before it was completed. In 1928 it was sold to United Hotels Company. President Frank Dudley hired Tucson builder John Murphey to complete the project, and the grand opening was held on November 22, 1928.[57] The hotel and grounds were beautiful, and they attracted some famous guests, but El Conquistador never paid its way. In 1935 the hotel com-

The magnificent El Conquistador before the city surrounded it.

Mrs. Isabella Greenway's Arizona Inn. Buehman photo.

Congresswoman Greenway.

pany, in the grip of the Depression, petitioned for bankruptcy, stating that it owed almost $125,000 in interest, taxes, and deficits. A court-approved reorganization was undertaken three months later. There were more changes in ownership in 1951 and 1957, but the most ominous development occurred in 1959, when ground was broken east of the hotel for a shopping center. Levy's and Montgomery Ward built the first stores in the El Con complex, and they were so successful that there was no hope of preserving the great old hotel. In 1968 the wreckers moved in, and El Conquistador became a fond Tucson memory. All that remains at the site is the ornamental water tower, but relics are scattered about the city—for example, the copper dome of the central tower, now ornamenting a commercial structure in the Casa Blanca Shopping Center, on North Oracle.[58]

If El Conquistador had a successor, it was the Arizona Inn, built in 1931 just north of Speedway and east of Campbell by Mrs. Isabella Greenway, who gained distinction as the first and only congresswoman from Arizona. It was smaller than El Conquistador

but better conceived and was a success from the start. Its quiet elegance attracted a long succession of well-to-do easterners and celebrities in search of a little peace and quiet.

Then there was Christopher Square, occupying a block on East Mabel near the university. Built in 1937, it was furnished and maintained by Mrs. Helen d'Autremont as a home away from home for superior people who found the Arizona Inn just out of reach. Helen and her banker husband, Hubert, were superior people themselves, leaders in all good Tucson causes. Christopher Square, unobtrusively refined, was one of their most interesting enterprises.[59]

So much had changed by 1968! Once far out in the desert, the El Con area was surrounded by housing subdivisions and commercial plazas. On the west, north of Broadway, were the fine homes of El Encanto. Colonia Solana grew up nearby, and east of Alvernon, across from Randolph Park, San Clemente's luxurious mansions arose. The city had made room for thousands of newcomers.

A new development of special interest was the Old World Addition, lining both sides of Campbell Avenue between Mabel Street and Elm. Swiss-born architect Josias Joesler and John Murphey, a local product, functioned as designer and builder. John's wife, Helen, a converted easterner, made the firm a triumvirate. The Murpheys had already acquired 1,700 acres in the foothills north of town and were beginning to develop what was to be the city's most prestigious residential area. They needed an architect, and Joesler was imported from California, where he and his Spanish wife were pausing on a leisurely world tour. His plans added a wide variety of European designs to Tucson's adobe background and contributed a special flavor which persisted

Saint Philip's-in-the-Hills, triumph of architect Josias Joesler and builder John Murphey. J. Robert Burns photo.

Broadway Village, Tucson's first shopping center, January, 1940.

until the widening of Campbell Avenue in the late 1970s removed a number of his little architectural triumphs.

Among the Joesler-Murphey master-pieces were Saint Philip's-in-the-Hills, an exceptionally beautiful Episcopal church, and Broadway Village, Arizona's first shopping center. The Murpheys owned ten lots along Broadway west of Country Club but had no plans for developing them until a visit to the quaint, beautiful town of Pátzcuaro, in central Mexico, gave them an idea. They decided to re-create the town, with modern improvements, at Broadway and Country Club.

Insurmountable obstacles at once blocked the way. The land was at the doors of the El Encanto development, where many of Tucson's first families were buying sumptuous homes. The builder was indignant at the thought of a commercial block in the middle of his exclusive area, threatened to "sue hell out of" the Murpheys if they persisted in their plans, and stirred up the whole neighborhood against them. John and Helen went ahead with their ideas, however, and Joesler made Broadway Village a thing of beauty. For a while the residents of El Encanto boycotted the enterprise, but eventually they decided to be proud of it too, and its *portales* and greenery were still charming visitors in the 1980s, forty-odd years after it opened in 1939.[60]

Tucson's downtown was still growing in the 1920s, along with the outskirts. Two architectural achievements of the period, in the heart of the business district, were the Consolidated National Bank and the Pioneer Hotel. The bank, erected in 1929 at Stone and Congress by eastern financier T. N. McCauley, was a "skyscraper" ten stories high. Harold Steinfeld opened his hotel at Stone and Pennington with much fanfare

The Pioneer Hotel and the Consolidated National Bank, Tucson's first skyscrapers.

on December 12 of the same year. The Pioneer was twelve stories high. With two such structures in the center of town Tucson at last had a skyline.

The Depression brought problems to hotel owners, as it did to everyone else, and Steinfeld had to ask for a reorganization after a mortgage foreclosure in 1932, but after that things went better, and the Pioneer remained a focal point for Tucson social life and a magnet for visitors until December 20, 1970, when an incendiary fire destroyed the upper floors and took the lives of Steinfeld and his wife.[61]

Transportation and communication were behind all this dramatic growth. The railroad began it; the automobile and the good-roads movement gave it new impetus; the airplane added a third chapter to the story.

Charles A. Lindbergh meets the Tucson ladies, September 23, 1927. Buehman photo.

Tucsonans were airplane-conscious from the beginning. Ownership was out of reach of the average citizen, but interest was always there. Barnstormers and aerial circuses using surplus World War I machines provided thrills far more sophisticated than the "spectacular maneuvers" the open-mouthed throngs had enjoyed when Charles K. Hamilton took off from Drachman's Elysian Grove in 1910. Macauley Field, which became an official landing field for army airplanes on May 9, 1919, was in constant use by military and civilian fliers, as was the larger facility south of town on the Nogales Highway, in service on November 19 of that same year. It was still Tucson's airport on September 22, 1924, when the "Round-the-World" fliers taxied their four planes up the dirt runway while 12,000 "screaming spectators" watched. The next day the four ships took off on the last lap of their long journey.

In 1925 negotiations got under way for the acquisition of the land which eventually became Davis-Monthan Field, the largest municipally owned airport in the United States. It was named for two Tucson boys who had joined the air force in World War I, continued in the service after the war, and lost their lives flying in the line of duty. It was dedicated on September 23, 1927, by none other than Charles A. Lindbergh, touring the United States in his *Spirit of St. Louis* after his transatlantic flight.[62]

The country had not seen anyone like Lindbergh before, and there was statewide excitement when the date of his arrival was announced. Special trains arrived, bringing groups from Phoenix, Nogales, Douglas, and probably from the remotest mining camps. Schools and municipal offices were closed, and a wave of humanity had crested at the airport before two o'clock in the afternoon, the time of arrival. Lindbergh was on time. He circled the field several times, made a flawless landing, and taxied his plane into the hangar, where the reception committee was waiting. The ceremonies over, he began the long motor ride to the old veterans' hospital facility at Pastime Park, where a group of eager patients was waiting to see him. He spent the night at the Old Pueblo Club after the inevitable banquet and was up and away the next morning, leaving enormous thrills in the hearts of innumerable Tucsonans, old and young.[63] He also left the "Lindy Beacon," a revolving light which the city had contributed. Mayor John E. White's last official act was the installation of this aid to aviation at Davis-Monthan. Much mourned, White died the following March. The beacon was later moved to Ryan Field, on the Ajo road, where it was in use for more than half a century.[64]

Mayor White's obituary noted that "his administration saw Tucson's population almost double" and that he had left his town "one of the most financially sound cities in the country." The airplane had helped in both departments. Standard Airlines (the predecessor of American Airlines) began regularly scheduled flights through Tucson in 1928. Airmail service began in 1930. Charley Mayse, a great barnstormer and teacher, set up the Mayse Flying School in 1927 at the old airport. The army air corps made such frequent use of Davis-Monthan that there was less and less room for civilian carriers. By 1947 it was obvious that Tucson would have to provide itself with a new municipal air facility, and the present airport was acquired and opened in 1948.[65] Each step added to Tucson's growing wealth and prestige.

An adjunct of all this growth and activity in the 1920s, and for many years an important one, was the dude-ranch industry, which came to Arizona in the twenties, flourished through the thirties in spite of the Depression, and continued to prosper into

the sixties. The first identifiable guest ranch was started in North Dakota by Howard Eaton and his three brothers, easterners from Pittsburgh, in 1882, but the craze did not really develop in the southwestern states until after World War I. Before the twenties were over, however, Tucson had become the most important dude-ranch center in the United States. "Phoenix and Tucson," writes historian Bernard L. Rodnitzky, "catered to winter guests and became major dude-ranch centers," but Tucson was far in the lead. A leaflet issued by the Valley National Bank in 1945 listed sixteen guest ranches near Tucson, while Phoenix could muster only seven, along with a few more which were obviously winter resorts with no ranch atmosphere. The Dude Ranchers Association, founded in 1924, insisted that all members be operators of working cattle ranches, but in many cases the cowboys were primarily dude wranglers, and the cows were sometimes imported solely for atmosphere, according to Rodnitzky:

Desert Arizona and California raised dude ranching to its most sophisticated level, and added greatly to the confusion regarding its nature. Here, newly built ranches named for the old cattle brands simulated modern country clubs. Elegant living quarters were supplemented by tennis courts, polo fields, sun decks, and dance floors. These "ranches" usually had a herd of horses sufficient only for the guests, and if they had cattle, it was necessary to import food for the animals.[66]

Spreads which started out as bona fide cattle operations changed as the years passed. The Flying V, in the Catalina foothills just west of Sabino Canyon, had a long history before Lynn and Patsy Gillham built a few guest cottages in their own canyon and started entertaining easterners for money. Before long they were advertising "polo,

Flying V guest ranch.

horseback riding, tennis, and many other outdoor activities." The Tanque Verde Ranch, once owned by the Carrillo family, with a history that ran back to Indian and outlaw times, went the same road. Nancy Sortore reported in 1971 that at Howard Miller's Wild Horse Ranch the guests were required to dress for dinner. "I can't stand eating with people who smell of horse," the proprietor explained.[67]

There were other ranches in the foothills—the Harding Guest Ranch, the Rancho Las Moras, the Desert Willows—and several below the foothills inside today's city limits. Rancho Palmilles offered horses but no cows on acreage owned by Mrs. J. P. Martin ten miles east of town and south of Speedway. Vista al Norte Ranchito was in business five miles northwest of town. Rancho Fiesta was only eight miles east of downtown, on Wilmot Road just south of Broadway—open country in those days. In widening circles farther from the Tucson center a score of these havens advertised their attractions—

climate, scenery, entertainment, relaxation close to nature. Three of them were located in the neighborhood of Oracle, at the north end of the Catalinas. Others were in business farther away: La Osa at Sasabe; the Circle Z near Patagonia; the Triangle T in Texas Canyon, east of Benson; the Y Lightning near Hereford; and the Double Y north of Willcox. These and many more flourished, even during the Depression, and gave a taste of both the real and the imaginary West to countless eager tenderfeet.[68]

The dude ranch was a unique and useful institution. It even promoted the spirit of democracy. It was the only such arrangement, in the words of observant western writer Hal G. Evarts, in which "the guests deliberately sought the servants' quarters for recreation"[69] and where the equality visualized by the founding fathers of the country came close to being a reality. It is hardly necessary to add that dude ranching as a business added strength to the economy of Arizona in general and Tucson in particular.

A sort of spinoff from the guest-ranch business was the ranch school, in which the sons of well-to-do easterners studied hard, lived as close to nature as possible, and learned firsthand about the West. The best known was the Evans School, started at Mesa in 1902 by H. David Evans, an Englishman with advanced ideas about education. In 1921 he moved part of the enterprise to a new location near the Tanque Verde Ranch, east of Tucson.[70] In 1939 ten such schools were flourishing in and around Tucson, and more were added during the next decade. Some, like the Evans School, put every boy on a horse. Others, like the Arizona Sunshine School, on Craycroft Road, offered only the outdoors in classes which were conducted under ramadas, or brush shelters. The Hacienda del Sol was a school for girls in the Tucson foothills. There was even a school for Jewish boys—the Desert Ranch School of Arizona—which offered its students "a refined home."[71]

The dude ranches and the ranch schools had their day, but that day ended in the sixties. "Today," wrote J. C. Martin in 1976, "fewer than 30 of the ranches remain in southern Arizona and many of them resemble westernized motels, more than dude ranches. Tennis and swimming have replaced the trail ride."[72]

The quality of life in Tucson during the gold-plated decade, it must be admitted, did not depend solely on mechanical devices and immigrants. The arts can hardly be said to have kept pace with the automobile, but they were developing too. Mrs. Heineman-Berger and her company of music supporters built the Temple of Music and Art, as has been noted, and created a flourishing musical life far from the great centers of culture. It seems, moreover, that one good musical organization leads to another—a principle which accounts for the birth of the Tucson Symphony Orchestra in the summer of 1928. The founder was an Italian-born Tucson lawyer, musician, and music enthusiast named Harry O. Juliani. Feeling that the time was ripe, he assembled in his offices a number of the city's leading performers, proposed that they form a symphonic organization, and received an enthusiastic response. Fifty men and women turned out for the first rehearsal. All of them were amateurs, eager to play for the pleasure of playing. They offered the conductorship to Camil Van Hulse, a young pianist, organist, and composer then living in Tucson.

Van Hulse was a member of a musical Belgian family who had been gassed fighting against the Germans in World War I and had drifted to the Southwest in search of health. Slender, handsome, with intense eyes and a bushy mustache, he was a musician's musician, already winning prizes for composition, who never compromised when an artistic principle was involved. The new group rejoiced when this true professional accepted their offer, and the organization got under way with Harry Juliani as manager. The first concert was presented on January 13, 1929, in the high-school auditorium. Van Hulse conducted one more concert and then went back to Europe for a few years. On his return he thought it best not to accept a reappointment, but he continued to live and work in Tucson, "a delightful gentleman with a razor-sharp mind," as an interviewer described him in 1975, occupying an apartment on North Euclid Avenue with a black grand piano as his sole companion. He played the organ in several Catholic churches until 1956, when he retired to spend the rest of his life composing. His choral works became known throughout the country, but he was at home in more

Camil Van Hulse. Courtesy Tucson Festival Society.

Harry O. Juliani.

ambitious forms. The Tucson Symphony Orchestra played a movement from his great *Sinfonia Maya* in 1978 and presented the whole work on April 30 and May 1, 1981, in a performance described by one reviewer as a "triumph."[73]

Since 1928 there has always been a symphony orchestra in Tucson. It changed identity after the first ten years, however, when economic pressures forced a merger with a new symphonic group then being formed at the university. As the city grew, many new ensembles were created—a chamber music society, a youth symphony, the internationally famous Boys Choir, founded in 1939, and many more. The Old Pueblo has done well musically.

The pictorial arts lacked a leader like Mrs. Heineman-Berger or Harry Juliani to escort them into the Promised Land, but the dec-

ade was a time of beginnings for them too. A Fine Arts Association was organized in 1924 with impressive local support, and by October 21, 1927, when the Temple of Music and Art was dedicated, the association was ready to take a major part in the ceremonies. The second floor of the temple was designed to be an art salon, and the second event of the dedicatory week was the formal opening of this part of the whole. The Bentley Collection, lent by a well-known Boston collector, was on display, and a "brilliant assemblage" gathered for the occasion.[74] The association continued in existence with the inevitable ups and downs, gathering strength as time went on. In 1949 the headquarters was moved to the basement of the Chamber of Commerce building at 80 South Stone. In 1955 it moved again, this time to the house once occupied by lawyer and water-

The Tucson Symphony Orchestra, 1941. Buehman photo.

color artist Samuel Kingan at 325 West Franklin, where the Tucson Arts Center was incorporated. In 1970 a $500,000 gift launched a campaign to build and endow a new museum and arts center, and the Historic Block, where Sam Hughes, H. S. Stevens, and other pioneers had lived, was approved as a site. The Fish-Stevens house and the Cordova house were integrated into a museum complex, and a library was added at 119 North Main. The center was officially opened on May 4, 1975, offering an unusual combination of the old and the new in architecture and function.[75]

The verbal arts, it must be admitted, lagged behind the pictorial and musical forms in the Golden Decade, but one group—the Scribblers Club—struggled valiantly to provide an encouraging atmosphere for writers. The membership included poets, novelists, short-story writers and a few university people, Frank C. Lockwood and Melvin Solve, of the English Department, among them. Lockwood began gathering pioneer history when he arrived in 1916 and produced an important series of books. Here and there in the community other literary lights were beginning to burn.

Tucson Museum of Art. The restored Fish and Stevens houses are at the left. David Burckhalter photo. Courtesy Glenda Bonin and Tucson Museum of Art.

Coach James Fred ("Pop") McKale (center) and surviving members of the 1913 University of Arizona football team, November 2, 1963. From left: Jay MacIntosh, captain; Orville S. ("Speedy") McPherson; McKale; Albert Condron; Turner Smith.

Richard Summers graduated from the university in 1925, joined the faculty in 1928, and pursued a vigorous career as a writer and teacher. His *Dark Madonna* (1947) was an early example of the novel of Chicano life in the Southwest.[76]

Tucson had cause to be grateful to a great variety of men and women who widened her horizons in the 1920s. There was hardly any aspect of life in which important changes were not being made. In the twenties, for example, the university began offering sports enthusiasts some local teams to boast about. With the arrival of James Fred ("Pop") McKale in 1914 university athletic teams began playing other universities and winning games. In 1922, James H. ("Jumbo") Pierce took over the basketball team with considerable success, and in 1925, Fred August Enke arrived from Notre Dame to coach basketball and football and began making history without even a gymnasium to work in. His teams became a power in the land and objects of passionate interest to Tucson sports fans.[77]

No newcomers, however, had more far-reaching effects on the community than two young journalists, Ralph E. Ellinwood and William R. Mathews, who took over the *Daily Star* in 1924. Ralph was the son of E. E. Ellinwood, a prominent and prosperous Phelps Dodge attorney. He spent time in a German prison camp in World War I; graduated from the Columbia School of Journalism; married a remarkable woman named Clare Rounsevell, of New York City; and went to work as night telegraph editor for the *Sacramento Union*. When the *Star* was offered for sale, the senior Ellinwood resolved to make Ralph the editor—if he could find a competent business manager. The right man came along in the person of W. R. Mathews, then business manager of the *Santa Barbara Morning Press*—a young man who knew the worth of a dollar, paid his bills promptly, and was able to double the circulation of his paper in three years. Each man borrowed money—enough to buy the *Star*—and on November 1, 1924, they informed the world of their proprietorship and policies. Their newspaper, as *Star* historian David F. Brinegar reports, would be "constantly devoted to the interests of Tucson and of Arizona" and would uphold the principles of Jeffersonian democracy. More than that, as time went on, they showed themselves willing to fight for principle. They attacked "demagoguery, racism and hypocrisy—naming names and risking reprisals—and fought hard and successfully to preserve the integrity of the University of Arizona." Under Ellinwood's careful eye the paper improved in editing and writing, in makeup and news coverage. He gave the tubercular shut-ins their "Happy Days" column and defied the administrators of a Texas high school who threatened to cancel a football game with a Tucson school if a black player was allowed on the field.

Mathews was beside him and behind him all the way, though no two men could have been more different in temperament. Mathews was quick-tempered and given to bursts of volcanic wrath. Ellinwood was quiet and polite, helpful and kind. Both were high principled, hardworking, and honest. They made a good team until Ellinwood's untimely death in 1930 of a heart attack. Clare Ellinwood, intelligent and competent, took his place as copublisher, but Mathews moved over to the editorial chair and became something of a journalistic legend before he died in 1969.[78]

In one final way Tucson moved forward at the end of the twenties. After two previous unsuccessful tries the citizens laid to rest the

These men brought the Arizona Daily Star *through the Great Depression. Top left: William R. Mathews, editor; top right: Ralph E. Ellinwood, editor; bottom left: George W. Chambers, business manager; bottom right: David F. Brinegar, reporter, executive editor.*

228

forty-five-year-old city charter, long out-grown, and on May 26, 1929, adopted a new one which became effective in January, 1931. It was the result of two years' work by a twenty-four-member board comprising a cross section of Tucson's citizens, chosen by the electorate. It provided for a city manager, an eight-hour day for city employees, a pension fund, and civil-service tenure for certain categories. It was criticized for electing councilmen "at large," though nominations were made by wards. Mexican-Americans saw a possibility that under this arrangement they might be disfranchised by the Anglo majority. All agreed, however, that the charter was a long step forward, and Tucson entered the thirties a more orderly and better-governed place than it had been in 1920, in spite of the bootleggers and speeders.

It was a good place to live and a good place to grow up, the sizzling summers notwithstanding. The city limits were moving out, but it was still a town with a center, located approximately at the intersection of Stone and Congress. On the northeast corner was T. Ed Litt's drugstore, where a soda fountain attracted the young people of high-school age. Next door was Jimmy Rand's Smoke Shop, with a poker table upstairs and a daily betting pool during the baseball season. A somewhat older crowd hung out there. The college group frequented the Varsity Shop, between Congress and Pennington on Stone Avenue. It was the pride of Julius ("Dooley") Bookman, with pool tables in the rear and cigars, sodas, and sandwiches in front. Bookman was one of the great Tucson characters, a little, lively, friendly man with a smile that would not come off. He came to Tucson as a drummer in a theater orchestra and was good enough to handle the tympani at symphony con-

The beloved Dooley Bookman.

certs, but his real love was for band music, and at times he fielded a band of his own. His shop was the other half of his life. He did not encourage saloon and pool-hall hangers-on, and the college students were at home with him. The theaters were all in the same general neighborhood, and there were other attractions within reach. The Blue Moon Dance Hall, on the corner of Stone and Drachman, was one. Farther out on the Oracle–Florence road was the Wetmore Ranch, a favorite spot for picnics and swimming.[79] But Dooley's was home.

Almost everybody enjoyed a good life in a prosperous and hopeful community. The great financial crash in 1929 was ominous, but it seemed to be happening a long way from Tucson's little world, and in fact it took months for the full effect to be felt. When it did come, hard times were back again, and the next decade was, to say the least, trying.

CHAPTER 13

Hard Times in Tucson

On Black Wednesday, October 24, 1929, the New York Stock Market crashed, and the worst times the nation had ever faced were under way. Tucson citizens shared the general anxiety as they followed events in the newspapers, but at first few of them were deeply involved. They were "in the stock market," like everybody else, and some may have been cleaned out as a result of speculation, but the gloomy presence, familiar in the East, of former capitalists selling apples on street corners was not part of the Tucson experience.[1] As the weeks and months went by, newspapers all across the land were full of alarming stories—steel production at 12 percent of capacity; 13 million unemployed; millions on relief; a quarter of a million families deprived of their homes through mortgage foreclosures; thousands of men wandering about in search of nonexistent jobs.[2] Yet for months life went on in the Old Pueblo pretty much as usual. When the hard times did arrive, the civic leaders showed themselves courageous, resourceful, and, above all, compassionate. No city in the nation handled the Depression better.

In the early weeks of 1930, Pima County, by now the home of 32,000 people (12,000 more than in 1920),[3] was still preoccupied with the tempests in its own teapot. There was a problem, for example, involving the new city manager, Tucson's first. The mayor and city council picked George A. Wade, of Brawley, California, who had been interviewed but had not formally applied. When this obstacle had been removed and Wade had accepted, it was discovered that he was ineligible for the job. The incumbent was required to be a "qualified elector." That barrier was surmounted when C. E. Pequignot, the city auditor, accepted the job at a salary of a dollar a month, and Wade moved in as his assistant on a pay scale of $7,500 a year.[4] No one objected to this transparent subterfuge.

Another news item in January told of a campaign to oil the county roads and eliminate, or at least reduce, the ever-present plague of desert dust. Novelist Harold Bell Wright, whose estate was far from town, where Speedway ended at Wilmot, was a leader in the movement. He and his neighbor C. A. Belin offered to invest $2,000 in an oil treatment for Wilmot between Broadway and Speedway if the city and county would take care of those two avenues.[5]

Looking west on Congress Street downtown in 1887.

Looking west on Congress in 1940.

The university was forging ahead, proud of its new stadium, built the year before, and of its newly approved music school, directed by Dean Charles Fletcher Rogers.[6] In February the Sixth Annual Rodeo opened with a big parade and drew a record crowd to the fairgrounds.[7] In March a price war among milk producers dropped the rate to fourteen cents a bottle. The Greater Tucson Airport was completed at Davis-Monthan Field in June, and in July the city took positive action in breaching the barrier of the railroad tracks which separated downtown from the developing residential districts on the east, northeast, and southeast by accepting plans for a system of subways or underpasses. The old Fourth Avenue Subway, built in 1916, had long been inadequate to handle the traffic, and the voters, after months of civic infighting, had passed a $400,000 bond issue in 1929. Plans and specifications for the Broadway underpass were approved on July 6 of the following year, and in November the Sixth Avenue Subway was officially opened for traffic. Tucson was still enjoying peace, progress and prosperity.[8]

Building had not yet slowed down. John W. Murphey, builder of 400 homes in eleven years, was as busy as ever. A $280,000 addition to the Veterans Hospital had been announced, and the Hacienda del Sol, a first-class school for girls, opened in the foothills north of town. Mansfeld Junior High was completed in July, and the Carrillo School, on the south side, was opened in September.[9] Before Christmas, Tucson businessmen were anticipating "the perennial harvest" of tourists, happy in the thought that every visiting automobile brought 3.2 passengers and that every passenger spent five dollars a day in Tucson.[10] All seemed serene and progressive on the Santa Cruz.

Along with these cheerful indicators, however, many signs of coming trouble were evident. The "secondary postwar depression" was developing in the summer and fall of 1930 as cotton and copper prices dropped, the national income fell, and a severe drought cut crop production in the South and in the Middle West. Tax collections declined sharply in Arizona, and all state institutions began feeling the pressure. University President Homer L. Shantz had to give up his cherished building program and settle for an appropriation which would do little more than keep the school alive.[11] Banks began to fail here and there about the country, and in December the New York–based Bank of the United States, with sixty branches, closed its doors. A creeping paralysis gripped the economy.

By late 1930 the infection had spread to southern Arizona. The eighth robbery in ten days occurred in Tucson on December 18, and the following day bandits held up a poker game in a private house in Ajo and escaped with $500.[12] The trickle of jobless transients was becoming a steady stream. Dr. Gay M. Brunson, of 125 East Speedway, was impressed by the number of men who asked for food at his back door—good men down on their luck, not bums or hoboes— and pointed out the need for a "large and spacious 'Flop House' for the endless string of unemployed drifting into town." A surprising number of women in men's clothes turned up among the hoboes.[13]

Suffering was not limited to the drifters. More and more Tucson men were out of work, needing help, and every responsible citizen was worried about it. On December 18 an unemployment bureau was established by the Republican Women's Club, with the cooperation of the city and several other organizations, with the object of reg-

Homer L. Shantz, president of the University of Arizona, who guided his institution through difficult times. Courtesy Special Collections, University of Arizona.

istering the jobless and finding out exactly what the situation was. A desk was set up in the Chamber of Commerce Building, and 1,100 men registered. Out-of-work carpenters and truck drivers were the most numerous among them.[14]

The next step was to find something—anything—for these people to do. Dr. John W. Flinn, chairman of the State Unemployment Commission, urged every citizen to provide a job, "at least for a few days during the holidays," for somebody in need,[15] and Isabella Greenway, whose Arizona Inn had just opened, reminded the members of the Rotary Club that "this is a good time to have the fence painted and a new roof put on the garage—if you have the money."[16]

Everybody felt that Christmas was no time for anyone to go hungry. The charitable agencies sent out an SOS on December 24. Harry White, confined to his bed in the Veterans Hospital, conducted a rousing campaign to raise money for Christmas baskets for the poor and managed to provide for 125 people. The Big Brothers Club of the Lions Club took to the streets selling newspapers, provided free by the *Citizen*, and raised $668. It was estimated that a tenth of the population had help of one kind or another in making it to the end of the year.[17]

It was not such a bad Christmas after all, thanks to Tucson's civic spirit, and the urge to help was still present after the holiday. On December 31 county officials and the United States Forest Service got together and set up a road project which would employ forty men. It was only a drop in a big bucket, of course, and on January 16, probably stimulated by the registration program of the previous month, 150 jobless, hungry men stormed City Hall when it opened in the morning. They demanded that something be done for them, and there could have been

trouble, but Street Commissioner F. W. Percy, in a moment of illumination, got out a sheaf of registration blanks and asked the men to fill them out. That seemed to satisfy them, and they dispersed peacefully after turning in their paperwork.[18]

Meanwhile President Herbert Hoover was doing what he could to alleviate the sickness that was enveloping the country. In the fall of 1931 he established the National Credit Corporation (which later became the Reconstruction Finance Corporation) to ease the strain on weak banks and signed a measure creating a $116 million fund for "new jobs on federal improvements."[19] The ideas were constructive, but they were only pebbles tossed into a raging torrent. Europe was approaching collapse, and the United States existed in a climate of fear. The stock market was still crippled; the American banking system was seriously ill. "From the beginning of 1930 to the end of 1932," says economic historian Dixon Wechter, "a total of 773 national banks involving deposits of more than seven hundred million dollars had failed, along with 3604 state banks . . . with deposits exceeding two billion."[20]

To many people it seemed that the only way to keep one's money safe was to take it home and hide it, and so much was withdrawn from circulation that several southern cities began printing their own currency. Estimates of the amount hoarded ran as high as $1,212 billion.[21]

Arizona banks, with many uncollectable loans outstanding and much of their cash in hoarders' hands, were vulnerable. Early in 1930 the weak ones began to fail, among them the Arizona Southwestern in Tucson—new and insecure. The two major Tucson banks were in no danger. Around the state some of the small institutions were saved by merging with larger ones—the First Na-

S. A. High (center) and J. W. Garms, members of Big Brothers, selling papers to Mrs. Mary Jackson, December, 1940.

tional of Prescott, for example, which was taken over by the Valley Bank of Phoenix. New president Walter Bimson was pumping confidence into this beleaguered firm and making a start at reviving the state's financial affairs, though he was finding the eastern bureaucracy hard to deal with.[22] Bimson had to wrestle with Washington at the same time he was contending with fear and desperation in his own state, but he kept moving forward. In 1934 he bought the Consolidated National Bank in Tucson, one of the oldest and largest in Arizona.

The purchase had some odd angles. T. N. McCauley, president of Consolidated, was a less-than-scrupulous promoter of min-

ing stocks who for various reasons wanted to get out of banking. Barney Goodman, of Kansas City, who owned some Tucson real estate, including the Santa Rita Hotel, wanted to get in and acquired controlling interest for a group which he headed. The papers were signed in September, 1934, and immediately Goodman offered to sell to the Valley Bank—at an increased price. The bargaining that went on between these two tough operators was hard and determined. When it was over, Bimson had gained control for $75,000. Through the luck of the draw one block of doubtful stock held by Consolidated took off unexpectedly on Wall Street, and Bimson sold it at a profit of

T. N. McCauley. Buehman photo.

$90,000. In effect he got the Consolidated Bank for nothing.[23]

One of Bimson's conditions when the deal was closed was bad luck for Tucson's first skyscraper. He refused to accept the ninety-nine-year lease, signed in 1927, for the real estate on which it was built. The leaseholders would not cancel, and the bank remained "inactive" for several years.[24]

In spite of Bimson's influence financial difficulties in Arizona went from bad to worse in the early thirties. Sixteen banks failed between April, 1930, and April, 1933. On March 2, 1933, the governor of California closed every bank in his state, and Governor B. B. Moeur, at Bimson's insistence, followed suit, since fiscal institutions in the two states were closely connected. Thirty-nine other states had taken similar action. Many Arizona bankers, however, re-

acted to the closing order with indignation, maintaining that they were sound and had no reason to shut down. A few refused to obey the order, but when President Franklin D. Roosevelt called for a general closing on March 6, they were obliged to get in line.

This was the critical period of the Depression. Very little cash was circulating. The necessities of life were almost unavailable to many. In some places looting and rioting were the result, but not in southern Arizona. "After an initial stunned moment on the morning of March 2," says William H. Jervey, with some exaggeration, "smiles replaced stricken faces" on the streets of Tucson. "Indeed, Tucson took the bank holiday in something of a gay spirit."[25] The town was grimly determined, but hardly gay.

Every businessman in the city had stories to tell about what he went through during this time of quiet desperation, but nobody had better ones than the newspaper editors. Dave Brinegar, who was executive editor of the paper when he retired in 1974, recalls some of them in his manuscript history of the *Star*, spotlighting the activities of Editor William R. Mathews:

There were times when the cash flow was slow and there wasn't enough money to pay the employees. Mathews dug into his own funds so that the payroll could be met.

Desperate measures had to be taken to maintain a cash flow of any substantial nature. Mathews' business manager was George W. Chambers. One day Chambers garnisheed the contents of the cash register of the Grand Central Market, which owed a sizable advertising bill, and found himself looking down the barrel of a pistol held by Rulon Goodman, market operator. Fortunately Goodman didn't pull the trigger.

The operator of a garage went broke owing the *Star* for advertising. His assets didn't cover his debts. Chambers knew that the garageman did a little bootlegging on the side and had a considerable quantity of whiskey on hand. Mathews accepted the whiskey and passed the word down through the *Star* that it could be bought for $4 a gallon—the going price was $6—and John Carmichael, controller, deducted $4 from my next pay check.

"If Mathews had been caught," says Brinegar, "he probably would have gone to McNeil Island Federal Penitentiary. Several prominent Tucsonans did."[26]

The resourcefulness of Mathews and his staff in difficult times was demonstrated when Roosevelt ordered the bank holiday:

While almost every Tucsonan was affected in some manner, and probably every business felt pains, the *Star* did something about it. With Mathews' approval, Chambers quickly devised a "Hoople dollar"—scrip the size and shape of standard currency but with the image of Major Hoople, a funny-page figure, on the front. This scrip was accepted by the *Star* in payment of advertising bills and as a result *Star* advertisers were willing to accept them from any *Star* employee who could draw the scrip or not as he pleased. Since almost every Tucson merchant advertised, or dealt with advertisers, the scrip, though technically illegal, filled a void caused by the closing of banks and hoarding of currency. . . . Carmichael, who handled employee checks and other accounts until his health broke in 1934, told me that the "Hoople dollar" had such wide acceptance that the woman who ran Tucson's best house of prostitution authorized her girls to accept "Hoople dollars."[27]

It should be noted that the *Star* suffered additional difficulties from a disastrous fire on December 18, 1933, and that the staff was scattered about in temporary quarters while the actual production was being done on the printing presses of the *Citizen*. Mathews kept salaries as high as he could and laid off as few people as possible. "He fought for us when we could not fight for ourselves," Brinegar summarizes.

The best fighters during these trying times were the officers and supporters of the Organized Charities of Tucson, spearheaded by a handful of professional workers and assisted by several hundred volunteer citizens who helped with casework, distribution of supplies, mailing, fund raising, and similar chores. The group began functioning in 1915, when the Comstock Hospital needed help, and its activities expanded through the twenties. It coordinated and carried on the charitable activities of Pima County, particularly the Pima County Health Center, and represented such organizations as the Travelers Aid Society, the Community Chest, and the Red Cross. Its aim was to streamline social services, eliminating as far as possible duplication and misdirection of efforts. On the one hand, anybody who really needed help could get it; on the other, those who played the "welfare game," getting contributions from three or four separate agencies, would run into obstacles. The office kept a card index of people who had been helped, and the officers had many interesting stories to tell about their special cases—about Frank Lujan, for example, who came back periodically on his way to see his dying mother in Nogales or El Paso and always asked for aid.[28]

Before the Depression arrived, the problems the Associated Charities faced were pretty well typed. Hard times only made them worse. Probably the most prevalent one was beggars, door-to-door panhandlers, open-air merchants who sold pencils on downtown street corners. In 1927 twenty-seven such cases were investigated, and the men were offered "care" in exchange for work. All but two left town within two hours. Those two left within six.[29]

Another problem was a steady stream of "automobile gypsies" who needed gasoline to continue their travels. Forty families turned up in this situation in 1927. Each was offered a house and a chance to work. "Not one accepted our offer." There was no end to the strange characters who needed a helping hand. In 1929 a man appeared who had been making a living for some years lecturing on "How to Achieve Success."[30] There were so many of them that a proposal was made to revive the chain gang. Actually work on "the woodpile" and on the roads provided a reasonable substitute for it. A vigorous application of the "no-work-no-eat" policy did as much as anything else to cut down on the number of hoboes and "vags."[31]

As the Depression deepened in the early thirties, the load increased enormously, becoming an almost impossible burden on the Associated Charities. Help appeared, however, in the person of Harold Bell Wright, who in 1931 formed an Emergency Relief Committee, mounted a drive for funds, and had $15,000 in the bank in a surprisingly short time. The committee continued its "wonderful work" for several years and was an indispensable part of the relief effort.[32]

Part of the problem was the appearance of new kinds of charity cases. Many Mexican citizens, for example, were working in the United States when unemployment figures began soaring. Pursued by the outcries of jobless Americans who accused them of "taking the bread out of our *white* children's mouths" and unable to find work themselves, they had only one alternative, to go back to Mexico, and this they did by the thousands. Congress had passed the Deportation Act on March 4, 1929, while state legislatures, including Arizona's, called for limiting Mexican immigration and sending the wetbacks home. In 1938, according to a newspaper report, 1,768 aliens were picked up in the Tucson area.[33]

When Mexicans heading for Mexico needed help, Tucson's charities, it appears, rose above political issues and racial prejudice. "The service agency is prepared to facilitate the movement of those who may apply to them for transportation to the border," the directors announced:

L. Roca, honorary Mexican consul in Tucson, has assured the Organized Charities that the Mexican government is willing to receive their citizens who may now be stranded in the United States. . . . Local charitable organizations have been called on frequently to assist some of these in getting to the border from where they have been transported to their old homes.[34]

A different sort of problem involved a group of about 500 Yaqui Indians from Sonora, Mexico, who had settled in two main communities on the outskirts of Tucson, bringing their ceremonials and their lifeways with them. They were poor strangers in a foreign land, but poverty in the United States was better than persecution, danger, and death in Mexico. The men worked for the railroad and for the farmers in the area and kept their families alive, but they did not understand land ownership or citizenship, and life was precarious, especially in the early years, for most of them. Uprisings in Mexico in 1927 and 1929 brought new recruits to Pascua, on the northwest side, and Barrio Libre, on the south. The fugitives who arrived in 1927 had given up their arms to United States Army representatives as they crossed the border, had accepted parole, and had claimed the status of refugees asking for asylum. The Associated Charities were doing what they could to keep them alive, and a spokesman called them "an almost permanent charity problem."

The discovery that these immigrants had an interesting cultural life, centered on their

Tucson Yaquis—the old ways. Dancers at the Pascua ceremonies, July 31, 1965.

Tucson Yaquis—the new ways. Yaqui children at school with Thamar Richey, teacher, and C. E. Rose, superintendent of schools.

elaborate Easter ceremonies, was some years in the future. In 1936 anthropologist Edward H. Spicer and his wife spent a year at Pascua immersing themselves in Yaqui ways and traditions, opening the door for later professional and amateur enthusiasts, but in 1931 nobody knew or cared much about the Yaquis, and their ceremonials were described as "wild and eerie." Interest was growing, however, and several hundred Tucsonans went to watch in 1932. The visitors, of course, did nothing to put food in the mouths of the Yaquis, and food was badly needed.

A possible solution seemed to be in the making in 1931, when a Sonora Yaqui named Guadalupe Flores moved to Pascua, assumed the title Captain General, or Chief, and began agitating for the return of all Yaquis to their homeland to support the freedom fighters there. Speaking, he said, for all the Yaquis in their four major colonies (two near Phoenix and two at Tucson), he announced that they wanted to go home and would do so if the Mexican government would grant them amnesty.

This was welcome news to the Anglos in Tucson. Washington was the place to start negotiations, and Congressman Lewis Douglas joined forces with Senator Carl Hayden to pursue the matter with representatives of the Mexican government. Before anything could be done, however, another Yaqui voice was raised. It belonged to Cayetano López, of Guadalupe Village near Scottsdale, who said that *he* was the chief of all the Yaquis and that his people did not want to go back to Mexico at all. The Mexicans treated them like dogs, he said, and hanged them for small cause. They were better off in Arizona and wanted to stay. There was a good deal of fuss about who was in charge and who was not, and at one point

there was talk of deporting the whole group, about a thousand in all in the four communities, because they could not agree on a leader. Only the more violent ones, including Guadalupe Flores, were sent back, however. The rest stayed in Arizona, clinging to their old ways in spite of all attempts by various Anglo Protestant groups to convert them and growing in numbers. Probably the Yaquis suffered less than their American neighbors during the Depression. They were used to doing without and living from day to day.[35]

Other ethnic groups were in trouble during those years, especially the Chinese who were expelled from Sonora by Governor Francisco Elías on August 25, 1931. All their property was confiscated, and they headed, usually on foot, for other Mexican states or for the United States border. A great many crossed at Naco, near Bisbee, and were picked up by the Border Patrol and the Immigration Service almost as soon as they had both feet across the line. At Tucson they were brought into court, charged with entering the country illegally, and sent to San Francisco for deportation to China. On October 26, 1931, more than 100 of them, mostly from the Cananea district, faced the judge and heard the sentence. Reporters described them as "uniformly courteous and anxious to please." Some were well dressed and well educated. At least a few of them had managed to get out with some funds, though their Mexican neighbors had done their best to see that they left without a *centavo*. They were not candidates for relief by the Associated Charities, but they deserved as much sympathy as the other unfortunate victims of the Depression.[36]

Through it all the charitable organizations were committed especially to their own poor—the average citizens who had always worked hard, saved their money, supported their families, and asked nothing of anybody. Now, in growing numbers, they were out of work and desperately in need of help. Some government money was coming in, but not nearly enough, and even that was granted on a contingency basis. Unless a community made strenuous efforts to solve its own problems, government aid would be cut off. Harold Bell Wright made the point in a letter sent out on September 20, 1933, on Organized Charities stationery, to Tucson's civic leaders. "There is grave danger," he wrote, "that through misunderstanding of the part the Federal Government is now taking in our Pima County Welfare Work our Tucson Organized Charities will suffer disastrous neglect. . . . federal aid for unemployment relief will be extended only to those communities that do their full share in caring for their own needy citizens." [37]

Tucson's responsible men accepted the challenge. A meeting of civic leaders was called at Isabella Greenway's Arizona Inn on January 15, 1932 (Mrs. Greenway contributed the food), and the town went into action. Every year it was the same, with as many as 200 workers involved in fund-raising drives. Street fairs and musical events were staged to provide more cash, and C. Edgar Goyette, who headed the Associated Charities, saw to it that the money was wisely spent.

Goyette was the man who made things happen when leadership was badly needed, and he deserves a paragraph to himself. An adopted Tucsonan, he arrived from Los Angeles in 1911 at the age of eighteen and enrolled in the University of Arizona. His talents as a leader were recognized early. He was elected the first president of the student body in 1913. As the years went by, he became more and more deeply involved in wel-

C. Edgar Goyette.

fare work and was ready for a top job when the Depression arrived. A calm, friendly, efficient, industrious man, he probably had more friends and fewer critics than any other leader in Tucson's history. He administered the government programs from 1929 on, resigning from the Welfare Board in 1937, though he continued to act for some time as secretary. From 1940 to 1960 he was secretary-manager of the Tucson Chamber of Commerce, and when it was time to step down from that strenuous job, he went to work as publicity man for the Pioneer Hotel. He was the kind of man whom everybody relies on and takes for granted. The Advertising Club named him Man of the Year in 1958 for his work in bringing the Kitt Peak Observatory to Tucson; the city

Mayor Henry O. Jaastad.

ticing his profession and became a specialist in designing school buildings, and he had the talent and training to plan El Conquistador Hotel in 1927.

Success did not change him. He remained a very human fellow, never able to keep his desk in order, and he never lost his Norwegian accent. The letter *v* was always *w* to him, and the consequences were sometimes laughable. In the course of one of his political campaigns, for example, his campaign manager needed the voter list from the last election. It was not to be found until someone thought to look under "woters."

From the beginning he took an active part in civic affairs and became a city councilman in the administration of Mayor John White in 1926. As street commissioner and head of Buildings and Lands he "got things done" and made a reputation as a wise, patient, firm administrator. In 1933 the Spanish-Americans asked him to run for mayor. He won easily and continued in office for seven terms, stepping down at his own request in 1947.

Jaastad was a quiet, scholarly-looking man with a somewhat quizzical expression, suggesting that he might be contemplating—as he often was—the quirks and foibles of the human race. He seemed calm and relaxed until he encountered shortsightedness or stupidity in his fellow man, and then he was likely to go off like a firecracker. The story is told that when the city council was considering buying the land between Broadway and Twenty-second Street that eventually became Reid Park, the members thought the price was too high and nearly let their chance slip away. Only when Jaastad blew up and threatened to buy the land himself and give it to the city did the council see the light and do its duty. A better-documented story involves the highly contro-

gave him a testimonial dinner in 1974, just before his death at the age of eighty-two; and the city planners named a street for him on the north side. These were small returns for his years of service, but he would have asked no more. Only the old-timers remember him now; nevertheless he left his mark on the city.[38]

Another force for order and advancement who found his way to the top at this time was Norwegian-born Henry O. Jaastad, who came to the United States at thirteen, went to a country school in Wisconsin, and continued his education in the field of architecture. Architects were not in great demand when he arrived in Tucson in 1902, but his father had been a cabinet maker and Henry was good with tools, so he went to work as a carpenter. Before long he was prac-

versial subway under the tracks at Stone Avenue. Merchants who thought that they would be injured by it got out an injunction which stopped the work already begun. Jaastad announced that if the subway should be lost through the misguided efforts of these men he would personally sue each of them for damage done to the city. He might have carried out his threat, but he did not need to. He spent his ninety-second birthday at his old home in Hardanger, Norway, but his heart always belonged to Tucson, where he died at the age of ninety-three.[39]

It was fortunate for Tucson that men of the caliber of Goyette and Jaastad were in charge when the difficult days came. They provided leadership when the city was trying to solve its problems and saw to it that government funds were handled efficiently and without scandal. The Reconstruction Finance Corporation was born on February 3, 1932, regional offices were set up, and money began flowing in. Some went to the Associated Charities, some to the Salvation Army and similar agencies which imported carloads of flour from Kansas and provided staples for needy families.[40] In September, 1932, more than 4,000 men in Tucson were jobless, but $30,000 was available to provide work on county roads and direct relief for those who could not work. More came in as the weeks went by—never enough to take care of everybody but enough to make a very real difference.[41]

The great problems, however, were unpredictable and unexpected. No sooner were plans worked out for equitable distribution of money and supplies than needy people appeared, sometimes in considerable numbers, with their hands held out. A great trial arrived with the "Bonus Army" in June, 1932. It began forming in April in Portland, Oregon, following a familiar American pattern of "dramatic protest," and gathered increasing strength as groups of unemployed veterans moved eastward—in cars if they had them, in boxcars if they did not—and by the end of May the first contingent was in Washington. Within a few weeks over 20,000 men, some with their families, were camping in several areas, besieging Congress to pass the bonus bill already before the Senate. There was no question of their need, and they were for the most part as orderly and restrained as could have been desired, but the mere presence of so many destitute people seemed to be an insoluble problem for everybody concerned.[42] The people along the many roads leading to the capital were able to handle the challenge and pass it on to Washington, but some were seriously embarrassed by the marchers and resentful of their demands. Among them were the civic leaders of Tucson.

A large contingent rolled toward Arizona from southern California late in May, picking up recruits as it went along. The main body was at El Centro on June 14. It reached Phoenix on the sixteenth and camped at the fairgrounds. On the seventeenth it headed for Tucson, where preparations had been made. "Vets will be fed and bathed here," said the *Star*, and added that 1,500 marchers were expected. A southside swimming pool was to take the place of showers. More than $100 (a ridiculous sum, as it turned out) was set aside for the purchase of food, and generous people dropped contributions into a barrel at the Post Office Drug Store. Mose Drachman donated six new shirts and two dollars in cash. Everybody wanted to help, and the *Star* published a list of donors who had contributed wood, milk, coffee, wieners, soap, bread, and so on. The contributors expected the marchers to camp overnight and be on their way the next morning. If Tucson had known what was ahead, Tucson might have been less hospitable.[43]

Early in the afternoon on June 18 about 2,000 tired, dirty, hungry veterans reached Tucson in a great fleet of old automobiles and were guided to the Twenty-second Street Park, where trenches were dug for latrines and cooking pits. A sound truck with a loudspeaker rolled in. An airplane flew back over the road to look for stragglers. Mechanics went to work on crippled cars. A hospital unit was on hand with a corps of doctors and nurses, who began attending to men with injuries and heat problems. Observers were impressed by the order and discipline which seemed to prevail.

The man responsible for the order and discipline was Royal W. Robertson, who functioned well and continuously in spite of a broken neck, said to be service-connected (historians have revealed that it was the result of a fall from a hammock while he was in training). His head was "resting loosely in a sling hung from an iron brace on his back." He seemed earnest and calm, "speaking in a moderate tone of voice, issuing orders, calling for volunteers for certain tasks and despatching business." Since he was suffering from overexertion and lack of sleep, his own men and the local leaders persuaded him to go to bed in a local hotel, but after two or three hours he was back in camp.

To the surprise of the townspeople a number of women and children were in the party, creating special problems as time went on, and a second look at the group quenched much of the early enthusiasm. Some of the men, it was noted, "looked like tramps," and they were noisy as their sound truck blared popular music, and a piano on a truck contributed to the uproar. The day after

their arrival, one reporter detected "a general contempt for anyone not a marcher and was of the opinion that "underneath the surface of discipline . . . this army of marchers appears to have the makings of an ill-controlled mob capable of causing consternation in the city." No "effective sanitation was apparent," and the encampment "seemed ripe for an epidemic." After one day and one night Tucson was looking forward with pleasure to the departure of the caravan.

Then came the bad news. It would take 3,000 gallons of gasoline to move the visitors out, and food was running low. It was already becoming next to impossible to provide for them. On June 20, the third day, James P. Graeber, chairman of the Tucson Relief Committee, pleaded for contributions of bread and milk for the women and children. They "must be fed whether the men eat or not," he declared. Six cases of whooping cough had appeared among the children the night before to add to the general alarm.

By this time the camp had begun to break up. Robertson and about a thousand of the men had caught a "melon train" for El Paso, where they planned to stage a parade and a fund-raising campaign to get their people back on the road. Before he was out of sight, his unwilling hosts were busy rounding up every available gallon of gasoline, and that night all but 250 of the marchers had been "eased out of the city." The remnant left as soon as their departure could be arranged.[44]

Robertson and about a thousand of his contingent arrived in Washington on July 8, in time to participate in the final, futile demonstrations of the Bonus Expeditionary Force and to endure the humiliation of the eviction by General Douglas MacArthur and his soldiers.

Tucson had learned a hard lesson, but it

had learned it well. When news came that a new regiment was forming in California, city officials notified the members of the American Legion that no further provisions would be made for bonus marchers and asked that the word be relayed to the West Coast. The warning must have been heeded, for no more marchers appeared.[45]

The appearance of the bonus caravan brought the Associated Charities to a new financial low, but better times were already in sight. After the inauguration of Franklin D. Roosevelt and the brief bank holiday, a succession of government bureaus usually called the "alphabetical agencies" sprang into being—the PWA (Public Works Administration) encouraged private contractors to employ workmen in erecting or renovating public buildings. The WPA (Works Progress Administration) provided more jobs. The RFC, the TRC, the CWA, the CCC, and all the rest were created to put the country back on its feet, and the results were soon visible. By December 3, 1933, at least 1,250 men were working on CWA projects. The Sabino Canyon Dam was a major undertaking. Work on the Mount Lemmon highway kept the CCC boys busy. The runways at Davis-Monthan were extended, road improvements inside and outside the city moved forward in long strides, and many public buildings were erected at government expense. The currents of life began to flow in their old channels.[46]

A special beneficiary of the alphabetical programs was the University of Arizona, hard hit by staff and salary reductions. All services had been curtailed, and the faculty was being paid in scrip, while the regents warned that if things got worse the professors might have to serve without any pay at all. When skies were darkest, however, President Homer Shantz started a campaign to obtain an $800,000 grant from the PWA—30 per cent as an outright gift, the rest to be repaid over a period of thirty years. It took a special session of the legislature to gain state approval, but the grant was made. Shantz "asked for and got a science building and greenhouse, the women's gymnasium and recreation building, an auditorium, a classroom building, the State Museum, plus additions to and remodeling of farm facilities." The university profited, and Tucson's unemployed profited even more.[47]

The city needed the alphabet agencies—could hardly have survived without them—but there were drawbacks. In time they became as much a hindrance as a help. By 1936 the worst times were over, and the comeback had started. Job opportunities were opening up, but workers were not always available to fill them. The men were busy with government projects, and the administrators would not release them for temporary employment. Cotton growers were in great need of seasonal help but got no cooperation from the government men until mounting resentment forced a layoff which freed the men to work for the farmers—if they wanted to exchange what they were doing for stoop labor.[48]

Poverty and crime go hand in hand, and during the hard times the Tucson police were almost as busy as the welfare workers. Wherever a dishonest dollar could be made, somebody was there to make it. Bootleggers flourished, sometimes with the connivance of the peace officers. Honest officials slowed down the traffic. When they were replaced by others with less rigid standards, it reappeared at once. During his term as county attorney (1932–34), Clarence E. Houston put many a shady character out of business, but when he left, "they all started up again." Prostitution flourished in spite of repeated

Louise Marshall and friend. Courtesy Marshall Foundation.

Thomas Marshall at work. Courtesy Marshall Foundation.

raids on Gay Alley. Robbery was a continuing problem.[49] And, as always in times of stress, major crimes periodically shattered the desert tranquillity.

The most sensational of these happened shortly after midnight on April 27, 1931, in the large, expensive home of Mr. and Mrs. Thomas E. Marshall at 1185 East Second Street, near the university. Tom Marshall was asleep in his bed when his wife of thirty-one years came into his room with a pistol in her hand and fired four shots into his body. He lived for three weeks and died in a Los Angeles hospital after an operation failed to save him. His wife went on trial for her life while the whole town watched with shocked incredulity.[50] Mrs. Marshall could not have done it. But Mrs. Marshall did.

The whole unlikely train of events began when Louise Henriette Foucar, daughter of a wealthy Massachusetts family, came west for her health in the late 1890s and entered Denver Women's College. Her preparation was good. She had gone to school in Italy and Switzerland and was at home in several languages. She adapted well to life in a Western university, pledged Pi Beta Phi Sorority, and graduated with a major in modern languages. In 1899 she went to the University of Arizona as an instructor in French, Latin, and botany. She was a good teacher, her character was firm, her ideals were high, and after two years she was given a permanent post as professor of ancient and modern languages. In 1902 she left the faculty, possibly because of her weak heart and history of tuberculosis but more probably because she wanted to devote all her time to business. Starting with $40,000 derived from her own savings and from a gift from her mother, she became deeply involved in commercial ventures, buying buildings and land all over town but particularly near the university. The block across from the main gate at University and Park is still the property of the Marshall Foundation, which she organized in 1930 to minimize her tax problems and provide funds for various charitable enterprises.

She was always giving to good causes and was particularly interested in university girls with problems. She listened to them, provided for them, sometimes took them into her home. Many organizations benefited from her generosity—the Methodist church (of which she was a devout member), the Associated Charities, the university, the Yaqui Indians. She started a Pi Beta Phi chapter on the campus and a local unit of the Audubon Society. She was a prohibitionist and for a brief time published a newspaper which supported the cause. She was something of a crusader for public morals, and it was unthinkable that she could have any personal weaknesses. Her image as an epitome of virtue was enhanced by her lifestyle. Naturally reserved, she avoided social contacts, and poor health limited her public appearances still further. She had few friends, but the whole town respected her and, figuratively speaking, took off its hat in her presence.[51]

During her years as a teacher Tom Marshall, a young Kansan, appeared in one of her classes. He worked on the campus as a gardener to support himself and played a little football. Although he was six years younger than his teacher, they had much in common. He too was reserved and introspective, firmly grounded in religion, careful and meticulous in his habits, interested in birds. She made him manager of some of her properties, and in 1904 she married him.

There was never any question about who was in charge. She kept him, as one survivor from those times puts it, under her thumb. Every morning, for example, he went downtown with a basket to do the grocery shopping, and although he was responsible for many of the Marshall enterprises, including the service station on the corner of Tyndall and University, where young Evo de Concini (later a justice of the Arizona Supreme Court) was employed, Louise made all the major decisions. Some people assumed that Tom was not overly bright, but his old friends say, "He was brighter than they thought." There was never any doubt about his being a good man.

They lived together in apparent harmony, according to Mrs. Marshall's own story, until the mid-twenties, when their relationship began to deteriorate. The cause of the final break, she said, was her housekeeper, a woman named Harriet Seymour, who had lived with the Marshalls for several years. A few months before the tragedy Mrs. Seymour was discharged for allegedly having an affair with Tom and putting arsenic in Mrs. Marshall's food.

The odd part of it, say Tom's old acquaintances, was that Tom seemed the last man in the world to become involved in such an affair. "He was a loner. He had no women friends, and no men friends either."[52] But his wife accused him of flaunting his wickedness in her face and even bringing home a case of venereal disease. She was sure that he meant to kill her. Three days before the end, she testified, chemical analysis showed that she had been given lethal amounts of poison. Sick and frightened, she had not slept for days. Finally, in desperation, she entered Tom's bedroom, pistol in hand, determined to end her nightmare once and for all.[53] "I shot him," she told Matty Edwards, Seymour's successor. "He had been living with that woman in my own house for the past three years and he made three attempts to poison me." Edwards quoted her, under oath, on the witness stand.[54]

Tom was able to crawl to a telephone and call his doctor. A neighbor, hearing the shots, had already called the police. Mrs. Marshall opened the door for them, and they found her husband on his knees, with his elbows on the telephone table, bleeding profusely but still conscious.[55] As they carried him away he repeated, over and over, "Why did she do it?"[56]

The town was in an uproar as the news spread, but no one seemed willing to believe the worst about Mrs. Marshall. She spent only a few hours in jail. It was against all precedent for her to be granted bail, but her lawyers (the best in the business) took their request to the state supreme court and got a favorable ruling.[57] During her brief confinement every effort was made to provide for her comfort. When Tom finally died, her attorneys requested and got a change of venue, and she came to trial before Judge W. A. O'Connor in a Nogales courtroom, surrounded by doctors, solicitous officers, and her personal maid. A rocking chair was provided for her when she was on the witness stand. The trial reached its emotional high point when she told her story. Twice she broke down and was given time to recover. As a defendant she could not have been more effective.

There were skeptics, however, who considered her, not Tom, the offender. Chief among them was Dr. E. J. Gotthelf, one of three physicians put on the stand to clarify technical aspects of the case. George R. Darnell, the leading defense attorney, had him under cross examination. Suddenly the lawyer shifted direction, and this interchange followed:

"You have an animus in this case, have you not?"

"I have."

"You had the county attorney called after the shooting?"

"I did. That was my duty."

"You tried to get Tom Marshall to sign a warrant against his wife?"

"I did."

"Didn't you tell Mr. Hall, Mr. Houston and several others at a meeting some time ago that you'd do all you could to hang the old————————?"

"I certainly did."

"Witness excused."

Gotthelf left the witness stand and stalked out of the courtroom. A man of strong opinions and brusque speech, he was convinced that Mrs. Marshall was not the one who had been wronged. Clarence Houston, the county attorney, agreed. "Tom didn't do anything," he said many years later. "It was all in her imagination."[58]

Public sympathy was with the accused, however, and when a verdict of not guilty was brought in on September 23, nine days after the trial began, "cheers burst forth from the throats of more than 100 spectators who had waited outside the jury room for the verdict," and there was "wild cheering" even in the courtroom.[59]

The *Star* on September 25, however, raised serious objections to the conduct of the case and declared that every step showed "the power of money":

The justification of the shooting introduced by the defense with the story of what Mrs. Marshall thought her husband was doing, as endorsed by the jury, sets a precedent of grave import. The effect of this defense is that wife can punish her husband if she thinks he is running around with other women by shooting him while he sleeps, and that it is her privilege to take the law into her own hands and administer it as she chooses. . . . If that is true, the administration

of justice is reduced to mob rule. If that is fair and just, then a mob has a right to lynch. The mind of a mob is under great mental stress too. . . .

Tom Marshall may have sinned, but that did not legally justify Mrs. Marshall in punishing him by shooting him while he slept; neither did it justify the action of the jury in freeing her and allowing her to go unpunished.

People in delicate health often live to ripe old age, and Mrs. Marshall was one of them. She survived for another twenty-five years, still reclusive, still devoted to her philanthropies, haunted by her one evil deed. Harold Webb, an employee who served as president of her foundation, told reporter Nancy Sortore many years later that the murder "bore on her mind" continually. "Sometimes she would call me, supposedly about a business matter, but it wouldn't be long before the conversation would turn to that."[60] Sometimes she would inquire of a man she trusted, "What do people think of me after what I did?" She was no doubt pleased when one of them replied, "They think you did exactly right, only you should have done it sooner."[61]

She looked and lived as she always had, according to Harold Webb, who remembered her as

a small, compact woman, with a sweet, motherly face. She always wore an old-fashioned black dress with a small white-lace collar, was birdlike in her movements, and very generous. She helped lots of girls through the university, many of them living in her house, and she always kept a little black purse attached to her belt from which she dispensed funds to anybody with a good sob story.

She died on July 12, 1957, at the age of ninety-two. According to Webb, only six people, besides the members of the board of her foundation, attended the funeral. Since

Gordon Sawyer.

she was always a very private person, she probably would have wanted it that way.

Less than five months later a second shock ran through the community when one of its leading bankers was kidnapped and held for ransom. Gordon Sawyer, an Illinois native with banking experience, had arrived in Tucson in 1909 and had been vice-president and cashier of the Southern Arizona Bank and Trust Company since 1912. A thin-haired, middle-aged, mild-looking man with a cheerful countenance and a ready smile which showed a battery of gold teeth, he looked inoffensive but was in reality a hard-nosed, tobacco-chewing executive. His inner toughness, however, did not prepare him for what happened on the night of February 4, 1932. He had been to a meeting of the Masons, returning home just after 11:00 P.M. He gave three gentle toots on the horn of his Packard sedan to let his wife know

that he was home. She always responded by turning on the outside light on the back porch. This time she was not feeling well and was slow to react. When she reached the back porch, husband and car were gone. Worried, she called Mose Drachman. Mose said, "Don't worry." But she did worry, and called the police.

At that moment Sawyer was lying on the floor of the back seat of his car, heading north on First Avenue, with a man sitting on him. Later he told what happened when he left his seat to open the garage door:

. . . two men stepped from the shadows, each holding two pistols. One man stood slightly back while the other jammed his two gun barrels into my ears and ordered me back into my car. I did not hesitate but as I stepped on to the running board one of them gave me a kick and with an oath threw me onto the floor of the tonneau. He whipped out a large rag and tied it tightly across my eyes. . . . I had no idea where they were taking me. I raised my head and said, "Boys, if you are going to kill me don't drive this car too far as there is not much gasoline in the tank." I was told to shut up and the man who was sitting on me pushed my head roughly back to the floor.

It was then they began to threaten me. I was told that if I made a false move I would be drilled through both ears. At times the cold steel of the two revolvers were pressed so hard to my ears that they are very sore today.

A few miles from the starting point the kidnappers switched to a green Chevrolet roadster driven by a third man, leaving the Packard abandoned in the brush. Minutes later Sawyer was taken, blindfolded, into a house, thrown down on a wooden floor, and told to go to sleep. "One glimmer of hope came toward morning when my guard said, 'I'll try to save you, Mr. Sawyer, but they will kill you, probably.'" In the morning, still alive but terrified, he was led to an abandoned well near the house and ordered to descend to the bottom. As he prepared to do so, he said, "If you are doing this for money, you had better take good care of me. It's going to be cold down there."

"You'll be a lot colder in two minutes if you don't sign this right now," said one of them as he thrust a paper into Sawyer's hand. They had taken off his blindfold, and he could read the note. "This to warn you," it said, "that we want $60,000 Saturday night or Gordon Sawyer will be killed. We have killed and robbed other people. Another killing is nothing to us." Then followed directions for delivering the money somewhere along a lonely country road. Early the next morning the letter was delivered to Fred J. Steward, president of the bank.

Meanwhile the Tucson police had gone into action. As soon as it was light enough to see, Tucson's pioneer aviator Charley Mayse took off in one of his planes from the old airport, where he had his flying school. He spotted the Packard in a few minutes. Officers Al Franco and Jesus Camacho were detailed to see what they could find at the site. They found tire tracks which were easy to follow on the dirt roads and traced them to West Grant, then known as DeMoss-Petrie Road. A mile or two down this country lane they came upon two men with brooms sweeping away the tracks. One of them took cover behind the green Chevrolet and opened fire with a rifle. A lively interchange of gunshots followed, but the two policemen, armed only with pistols, found themselves outmatched and beat a quick retreat. Returning with several more officers and better armament, they followed the road to a small ranch house which showed signs of having been abandoned in haste. The coffee in cups on the kitchen table was still warm.

Sawyer was still in the well, afraid to climb the ladder and face the weapons of his captors, but he called out when he recognized the voice of detective Douglas Ford. A few minutes later he was back at his home, shaken but otherwise unharmed.

It was not hard to identify two of the three kidnappers. In the house was a packet of sentimental letters addressed to twenty-year-old Billie Adkins by a Tucson boy. Through him they found her, jailed her, and "severely grilled" her. She proved to be remarkably self-possessed, refusing absolutely to give any information, admitting only that she liked shows and dancing. Since she had been living in the house by the well with her father and brother, however, those two were logical suspects. "Colonel" Cole Adkins and his son Clifford already had records, having served time in a California prison for bootlegging. The colonel, originally a Kentucky barber, was an experienced sinner. Clifford, twenty-nine and good-looking, was taking his first steps. The third man was never positively identified.

A large proportion of the able-bodied males of the town turned out to try to run them down. As many as 1,500 armed men began combing the hills the morning after the abduction, but the colonel got away entirely, and it took nine days to find Clifford, who was hiding in the house of an acquaintance named Joe Baker, near the old Yuma mine in the Tucson Mountains west of town. They might never have found him had Joe not become bored with his company and turned him in. He told Clarence Houston, the county attorney, about his predicament: "Don't breathe a word of this or I will get killed. I may get killed anyway, but I want you to get that sonofabitch out of there." The officers flushed their man without any trouble.

Clifford Adkins, bankernapper.

June Robles and mother.

Clifford's trial was held in May with energetic attorney Harry Juliani in charge of the defense. The jury could not agree on the validity of the defendant's alibi, but he was tried again in June, convicted, and sent to prison at Florence under a life sentence. He was a model prisoner, serving as librarian and postmaster, and was granted an out-of-state parole on December 2, 1941. An account of his further adventures would be interesting, but he left no forwarding address.[62]

An equally sensational kidnapping occurred in 1934. This time the victim was a six-year-old first-grader at Roskruge School. June Robles left the school grounds at three o'clock on the afternoon of April 25, 1934, on the way to the home of her aunt, Mrs. Herman W. Kengla, on North Second Avenue. Her mother was to pick her up there at five. Her cousin Barney Kengla, also six, was with her, but he hurried on ahead on some pressing juvenile errand of his own. Looking back, he saw a somewhat seedy-looking man get out of an old black Ford sedan, speak to June, put her in the car, and drive off. Less than two hours later her father, Fernando Robles, received a note at the Robles Electric Company. It was handed to him by a small boy who said he was to wait for an answer and deliver it to a man in a car across the street. The note said that June was safe and would be released for $15,000 ransom. When the boy returned with a reply, the man was gone.

The next day a second note was received

The pit in the desert where June Robles was found. From left: Al Taylor, Department of Justice; Clarence Houston, county attorney, Pima County; C. S. Farrar, undersheriff; Gus Wollard, chief of police; and Maurice Guiney (kneeling).

by Bernabe Robles, June's prosperous cattle-man grandfather. Detailed instructions were included for delivering the ransom, and the amount was reduced to $10,000. The family intended to follow instructions and asked the police to withdraw from the case while negotiations were going on.

For several days after that no one on the outside knew what was happening. There were rumors that Bernabe Robles had gone into Mexico following some mysterious lead, but they remained unverified. Public interest continued high, however. "Thousands of persons voiced their sympathy," the newspapers reported, particularly for the mother, who was "dangerously sick," and crowds gathered and regathered near the Robles home on Franklin Street, north of the downtown area.[63]

Behind the scenes the parents were trying to establish some communication with the kidnappers, hoping to determine that June was alive and could be ransomed. They asked the *Citizen* to print a list of questions which only June could answer, like "What do you do with your bunnies in the morning?" The right answers, they said, came back. Then there was silence, day after day.[64]

Finally, nineteen days after the abduction, the long ordeal came to an end. A letter postmarked Chicago came to Governor B. B. Moeur, giving general directions for finding where the child was hidden. On May 14 County Attorney C. E. Houston, accompanied by Carlos Robles, June's uncle, began searching an area in the desert east of Wilmot Road, miles from the settlement in those days. They found nothing for a long time, and Houston was about to give up and go home when he stumbled on what they were looking for. It was a sheet-iron box, six feet long and less than four feet high, buried in the desert soil and covered with earth. Inside, chained to an iron stake, was June herself, dirty and disheveled but alive, well, and cheerful. The key to the padlock attached to her chain was lying on the box, and she was soon at home with her mother. There was great rejoicing. Several hundred friends and relatives gathered at the Robles home to offer congratulations. It seemed that the whole country was interested. Newsmen and photographers appeared in large numbers. Visitors included two Hollywood figures who wanted to take June on a round of public appearances. The family took very little time to decide that this sort of public attention was not in the best interests of the child, and life gradually settled back into its normal routine.[65] A vigorous hunt for the kidnapper or kidnappers, however, went on and on.

There was no lack of suspects, the number-one candidate being Oscar H. Robson, a debonair character who had operated a dance hall in Tucson. After some delay he was cleared, however,[66] and the federal grand jury which met in December, 1936, decided, after listening to much testimony brought in by FBI agents and many others, that no indictments would be returned. The *Star* summarized: "The jury's report labeled the child's baffling disappearance as an 'alleged kidnapping,' then quickly dropped the curtain on one of the West's most puzzling dramas." Officials refused to release "the long-promised 'complete story' of the case," and the record has remained permanently closed. Roy Drachman picked up a rumor, current at the time, that the kidnap-

ping was "an 'inside' job by an unhappy distant relative from Mexico who was trying to get even with the grandfather for some past mistreatment. Nothing in half a century has surfaced to substantiate this or any other explanation of what happened.[67]

The crime history of Tucson came to a mighty climax in January of that same year, 1934. It was unusual in that no one from the city was on the wrong side of the law. This time the criminals were imported.

The story begins with a fire in the three-story Congress Hotel at 311 East Congress Street. The blaze broke out in the early morning of January 21 and destroyed one of the city's best hostelries. It was a relatively ancient structure, however, and burned quickly when a furnace in the basement malfunctioned and ignited the dry woodwork. The fire department responded quickly to the alarm and got everyone out, knocking on doors and hurrying the patrons, half-dressed or less, to the exits. Several guests on the top floor, apparently concerned about their luggage, created some problems, but they too were successfully evacuated. Once on the ground, however, they continued to worry about their abandoned possessions and persuaded firemen William Benedict and Kenneth Pender to go back into the burning building and bring down a number of expensive—and heavy—traveling bags.[68]

Three days later Benedict and Pender passed an off-duty hour perusing a copy of *True Detective Mysteries*. In "The Lineup" department they saw a face they thought they recognized. It belonged to Russell Clark, a member of the Dillinger gang, wanted for bank robbery and murder. He had registered at the hotel as Arthur Long from Florida, and it was his bags the firemen had saved from the flames. It was revealed later on, when the police took charge of them, that

The Congress Hotel on fire, January 21, 1934. Buehman photo.

check of the files of the identification bureau established that these birds, not yet in the hand but still in the bush, were not wealthy tourists from Florida but the notorious criminals Russell Clark, Charles Makley ("Fat Charlie"), Harry Pierpont, and their women—all members of "Bad John" Dillinger's gang. Dillinger was not with them, but they suspected that he would not be far away. The gangsters were "hot" back in Indiana and Ohio and had undoubtedly come to the Southwest to cool off. The question was how to handle them. They had no scruples about using their guns. Pierpont, in particular, was a pathological case who killed for pleasure. Bringing them in would be risky.[69]

The officers got Makley in a radio repair shop by asking him to come to the police station for a routine check of the papers on his out-of-state car. Once they had him, they fingerprinted him, over his loud protests, and identified him beyond question. Frank Eyman of the traffic squad and plainclothes detectives Chet Sherman and Mark Robbins found Clark and Opal Love, a buxom redhead known as "the Mack truck," living in a rented house at 927 North Second Avenue. There was a brief struggle which left Clark with a split scalp and a headache. To police headquarters with the suspects went the bags containing their weaponry. Pierpont fell victim to the same ploy that had trapped Makley. Two officers spotted his car on the street, pulled him over, and asked him politely to come with them to the station to clear his automobile. Frank Eyman rode in the back seat with his pistol between his knees, but nothing happened until they got inside the building. There, in a room at one side, Pierpont saw the two machine guns and the rest of the gang's arsenal. He almost made a fight of it, but Chief Wollard

they contained a fine collection of pistols, machine guns, ammunition, and bulletproof vests. Benedict and Pender relayed their suspicions about Long's true identity to Deputy Sheriff Maurice Guiney, who went to the police station to report but found everyone out to lunch.

Meanwhile Patrolman Harry Leslie had picked up another story from a couple of New York Staters who had met Long the night before at a local nightclub. He was the noisiest member of a party of six—three men and three women—and spent some time explaining how easy it was to make a living by robbing banks. The New Yorkers noted that the three men were armed. Did Leslie think this was strange? Leslie did. He called Police Chief C. A. (Gus) Wollard at his home. The chief left his lunch half-consumed and hurried down to his office. A

From left: John Dillinger, Harry Pierpoint, and Charles Makley.

Gus Wollard, chief of police (center), and the captured Dillinger arsenal.

and his men were too quick and took an assortment of weapons away from him, including a hideout gun on a string down his back.

But what about Dillinger? He had not yet shown himself, but the officers were sure he would eventually appear at the rented house on Second Avenue. They learned later that he had holed up in a motel on South Sixth, but sure enough he drove up with Evelyn Frechette, who traveled with him, and walked into a police stakeout. As he got out of his car and started up the walk, Milo Walker, James Herren, and Kenneth Mullaney closed in and took him without difficulty. His only comment was, "Well, I'll be damned!"

It was a great moment. A provincial police department had rounded up the most notorious criminals in the United States without firing a shot. No prison had been able to hold them, and lawmen of three states had pursued them in vain. Some of the Tucson policemen never got over that moment of glory. There were photographers and reporters and articles in newspapers and magazines. And there were rewards. The heroes no doubt spent a good deal of money in their imaginations before they learned that the Indiana authorities could offer only $300. Ohio did better, and the papers reported that $3,000 was on the way, to be divided eight ways. Inevitably some disappointments and hard feelings were generated by those rewards. The two firemen who had recognized Russell Clark, for example, held out their hands but got nothing.[70]

Almost before the excitement began, it was over. Officers from Indiana put Dillinger on a chartered plane to make sure they got him back safely. The others were taken to Ohio by train. The rest of the story, ending with Dillinger's death in a burst of gunfire on July 27, 1934, outside a Chicago theater, is too well known to need retelling here. His great crime spree had lasted only fourteen months. Likewise Tucson, on the front pages everywhere for a few hours, was back in its rural isolation in as many days.

It had happened at a time when most people had plenty of troubles of their own to think about. The bad years were leaving deep scars everywhere. "No one who did not experience the depression will ever know or appreciate what it was to go through," says one-time Arizona Supreme Court Justice Evo DeConcini:

It was an insidious thing. Every branch of the economy seemed to depend on another branch, and it was sweeping through the country like a blotter absorbing water. It seemed no place was left untouched. Money became so tight that it was practically impossible to get any. People were drawing their savings out to live on, people were losing their jobs, and small businesses were going broke. . . . 1934 was one of the worst years of the depression. Tucson was at its low ebb.[71]

Everyone was involved. Those with money had less; those with little had nothing. "It was damned tough," Oliver Drachman remembered in 1979. "Everybody owed everybody money. I owed the bank, just like the others, and I couldn't pay them, and it was taken for granted. Everybody was in the same boat."[72]

Nevertheless Tucson kept on growing, slowly but steadily. New and unusual things happened every year, indicating that the juices of life had by no means dried up in Arizona, though the money supply may have done so. Isabella Greenway, for example, went to Washington in 1933—the first and only Arizona woman to be elected to Congress. Arizona writers, subsidized by the Federal Writers Project, worked at salvaging Arizona's historic past and turned out a useful state guide. Artists, sponsored first by the Public Works of Art Project and later by the various divisions of the Federal Arts Project of the WPA, did just as well, producing paintings and murals for public buildings. Their work was good enough to call for a retrospective exhibition in 1980.[73] Perhaps the most far-reaching experiment of the period, however, was the incorporation of South Tucson by its residents on August 10, 1936—a step taken, as the rest of Tucson saw it, against all reason and utility.

A business community was growing up on South Sixth Avenue along Highway 80. It was then at the extreme south edge of the community, outside the city limits. "As a town, it could be said to have been sired by the owners of two tourist courts who did not want to be subjected to Tucson's building codes," says historian John Bret Harte, "and by liquor dealers who felt that the city's licensing fees were too steep." When Mayor Jaastad, with the city council at his back, introduced a proposal to annex the area, South Tucson residents took hasty action, and the square mile of desert territory became an independent municipality. It was racially mixed, poverty-stricken, and unable to provide all the services its citizens needed, but it was fiercely proud of its new status and survived several years of attempts by its larger neighbor to arrange for its disincorporation and annexation. The ups and downs of the legal roller coaster were bad enough, but in addition there were always financial problems, police problems, and scandals of one kind or another. Nevertheless, as Tucson grew around and beyond it, South Tucson continued to fight for its autonomy. As late as 1980 it was under pressure by the mayor and council of Tucson to disincorporate and come into the municipal fold, and it was still determined to stay out.[74] Its history was a demonstration that some people in Arizona were still willing to take chances in order to live as they pleased, even in the middle of a depression.

By 1935 the worst times were over, though a slump in 1937 scared everybody again. Small signs indicated that a change for the better was coming. On June 13, 1935, for example, the Tucson Rotary Club left on a special train for a convention in Mexico City. The municipal golf course opened on October 31, 1936. Plans to install parking meters on downtown streets were announced on July 13, 1939, and a few days later, on July 22, the word was out that a replica of Old Tucson would be built for the filming of the Columbia motion picture *Arizona*—story by immigrant writer Clarence Budington Kelland. Tourists were coming in greater numbers; apartment rentals were up; the building industry was reviving. Even before the boom times which came with World War II, Tucson was almost back to normal.[75]

CHAPTER 14

War Again

World War II was a year old in 1940. Hitler and Mussolini were carrying all before them, and the rest of the world was wondering what to do about it. The United States was aware that it would probably have to fight Germany again—with Italy and possibly Japan thrown in, and Tucsonans, like everyone else in the country, were troubled by a sense of recognition—the feeling that they were watching the same old play with a different set of characters. It was 1917 all over again, and as the buildup toward full involvement continued, the resemblances became more and more obvious. Isolationists wanted us to stay out; Francophiles and Anglophiles wanted us to get in; arguments for and against conscription went on wherever men and women gathered, all the way up to the halls of Congress. There was deep concern for the hungry people of Europe, resentment against the arrogant conquerors, fear for our own safety.

The fear was real enough, and it was justified. The Axis powers appeared to be unstoppable, their ambitions insatiable. Chances seemed better than even that the whole world would come under the thumbs of the ruthless tyrants and that we might soon be a conquered and subservient people. It could happen, and we knew it could happen, and it came closer to happening than we are usually prepared to admit today since, after all, we won.

The feeling of going down a familiar road, however, did make a real difference in the nation's approach to the war. Illusions about making the world safe for democracy, or for anything else, had gone with the Treaty of Versailles. The University of Arizona *Wildcat* commented, "No, we're not wanting to make this a war to end wars. We know that's a lot of poppycock of a generation ago." The determination to do the job was there, but the resolve to do it was quieter, the emotional highs fewer and farther between. Hardship and sacrifice and death had to come. We had survived them before, and we could survive them again, but they were nothing to cheer about.[1]

The war itself, as most people realized, was basically a continuation of World War I, a result of the heavy burdens imposed on the conquered nations by the vindictive conquerors, of the withdrawal of the United States into isolationism, of the fears and suspicions that led to rearmament on both sides. Hitler came to power in 1933, reoccupied the Rhineland in 1935, and began extending German rule over his neighbors. He overran Austria in 1938, dismembered Czechoslovakia in 1939. In the same year he signed a nonaggression pact with Russia, freeing his hands for further adventures in central and eastern Europe. Britain, already rearming, tried to stop him by forming an alliance with Poland, but the German leader brushed the threat aside. When he crossed the Polish border, England declared war, and the armies began to march. Denmark and Norway fell. France capitulated in 1940, the debacle at Dunkirk followed, and the Battle of Britain began.[2]

Tucson in 1940 was a provincial American city of less than 40,000 people, isolated in its arid terrain, but it was just as much a part of what was happening as New York or San Francisco and, thanks to the newspapers and the radio, just as aware of the dangers the country faced. Day by day gloomy reports dominated the headlines—Nazi successes in Africa and the Balkans—triumphant Germans in Paris—waves of bombers reducing London to smoking ruins. Buckingham Palace, the royal residence, was hit, but the king and queen emerged from the palace bomb shelter unscathed. Almost daily the raiders returned, to be engaged by heroic but outnumbered fliers of the RAF. Almost daily German submarines accounted for more merchant vessels bringing foodstuffs and war supplies to the beleaguered island. England was being bombed out, starved out, and softened up for invasion. Hitler even stated the conditions—beginning with the surrender of London—for calling off his war dogs. The British leaders scornfully rejected his ultimatum and even turned the tables by bombing German ports, factories, and the hundred-mile strip

of coast from Boulogne to Calais, where the führer was marshaling his invasion forces. Stung by these countermeasures, Hitler stepped up the bombing. By early August, 1940, as many as 500 planes a night were flying over England, and as time went on, the numbers went as high as 1,000. At sea submarines and swarms of torpedo boats were furiously active, sinking, according to the Germans' figures, 250,000 tons of shipping a week.[3]

Desperate but undaunted, the British fought on. "Britain's peril is such," Prime Minister Winston Churchill announced in a brief, grim statement, "that the nation's ministers must sleep beside their desks." To make matters worse, the Italians were swaggering through Africa, and the Japanese were leapfrogging down the Chinese coast toward the countries of southeast Asia. "Democracy has its back to the wall," the Arizona Daily Star admitted. "Totalitarian influence is spreading throughout the civilized world."[4]

Everyone was aware that Europe's problems would soon be our problems. No one denied that every effort must be made to prepare ourselves—no one, that is, except the old hard-core isolationists and a few pragmatists who foresaw a triumphant Axis and counseled making peace with the victors. Early in August, 1940, Colonel Charles A. Lindbergh urged the government to accept the inevitable and seek a treaty with Hitler, but his countrymen put him down firmly but politely. He should not be charged with "disloyalty or cowardice," a Star editorial declared, but the writer noted that Hitler was "no respecter of friendships" and was as eager for conquest as Alexander or Caesar had been. The United States had only one recourse: "Get Ready!"[5]

Factories responded first, turning out airplanes and military supplies for the British as fast as they could. England wanted 3,000 planes a month, and President Roosevelt set a national goal of 50,000 planes a year. Shipbuilding and repairing were also heavily involved, and all sorts of supplies were moving toward Europe day and night. The country would not approach full production until it was actually at war, but a sort of cranking-up process was going on. Fifty thousand National Guardsmen were on call and ready to assemble for training and maneuvers. Congress appropriated an astronomical $13 billion for "peacetime defense."[6] In exchange for fifty over-age destroyers, badly needed by the British, the United States gained ninety-nine-year leases on bases in eight British New World possessions, and American forces were sent to Iceland to help guard the sea routes to the British Isles. Under the lend-lease subterfuge all sorts of American manufactures, including war material, could legally be shipped abroad, opening the door a little wider to American participation in a conflict which had already engulfed almost the entire globe.[7]

So much was sent that we had very little left for ourselves. Dave Boone, the *Star*'s popular columnist, revealed that militiamen engaged in war games were "using ice wagons for tanks, stove pipes for anti-aircraft guns, and gas pipes for machine guns. The state guards rent ice and coal trucks and label them 'light tanks' so friend and foe in the sham battles will know what they are when they see 'em."[8] Old soldiers remembered that similar expedients had been necessary as the country geared up for World War I, but it was embarrassing, nevertheless, that the most powerful country in the world should be caught short in this fashion.

Confusion in Washington was not helping the situation. Government agencies were already set up to monitor the change-over to war production, but American businessmen and manufacturers wanted some answers before they became cogs in the great machine. They wanted profit ceilings lifted and five years to amortize the cost of retooling. While the negotiations were going on, however, the airplane factories were already preparing for all-out massive production, and the automobile companies were reshaping their assembly lines. Chrysler, for example, was about to become the tank arsenal of America and the free world at a cost of $20 million.[9] On the West Coast the Lockheed P-38, the fastest military plane in existence, was unveiled. It could attain a speed of 500 miles an hour.[10]

One by one the necessary steps were taken. There was a shortage of skilled mechanics for the mechanized army, and the government began signing up the ones that were available, in Tucson as well as elsewhere, at the same time preparing to train more. Roosevelt called up four divisions—60,000 men—of the National Guard for a year's service.[11] Aliens were required to register at the end of August. At the same time the Office of Price Administration was readying the food stamps which finally were in the hands of housewives on November 1. Meanwhile the skeleton of a bureaucracy was taking shape with the organization of a Tucson Council of Defense, which reported to the Pima County Council of Defense, which in turn reported to the State Council.[12]

Recruiting was already in progress, and men were enlisting in both the National Guard and the army. In July a new unit of mechanized cavalry from Fort Bliss at El Paso, Texas, began touring the country to stimulate enlistment. It spent three days in Tucson, making as much noise and news as possible. Monte Mansfield, the Ford dealer who was involved in every civic enterprise and was chairman of the Pima County Volunteer Procurement Commission, headed the welcoming committee, with H. S. Corbett, Andrew P. Martin, and Colonel Ted Monro supporting him. The Fort Bliss band led a parade through the downtown section on July 25 and impressive ceremonies followed at the Armory. Mayor Henry O. Jaastad opened the program, and Tucson's premier orator, lawyer James F. Boyle, made a spirited speech on "American Preparedness." Similar efforts all over the country were showing good results. Six thousand men a week were joining up, and it seemed that the first goal of 375,000 men would be easily reached. At the same time Congress was debating a draft law. Senator Burton K. Wheeler of Montana and Secretary of War Harry H. Woodring spoke for a considerable group arrayed in opposition. Conscription was un-American and unnecessary, they said.[13] It all sounded very much like 1917. A conservative western community like Tucson, of course, had very little patience with such people.

Tucson was concerned also about the reports of imminent starvation in Europe. Sympathetic Americans were eager to help and found ways to do so. Ruth Millett, in her daily *Star* column "We the Women," suggested joining a Red Cross knitting unit, adopting a war orphan, helping the Welfare Board can tomatoes. Another good idea was conceived by the organizers of a British Relief Project, who staged a "Rummage for Relief" sale in the Tucson High School cafeteria on August 3, 1940, providing entertainment and making a social as well as financial occasion of it. The ladies in charge included Priscilla Sanders, Mary Winstanley, Jane Ivancovich, Gladys Carroll, and Ann-Eve Johnson. A thousand people came, saw, and bought, and the event raised $1,000 for the cause. The women felt amply repaid when a letter of appreciation from British actor Alan Mowbray arrived three weeks later.[14]

Concerned as these good people were for their friends and potential allies abroad, they had some problems of their own to contend with at home. Their worst ordeal of the year came on August 14, 1940, at 7:00 P.M., when a terrific electrical storm accompanied by high winds dropped over two and a half inches of rain on the downtown section in a matter of minutes. Tucson had never prepared for great storms because they came so seldom, and runoff arrangements were inadequate. The Rillito, north of town, was 206 yards out of its banks; the Santa Cruz, ordinarily dry as the Sahara, was in full flood. Water ran a foot deep through stores and homes and stood at twelve feet in the basement of the O'Rielly Motor Company, where thirty-seven new automobiles were stored. Water reached even the big diesels at the Tucson Electric Power Company, and the city was without light or energy—was, in fact, paralyzed.

The staff of the *Star* showed what American ingenuity could accomplish under seemingly insuperable difficulties. There was no way the paper could be printed, since the presses could not move, and the plant was in total darkness. But the paper *was* printed, and reporter Jack Weadock had a good time the next day telling how it was done—by candlelight. The Acme Printing Company came up with an old-fashioned press that could be operated by foot power and supplied some of the type; Herb Morrison, a job printer, contributed the rest. Ray Reynolds of Pima Printing Company lent a hand-operated paper cutter and the flat paper needed. Type was set by hand, and when the supply of candles ran low, Sears, Roebuck sent over flashlights and batteries. The result was a one-page paper set in a variety of type faces. It was without advertisements and carried only a few paragraphs of foreign news, but it was a newspaper. The press run began at 4:00 A.M. and proceeded at the rate of 1,200 copies an hour. The newsboys got their supplies in time for the morning delivery.[15]

Almost everything seemed to go right in that summer of 1940. Business was good and getting better. Roger Babson, the financial pundit, announced a 6 percent rise in production and predicted that a boom was coming. The Sunshine Climate Club revealed in September that 240 new families had moved to Tucson and that 1,404 visitors had been counted in the last eight months. At a kickoff banquet on September 30 club officials predicted that the "biggest winter season in the city's history" was coming up and that visitors would total 1,700. The new Flowing Wells School, "one of the most completely modern rural schools in the state," was ready to receive students, and registration at the university was well over 2,500. The price of copper was climbing— always a sign of better times in the copper state—and it seemed that the ill wind of war was blowing some good in the direction of Arizona.[16]

The most hopeful sign of all was the announced intention of the government to make Tucson a military-aviation center. "U. S. to spend millions to expand and militarize the airport," the *Star* revealed on August 6, and news items thenceforward traced the progress of plans and negotiations. The field was to be expanded from 300 to 1,600 acres and would be able to handle the largest bombers. As many as 3,000 men would be quartered on the reservation. Tucson in

World War I had not been lucky enough to win an army installation. This time the situation would be different.[17]

No hardships or sacrifices had been called for yet, and the town carried on pretty much as usual through the fall months. Political contests were heating up on the local and national levels. Sidney P. Osborn was trying again for the governor's office and spoke at a rally in Tucson on August 17. Roosevelt had been nominated for a third term, and Wendell Willkie was running against him, but it was an uphill struggle. About a hundred families were filtering back from their summer homes on Mount Lemmon and getting ready for school. Sports fans read with interest that young Sam Snead, on his honeymoon, had won the Canadian Open Golf Tournament at Toronto on August 15 and that Bob Goldwater had walked off with the amateur championship of the Southwest three days later.[18]

The social and cultural life of the city proceeded likewise at its usual pace. The Saturday Morning Music Club was ready on September 15 to announce the winter concert series, offering such attractions as violinist Ruggiero Ricci. Soprano Helen Traubel was also to appear. Melvin Solve, of the university English Department, addressed the annual open meeting of the Little Theater. Moviegoers were lining up at the State Theatre to see Bing Crosby, Mary Martin, and Basil Rathbone in *Rhythm on the River*, with pianist Oscar Levant in the cast as an added attraction. Errol Flynn was starring in *The Seahawk* at the Fox, and viewers with more refined tastes were looking forward to *Pride and Prejudice*, with Greer Garson as Elizabeth and Laurence Olivier as Darcy, on September 17.[19]

There was something for everybody in that pleasant fall month of September,

Clarence Budington Kelland, author of the novel Arizona, *on the set of the motion picture* Arizona *with Nick Hall, manager of the Santa Rita Hotel, known as the "mayor of Old Tucson."*

Airport welcome for Hollywood personalities and the cast of Arizona. *From left: Pat Gooden, Wally Devane, Polly Fernald, of the University of Arizona; Charles Ruggles, behind hat; Hedda Hopper, Hollywood columnist; Mary Carlisle, John Mack Brown, and Melvyn Douglas, film stars.*

Crowd at the premiere of Arizona, *November 16, 1940.*

1940. The new Hudson automobiles had gone on display on August 24, and Tucson women were excited to read that actress Norma Shearer was wearing her hair short for work and play while Olivia de Haviland was wearing hers in pompadour style. For the Mexican-American segment of the population there was a fine Sixteenth of September celebration which enlivened the whole town.[20]

November was even better. The opening symphony concert was scheduled for the twentieth, but much more important was the premiere of *Arizona*, the motion picture made at the specially created Old Tucson village west of town. The first showing was set for November 15. It was to be shown at four Tucson theaters simultaneously. The buildup was tremendous. An Indian village pitched tents on Congress between Broadway and Stone—the very heart of downtown. There was a great parade, perhaps the largest in the city's history. Kate Smith appeared in concert. Three 21-passenger planes brought a gaggle of celebrities from Hollywood. The list included William Holden, Charles Ruggles, ZaSu Pitts, Rita Hayworth, and Paul Lukas. Jean Arthur, the heroine of the film, spent the night of the fifteenth making personal appearances at the four theaters. These famous figures descended upon Tucson much as angels might have fluttered into Jerusalem in biblical times, and the effect was tremendous.[21]

Grim bits of news, however, reminded all those happy people that the war was a reality. Bombs were falling on London as Jean Arthur made her rounds. Fifty Tucson draftees were called up five days later. Martin Dies of Texas told Congress that a "fifth column" of six million foreign agents was working undercover in the United States, and Hollywood, which was believed to harbor a hard core of communists, was "writhing" under charges of disloyalty. The country at large took all this with the utmost seriousness, and Roosevelt haters aimed charges at the government and at the White House itself. Arizona's Clarence Budington Kelland, famous writer and top-ranking Republican, declared in print that "the New Deal Administration is dominated by communism." Isabella Greenway, Arizona's leading lady, agreed that "pink parasites are the real danger in the United States government," and Wendell Willkie, trying to put planks in his presidential platform for the November elections, told the country that "Roosevelt favors some form of state socialism."[22]

Early in August, in response to the general uneasiness about reds and spies, the FBI was put on twenty-four-hour alert and received permission to tap wires as its agents pursued "sabotage, treason and espionage." Fear and suspicion were becoming part of the wartime mood, and they appeared in some unlikely places. University President Alfred Atkinson, for example, welcomed the incoming freshmen on September 9 in a speech which seemed to indicate a belief that agents of the Bolsheviki were lurking on the campus. He warned his audience that disloyalty and disaffection in the halls of learning would not be tolerated.[23]

The mood of the nation was changing rapidly as these developments unfolded, in Tucson as elsewhere. People were buying and wearing patriotic jewelry and singing "God Bless America" at public functions. The pledge of allegiance to the flag opened every organized gathering, and the flag makers were having difficulty keeping up with the demand. In Galveston, Texas, said a story in the *Star*, a man who yelled "Hooray for Hitler!" was fined $200 for starting a disturbance, and in Philadelphia a laborer who slugged a fellow worker with a shovel for unpatriotic remarks was freed by the court with tacit approbation.[24] The difference between Tucson and these centers of population was that no one in the Old Pueblo shouted "Hooray for Hitler" or made unpatriotic remarks.

The whole situation in America in 1940 was summed up in a two-panel newspaper cartoon titled "The Weather," which appeared in the *Star* on September 23. On the right an American gazed up at a sign which said, "Baseball Today." On the left an Englishman looked at a similar sign which read, "Invasion This Week?" The mind of America was divided—concerned on the one hand for its own affairs, and grieved on the other for its suffering friends abroad.

The balance began to change when Congress passed the Selective Service Act on September 8, 1940, but long before the draft machinery could be activated, Arizona men were in camp preparing for war. The first contingent from Tucson went off to Fort Sill, Oklahoma, on September 25, when the local unit of the National Guard entrained at the Southern Pacific depot. Five thousand citizens turned out to see them off, just as they had done before at the beginning of World War I. The country was beginning to be united in a common cause.[25]

The draft itself, which was to bring in 16 million young American men for registration on October 16, tightened the bonds, but there were a few holdouts. Notable among these was a venerable Papago leader who lived far out on the enormous reservation at a place called Stoa Pitk. Pia Machita, whose name meant Man Without a Grindstone, was described by a reporter as an Indian "of striking physique and entirely fearless." He was the absolute ruler of his village and a vigorous opponent of any man or agency attempting to force conformity upon him. As a symbol of authority he flourished a cane said to have been bestowed for the first time by Father Kino, the great missionary, two and a half centuries before. He considered himself a Mexican citizen, refused to admit the authority of the United States, and had no idea that there were more white men than Papagos in the world. By 1940, says historian Elmer Flaccus, "Pia was feeling more and more harassed. Some bureaucrat was always trying to count his people, test his cattle, and worst of all, enroll his braves in the armed forces." It did no good to explain to him that all the government wanted him to do was allow his young men to register. Every white official knew that since these youths were illiterate they could not be called up for service. Pia, however, was unaware of this fact, and was determined to keep them away from draft boards.[26]

This was before Pearl Harbor, but already there were fears that the Japanese might be planning to invade the United States through Mexico and that the Papagos might cooperate with them. No less an authority than W. A. Mathews, editor of the *Star*, had warned that war might break out in the Pacific at any time. It was necessary to be firm with these holdouts, and Deputy United States Marshal Henry W. Smith of Tucson was given the job of arresting Pia and his young men for draft evasion. Smith came to Stoa Pitk, at the end of its primitive dirt road, at two o'clock on the morning of October 16. He dashed in with tear gas at the ready, called Pia out of his house, handcuffed him, and prepared to take him back to Tucson. Pia's neighbors, however, were not of a mind to put up with such treatment of their leader. They attacked the officers with such vigor that Smith had to remove Pia's handcuffs and flee, bruised and beaten, from the scene. Back in Tucson he attended to his wounds and filed charges. On October 24 the officers tried again and found the village deserted. Deputy Sheriff Ben McKinney, afraid that he might have a real war on his hands, requested a plane, gas bombs, machine guns, and hand grenades from the army at Fort Huachuca. While his request was being processed (it was eventually denied), he staged another raid on November 10 and again found nobody at home.[27]

The big roundup came six months later on May 18, 1941. McKinney had got hold of an airplane, from which he directed his ground forces, already in position. This time the Indians were at home and allowed themselves to be arrested. There was a trial before

Deputy United States Marshal Ben McKinney.

United States Commissioner C. Wayne Clampitt which had many of the aspects of comic opera. Everyone except Marshal Smith, even Ben McKinney, was on Pia's side. The old man was sturdy and honest, and it seems to have been impossible not to like him. Nevertheless he went to jail, thereby bringing important reinforcements to his cause. On May 21, 1941, the *Star* commented indignantly that Pia

embodies much of that pride and independence for which the Red Man has been noted. . . . To those who have sought to bring him into what we call civilization he has declared, "This is my land; these are my people; white man leave me alone, I leave white man alone." He does not want to be civilized, he wants to live and enjoy the true Indian life of independence and self reliance. . . . Will any American citizen arise to defend Pia Machita and his braves who are now in jail and face probable prison sentence for attempting to defend the liberties they inherited from their forbears? No indeed! Americans are more interested in defending the cruel barbarous savages of Ethiopia in far off Africa against the same kind of force which they used against the Red Man in their own country, and a few hours ago, near Tucson.

Unfortunately Deputy Smith did not share the views of the editorial writer. He pressed charges, and Pia was held for trial. Ironically, he was enchanted with the jail. The electric lights, the indoor plumbing, and the cot he slept on were luxuries to which he was happy to become accustomed, but what pleased him most was the food. According to Flaccus, he went out of his way to express his approbation to the jail cook, making the man "a friend for life." His jailers, beguiled by the old man's singular charm, strained the rules by taking him out for "exercise" and showing him the city. They may even have taken him for a ride in an airplane.

When he was sent off to California to serve his eighteen-month sentence at Terminal Island, he had similar pleasing experiences. McKinney visited him there on September 13, found him working outdoors taking care of the warden's garden, and obviously enjoying himself. He was already so impressed by the white man's world that he sent back word to Stoa Pitk that all the children should be enrolled in a new school just opened on the reservation at the larger settlement of Hickiwan. When he came home at last, after several transfers to other prisons, he was a different person. From then on he gave nobody any trouble. His young men registered, and a few of them joined the armed forces when the literacy requirement was waived. Thus ended the last Indian disturbance in the Tucson vicinity.[28]

Pia Machita made the front page, but his case was exceptional. During the final months of 1940 war bulletins dominated the headlines. They crowded local news into the back pages of the newspapers as the Germans and the English bombed each other into dust and rubble, the Nazis penetrated far into the heart of Russia, the British drove hard against the Axis forces in North Africa with little success, and the Japanese enveloped Hongkong on their way south toward Singapore and possibly the Dutch East Indies. The reports were mostly bad: "U.S. Warns Citizens to Get out of the Orient"; "Yugoslavia Joins Axis as British Prepare to Quit Bulgarian Realm"; "Iraq Oil Flow Cut Off in Continued War"; "London Reveals Ship Loss of Staggering Proportions"; "Fall of Leningrad Near." So gloomy were these dispatches that reports like "Greeks Hold Border Against Italy" or "Most English Troops Saved from Balkans" seemed cheerful and encouraging by contrast.[29]

On the home front the news was better. The shadow of the Depression had lifted with the coming of "armament prosperity."[30] Full employment was becoming a reality, and boom times seemed to be at hand. Shortages had not yet developed, and prices were still reasonable. On November 1, 1941, in Tucson markets a ten-pound bag of pinto beans cost $.39, sirloin steak sold for $.29 a pound, and a quart of whiskey (a necessity by some standards) cost $1.59. Housing starts were up, winter visitors were coming in record numbers, and Miracle Mile, the main highway north from town, which had begun developing in the late 1930s as a haven for tourists, was building up rapidly.[31]

The surge in construction owed much to government-sponsored projects as the armed forces expanded. A major undertaking was the conversion of the municipal airport to an army air base, announced in August, 1940. This was great news for the business community, but the businessmen who directed Tucson's destinies soon learned that there was a price to pay for the coming prosperity. "City Evicted," said another news story on December 8. The armed forces needed all the facilities, actual or potential, at the municipal field, and the city would have to find, pay for, and build a new airport.[32] The ever-present and ever-efficient Ford dealer Monte Mansfield—Mr. Tucson—headed a Chamber of Commerce committee to search for a new site, and within a month the city had leased 360 acres two miles south of Davis-Monthan. It was the foundation on which the town built its future international airport. Through the fall and winter months expansion and planning went forward.[33]

The days and weeks passed, and as December, 1941, came up on the calendar, war clouds were darkening on the American horizon. The situation in the Pacific and on the Asian mainland was particularly alarming. The marines had been recalled from China, and there was speculation that the United States might be "clearing the decks for a possible clash with Japan." Winston Churchill had already warned the Japanese leaders that in case of a Pacific war "they would be engaged to the death by Britain within an hour of the decision." In an attempt to slow the Japanese drive southward, the United States had cut off supplies of scrap iron and aviation gasoline, and the Tokyo papers reported that "the Japanese people are burning with anger." At the same time Japanese emissaries were in Washington, apparently trying to patch up some kind of peaceful arrangement. It was possible to believe that there was no cause for unusual concern.[34]

Difficulties at home, in fact, seemed more pressing than difficulties abroad, particularly in the field of production. Young John L. Lewis, with characteristic truculence, called out his coal miners on November 16 and the next day defied the United States government to send in the army and put him down. There were other walkouts in factories and defense plants throughout the country, and Congress was considering legislation to outlaw strikes and punish strikers.[35]

On December 6, 1941, southern Arizonans worked and played with no suspicion of what was about to happen. Jim Brophy's funeral in Bisbee was in the news. Everybody knew Jim, the brother of Billy Brophy, the Phelps Dodge storekeeper who had become one of the state's leading bankers. Jim had not allowed his brother's success to change his down-to-earth life-style. In Tucson the American Association of University Women was planning a Christmas party for December 13 at the Santa Rita, featuring a program by the high-school chorus under the direction of Madge Utterback, and Mrs. Grace McEwen Klein would direct a play presented by the drama section. The Birth Control Clinic announced the election of Mrs. Jay Sternberg as chairman and reported that 3,000 women had come to the clinic for advice during the six years of its existence. Gregory Piatigorsky, internationally famous cellist, was coming, and the Amphitheater PTA was planning a Fathers' Night in the school auditorium on Monday, December 8. In the comics section of the *Star*, Little Orphan Annie escaped from the wicked Dr. Eldeen, who held patients for what amounted to ransom in his "hospital." Daddy Warbucks's friend Dr. Zee staged a counterkidnapping and found Annie with broken ribs and full of dope but otherwise unharmed.[36]

That was Saturday. Sunday was Pearl Harbor Day.

The news of the Japanese attack changed the life of every American. In a conservative community like Tucson, without a significant foreign population and without a bloc of socialists or communists, the patriotic response to the shocking news was unanimous. The town was at war almost before President Roosevelt appeared before Congress to ask for a formal declaration. While Governor Sidney P. Osborne was calling his Defense Council together and doubling the guards at the Mexican border, the city administration was taking swift action. Mayor Jaastad feared sabotage and asked for guards at strategic points to protect telephone and gas lines, railroad bridges, dams, and reservoirs. He was particularly concerned about the water supply and ordered the erection of a six-foot wire-mesh fence, topped by barbed wire, around storage facilities.[37] His call for guards was answered by an organization calling itself the Old Pueblo Vigilantes, headed by William ("Scrap") Roberts. Police Chief Harold C. Wheeler promised to deputize these volunteers and any others accepted for duty as "auxiliary police." Manpower was no problem. Six hundred members of the American Legion stood ready to assist, and Tucson businessmen were also poised for action. City Manager Phil J. Martin reported that employers in "strategic parts" of the city had been furnished with maps of the municipal water lines and with wrenches to shut off the flow in case of damage to the reservoirs. "The city," he said, "will be divided into nine districts and a minimum of twenty auxiliary firemen will be assigned to each section. Training will look toward extinguishing and controlling of fires started by sabotage or bombing."[38]

"Actual bombing of Japanese planes is not anticipated here," the *Star* acknowledged on December 8, but everybody believed that Japanese aircraft carriers were lurking off the California coast and that there was danger on the East Coast too. Air-raid alarms, later described as "dress rehearsals," on December 8 scared the citizens of Boston and New York. San Francisco was "scouted by unknown planes during the night," and Los Angeles and San Diego reported similar inspections. Residents of coastal cities were so earnest about blackouts that a crowd in Seattle was reported to have wrecked several stores where lights were showing.[39]

A blackout in Tucson was seriously considered, especially after a Japanese flag was discovered at the top of the university flagpole west of Old Main on the morning of December 8. The halyards were intentionally fouled, but Herbert Miller climbed the pole and brought down the offensive object as an "indignant crowd" watched and murmured. Although pranksters were thought to be responsible, Colonel Arthur W. Holderness, commandant of cadets, chose to take the situation seriously. He detailed cadet officers to direct traffic and guard buildings on the campus in case a blackout was imposed and set up a command post at the flagpole.[40]

At this point the city administration decided that a warning system would have to be improvised to start the blackout and sound the all clear when the crisis was over. A test was scheduled for Friday, December 19. Whistles at the utility plant, the Southern Pacific shops, the Veterans Hospital, and the University of Arizona were to be sounded simultaneously. The "standard warning"—three short blasts repeated at intervals for the alarm and one long blast for all clear—was to be used. To make sure that somebody would be in charge, the mayor and council on December 11 passed an ordinance designating City Manager Phil J. Martin coordinator for the Municipal Civilian Council and made him responsible for ordering a blackout "or any other emergency precaution he deems necessary." Next day Coordinator Martin issued his first general order: no whistles or sirens to be sounded in Tucson after 5:00 P.M.[41]

This brought on a contest of wills, throwing the town into "dire turmoil," which might have been called the Battle of the Martins. Opposing Phil J. Martin was Andrew P. Martin, World War I sergeant, pillar of the American Legion, and state vice-chairman of the Arizona Division of the National Office of Civilian Defense. Andy issued a statement to the public reminding all concerned that he was, or should be, in charge of all blackouts and related activities: "The municipal group created several weeks ago by the mayor and council at the request of F. H. LaGuardia, National Director of Civilian Defense, is purely supplementary to the Civilian Defense Council that is being set up here under the direction of Andrew P. Martin, state vice-chairman for this area." All other agencies must be coordinated with his, Andy said.[42]

Neither of these strong-minded men would yield, and the governor himself had to intervene. At his request a meeting was held at the American Legion Hall on December 10. The chain of command in the OCD was explained. When the governor followed up by issuing a statement backing Andy, the latter offered what amounted to a compromise: "Currently active groups of Tucsonans, organized under some phase of civilian national defense" should remain intact and continue their programs. Somewhat condescendingly he provided a place

on the Agricultural Resources Production Committee, chaired by Edgar Goyette, for Phil Martin. William ("Scrap") Roberts, already introduced as leader of the Tucson Vigilantes, was Andy's vice-chairman of the Home Defense Committee.[43]

Satisfied by, or ignoring, Andrew Martin's proposal, Phil Martin and his group went ahead with plans for the blackout. On December 19, as scheduled, the whistles blew and the sirens sounded to begin the practice alert. Unfortunately they were too weak to be heard more than a few blocks away, and nothing much happened. The test was pronounced "inadequate" by the *Star*, and since it was becoming increasingly obvious that Tucson was in no danger whatsoever from enemy aircraft, no further tests were scheduled.[44] The "Martin War," such as it was, was over. The Office of Civilian Defense, however, continued to believe in taking precautions, even when they were unnecessary, and on January 3, 1942, the *Star* gave a full page to advice from Fiorello H. LaGuardia, civil defense director in Washington. In case of an air raid, he admonished:

> Keep Cool
> Stay at Home
> Put out the lights
> Lie down
> Stay away from windows
> Help with volunteer services.

Other aspects of the war effort came off better than the blackout. The Army-Navy Recruiting Center in the Federal Building stayed open around the clock, and there was a rush to enlist. Tucson women were as eager as the men. Three hundred of them poured into the Red Cross office to offer their services, and as branches of the armed forces were opened to them for enlistment, many

Tucson girls appeared in uniform. People were as ready to enlist their money as they were to offer their bodies. On December 8, 1941, they set "an all-time one-day record in the purchase of U.S. defense bonds," and they kept on buying.[45]

Businessmen found other ways to help. Mindful of the strikes that were plaguing the country's industries and slowing production, fifty of Tucson's leading business figures met at the Chamber of Commerce building on December 9 to form a labor board which would consider grievances and settle disputes between management and the work force "without either strikes or lockouts." When Japanese submarines attacked several freighters off the Pacific Coast late in the month and sank the lumber-carrying ship *Absaroka* and the tanker *Emidio*, these precautions seemed more than justified. The enemy might be closing in for a major attack.[46]

Tucson would not have been Tucson, however, if it had allowed these serious matters to eliminate all gaiety. The townspeople managed to enjoy themselves even in the worst times. On December 16 a band of public-spirited thieves raided a carload of whiskey parked in the Tucson railroad yards, punctured the kegs, filled bottles, cans, and jars with cheerful fluid and distributed them around the neighborhood to promote goodwill among men. The next day "Bundles for Bluejackets" raised money by staging a grand ball at the Pioneer Hotel. The annual Happy Days party (for house-bound victims of tuberculosis) was held at the Woman's Club on the twenty-eighth. Accounts of these and similar events provided a little relief from the accounts of carnage and defeat on the front pages of the newspapers.[47]

Arizona went to war in 1941, but beginning in 1942 the current flowed the other way—the war came to Arizona. On account of its favorable climate and great expanses of unoccupied land, the state became one vast training center for troops who had to be conditioned for desert warfare in Africa, for engineers testing military equipment, and especially for young men learning to fly airplanes. According to the statisticians, 17,500 pilots were trained in this part of the Southwest. They came from twenty-nine countries, including China and Great Britain, though most of them were Americans. "From plow jockey to pilot in twenty-nine weeks" was the slogan of the instructors.[48] Tucson came up with three training installations: Davis-Monthan, the old municipal airport; Ryan Field, west of the city; and Marana Air Base to the north. Marana was activated in April, 1942, when it was 75 percent completed. Before it was deactivated in September, 1945, it had trained 10,000 young men and ranked as the largest pilot-training center in the world. Some infantry and cavalry detachments were also stationed in or near town, and the Consolidated Aircraft plant at the new airport was running three shifts a day in its three huge hangars, modifying B-24s flown in from San Diego, Fort Worth, and Detroit. Housing was a problem for the wave of immigrants who followed the soldiers or came to work as civilians at the bases or at the Consolidated plant. The government provided some assistance by converting old buildings into "wartime housing," and the citizens helped by renting spare rooms. Somehow everyone was taken care of, though on weekends people were not surprised to find men from out-of-town bases sleeping on their lawns. When German and Italian prisoners of war began arriving later on, the war-related population swelled even more. In the Tucson vicinity prisoners were detained at

World War II draft board on duty. From left: Barney Mead, Danny May, George Martin, Monte Mansfield, Hi Corbett, and Ralph Bilby.

Continental, on the road to Nogales, and at Marana.[49]

Officers and trainees were hungry for amusement, and the demand created a supply. Roy Drachman recalled:

There were night clubs, a few of them struggling, but when the servicemen started coming in and the money began to flow, there were quite a few clubs to cater to the servicemen. The Santa Rita Hotel was a very busy place in those days, [and] the Pioneer Hotel. The old La Jolla Club down on South Sixth Avenue was probably the outstanding nightclub in town.

El Conquistador Hotel became a good substitute for an officers club for the lieutenants at nearby Davis-Monthan.[50]

A young man in civilian clothes at a dancing party during these years felt embarrassed and out of place. Uniforms were everywhere,

particularly at weddings. Sometimes the grooms were local boys; often they were outsiders who had fallen in love with local girls. Phil J. Martin's daughter Phyllis, for example, was married at Tucson on August 3, 1944, to Sergeant John Lynch, of Beverly, Massachusetts. The couple left after the wedding for Dalhart, Texas, where John was stationed with a gunnery group. If the man could not make it to Tucson for the wedding, his fiancée had to do the traveling. On January 2, 1944, Betsey Phelps Ellinwood married First Lieutenant Thomas Y. Clark, of Lowell, Massachusetts, at McCook, Nebraska. Announced on the same day was the wedding of Alice Graybeal to Lieutenant Loren E. Jackson at Saint Petersburg, Florida. Both brides were from important Tucson families.[51]

The marriage lottery induced some very

fine young men to settle in Tucson permanently. A good example was Tom Stevens, an Illinois boy who trained as a radio mechanic at Scott Field, in his home state, and came by roundabout ways to Arizona. In Tucson he met and married Mary Hand, a local teacher whose parents lived at Winkelmann. His specialty took him to Kunming, China, where he was in charge of radio repair work for the B-24 bombers, but after his discharge he returned to Tucson, built a house at 1128 East Tenth Street, and induced four local men (George W. Chambers, George Aurelius, Roy Drachman, and Robert W. Williams) to back him in purchasing El Patio, a drive-in restaurant on East Speedway.[52]

He was one of many. A writer for the *Arizona Republic* who headed his column "Que Pasó?" remarked in 1978 that these men followed a standard pattern:

. . . they all hurried home, from wherever they were in 1945, but they stayed only long enough to change into civilian clothes. I keep running into them all over Arizona. Our intelligence officer became a Tucson newspaper executive. One of them sold me a car. And when I ventured into a patio store in 1948, guess who bustled up, all smiles and calling me sir? Our first sergeant.[53]

So much for the military. Civilians had special concerns of their own during those years. The War Production Board siphoned off all resources needed for the war effort. The people back home got what was left, and the Office of Price Administration took charge of that. The OPA became a superbureaucracy which eventually involved some of the country's best brains. Richard A. Harvill, professor of economics in the university and later on its president, was a good example. He moved to Phoenix in 1942 to join the OPA staff and in 1943 became district price executive. For four years he listened to the cries of outraged housewives who complained about the price of milk and the indignant protests of dairymen who demanded more money for their product.[54]

Because of the OPA, ration books became family treasures, and housewives mastered the intricacies of a point system and kept up with the regularly published OPA guidelines which mirrored the shifting policies of the economic dictators with regard to the value of stamps, the availability of commodities, and the length of time specified stamps would be accepted. Long lines shuffled forward at meat markets and grocery stores, and sometimes people at the end of the line found little on the shelves when their turn came. The lucky ones went home to concoct such dishes as Gypsy's Joy Stew, Vegetable Pie with Cheese Crust, Haddock Creole, and Economy Fruit Sherbet, guided by Josephine Gibson's *Wartime Canning and Cooking Book*.[55]

Ten-year-old Margaret Sparks was ready to hurry down to the A&P store when word came to her mother that coffee or sugar was available. Her family eschewed tobacco and traded their cigarette stamps for something they could use. Stamps were supposed to be detached from the book by the butcher or the grocer, but trading was possible. Disillusioned shoppers complained that, although the *C* card (lowest in priority of the three gasoline cards) was good only for retreads when the ration board admitted grudgingly that the family Chevrolet needed tires, people who "knew somebody" could get around the regulations, and there was always the black market if one had enough money. A traveler who saw three truckloads of butter rotting on the San Francisco docks because the bureaucracy had slipped a cog became disillusioned and critical, like so many others.[56]

Men and women who were not too deeply lacerated by the OPA realized that its objectives—to give everyone a fair chance at what there was and to hold down inflation—were at least partly realized. It is easy to imagine what would have happened to the economy, as wages soared and the supply of commodities declined, had there been no OPA. "Looking at the cost of living generally," said retiring price administrator Leon Henderson in January, 1943, "we find that it has been held within reasonable bounds up to the present, particularly when compared with the same period during the last war."[57] Existence, especially toward the end of the war, became increasingly difficult, but it was at least possible. One could do without a new car and new clothes, especially since every other American citizen was in the same situation.

Although Tucsonans responded emotionally and financially to every demand imposed upon them, they had a good time too. Avid sports fans, they followed the news about football and boxing and golf. They went to plays and movies and concerts, and they flocked to parties, when parties were possible. The New Year's Eve celebrations on December 31, 1942, were the largest in the city's history, according to the *Star*, but some sadness was mingled with the joy:

Night clubs and hotels played to overflow crowds of confetti-showered, serpentine-draped merrymakers, midnight theatres were jammed, fraternal halls and clubs echoed to gay laughter of dancers mingled with orchestral strains, but in many homes and in many hearts, the New Year brought poignant memories of former New Years shared with loved ones now in the service. Many a silent prayer was offered.[58]

The prayers were needed. Prospects were bleak enough on January 1, 1943. Columnist Charles P. Speare warned his readers:

"During 1943 we shall have to become accustomed occasionally to being a little hungry, and to enduring chilly homes, wearing clothes that have begun to look shoddy, walking where we once have ridden, directing what money we can into Victory bonds, going where we are sent, and doing what we are told to do." Lack of money was not the problem. "Americans will have more spending money than ever before," Speare acknowledged. The problem was that there was very little to spend it on.[59]

Speare was a good prophet. Events turned out pretty much as he predicted. Belts had to be tightened, and some hardships had to be endured, but the country held on, sustained by a strong faith that the Allies would eventually win and by increasingly hopeful reports from the battlefronts, especially in Europe, where the Nazis were losing and the Italians had already lost. Tucson men were carrying their share of the load all over the world. Editor W. R. Mathews of the *Star*, who liked to travel to far places and report to his neighbors back home, was in Manila in August, 1945, and sent back stories about the many Tucsonans and University of Arizona graduates he had encountered in the Pacific area. They were everywhere doing everything. Frank Eyman, former Tucson police captain, was serving as chief investigator for the navy shore patrol in Honolulu. Colonel Frederick R. Stofft was commanding officer of the 127th Infantry somewhere in the Pacific theatre. Major Fred Finney of the *Star* and Major Masten Jacks of the *Citizen* were present at an "Arizona Day" celebration on the island of Guam. Howard Pyle, veteran Phoenix radio announcer (and later governor of Arizona) was broadcasting for KTAR and for NBC from the Philippines. They were all glad to see somebody from home.[60]

Frank A. Eyman, outstanding police officer.

Tucson women were making their contributions too. Emily Brown was one. She was training with the WAAC at Fort Huachuca in January, 1943, and wrote with pride that her unit was making a fine record. "It meant so much to us," she said, "because they said we could never make the grade. The Army wasn't worried about training women operators for service, but was definitely apprehensive as to female mechanics." Emily was only one of many women who found places in the service.[61]

A few Tucson civilians were caught in battle areas and suffered the consequences. The Mark W. Clardys and their two children were in the news in August, 1945. Clardy was a mining engineer—a "brilliant student," according to his teachers at the university—who went to the Philippines after graduation to live in a mining community. When the Japanese troops took charge, he

joined a guerrilla force and moved back into the hills. Twelve missionaries were in the party at a camp which they called 'Hopevale,' and there a Japanese detachment found them on December 20, 1943. After two days they were all beheaded. Two days later, when their unhappy fate was revealed, a *Ladies' Home Journal* article about them added an ounce of iron to the resolve of the American people to put an end to such atrocities.[62]

Day by day and mile by mile and island by island the Allied forces advanced, and the day came when the Axis could fight no more. Germany capitulated first. In July, 1944, the American flag was raised over Berlin. A year later the great exodus from Europe was in full swing. "In increasing numbers Tucson's veterans of World War II are returning from the battle fronts of the world," the *Star* commented, "hanging up their uniforms and getting back into civilian life."[63] High-ranking officers were among them. Major General Frank Culin, Jr., a graduate of the university, returned on July 13, 1944, for a four-generation reunion at the home of his parents, at 1001 North Ninth Avenue. Culin had won his star in the Aleutians by clearing the island of Attu of its Japanese defenders and had distinguished himself as leader of the 87th Infantry during the invasion of Germany, especially at the storming of Coblenz. Major General Ralph Smith, who had a record of successful combat in the South Pacific, was awarded the Legion of Honor by the French government before he left Europe for home. Major General Charles B. Stone III, Tucson-born and bred, had strengthened his ties with the town by marrying George Smalley's daughter Ama, who lived with their two children at 833 North Fourth Avenue while he was away. He succeeded to command of the Fourteenth Air Force when General Claire Chennault retired.[64]

The men in the Pacific eventually had their homecoming, but it was delayed by unremitting Japanese resistance. By the summer of 1945 the Americans, the Australians, and the British were within bombing distance of the Japanese homeland and had reduced the enemy navy and air force to impotence. Japan's war production had been cut to almost zero, but still a diehard government refused to surrender and continued to refuse until the Bomb fell on Hiroshima and Nagasaki, ending all effective resistance.[65]

When President Harry S. Truman announced the capitulation on August 15, 1945, wild celebrations followed all over the country. In Tucson the downtown streets were flooded with jubilant men and women. Pedestrians shouted and embraced each other, while motorists raised a magnificent din with their horns. The roads were jammed with people coming in from outlying communities, wanting to join in the demonstration. That night there was a parade through the business district, and a memorial service was held in the high-school stadium for those who would never come back. The churches were crowded with thankful congregations. It went on for two days.[66]

General MacArthur was in the Philippines when the end came, and he set out immediately for Tokyo with an armada of 383 ships. With this flotilla was William R. Mathews, editor of the *Star*, who was present aboard the battleship *Missouri* on September 1. He reported to his readers back in Tucson that he "looked down on the surrender from a front-row seat, gun turret two." It was a gray day, he said, and clouds hung low over Sagami Bay as the signers came to the table, first the two Japanese representatives, then MacArthur, then recently released prisoner of war General Jonathan Wainright and Sir Arthur Percival of Singapore, then seven others, including a Russian staff officer. Just after the New Zealand representative signed, the sun broke through the clouds, relieving the somberness of the proceedings and symbolizing, for some of the participants and observers, the better days which everyone hoped were just ahead.[67]

CHAPTER 15

The Price of Progress: Tucson as Metropolis

As World War II faded into history, Tucson entered a new era—a new world. It began changing from a small city to a metropolis, and its problems and its advantages changed as a result. The advantages were there, but the problems captured the most public attention and caused the most debate as the city limits edged toward the horizon and the newcomers arrived in greater quantities until they numbered a thousand and more every month.

At first the times were good in spite of the gloomy predictions of those who remembered the great slump which followed World War I and expected another in the late 1940s. For one thing, new business continued to bolster the economy. In 1944 a $1 million cement plant prepared to open at Rillito, north of town. In 1945, Davis-Monthen scheduled a $1.5 million expansion. In 1946 the postwar building boom produced 1,000 new dwellings, and in 1948 the number rose to 5,000.[1] After Howard Hughes erected the first units of an enormous defense plant, a new surge of activity began, and when his men started buying up real estate, particularly on the south side but in other parts of town also, the pace increased.[2]

The advance, however, was not steady. There were slumps and recessions, the first coming in 1949, when Consolidated Vultee closed its huge shops at the municipal airport. When that happened, says Evo DeConcini (who was in real estate), "a pall of depression descended on the city." Worse reverses came in 1961–62, and the slowdown lasted for some six years, but even during the worst times Tucson expanded rapidly as more and more people crowded in.[3]

The tidal wave of immigration was not just local. The whole Southwest was bulging and booming and continued to attract hordes of immigrants as the years passed. The war had already contributed substantially to what George E. Mowry called "a vast urbanization of the nation's people" as men and women from small towns and farms were absorbed into factories and defense plants, especially in the South, the Southwest, and California.[4] Fifteen million servicemen had been uprooted and sent to camps where training could continue through the winter months. By the end of the war thousands of them had come to realize that they would rather be hot than cold, and they flocked to cities like Phoenix and Tucson.

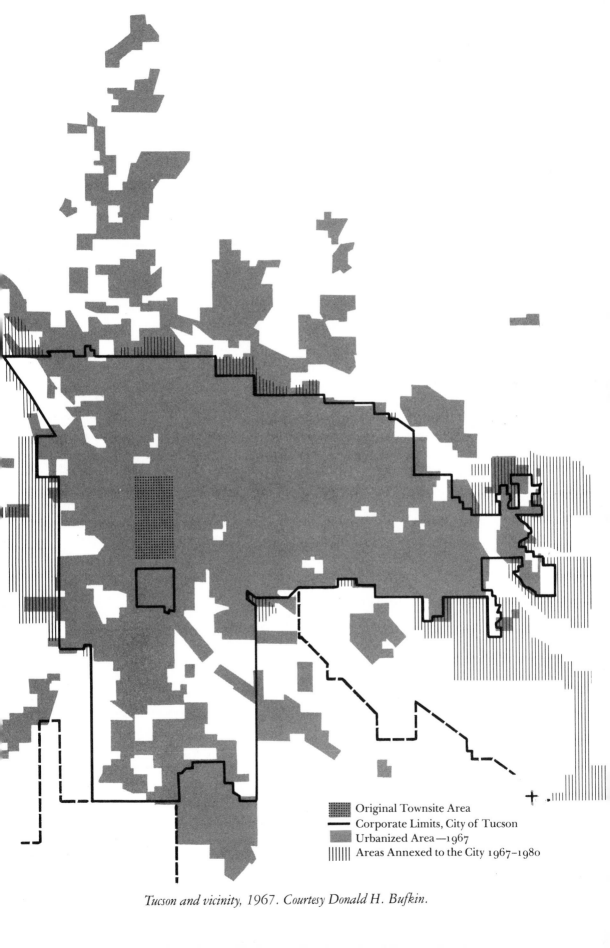

Original Townsite Area
Corporate Limits, City of Tucson
Urbanized Area—1967
Areas Annexed to the City 1967–1980

Tucson and vicinity, 1967. Courtesy Donald H. Bufkin.

They were more than welcome. Since before the coming of the railroad, Tucson had yearned for more people. The great argument of the foes of statehood was the insignificance—and the perversity—of the population of the territory. More and better citizens were needed, since everything, including representation in governing bodies, seemed to depend on numbers. Tucson had to grow to amount to anything, and there was always rejoicing when new figures revealed advances in population statistics. There was no doubt or debate about it. The desirability of growth was taken for granted until relatively recent times, and even in the 1980s chambers of commerce in most southwestern communities were still advertising and promoting and trying to attract business, industry, tourists, and retirees.

And the growth did take place, increasing steadily as the century progressed and the Tucson city limits moved toward the horizon: 32,506 inside the corporate limits in 1930; 36,818 in 1940; 45,454 in 1950; 212,892 in 1960; 262,933 in 1970; 331,506 in 1980. It was astonishing; it was incredible; and every effort was made to make it even more so. As housing became "critical" and "desperate," the builders opened new subdivisions, and the city annexed them. The banner year was 1953, when ten named areas were absorbed.[5]

The Sunshine Climate Club was given credit for opening the doors, and Tucson citizens were urged every year to subsidize its efforts. On October 1, 1940, a *Star* editorial voiced the sentiments of the community:

Since 1922 when this club was organized, Tucson has grown steadily year after year. The story of Tucson and its sunshine has been told constantly every year to the people of the entire nation and Canada. The several hundred thousand inquiries that have come directly from this ad-

vertising coupled with the many thousands of arrivals stand as eloquent proof of the success of this year in and year out advertising campaign. The last winter's season was the biggest season that Tucson ever had. Tucson by its advertising has sold the desert to the nation and made it a great asset.

It seemed normal and natural in 1953 that a Committee of 100 should be organized by civic leaders to attract industry. How else was Tucson to become bigger and better? Some "old fashioned boosterism" still prevailed in the business community at the end of the 1970s.[6]

One segment of the population also wanted Tucson to change from its comfortable Mexican-border character to something closer to the model of Peoria or Nashville or Rochester. Tourists came to town expecting to find a primitive society where men still carried six-shooters and the saloons stayed open all night. Progressive Tucsonans were pained and dismayed by such expectations. Two sisters, Sarah and Virginia Lovett, reacted in the columns of the *Star*:

Contrary to your beliefs, Tucson is not a part of the Old World, but is a city encouraging progress of every kind. After having lived here for 18 and 20 years, we still cannot see the beauty of living conditions on Convent and Meyers streets. We are as ashamed of those districts where the poorer members of our community are forced to crowd into the filth and dirt of those adobe houses in "Mexican Town" as you city slickers should be of your tenement districts. (We've seen them!). We cheer for joy every time we see an old building torn down and a new one taking its place. We are not proud of our "Mexican Town"—on the contrary, we are looking forward to the time when we can wipe it off the face of our map and give our Spanish-American population a chance to enjoy the finer things of life that they, as American citizens, have the right to look forward to. We believe in progress.[7]

The Lovett sisters no doubt approved, as a step toward civic beautification, the action of the sheriff's deputies on March 13, 1947, when they descended on a collection of hobo shacks near the Southern Pacific tracks and burned them all to the ground. Not everybody, however, was so eager to strip off the old and don the new. As early as September, 1944, serious consideration was given to establishing a Mexican historic center in the heart of town. The Chamber of Commerce proposed to restore San Agustín Plaza, where the freight wagons from the east had ended their journeys before the railroad and the venerable church had stood guard over the Old Pueblo. Not everybody wanted to pull the town apart in the interest of progress.[8]

In sober truth, Tucson was always of two minds about progress and expansion. There was never a time in three centuries of history when segments of the population in residence did not resent the influx of newcomers and wish the community could be kept just the way it was when *they* arrived. The Pima and Papago Indians in the eighteenth century had this feeling, and since they were in the habit of taking direct action in such cases, they either fled to the wilds or threw the Spaniards out. The Anglos, when they arrived, usually confined themselves to fussing and griping, and consequently the boosters and builders had things pretty much their own way. Supporters of no-growth and of historic preservation had to wait some time for their turn to come, and in the 1950s they were still a minority. In the sixties they came to life; in the seventies they almost took charge.

One obvious conclusion emerges from this discussion: the basic ingredient in Tucson's history during the fifties and sixties was newcomers. The tremendous influx of immigrants during those decades provides a key to Tucson's recent history. Almost every civic development, good or bad, has been the result of the population explosion and of the need to prepare for its certain continuation.

Responsible people were aware of what was happening, or about to happen, and did their best to plan for it, but it was hard for them to believe that the city would balloon as it did. Says Evo De Concini:

I recall very well, when the Chamber of Commerce predicted that Tucson would be 50,000 people, I thought, "That would be nice," but I didn't believe it. When we got 50,000, they said it was going to be 100,000, and I said, "Now, I know that will never be." But in time it happened, and from then on I would believe any figure projected. It is now predicted by the Hudson Company of New York . . . that Tucson in the year 2012 will be 1,250,000, and now I believe it.[9]

Not even the planners and city officials could foresee that Tucson would boom as it did, and consequently they held back when they should have gone all out to restrain somersaulting subdivisions, lay out adequate highways and arterial streets, and protect the desert environment. Their lack of long-range vision, excusable and natural as it was, laid a heavy burden on the city, its officials, and its citizens in the second half of the century.

Dedicated effort was never lacking. The idea of planning for growth was first heard of in 1930, when the city council adopted its first zoning ordinance. Five years later a group of public-spirited men and women put together the "Tucson Regional Plan" (incorporated in 1938), dedicated to the creation of an overall program for the orderly development of the city. A well-known city planner named Ladislas Segoe was imported in 1940, given a staff, and set to work studying the local economy, land use, population, transportation, recreational facilities, building codes, and similar basic considerations. Segoe laid the foundation for future planning activity. A city Planning and Zoning Commission was established in 1941, and a joint city and county department began operations in 1943. A regional land-use plan for the Tucson area was worked out and adopted by the Tucson City Council on November 16, 1959, and by the Pima County supervisors on July 19, 1960.[10]

Naturally, in a time of rapid change, the regional plan soon needed updating, and in 1965 the mayor and council appointed a Community Goals Committee, with William Voris, dean of the University College of Business and Public Administration, as chairman. This group accomplished very little, but it was the forerunner of many more in the decades that were ahead, some useful, some not. The most effective program, by all odds, was the Comprehensive Planning Process (CPP), which was activated in 1972 with considerable fanfare and an impressive amount of citizen participation. The first complete draft of the plan was ready in March, 1975, and after much debate it was adopted in a somewhat watered-down form. Another group worked out a new plan for the urbanized area of eastern Pima County—the Tucson metropolitan area—in 1976–77, and through the following years a mixture of local agencies and government units labored to foresee and provide for the needs of a ballooning population. They included the city and county planning departments, the City of South Tucson, the Tucson Area Transportation Planning Agency, the City of Tucson Citizens' Advisory Planning Committee, and the communities of Green Valley, Oro Val-

ley, and Marana when their interests were affected. Every effort was made to involve the public. The city was divided into fourteen planning districts, each with its own planning organization, and open meetings were held before any decisive step was taken. The wheels of change turned slowly because of prolonged debate, but the people involved at least had a chance to be heard.[11]

Meanwhile the ever-increasing expansion went on, restrained but never controlled by the planners. The best and almost the only tool available to them and to the city administration was the zoning code, and it was always controversial. The view of one group was summed up by Norman Williams in a paper read at the Arizona Historical Convention, meeting in Tucson in 1979: "The rule of the 70's was 'zoning for the asking.'" Professional planners, on the other hand, pointed out that zoning was never intended to be rigid and forever but had to change with changing conditions. Special situations did, indeed, arise as the city grew.

Speedway, Broadway, and Twenty-second Street served as main arteries eastward, while Davis-Monthan and the municipal airport provided focuses for industrial and residential development farther south. On the northwest side Ralph Wetmore, Moss Ruthrauff, and Nicholas Genematas came early and left their names on the geography. M. L. Reid, who came to Tucson in 1923 suffering from tuberculosis, acquired 200 acres in what he called the "thermal belt" because it was on the plateau and often escaped the frost that settled in the Rillito Valley. He said that he could grow anything, but he specialized in oranges and palm trees. Italian-born Sam (christened Silvio) Nanini, a self-made Chicago businessman and contractor, became interested in the northwest side when he came to Tucson in 1936 in search of a climate that would benefit his wife's health (Giaconda Way is named for her). In 1948 he came back for good, bought 2,900 acres, and, in spite of warnings that he was insane to try it, developed the Casas Adobes area into (in his own words) "the best community anyone has ever seen." It was opened in 1954.[12]

A school-site plan established in 1955 provided a pattern for residential development south of the thermal belt and the foothills. The land was fairly level, the streets already followed section lines, and it seemed logical to approve a series of residential developments approximately a mile square, with a school in the middle and shopping facilities. The pattern could be used in most of the subdivisions, and the big shopping centers along main arteries fitted into the grid pattern.[13]

The barrage of new centers began with small shot as Swanway at Swan and Broadway, and Delray, on East Twenty-second were opened in 1954, followed by the County Fair, at Twenty-second and Craycroft, in 1956. Large-caliber building began in February, 1957, when a $3.5-million center was finished at Broadway and Wilmot. In March, Southgate was completed on South Sixth along Interstate 10. The first unit of the Casas Adobes center was ready in September. Other openings included Amphi Plaza, on North First at Fort Lowell, in January, 1958; Monterey Village, at Speedway and Wilmot, in October, 1958; Campbell Plaza, in April, 1960; Tanque Verde and El Con (the first "regional" or supercenter), in November, 1960; Flowing Wells, in December, 1960; and El Campo, Oxford Plaza, and Eastgate, in 1961. Building came almost to a standstill in 1961 and 1962, the downswing lasting for several years, but the opening of Orange Grove Village Shopping Center on North Oracle in 1965 was the prelude to renewed activity.[14]

Construction picked up after that, encouraged by outsiders, many of them from California, who found Tucson real estate priced below values in their home territory and bought up business blocks and houses by the dozen. One West Coast syndicate was reported in 1978 to have acquired 400 family homes. The annexing of new built-up areas went on apace, each one ambitious to outdo Del Webb's Pueblo Gardens, a $20-million enterprise just west of Davis-Monthan, which was started in 1946. A few of the new subdivisions asked for annexation; others submitted without too much resistance; many battled furiously to avoid it. Expansion-minded Mayor Don Hummel worked so hard and encountered so much opposition in the late fifties that he attended a citizens' meeting at Catalina Junior High School (now Doolen) wearing a suit of armor. He was the only one present who appreciated the joke. A few years later Mayor James Corbett remarked that the protesters would have to be dragged in "kicking and screaming." Immediately bumper stickers appeared on area cars: "Kicking and Screaming, Yes. Annexation, No!" Eventually some of the recalcitrants gave in, but by no means all. Resistance was successful in the Casas Adobes area and in the Catalina foothills— which were still outside the city limits in 1980.[15]

This was the time when Tucson began to be a multilingual, multinational city. The new people came from everywhere and often organized to enjoy and preserve their heritage. The Greeks, the Italians, the Poles, the Finns, the Norwegians, the Scots, the Cubans, the Serbs, the Czechs, the Japanese, the Filipinos, the Ukrainians, the Hungarians, the French—all formed their own groups and societies. In 1974 these and more, plus the Papagos, Pimas, and Yaquis, were brought together for the first Tucson "Meet Yourself" celebration downtown at Presidio Park. The idea was conceived by folklorist and anthropologist Jim Griffith and his wife, Loma. It was sponsored by the Cultural Exchange of Tucson and by Pima Community College. The government of the United States helped with the expenses. In 1980 twenty ethnic groups took part in the entertainment program, and many of them offered the foods of their homelands as additional attractions. Could this sort of thing happen anywhere but in Tucson?[16]

In the 1950s and after, expansion moved forward outside the municipal boundaries with considerable speed. In September, 1960, Washington released $64.8 million for the installation of the eighteen Titan missiles which eventually ringed the city. After the missiles were in place, several hundred workers were laid off, severely jolting the economy. Massive strikes among industrial workers delayed full recovery, but new arrivals and new projects kept the wheels turning. One such enterprise was Green Valley, a community for the comfortably retired. Begun in 1963, it survived some early setbacks and by 1980 had blossomed into a community of homes, shopping centers, and golf courses enjoyed by over 13,000 happy residents.[17]

The mining industry was always a steady source of income. Important copper mines ringed the town, and the big companies expanded and stepped up production in the 1960s. Anaconda began a big stripping operation at Twin Buttes, south of town, in 1966, and by 1970 the Sierrita works had piled up tailings 340 feet high, to the dismay of residents of Green Valley, just across the Nogales highway. Mining specialists re-

ported in 1976 that the four open-pit operations along the Santa Cruz Valley produced 10 percent of the nation's copper and provided jobs for 5,000 local people. Tucson was a supply center for a great deal of mining activity.[18]

Another source of income was the great observatory at Kitt Peak, sixty miles west of the city. Dedicated in March, 1958, it needed time to shift gears but finally got its big telescope into operation in May, 1963, and continued to develop thereafter. Tying the community together, Interstate 10, known always as "the freeway," was opened to through-city traffic in 1954 and completed the final link with Phoenix in 1966.[19]

Not content to let events take their natural course during the slowdown of the sixties, James N. Corbett, later a sometimes controversial mayor, organized the Development Authority for Tucson Economy (DATE) to attract new industry, and new industry continued to arrive.[20] The biggest plum was the Burr-Brown Industrial Research Company, which broke ground for a quarter-million-dollar plant at Airport Industrial Park in January, 1965. DATE director David Richmond noted proudly in 1974 that his group, after six years of supercharged activity, had attracted fifty-two new companies to the city. Important later additions were Gates Learjet and American Atomics, the latter specializing in the manufacture of illuminated dials for watches and other instruments. Both arrived in 1976. After 1978, DATE was absorbed by the Tucson Economic Development Corporation, but the campaign continued, and new businesses responded. In 1978, International Business Machines equipped and staffed a large plant on the southeast side of town. National Semiconductor and Veeco Instruments followed in 1979. A few got away. In 1965, Motorola considered moving in but gave up the idea in 1974, when it failed to get the location it wanted. American Atomics was lost in 1979, when it was discovered that children's lunches in a nearby school cafeteria contained enough radioactive tritium to pose a health hazard. The company was forced to close down, and a great quantity of expensive food was taken out and buried.[21] These, however, were exceptions.

Labor was cheaper and more plentiful in El Paso and Tijuana, but the Tucson work force was adequate, and the city offered so many advantages that new businesses, particularly light manufacturing companies, continued to come in.

Tourists also continued to be a mainstay of the economy. In 1954 they were worth $28.5 million to the city. In 1959 the figure had risen to $900 million.[22] Much of the new construction was tourist- and winter-visitor-oriented, and motels and apartments rose where saltbush and paloverde had flourished a few months before.

Unfortunately growth had to be paid for, and the first installment was exacted in a marked decline of the inner city. New buildings were indeed going up. Tucson House, the great apartment complex on Miracle Mile, was completed in the fall of 1963. In 1964, Tucson Federal Savings, later Home Federal, poured concrete for what was then the city's tallest building. But business in the downtown section was already unmistakably declining. Fewer and fewer people did their buying in the downtown stores. The proliferating shopping centers on the outskirts provided them with shiny new shops and ample parking facilities, and they seldom appeared on Congress Street or Stone Avenue, wallet in hand. The slowdown in the center was accompanied by a corre-

sponding decline in the old residential districts on its fringes on the south and west. Landlords did not want to spend money on the renovation or upkeep of houses and small shops, 80 percent of which were rented.[23]

Some stopgap measures were proposed. As mentioned earlier, in September, 1944, serious consideration was given to establishing a "Mexican historic center" in the heart of downtown with traditional Mexican architecture and old-fashioned *tiendas* stocked with curios and traditional foodstuffs. The Chamber of Commerce proposed to restore San Agustín Plaza, where the freight wagons had ended their journeys before the railroad arrived and San Augustine's Church rose at the heart of the Old Pueblo.[24]

Although this and a few similar schemes came to nothing, the slum problem, which had been addressed with some success in the late 1930s, was followed up in the succeeding decades. New Deal machinery for improving the lot of poor Americans included the United States Housing Administration, created to finance low-cost shelter for the underprivileged and, during World War II, for civilians working in war-related industries. Tucson was targeted for improvement, and Mayor Henry O. Jaastad and his advisers debated whether or not to accept the offered bounty. The promise of a $750,000 government loan to initiate the project silenced the skeptics, and in 1941, Warren A. Grossetta became the first chief of the Tucson Housing Authority.[25]

La Reforma housing complex, at Twenty-second Street and Tenth Avenue, was the immediate result, but it remained the only permanent low-cost project until the 1950s. Following the passage of the 1949 Congressional Housing Act, a serious survey of Tucson's needs and opportunities was undertaken by a citizens' committee headed by attorney Morris K. Udall (later congressman). The group investigated 1,022 dwellings and reported to the mayor and council that 75 percent of them were substandard. They recommended asking for federal government help for the construction of 500 or more units as the start of a continuing campaign. Their work led to the opening in 1967 of the Connie Chambers development, near La Reforma, and ultimately to others, including the Martin Luther King Apartments, on Congress Street, in the downtown area. At first the objective was to concentrate many units in a small space, but in a few years the philosophy changed, and dispersal became the rule. As the year 1970 drew to a close, 200 housing units were under construction on twenty-six sites, and the city had enough federal money to lease 200 private dwellings for occupancy by low-income families—800 units in all. Impressive as these figures were, new quarters were never able to keep up with the steadily increasing need. There were never enough apartments; the ones that were built were sometimes in the wrong places for the comfort, convenience, and safety of the tenants; there were problems of security, transportation, and social adjustment. Public housing was a remedy but not a cure for the ills of the inner city.[26]

There seemed to be no effective cure, either, for the flight of business from Congress, Broadway, and Stone to the suburbs, but in the sixties and seventies Urban Renewal seemed to offer a way out. First proposed in 1957, the idea was revived in 1962, when the crowds began disappearing from downtown streets. Slum clearance was still part of the plan, but this time the adobe hovels were to be replaced not by improved housing but by a whole complex of structures which would concentrate, in the area

to be cleared, the city and county governments and the cultural life of the community. This gleaming core, the enthusiasts said, would make the heart of the city beautiful again and bring back the crowds of shoppers, visitors, and culture buffs.[27]

The issue was highly controversial, and it was hard to tell whether supporters or opponents were in the majority. Proponents pointed out the obvious advantages. Critics, led by Councilman G. Freeman Woods, objected to the inevitable intrusion of government bureaus into municipal affairs. Residents of the endangered areas fought to keep their homes and small businesses. There were bitter debates, and finally the city council went on record as opposed to the whole concept.[28] In 1965, however, the councilmen reconsidered. They agreed to let the voters decide on the merits of urban renewal and the proposed community center. The voters obliged by registering disapproval of both. They had already turned down a big school-bond issue in 1954 and had been slow in years gone by to authorize street paving or anything else that cost money. The city planners were not the only ones who failed to realize what was ahead for Tucson. After all the shuffling and vacillating, however, the council approved the program of slum clearance and urban renewal on November 8, 1965, limiting the area to fifty-two acres. The voters affirmed the decision on January 1, 1966.[29]

The whole program was deeply disturbing to one segment of the population. It meant, first of all, the obliteration of one of the oldest residential districts in Tucson. The residents were mostly Mexican-American families who would have trouble finding quarters they could afford elsewhere and small businessmen who had no hope of making a living anywhere else. The effect of urban renewal on this group would be traumatic. The barrios were home to them, and their decaying houses were nothing if not "historic." Mrs. Elva B. Torres in the fall of 1967 headed a Committee to Save La Placita. She was backed by other Mexican-Americans and by some influential townspeople, including Gilbert Ronstadt and Emil Haury, of the university Department of Anthropology. They pointed out that the old church plaza was a traditional civic center for the Mexican-Americans—that 14,000 people had attended a recent Sixteenth of September celebration there, and that something priceless would be lost if it were taken away. The urban renewers were not inhumane, but they were convinced that the old adobes had to come down and be replaced by a fine modern community center, complete with an exhibition hall, a county and city civic center, a music hall, a first-class hotel, and a shopping center which would bear the familiar name of the old Plaza de la Mesilla—La Placita.[30]

It all boiled down to a conclusion that urban renewal would be possible if Washington advanced the money. In July, 1972, the money was forthcoming in the form of a $2.25-million loan. A ground-breaking ceremony was held on September 7, 1972, and construction started the following February. Meanwhile the bulldozers moved in, and the old landmarks vanished, including Sabino (Gay) Alley, several old hotels and stores, the building which had once been the Alianza headquarters, and dozens of saloons, rooming houses and business blocks whose 900 inhabitants scattered—uprooted and, in many cases, resentful.

Their wounds were still painful many years later. They remembered, as reporter Judy Donovan recorded in the *Star* in December, 1978:

the old adobe homes that sheltered generations, the small, productive gardens, and the security of their neighborhood where everyone knew each other, shared the same culture and spoke Spanish. . . . Those who lost their homes, businesses, and other property to urban renewal were paid off, but the money couldn't compensate for the psychological blow. . . . They not only had to leave; the stage was set for more development that endangered neighboring downtown barrios.[31]

True enough, the urban renewers were not content with replacing hopelessly blighted districts. They were bent on improving what was left. Backed by the United States Demonstration Cities and Metropolitan Development Act of 1966, the city of Tucson entered the "Model Cities" program—an experimental effort to identify blighted urban areas which could be salvaged and to try to upgrade them. Under a grant of $3,117,000 educational programs were started in several selected districts; paving, curbs, street lights, and sewers were installed; and some houses were renovated.[32]

Another enterprise, aiming in the same direction but largely funded by private investors, was the *barrio historico* south of the Community Center, where the old houses were restored as dwellings or converted into commercial establishments. The families who continued to live nearby in their ancient adobes discovered that, as the districts were improved, rents went up, and they could no longer afford to live in their familiar neighborhoods. The only people who seemed pleased with all this architectural spit and polish were the occupants of houses in the Armory Park area on South Fourth Avenue. In 1974 the area was declared a historic district, enabling them to qualify for tax reductions and to borrow government money at low interest for repairs and renovation. They complained, however, that when the bills were paid they had invested more money than their places were worth.[33]

The most ambitious of the plans for revitalization were aimed at vacant and run-down areas west of the center but close to downtown. La Entrada focused on the once high-class neighborhood west of Main Street sometimes called Snob Hollow. General Levi H. Manning's enormous white mansion (in later years an Elks Club) dominated the area, but the rest of the great houses were gone. The city proposed to build, with government help, a $15-million complex of apartments and townhouses as an adjunct to the urban-renewal program. The project would restore a district in which building was stagnant and would provide walking-distance housing for people who worked in downtown stores and offices and thereby solve their transportation problems. It seemed an excellent idea, but it ran into heavy opposition. In 1981 it was still unable to make headway as opponents charged that the site was not by any definition a "blighted" area and was therefore in violation of the terms of the proposed grant.[34]

The other west-side project, called Rio Nuevo, fared just as badly. It was intended to reclaim and beautify the junk-filled river-bottom lands clearly visible from downtown office buildings. Local residents protested that their neighborhoods would be endangered by the many new apartments and the multitude of new residents and that only the builders would profit. In spite of a considerable investment in surveys and plans, little progress had been made by the early 1980s.[35]

Meanwhile, however, the Community Center and its adjuncts became a reality. City and county employees moved into their new office complex in 1967. The Music Hall opened in 1971. The old adobe house

nearby, where territorial Governor John C. Frémont may or may not have spent a few days during his brief tenure of office (1878–83), was officially dedicated as La Casa del Gobernador in 1972 by Mrs. Richard M. Nixon and opened to the public in the following year. The Tucson Heritage Foundation, an efficient committee of civic-minded workers headed by Mrs. Emery C. Johnson, took charge of rebuilding and furnishing the venerable structure, first saving it from the bulldozers and then restoring it to a glory which it had probably never enjoyed even in its heyday a hundred years before.[36] The huge sports arena was ready for business in 1971; the theater opened in February, 1972; the convention hotel flung wide its doors in November, 1973; and what should have been the heart of a successful project—the assembly of shops and restaurants known as La Placita—opened in 1974, only to fall upon evil days. Three years went by before it operated in the black, and even then revenues were insufficient to meet mortgage payments. Too few merchants set up shop on the premises. Too few people left the suburbs and came downtown to spend their money. There were foreclosures and changes in ownership, and in 1980, La Placita was trying to make a new start with the cards stacked against it.[37]

The revitalizing activity which came off best was the stabilization, restoration, and utilization of the historic block on North Main Avenue where the first families had lived and entertained in the 1870s. After prolonged negotiations which began in 1965, the city leased the area to the Tucson Museum of Art for a dollar a year and agreed to contribute $60,000 annually for upkeep if the society would undertake to renovate the Fish-Stevens and Cordova houses and build a new museum. A $500,000 gift from

Tucson city hall, completed in 1917. Courtesy Donald H. Bufkin and Journal of Arizona History.

City hall coming down, and its 1972 replacement. Courtesy Donald H. Bufkin and Journal of Arizona History.

The Frémont House dwarfed by the Community Center Music Hall.

Mrs. Richard M. Nixon cuts the ribbon at the opening of the Frémont House, Casa del Gobernador, April 7, 1972. Governor Jack Williams stands at left.

The downtown area in December, 1955. Outlined are (1) the presidio, (2) the military plaza, (3) the cemetery. Courtesy Donald H. Bufkin and Journal of Arizona History.

Helen and John Murphey was the largest of several major donations, and the whole enterprise came to a triumphant climax with a grand opening on May 4, 1975. That moment remained a matter of immense pride to the hundreds of individuals who had contributed time, money, and energy to the cause.[38]

In spite of this success the debate contin-ued on the possibility and desirability of arresting the decay of Tucson's downtown. In 1980 it was still going on. One side argued that a town without a downtown was not a town at all and pointed out that new-building starts in Chicago, Pittsburgh, Baltimore, Oakland, and New York were signs that urban vitality could be restored and Tucson's center city could be saved. Peren-

Downtown in 1972, showing dramatic changes—the Community Center nearing completion, upper left. Courtesy Donald H. Bufkin and Journal of Arizona History.

nial Mayor Lew Murphy urged the citizens not to give up on the inner city, though even as he spoke, merchants were taking flight to the suburbs, and the once lively focus of community activity was as quiet as a graveyard after closing hours. Realistic city planners, on the other hand, argued that "cities are declining and will continue to decline—and deteriorate," having a life cycle like other organisms, unable to resist the pressures of the times.[39]

The causes of decline were obvious. In Tucson, as elsewhere, Everyman's love affair with his automobile had something to do with it, and the picture of the Good Life in Everyman's mind had even more. Easterners came to escape crowded cities and the pressure of too many people. They enjoyed Tucson's spaciousness and its casual western manners. They came for elbowroom, separation from their neighbors, a bit of wild nature at hand. They liked the undemanding desert landscaping of their full-acre lots, the quail and the rabbits and the white-wing doves that came in for breakfast and dinner. They were willing to drive many miles to work if they could come home to these amenities in the evening. The shopping centers followed them, and the neglected city center withered and declined. The happy suburbanites felt little or no grief over the municipality's problems, but the planners and city officials did. "A nation drunk with prosperity has disregarded its cultural heart," said architect William Wilde of Tucson, and many agreed.[40]

Plans for reviving downtown came thick and fast. In 1975 the Tucson Trade Bureau came up with ideas for a "face-lift" for the declining area. It included a shopping mall, closed to motor traffic, as its central feature. The idea was discussed pro and con and rejected in 1977. In 1978 the Downtown Advisory Committee presented a more ambitious *Plan for Downtown Tucson*, which involved a redesigning and reshaping of the whole central area. The "grand new design" angered barrio residents, however, while eastsiders argued that the money ought to be spent on their developing areas, not on run-down business blocks. All that came of it was a beautiful and expensive brochure.[41] Another plan, described by *Citizen* writer John BretHarte as "strictly in the grand manner," was proposed by a California firm in 1980. Its heart was to be a "huge, pyramid-shaped high-rise, . . . a vertical Park Mall." Nothing came of that idea either.[42]

If Tucson's center suffered from decay and desertion, the outlying areas had diseases of their own. One of them was called "urban

sprawl." The suburbanites, looking for peace and privacy, were partly to blame, but the developers were responsible too. One of them would buy a tract of land, cheap because it was outside the settled areas, and put in roads and build houses. Power and gas lines, sewers and telephone cables had to be extended for unreasonable distances; the desert was destroyed where it should have been preserved; and the many acres of land which the developer bypassed became polluted and unsightly. Zoning ordinances, by approving large tracts for single-family homes, and area plans with the same ideas actually encouraged low-density housing, and there was no way of regulating this sort of haphazard growth until the county was empowered by the state government to formulate zoning laws. Even then the trend continued until the late seventies, when low-cost peripheral land began to disappear and high interest rates cut down the market for suburban housing.[43]

It was this sort of abuse which finally brought the advocates of no growth or limited growth into violent confrontation with the developers. Leading the hue and cry was a determined little group of four college and high-school students who in 1972 advertised their feelings of revulsion by smearing painted signs on new housing starts— "Fight Urban Sprawl"—and sometimes signing themselves "The Eco Raiders." They later declared that they had not vandalized any of the houses or destroyed any equipment, but somebody did, and they got the blame. Clever and intelligent, they eluded pursuit for several months but were finally caught and brought before Judge Mary Anne Richey. She sentenced them to a few months in jail and a long period of probation.[44]

The opponents of sprawl marched with

the limited-growth crusaders, led by Ron Asta during his years as a member of the Pima County Board of Supervisors (1976–78). Asta, a striking and flamboyant young man, was good at making speeches and capturing headlines. The "Comprehensive Plan," which began functioning in 1972, called for public participation in decision making, and the "Astacrats" joined other citizen groups in well-publicized and sometimes acrimonious debates. When Asta failed of reelection, some of the excitement subsided, though Councilman John Varga and county Supervisor David Yetman kept the controlled-growth issue warm in succeeding years. The pressure was further relieved by the success of various area plans in controlling density and the progress of "urban infill" as apartment buildings rose on vacant land in the urban area. The 1980 census clearly showed, however, that Tucson was still booming and that the problems caused by rapid growth were not likely to go away.[45]

One result of the exploding population bomb was the impossible traffic situation. The "Comprehensive Regional Plan" of 1959–60 was supplemented by a transportation study, a first stage of which was completed in 1965. It proposed to upgrade the main arteries and build enough freeways and parkways to take care of the problem up to 1980. This was the time for decisive action. Settlement was sparse, and land acquisition along the routes was easy, but the officials did not strike while the iron was hot, and they lost their chance. Citizen participation in the planning process actually hindered positive action. Nobody wanted a freeway to go past *his* place. Nobody wanted a bantam interchange on *his* corner. The ideal seemed to be a country road winding past a house in the foothills. Without realizing it, perhaps,

these people were agreeing with Frank Lloyd Wright that "to look at a cross section of any plan of a big city is to look at something like a fibrous tumor."[46] They did not choose to look.

The great bone of contention was a plan for intracity limited-access roads, particularly the Butterfield route, which would cut across town from the southeast side, meeting the freeway below the city center. Proposed as early as 1960, it ran into heavy opposition in 1972 and was dropped, as was the projected freeway along the Pantano-Rillito channels, but both reappeared in modified form from time to time. New studies began in the fall of 1979, and by mid-1980 the planners were ready with a series of five carefully worked-out programs involving grade-separated intersections, bantam and superbantam interchanges, throughways, and parkways. Again the cries of outrage arose, and decision was put off, but a positive step was taken early in 1981, when the Pima Association of Governments voted to approve one of the five options—a long-range plan to build two parkways ("designed to move vehicles at high speeds through landscaped areas dotted with parks"), revivals of the Butterfield and Rillito-Pantano routes, intended to solve the city's problems until the year 2000. The usual howls of protest ascended at once, and the usual stalemate seemed to be in the offing. The California pattern of jammed highways and creeping progress at rush hour seemed unavoidable for Tucson in the eighties and nineties.[47]

Too many people. Too many cars. Another result was pollution—nowhere near as bad as in Los Angeles, not nearly as bad as in Phoenix. But bad enough. Automobiles were responsible for most of it, but the big cement plant at Rillito and the Magma

Mining Company smelter at San Manuel contributed their share. Dust entered the air from unpaved roads and from the mountains of mine tailings on the far southside. The Environmental Protection Agency ordered the County Air Quality Control District to clean up by 1982, and progress was being made in 1981. The yellow pall of fumes, smoke, and dust still hung over the city at certain times, however, and defied all efforts to remove it.[48]

Even harder to control was another big-city problem: the safety of citizens and their possessions on the streets and in their homes. Crime was on the increase all over the country in the seventies, and in 1978, after several years of steady progress upward, Tucson was leading all cities in its class, according to the FBI. "Tucson is crime city," Pima County Attorney Steven D. Neely declared in 1979. "Despite its peaceful veneer, Tucson has more rapes, robberies, assaults, burglaries, auto thefts and homicides than any of its American counterparts."[49] This was no great surprise to senior citizens who had known the town as a frontier community and expected a certain amount of violence and sin to liven up the news every day. Gambling was part of the inheritance and almost impossible to root out. Prostitution had never been eliminated. Statistics on violent crime demonstrated that Tucson still had its share of tough and willful characters, though the figures indicated that burglary, often drug-related, was the favorite crime.

It appeared, furthermore, as a result of periodic exposures, that peace officers and county officials were not out of reach of temptation. One regrettable case came to light in March, 1951, when Jerome P. Martin and Maurice T. Guiney, who had just completed terms as sheriff and undersheriff of Pima County, were indicted and con-victed on a charge of receiving protection money from Dolores Rains, proprietress of two massage parlors on Ina Road. Martin's case was a specially sad one. He had grown up in Tucson, was prominent in fraternal affairs, and had been a member of the Arizona legislature. A promising career was ruined when he went to prison, and he died at fifty-seven, broken in health and spirit, in 1956, two and a half years after his release.[50]

As distressing in a different way was the case of Sheriff Waldon V. Burr and his six deputies, whose resignation under pressure was the top news story of 1971. Most people considered Burr a good and honest peace officer, well trained in his business. He had served as undersheriff for Ben McKinney and had been a captain in the Arizona Highway Patrol, but a bad situation developed in his office—unhealthy rivalries among the officers and suspicious relationships between some of his men and underworld figures. Control seemed to be lacking. In 1968, Burr was under fire, and a grand jury indicted him on a series of counts, then quashed the charges. A new jury reinstated them, but they were later dismissed. In 1971 the sparks again began to fly. The state attorney general and officials of the Department of Public Safety conducted investigations for ten months, and in September they were ready with seventy-seven felony charges against the sheriff and his men.

For reasons which were not revealed to the public, the investigators offered the accused men a choice: resign and the charges would be dropped; stay on and suffer the consequences. Burr and six men submitted their resignations. Included were Undersheriff Richard C. Williams, Detective Captain Albert Felix, Captain Manuel Medeiros, and three deputies. Chief Deputy Michael S. Barr became acting sheriff and served until November, 1972, when William Coy Cox was appointed.

There was grumbling about the dismissal of the charges. All that County Attorney Rose Silver would say in explanation was that there was a "dangerous situation" in the sheriff's office.[51]

It was to be expected that the incidence of crime would grow as the city grew, but in the early fifties wrongdoing appeared to be moving ahead of schedule. It seemed that an unusually large percentage of the population was misbehaving, and nobody knew why. High-school students were in trouble when a marijuana ring was uncovered in February, 1950; vandalism was up, especially on special occasions like Halloween; street gangs were active. The same perverse tendencies appeared in the older citizens. Drugs were already becoming a problem, though the abuse would become much worse in the years ahead. The police staged a big raid on distributors in January, 1951, and made at least a semiserious attempt to control prostitution in the fall of that year. Robbery seemed to be epidemic, a particularly flagrant example being a raid on a Safeway store on the east side in January, 1951. County Attorney Robert Morrison stated publicly that Tucson was experiencing "a breakdown of law and order."[52]

Even supposedly good and orderly people were involved. There was a small scandal about church lotteries in 1952, for example. They were adjudged to be bona fide gambling games and therefore illegal, and the brethren were warned to desist. In private clubs, where such activity might have been expected, gambling went on undercover for years. A cleanup campaign was threatened but not begun until July, 1954. A year later the police raided eight private clubs and came away with twenty-one slot machines and other devices for idle-hour wagering. There was some argument about one such machine called a "digger"—a debate which reached a climax in 1957, when the diggers were identified positively as gambling equipment by the United States government and were removed from all clubs and bars.[53]

New causes for demonstrations, arrests, protests, and uneasiness arose in Tucson as elsewhere during the sixties. Racial tensions, which had never come to the surface before, now disturbed the community. On July 23, 1967, a group of militant blacks created a disturbance, alarming both blacks and whites. There was not much danger that the situation would get out of hand, but black leaders formed a committee within their own community to keep fires from breaking out. In spite of their efforts, however, minor disturbances occurred at El Rio Golf Course and at Mansfield Park, following a pattern becoming familiar all over the country. The worst trouble came on August 30, 1970, when a clash between black and white youths at the Fox Theater brought on a more serious riot and some looting. Investigations, arrests, and trials followed, but there were no serious consequences.[54]

Chicanos staged no major demonstrations during the sixties. A unit of La Raza Unida was organized, held its first meeting in September, 1968,[55] and was heard from occasionally in the months that followed, but there was no marching or arm waving, not even at the university, where trouble might have been expected. Outbreaks of intense racial feeling did not come until later in the seventies, when complaints of police brutality and cries for social justice were raised by the Mexican-American community.

Police expected social unrest, epidemic throughout the country, and early in 1968 began laying in supplies of Mace. Nothing happened until July 6, however, when the officers moved in on a group of young people congregating at a "coffeehouse" on Sixth Street. Suspecting traffic in drugs, detectives and uniformed officers searched both girls and boys without separating them and aroused much public indignation thereby.[56].

The succeeding calm lasted until January, 1971, when a group resembling the "street people" who harassed the University of California at Berkeley descended on the University of Arizona. Only a few were bona fide students. The rest were transients who came to enjoy the winter climate. Usually they moved on in a month or six weeks, but others took their places, bringing their sleeping bags and guitars with them. In the spring of 1970 forty or fifty began gathering at the main gate of the university. They panhandled, shoplifted, and intimidated customers, to the great irritation of the merchants. They camped on and befouled the campus grass, to the disgust of President Richard A. Harvill and Robert L. Houston, his tough, efficient chief of campus police. When the Tucson peace officers tried to round up the street people, they climbed over the wall onto the university grounds, where, by a gentleman's agreement, the city force did not go. Since Tucson had no effective ordinance against loitering, nothing was done until Houston's men tried to eject a group drinking wine inside the gates. They refused to go, and a scuffle ensued. On Harvill's orders the city police were asked to take a hand and bring a paddy wagon.

That started a riot. News went out over the radio, and a huge crowd of young people gathered. One story said that 500 youths were battling 400 police officers. Fifty-three offenders were hauled off to jail, and the next day the riot squad had it all to do over again.

Richard A. Harvill, president of the University of Arizona in the 1960s.

On the third day, while confrontations continued, the leaders met with the mayor and City Council and demanded, among other things, that the university lawn be reserved for them. The city officials responded by passing an effective antiloitering ordinance, and President Harvill was able to get his campus back under control.[57]

"Long-haired people wintering here" brought out the police again in February, 1973. The hippies were becoming a nuisance to merchants on North Fourth Avenue. After three weeks of tension they called for help, and seventy-three offenders were booked into the city jail. The ones who escaped the net went into vigorous action at once. Calling themselves the Social Revolutionary Anarchist Federation, they demanded that the city end "cop harassment." After one day of this, the merchants asked that the crackdown be called off. The arrests had hurt business more than the disturbances had, and besides, most of the disturbers had left the city.[58]

When the new sexual freedom arrived and made itself felt in the 1960s, new dimensions were added to the law-and-order situation in Tucson. Topless waitresses appeared in the news in October, 1967. *Deep Throat* scandalized one segment of the population in 1973 (it was declared obscene), and massage parlors came under official attention in 1974, capturing a headline from time to time thereafter. In 1980 the whole spectrum of pornography, prostitution, girl shows, and massage parlors was extensively reviewed by the *Star* in a revealing series of articles which named names and carried photographs, demonstrating, if demonstration was needed, that things had not changed all that much since the 1880s.[59]

The real peril through the seventies, however, was the steady growth of drug imports and drug consumption. Marijuana continued to be smuggled in and peddled freely, though the traffic was somewhat reduced late in the decade, when the smugglers moved their headquarters to Florida. Hard drugs were available to anyone with the money to buy them. Arrests for possession and vending of LSD were reported in January, 1969. The narcotics squad tried diligently to stop the traffic, sometimes breaking into the wrong house in their zeal and scaring innocent people, but seemed unable to stop or even slow the traffic. A major scandal in the middle seventies involved the use of methadone as therapy for addicts. Dr. Clifton T. Alexander was arrested and tried for writing illegal prescrip-

tions, but the abuse continued. Heroin continued to arrive from Mexico, and as early as 1973, Tucson was known as a "heroin port."[60]

The inevitable result was talk about the role of the Mafia in the business and a suspicion, amounting to certainty, arose that Tucson had become, or was becoming, a provincial capital of the eastern "families." Mickey Cohen, a famous gangster in his day, was discouraged from going into business in Tucson in 1951, but fifteen years later Joe Bonnano, reputed to be a major figure in Cosa Nostra in Chicago and New York, moved to Tucson, and the rumor of mob infiltration revived. Bonnano maintained a low profile and did as little as possible to arouse suspicion or investigation, but he was not allowed to live undisturbed. Various schemes were tried, including careful scrutiny of his garbage, to bring him into court. His sons were also kept under surveillance, and one of them, Salvatore (Bill) Bonnano, went to prison in California for a few months in 1978. Joe himself was convicted—for the first time in his life—in 1980, but his case was appealed, and his precarious health made it unlikely that he would ever spend time behind bars.[61]

A better case was made against another reputed mobster who lived in Tucson. Peter Licavoli, Sr., was tried in 1979 for possession of stolen property (a number of valuable paintings) and was sentenced for it.[62]

When investigative reporter Don Bolles was blown up in his car in Phoenix in June, 1976, supposedly to prevent him from publishing his findings about organized crime in the state, it seemed obvious that the mob had taken Horace Greeley's advice. The chief counsel of the state attorney general's special-prosecutions division was probably not exaggerating when he told reporters in August, 1979, that Arizona was "one of the most criminally infiltrated states in the nation," with "more con men per square inch than any other state." They like the climate and the people, he said, "just like you and me."[63] Pima County Attorney Steven D. Neely in a 1979 interview agreed, though he did not think the state was "overrun" with mobsters. "We don't have the numbers rackets, the prostitution, a large number of contract killings. We don't have the highly visible kind of organized crime activity in this community." Nevertheless, he said, "we have an organized-crime problem in this community," and the reason for its success is simple: "I think the Mafia has better lawyers than we do."[64]

One kind of crime seemed especially prevalent in Tucson—rape. Very few convictions, or even apprehensions, went on the books, and in 1980, with the numbers of reported rapes up over 18 percent (to 184 in 1979), relief did not seem to be in sight, though women were buying dogs and revolvers, carrying tear gas and Mace, and studying the martial arts of China. It was small comfort to them that the frequency of the crime was rising in all the major cities of the United States, not just in Tucson.[65] On the university campus in 1981 male students were providing escort services so that no woman student would have to walk alone on or near the campus.[66]

In the midst of all this darkness one lamp was lighted which should have cast its beams afar—the Tucson Urban Area Crime Commission—organized in 1969 at the suggestion of Mayor James N. Corbett when the word went out that the mob was infiltrating the Tucson underworld. Eight years later the commission was still "looking for direction." A federal agency in Phoenix with the same mission was said to be undercutting the Tucson body, reducing its responsibilities to such trivialities as registering bicycles. Unwilling to give up, however, county officials in 1977 were planning another team to fight the Mafia. "We are going after the top dogs," said Sheriff Richard Boykin, and County Attorney Stephen D. Neely added that the special force would search out "big-time, big-money organized crime—crime that is run like a business."[67] Citizens were skeptical of its success, though by 1980 some results were apparent. There was no way to eliminate crime in Tucson. It was part of the cost of becoming a metropolis.

CHAPTER 16

. . . But on the Other Hand

Being a big city was not all bad. The difficulties and dangers were real enough, including such problems as, along with those already mentioned, waste disposal, school desegregation, crime and vice in South Tucson, contention between police and minority groups, the plight of the indigent elderly, illegal entrants from Mexico—these and more.[1] But Tucson's astonishing growth brought some good results along with the hazards.

For one thing, metropolitan status made possible group efforts which a smaller community could not have afforded. A good example was the Arizona-Sonora Desert Museum, set in the midst of a cactus-and-saguaro forest across the Tucson Mountains from downtown, with spectacular views southward down the Altar Valley into Mexico and westward to the Baboquivari and Roskruge ranges. The site was dominated in 1950 by the Mountain House, a big adobe building erected by the United States government which was no longer needed. Three outdoor enthusiasts, William H. Carr, William H. Brown, and Arthur N. Pack, conceived the idea of adding to it and building a regional museum, "an outdoor interpretive center where people from all the states could see and learn about the land itself; about the birds, reptiles, insects, mammals of the vast American desert; the plants, life!" In December, 1951, the Pima County Park Advisory Committee voted to support the project, and the Desert Museum

Carr had experience with outdoor museums; Pack had influence and came up with the first funding. Visitors began arriving while the new facilities were still being laid out, and sometimes they picked up shovels or hammers and helped. William H. Woodin came in as director and took the enterprise farther down the road. Joseph Wood Krutch was an enthusiastic supporter. Hal Cras joined the staff and with his wife, Natie, created the *Desert Ark*, a station wagon which carried them and a collection of small animals to schools and clubs in communities as far away as Washington, D.C., bringing the wildlife message to children and grownups. Trials and dissensions occurred as the years passed, but the Desert Museum enjoyed solid public support from the beginning, drew enormous numbers of visitors, and served its educational purpose with remarkable success. It grew up with Tucson.[2]

Founded in 1951 at the very beginning of the great expansion, the Tucson Festival followed the same pattern. The idea was credited to Mme Elenore Altman, pianist and university music professor, a native of Rumania. Red-haired and dynamic, Altman passed on her enthusiasm to the first board of directors, which met at her home and studio in 1950. The members included novelist Elliott Arnold, the first president; English Department head Melvin Solve; planned-parenthood crusader Margaret Sanger Slee; bookseller Eugene Steinheimer; lawyer Samuel B. Goddard, Jr. (later governor), and newspaperman Murray Sinclair. A program committee was appointed: folklorist and novelist Frances Gillmor, historian Father Victor R. Stoner, author Rosemary Drachman Taylor, and anthropologist Edward Spicer. Harold Steinfeld took charge of a money-raising campaign and persuaded thirty-five businessmen to advance $1,000 each, to be repaid from proceeds. Altman's idea of a carnival of artists and musicians was replaced, largely through Elliott Arnold's influence, with a broader objective: "to weave together and perpetuate the indigenous cultures of the Southwest—Indian, Spanish, Mexican and Anglo-American"— in all aspects of their creative activities. Altman was not pleased, but she went along.[3]

The planners were ambitious and went all out to make that first celebration memorable. J. Frank Dobie and Oliver La Farge were brought in to lecture. Soprano Bidu Sayao appeared in concert. A jury picked a fine set of canvases for the art exhibition. Nine local writers, headed by old-pro Leslie Ernenwein, pooled their efforts in the writing of a western novel which appeared serially in the *Star* with no great critical acclaim. In retrospect the most interesting development involved a motion picture

titled *The Last Outpost*, starring Ronald Reagan and Rhonda Fleming. Most of the filming had been done at Old Tucson during the preceding October, and the premiere would coincide with the dates of the festival. It occurred to Elliott Arnold that the only possible place for that first showing would be Tucson, where much of the action occurred, and he persuaded Adolf Zukor, chairman of the board of Paramount Pictures, not only to approve the Tucson presentation but to attend it himself. The fact that his granddaughter Mrs. Boyd Morse and his two great-grandchildren lived in Tucson may have influenced his decision.

On April 4 the great event took place, with several of the principal actors, including Reagan, present for the preliminary festivities. The *Star* on April 4 and 5 went into a mild frenzy as reporters scurried about and filed stories about the Rotary luncheon, the reception at the Santa Rita, and the matinee performance of the motion picture. Providence mercifully hid from curious Tucsonans the destiny which was awaiting the agreeable Mr. Reagan.

As it turned out, the planners were too ambitious, or at least not cautious enough. They spent $10,000 of their funds on a stage for an outdoor performance in the university stadium and another $4,000 for a play-pageant called *The White Shell Cross*, specially written for the occasion by novelist Oliver La Farge. Since La Farge was no dramatist, Peter Marroney, of the university Drama Department, had to make the piece playable, but it was ready for presentation as the climax of a two-week celebration, which began on March 25, 1951. Unfortunately the committee had failed to make proper arrangements with the weather department, and the results were catastrophic—wind, rain, snow every day all day. Performers were

Ronald Reagan, leading man of The Last Outpost, *during the filming at Old Tucson, 1951. With him are Jane Loew Shelton (granddaughter of Marcus Loew and Adolph Zukor) and her children, Boyd and Linda Morse. Courtesy of Robert Shelton and Old Tucson.*

Rehearsal for Oliver LaFarge's White Shell Cross, *University of Arizona Stadium, 1951. Courtesy Tucson Festival Society.*

driven indoors to the university auditorium, where only 2,500 of the 4,000 paid-up patrons could be seated. As a result the first festival was a financial disaster. President Elliott Arnold resigned on April 13 "to get back to his own literary career," and several of the directors followed his example, leaving the rest with a deficit of $44,000 which somehow had to be liquidated.

Not everyone ran for the lifeboats. Lewis Douglas, former ambassador to Great Britain, stepped in as chairman of the board of directors. Lawyer Samuel P. Goddard (a fu-

ture governor) accepted the presidency, and the courageous rear guard prepared to throw themselves into the battle.

Miraculously, thanks mostly to the persistent efforts of Eugene Steinheimer, of Steinheimer's Bookstore, and businessman Thomas B. Freeman, of Tucson and Chicago, the festival survived and flourished. By 1954, through superhuman effort, it was "solidly established." By 1980, under the direction of Jarvis Harriman, it was in excellent financial health and a proud and permanent fixture in the municipal calendar. In

Mary Jeffries Bruce, founder of the Sunday Evening Forum. Esther Henderson photo.

that year more than 100,000 people participated in the month-long series of events at a dozen locations, reaching a final high point in the Turquoise and Silver Ball. The staff worked year round preparing for this month of celebration. Only a major city could or would have supported such a massive undertaking.[4]

The Sunday Evening Forum was another early starter. It began in the thirties, when a group of young-adult members of the University Methodist Church began inviting speakers in for lectures and discussion. After dynamic and aggressive Mary Jeffries (later Mary Jeffries Bruce) took charge in 1942, the public was invited, and before 1950 so many people were attending that the events

were moved to the university auditorium. Mrs. Jeffries went after top attractions, traveling as far as New York and Washington to get them. Eleanor Roosevelt, John F. Kennedy, and Gerald Ford yielded to her persuasion. Martin Luther King, Jr., Ralph Nader, John Chancellor, and Eric Sevareid took their turns. In 1961, Barry Goldwater debated Socialist Norman Thomas. Barry was still learning his business and may have misjudged the effectiveness of old-pro Thomas. Many thought he came off second-best. David Brinkley, who was onstage five times, called the forum "the best organized and best managed in the country."[5]

The seed planted by Mrs. Berger's Saturday Morning Music Club and the other pioneer musical organizations produced an especially rich crop. The symphony orchestra grew in competence and brought top soloists to Tucson. The university artists series did the same, and some famous performers liked Tucson well enough to make it their home. Metropolitan Opera baritone Igor Gorin was one. Mrs. Berger's Temple of Music and Art fell upon evil days after 1960,[6] but great musicians continued to appear.

A long musical step forward was taken in 1939, when Eduardo Caso founded the Tucson Boys Chorus, sometimes called Caso's Singing Cowboys. Caso, a tenor, gave up a promising radio career when he developed tuberculosis and came to St. Luke's-in-the-Desert to recover. He was a good director and handled the boys—and their parents—well. His small sopranos and altos criscrossed the country and in due time went to Europe on tour, singing everything from Bach to "Empty Saddles in the Old Corral." Caso died in 1965, but his successors made the Boys Chorus internationally famous.[7]

Many musical groups—choruses, bands, orchestras—came to life down through the

Eduardo Caso and members of the Tucson Boys Chorus. Left to right: top, J. D. Guthrie and Ted Bushnell; center, Thor Hansen and Jack Vossruhlen; bottom, Danny Reily and Donald Pitt. Ben O. Gross photo.

A member of the Tucson Boys Chorus on tour queries a London policeman. Courtesy Tucson Boys Chorus.

years. One was a chamber-music society, led by composer-conductor Camil Van Hulse, which was active in the late forties. In 1948 the Tucson Friends of Music Society was organized by George Rosenberg (managing editor of the *Citizen*), Stewart Udall (later secretary of the interior), Sybil Juliani Ellinwood, and members of the university music faculty. The group brought in good chamber ensembles and able performers on various instruments. For the first two years, programming was arranged by Peter Yates, of Los Angeles, whose musical "Evenings on the Roof" were popular in California. His tastes did not match those of Tucson listeners, however, and the organization was soon arranging its own presentations before good audiences at Crowder Hall, on the university campus.[8] It was still solvent and successful in the eighties. Opera did not fare quite as well. The Tucson Opera Company, later the Arizona Opera Company, was born in 1972 and immediately began assuming artistic credits and financial debits. The repertory was standard (*Lohengrin*, *La Bohême*, *Traviata*, and *Turandot* in 1979–80), voices and costumes were good, and audiences in Tucson and Phoenix were pleased, but by 1980 the company was $227,000 in debt. A successful financial campaign, however, reduced that sum by $99,000, and prospects were encouraging.[9]

Ballet had even greater problems, contending with sluggish audiences and half-filled houses. The Tucson Ballet presented programs in 1976–77, and was reorganized the following year by Patrick Frantz. It did not survive, however, and was succeeded in 1980 by the Western Ballet Theatre. Performances were described by critic John Peck as "a delight." The Tucson Metropolitan Ballet was offering sophisticated programs in the Music Hall in April, 1981.

Student interest remained strong as the Living Dance Company, Territorial Dance Theater and the Tucson Creative Dance Center trained and presented young dancers in performance.[10]

Tucson always attracted artists. Living was comparatively easy and cheap, the public was interested, winter visitors had money, and a growing art colony offered support and companionship. Organized backing came with the Fine Arts Association, founded in 1924.

Watercolorist Gerry Peirce came to Tucson in the early 1930s and set up an art school in the desert on the east side of town—the first attempt to offer art training. The Tucson Watercolor Guild was organized in 1947 at the home of Margaret Sanger Slee to provide a classroom and studio for this pioneer teacher. The art colony grew rapidly after 1950, and by 1980 many outstanding artists had worked, and were working in the city. Some, like painter, sculptor, and art historian Paul Rossi, had come and gone, but for one who left, ten came in. A few, like Ted De Grazia, became famous. Through the seventies tourists flocked to his studios—the little one on Campbell Avenue and the bigger and newer one on North Swan—and took home specimens of the work of this student of Diego Rivera and José Orozco. Western painter Ross Stefan built up a following of his own, and younger artists claimed the spotlight as the decade progressed. Barbara Ellen Grygutis, teacher and sculptor, did the fountain for La Placita. Ironworker Tom Bredlow fashioned the gates for the National Cathedral in Washington. Fulbright Fellow Andrew Reisch exhibited all over the world. Indians came to life in the canvases of Lawrence Lee, while Harry Brophy and Frances O'Brien, abstract painters, crystallized moods and reached out into the cosmos. James E. Waid and James G. Davis, of the university art faculty, attained distinction as the two Tucson artists chosen by the Western States Biennial Exhibition in 1979.

Tucson painters were joined by artists in other media. Textiles and weaving attracted Crane Day, Berta Wright, and Virginia Johnson. Charles Clement was a sculptor and muralist with subspecialties in concrete and copper. Nancy Skreko Martin was at home in paper, metal, ceramics, and photography. John F. Heric handled wood, marble, and crafts. Kit Schweitzer favored ceramics, concrete sculpture, prints, and masks.[11]

Best known of the sculptors was Suzanne Silvercruys Stevenson, Baroness Silvercruys, whose statue of Francisco Eusebio Kino was presented to the nation and dedicated in the rotunda of the Capitol on February 15, 1965. Born in Belgium, Silvercruys left her family and homeland, immigrated in 1917, became a citizen, and moved to Tucson in 1961. By 1965 she was living in the East again, and she died in Washington in 1973. In spite of her short residence, she made a considerable impression on those who knew her.[12]

Music and art may have claimed most of the public attention, but drama had its followers as well. The Tucson Little Theater, organized in 1950, was very much alive when the Tucson Festival made its debut in 1951 and made its contribution to the program. At the same time the drama department at the university was growing in size and prestige under the eye of Peter R. Marroney, a man of great talent and energy. In 1946 the Tom Thumb Players operated a children's theater, and the Corral Theater was presenting comedies in the round in the Rendezvous Room of the Santa Rita Hotel.

The Tucson Community Theater, formerly the Tucson Little Theater, was active in 1957. The most aggressive and ambitious group, however, was the Arizona Civic Theater, organized in 1966. Guided by founder-director Sandy Rosenthal, ACT survived on local and federal money, became a member of the League of Resident Theaters, built up its staff and audiences, scheduled a Phoenix season, and started a training program called Encompass. David Gardiner came as director in 1977, joining manager David Hawkanson. In 1980, Gary Gisselman became the artistic director. By that time audiences statewide had grown to 70,000 a season, and financial support had more than doubled. Crises had come and gone, but ACT in 1980 seemed to be flourishing.

ACT called itself, with pride, professional theater. The Invisible Theatre, dating from 1975, was just as proud of its amateur status, and the Theater of the Performing Arts made the most of its willingness to experiment. Two dinner theaters were attracting audiences, and the Gaslight Theater, at Trail Town on the east side, offered well-paced comedies, melodramas, and musicals. Tucson was a long way from Broadway, but theater had a secure place in the life of the expanding town.[13]

Of all the creative people on the scene, writers seemed to find themselves most at home. Harold Bell Wright was the only literary man of stature during the twenties, but by 1950 a group of nationally known pen people—novelists, scientists, historians, poets—were living and working in Tucson. Elliott Arnold was one. Sent by accident to Davis-Monthan during World War II, he had met and married a Tucson girl but had lived in the East until her parents gave him a copy of *Arizona Highways* containing an article on Apache chief Cochise. Scenting

307

Erskine Caldwell.

Margaret Sanger.

Elliott Arnold.

Clifford Goldsmith.

Nelson Nye.

Joseph Wood Krutch.

Rosemary Taylor.

Roy Chapman Andrews.

Charles Finney

Writers who were making news in 1951.
Courtesy Tucson Festival Society.

Frances Gillmor.

Westbrook Pegler.

a good subject for a novel, he came back to do research. *Blood Brother* (1947) was the result. Tom Jeffords, his hero, was in real life a charter member of the Arizona Pioneers Historical Society, and Arnold interviewed several of his surviving friends in the organization, trying to understand his character. When the book was published, they agreed that he had made Tom into a very interesting fellow but that any resemblance to the real man was incidental.[14]

The "gang," as Arnold called his group, included Erskine Caldwell (*Tobacco Road*, 1932) and Ruth Suckow, the novelist from Iowa. Years later Arnold reminisced to Don Schellie of the *Citizen* about others in the charmed circle: playwright Clifford Goldsmith (*The Aldrich Family* radio serial, 1938–45); painter Dale Nichols; sculptor Oscar Davisson, who gave an annual corn-and-wine party when the corn in his garden was far enough along; Rosemary Drachman Taylor (*Chicken Every Sunday*, 1943); and Frances Gillmor, a university English teacher who had published two good novels: *Windsinger* (1930) and *Fruit out of Rock* (1940). No member of this or any other coterie was Charles Finney, whose brilliant fantasy *The Circus of Dr. Lao* was a national literary event of 1935. Dozens of commercial westerns were being produced by Walt Coburn, Nelson Nye, and Leslie Ernenwein, while Frank Lockwood, English professor and dean, was writing about the real Arizona pioneers (*Arizona Characters*, 1928), whose adventures were more harrowing than anything the novelists could dream up. Nonfiction writers included Margaret Sanger Slee, already a celebrity when she came to Tucson "for a stay of several weeks" in 1934. Widowed in 1941, she gave herself entirely to the cause of planned parenthood and was always on the way to or coming back from India or Sweden or some other faraway place. One of her doctor sons lived in Tucson, however, and she was more at home there than anywhere else when she died, at eighty-six, in September, 1966. Another writer of stature of the time was Roy Chapman Andrews, whose specialty was the Gobi Desert. In the fifties he had few peers as a travel writer.[15]

As the years passed, more famous names found their way into the Tucson directory. Westbrook Pegler, cantankerous and controversial journalist, lived on Magee Road beyond Casas Adobes, as far as he could get from the city. He died there in 1968. Joseph Wood Krutch, long-term professor of English in Columbia University and leading New York drama critic, put the East firmly behind him and moved to Tucson in 1952. A convert to the desert, he became a great conservationist and nature lover and a masterful writer about the wild creatures he saw near his home on East Grant Road and on trips about Arizona (*The Desert Year*, 1951).[16]

All sorts of writers produced books in steady streams. Ann Nolan Clark and Betty Baker specialized in stories for children and young people. Some excellent craftsmen joined the university faculty as time went on. Anthropologists were particularly productive (Emil Haury, Keith Basso, Bernard L. Fontana, Clara Lee Tanner), but English professors like Cecil Robinson, L. D. Clark, and Robert Houston also did important work. Some nationally known figures—William Eastlake, Vine Deloria, Jr., Leslie Silko, Lawrence Clark Powell, and N. Scott Momaday—came to the campus on special assignments.

Unexpected immigrants turned up from time to time. John Creasey, the prolific author of almost innumerable suspense novels (557 by his own count in 1971) was a Tuc-

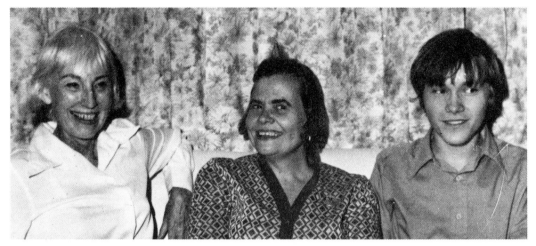

Ruth Stephan (left), LaVerne Harrell Clark (center), and unidentified student poet at the Poetry Center. Courtesy LaVerne Harrell Clark.

sonan for a number of years before returning to take up permanent residence on his family estate in England. Clarence Budington Kelland was another maverick. Editor of the *American Boy* and writer of serials for the *Saturday Evening Post*, he first became acquainted with Arizona when his car broke down in Phoenix on a transcontinental trip. Very soon he was maintaining a home in Arizona and writing about the state (for example, *Arizona*, set in Tucson, 1939) and functioning as the state Republican chairman. He died at Scottsdale in 1962 at eighty-two.[17]

Other unusual writing talents included that of Evangeline Ensley, author, among other things, of a well-reviewed tetralogy about medieval Wales. Jeanne Williams, who came to Tucson as the wife of John Creasey, developed into a highly successful novelist in her own right. She researched a wide variety of backgrounds but finally came home to Arizona with *The Valiant Women* (1980). Even more unusual, since he was the only one of his kind, was Refugio Zavala, a native of Sonora who came to Tuc-

son as a child in 1907 and in 1980 published *The Autobiography of a Yaqui Poet*.[18]

Then there was a remarkable company of poets, most of them imported to read their work and confer with students at the Poetry Center, just off the university campus. The center was the dream fulfilled of Ruth Stephan, a member of the Walgreen family, who lived first in Chicago and Greenwich, Connecticut. In her house she had a poetry room where her three sons read and enjoyed verse. Hoping to do the same for college students, she bought and furnished a small house where poets and poetry buffs could meet and browse. The students responded with enthusiasm, but they were not content just to read. They wanted to be read to. Mrs. Stephan was firm in her conviction that her contribution should not be used to provide fees and expenses for visiting poets, so the university took over that aspect of the project under direction of Professor of English Laurence Muir. The little house was converted into a hospice for the entertainment of bards in residence, and a new and larger building was transformed into a library, reading center, and headquarters, with office space for a small staff. LaVerne Harrell Clark, wife of another English professor, was installed as director. She gave up the post in 1966 to work on a book of her own, but in 1976 she harvested her experiences as a friend of poets in an anthology called *The Face of Poetry*, which sampled the work of 101 writers, many of whom had been guests at the center. There were, of course, many good poets in Tucson, some connected with the center, some not. Richard Shelton, widely known for his desert poems, was closely identified with it. Wallace Fuller, a university biochemist, worked independently.[19]

A good essay could be written on the novels which have had something to say about life in Tucson. An early example was *Dark Madonna* (1937), by university instructor Richard Summers. The setting was the Tucson barrios; the mood was bitter and sombrely realistic, forecasting the attitudes of Chicano writers twenty-five or thirty years later. In a somewhat similar vein was Edith Heal's short novel *This Very Sun* (1944), about unhappy people, presumably in Tucson, who "belong to no one." Heal had been in public relations in Chicago, had written successful children's books, and was working for a Tucson newspaper. Gil Meynier, her French-born husband, was also a journalist and author of *Stranger at the Door* (1948). The characters were ordinary people, victims and aggressors, in a Tucson boarding house.[20] Elliott Arnold's *Blood Brother* (1947), though it ranged far and wide through the desert country, made Tucson a

focal point, as did his last work, *The Camp Grant Massacre* (1976).

Many commercial westerns were set wholly or in part in Tucson. Kelland's *Arizona* was one. Another was Allan Vaughn Elston's *The Lawless Border* (1965). Both men made a serious study of the history and background, but the average writer of shoot-'em-ups relied on J. Ross Browne's account, quoted in an earlier chapter, or on the descriptions of John G. Bourke, who tried to be funny about the place a few years later. Even Louis L'Amour wrote in the same vein in *The Lonely Men* (1969), as did Robert Steelman in *Apache Wells* (1969—fourth printing, 1974) and Hunter Ingram in *Fort Apache* (1975). The trail was well marked.

Writers with better comprehension came along in the seventies—for example, Byrd Baylor, who wrote with humor and understanding about the Tucson Papagos in *Yes Is Better than No* (1977); and Don Schellie, columnist and novelist, in *Me, Cholay & Co.* (1973), which dealt with the Camp Grant massacre.[21]

Even writers of spy and intrigue fiction, whose numbers multiplied in the seventies, sometimes chose Tucson for a locale. Brian Garfield's *Deep Cover* (1971), Philip Chase's *Merchants of Death* (1976), and Don Pendleton's *Arizona Ambush* (1977), are good examples.

The list could be extended, but the point is clear: these creative people in their various specialties and on their separate levels would probably have lived and worked somewhere else had Tucson remained a village. But Tucson grew, and they responded.

CHAPTER 17

Back to the Bowl and Pitcher

Tucson, in the long run, is a city in danger. Its water supply is dwindling and may not last very long. When the water runs out, Tucson runs out, and the desert will reclaim its own. It is impossible to predict when this unfortunate event will take place, but one thing is certain: the more the city grows, the faster the water goes, and the less time it will take for the end to come.

The problem is compounded because pumps supply all the water there is and perhaps all there will ever be. Tucson is the only American city of comparable size which has to depend entirely on groundwater. The Central Arizona Project (CAP) may bring in a limited amount from the Colorado River in the late eighties, but it will be of poor quality if it does come, and there is no certainty that any of it will arrive.[1] Phoenix has the Salt River; Albuquerque and El Paso have the Rio Grande. Tucson once had the Santa Cruz, but it stopped running decades ago, leaving the city to "mine" its water from the great reservoir under the valley. How much is there, and how long will it last? "Nobody knows," says hydrologist Sol Resnick, of the university.[2]

The Indians and the early Spaniards relied on surface water for their needs. The river supplied the irrigation ditches. Water bubbling up from the *ojito* and other springs near A Mountain provided for drinking and cooking. There was enough to take care of as many as 5,000 people without tapping the underground supply.[3] The Americans, when they came, had bigger ideas. They dammed the river above town and created Silver Lake to power their gristmills and offer a new form of recreation to the people. They developed more and more farmland in the valley and pumped or diverted more and more water until there was none left in the river except in the rainy season, when the dry channel flooded.[4] The city had to drill wells to bring up water for domestic use, and by 1980 about 200 wells were tapping the underground supply. A few belonged to individuals and small neighborhood companies, but most had been drilled by the city or acquired over the years. The water table was receding four or five feet a year, the land was beginning to subside, and the quality of the water was declining as salt from recycling plants and irrigation runoff reached the underground reservoir.[5] The situation was not desperate. There was still a great

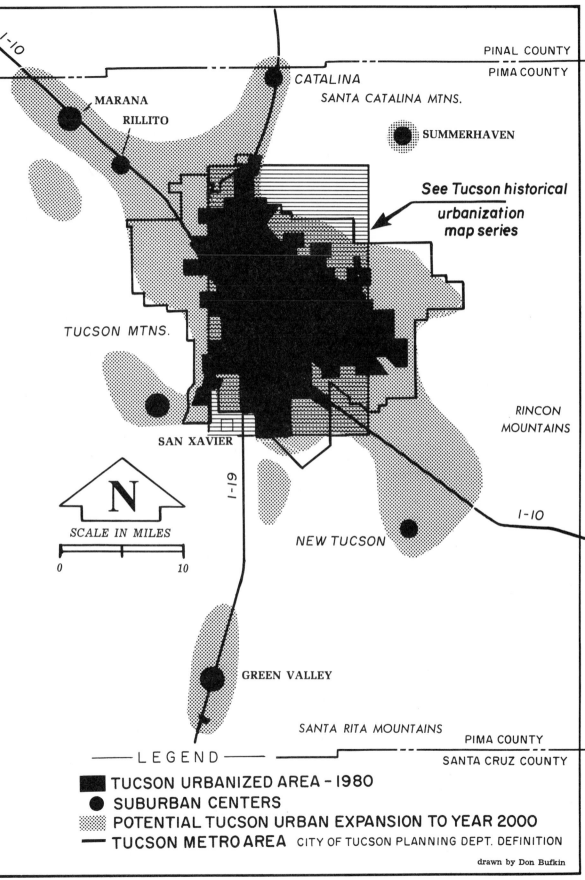

Where the people are and where they may be by the year 2000. Courtesy Donald H. Bufkin.

amount of water in the storage reservoir. Nobody knew how deep it was, but some estimates said it went down 3,000 feet.[6] The point, however, was that it did have a bottom and someday the bottom would be reached. Tucson's growth hastened that day.

There was no way to keep the immigrants from coming, and some arid-lands specialists thought they had to come. "It is widely felt," wrote Peter Duisberg in 1958, "that if mankind is to meet the increasing need of an expanding population and a rising standard of living, it will be necessary to turn to the arid regions of the world. These areas constitute nearly thirty percent of the land surface of the earth. At present they are generally characterized by sparse population or limited development, or both."[7]

So many pilgrims were coming to the Tucson area in the 1960s that the city began looking for water resources outside the basin. The first idea was to buy land and water rights in the San Pedro Valley, north of Benson, and a good deal of money was put into the venture. It all went for nothing, however, when legal experts warned that the water could not be moved from one basin to the other. In 1966 the city had better luck with water rights in the Avra Valley, just west of the Tucson Mountains. Eleven thousand acres went for $9 million, and in spite of outcries and lawsuits from the Avra Valley farmers acquisition went on until 1980. By that time the Papagos and their lawyers were claiming much of the available supply in that area, and the water specialists agreed that Tucson's chances of getting Colorado water would be improved if Avra Valley were out of the picture.[8]

Groundwater was the number-one problem for the state as well as for Tucson. Cities and towns consumed only a small part of the supply. Industry, including the copper mines, used as much or more, but the biggest share went to the farmers, and the farmers tended to dominate the legislature. They would agree to nothing that limited their right to pump, and as a result there was no effective control of water in Arizona until 1980. All agreed that control was vital, but no two groups could agree on a formula.[9]

Confrontations began with the signing of the Santa Fe Compact of 1922, which tried to divide the waters of the Colorado equitably among the states of the upper and lower Colorado basins and with Mexico. Arizona refused to participate until the drought of the 1930s forced a change of attitude and led to the ratification of the pact in 1943. A hard push toward regulation of groundwater use followed as Governor Sidney P. Osborn tried repeatedly but unsuccessfully to get legislative action. Only in 1945, when the Central Arizona Project was declared feasible—provided Arizona solved its water-depletion problems—did he gain cooperation, and legislation was not passed until 1948. Thanks to the efforts of such men as G. E. P. Smith, of the university, and Robert H. Forbes, a great arid-lands specialist, a code was formulated and passed. It gave the state only "token control," however, and years of bitter wrangling followed.[10] A new campaign started in the late seventies, when the CAP was again in jeopardy. Governor Bruce Babbitt brought his considerable talents and energies to bear on the problem and finally, in 1980, got what he wanted. The new code was immediately challenged by Indians and special-interest groups, however, and its effectiveness was still to be demonstrated.[11]

The Tucson situation was complicated by disagreements about the seriousness of the situation. On the one hand, the optimists refused to believe that there was anything to worry about. Technology could meet the challenge. Importation, conservation, desalinization, and scientific advances could save the day. Maurice M. Kelso, William E. Martin, and Lawtence E. Marsh, writing in 1973, recommended limiting allocation to "the sector of higher production of net income per unit of water." Under this system, they said, "the economy can continue to grow without significant restraint." Others pointed out that, although Tucson was consuming three times as much fluid as nature could replace, 90 percent of domestic water went back into the Santa Cruz channel and ultimately into the subsurface reservoir. They noted that water use went down as prices went up and that, willingly or not, the city was practicing conservation. Agriculture would be phased out by rising costs. Everybody but the farmers agreed that the farms would have to go.

The voters showed where they stood in January, 1977, when four council members were defeated in a recall election because they favored sharp increases in the price of water, especially for foothills residents whose supply had to be pumped to higher elevations.

In 1981 the optimists were telling the world that "if water consumption continues at current levels Tucson could support a population of 1.6 million." "If we can put a man on the moon," they said, "we sure as hell can pump sea water from the Gulf of California."[12]

On the other hand, a highly vocal group was convinced that the end was at hand. Charles Bowden spoke for them in *Killing the Hidden Waters*:

The lay of the land tells us that resources in convenient concentrations are limited. In the case of some minerals, fuels and water deposits, humans can see the point of exhaustion just dec-

ades ahead. Ground water is the dominant factor determining the prosperity of modern economies in arid lands. Access to ground water triggers the use of other resources in such regions . . . the more these reserves are developed, the faster they will be depleted. . . . Current trends make both possibilities increasingly unlikely.

"We can ignore these facts and pump, mine, and combust with abandon," Bowden added, "or we can recognize these facts and attempt to construct a sustainable society. There will be no painless answers."[13]

Some water specialists seemed to agree with Bowden's thesis. Gene Cronk, the city water administrator, warned in the late seventies that the interior wells in Tucson must soon be abandoned to prevent further land subsidence and that water from Avra Valley would not provide a long-term solution.[14] By 1980 many observers were convinced that before long swimming pools and lawns would be unknown in the city, that flower beds and palm trees would disappear from the university campus, that golf courses would return to the desert from which they came, and that the bowl and pitcher would replace the bathroom. Nonconformists could go back to Peoria or Poughkeepsie, where they might continue to live in aqueous luxury.

In his novel of 1980, *Good News*, Edward Abbey, Arizona's foremost prophet of doom, envisioned the collapse of civilization in the Southwest at the end of the present century. The "precarious monstrous cities" of the desert—"cities that were not meant to be"— have collapsed and the survivors are at war among themselves. Most of the people have fled to "greener regions from which, as everyone knew, their packaged food came." Failure to conserve water had to be one of the reasons for this anarchy.[15]

Even to people less pessimistic than Abbey, it began to appear that the Papagos were right after all. They knew how to live on terms dictated by their environment. Anglos might have to learn to do the same—make drastic changes in their style of living, perhaps become, for all practical purposes, desert Indians. Prophets from Mabel Dodge Luhan to Vine Deloria had been saying the same thing for years but finding few listeners. [16]

Anthropologist Bernard L. Fontana, a friend and historian of the Papagos and a believer in their way of life, retained in 1980 a hope that we might still have a chance, though he was not optimistic about it. The Papagos and other desert Indians had the right ideas, and we could learn from them. "Will our home be a place of heat and light and sun and life," he asks, "or will it be a place of barrenness, dust and desolation?" We are desert dwellers, he reminds us, and we had better not forget it. [17]

Sooner or later we will have to remember it—when the well is nearly empty. Someday, croaks Abbey,

the Colorado River will be drained dry. the water table fall to bedrock bottom, the sand dunes block all traffic on Speedway Boulevard and the fungoid dust storms fill the air. Then, if not before, we Arizonans may finally begin to make some sort of accommodation to the nature of this splendid and beautiful and not very friendly desert we are living in. [18]

At least the desert will remain. Perhaps Jon Manchip White's vision in *A World Elsewhere* is the true one:

Wandering across America, across the West, you realize with genuine relief that the population could double, treble, quadruple, yet the major portion of the landscape would remain empty. They can never saturate it. They can never bury it beneath Coca-Cola bottles, chewing-gum wrappers, used-car dumps. . . . It will swallow them up. One half of the United States, the western half of the country, is technically a desert: and a desert it will remain, to desert it will return. Nature, like God, is not mocked. Men can pollute her oceans, poison her rivers, rummage in her guts—she will survive. She is the frame of things. Her wounds must heal. [19]

Notes

Precarious Paradise: An Introduction

1. *Arizona Daily Star*, February 16, August 2, 1979; hereafter cited as *Star*.

2. Gladys Sarlat Public Relations, Inc., news release, May 16, 1978 (announcing *Tucson Trends, 1978*).

3. *Star*, September 21, 1975.

4. Franz Douskey, "Tucson," *Southwest: A Contemporary Anthology*, p. 284.

5. *Star*, December 22, 1980.

6. Sherman R. Miller, *Tropic of Tucson*, p. 34.

7. Bernard L. Fontana, "Where Are We?" *Tucson*, November 1979, p. 29.

8. Edward Abbey, "The Blob Comes to Arizona," in *The Journey Home*, p. 153.

9. *Ibid.*, p. 148.

10. John Coleman Reid, *Reid's Tramp*, p. 185.

11. Julius Froebel, *Seven Years Travel*, p. 503.

Chapter 1
Post Farthest Out

1. For O'Conor and his career see Luis Navarro García, *Don José de Gálvez y la Comandancia General de las Provincias Internas del Norte de Nueva España*; David M. Vigness, "Don Hugo Oconor and New Spain's Northeastern Frontier," *Journal of the West*, vol. 6 (January, 1967), pp. 28–35; Mary Lu Moore and Delmar L. Beene, "The Interior Provinces of New Spain, the Report of Hugo O'Conor, January 3, 1776," *Arizona and the West*, vol. 13 (Autumn, 1971), pp. 265–82.

2. For the location of San Agustín de Oiaur see Bernard L. Fontana, "Synopsis of the Early History of Tucson" (MS), pp. 1–2; Charles W. Polzer, "Clarifi-cation," *Star*, December 3, 1973. Henry F. Dobyns (*Spanish Colonial Tucson*, p. 3) and M. P. Freeman (*The City of Tucson*, pp. 3–4) identify Black Mountain as A Mountain. Charles W. Polzer and Daniel S. Matson (interview, June 4, 1979) believe that it has not been possible to identify Black Mountain with certainty.

3. Donald W. Page (letter to Eleanor Sloan, March 6, 1954) writes, "I claim that the original site of the presidio was at Kino's Indian rancheria of San Agustín de Oiaut (or Oiaur) some two leagues north of Tucson." Harry T. Getty ("People of the Old Pueblo," *Kiva*, vol. 17 [November–December, 1951], p. 1) holds the same opinion. Compare Charles W. Polzer, "Tucson Before the Territory," in Thomas F. Saarinen, ed., "Territorial Tucson" (MS), pp. 2–3; Cameron Greenleaf and Andrew Wallace, "Tucson, Presidio, Pueblo and American City, *Arizoniana*, vol. 3 (Summer, 1962), pp. 18–19.

4. Kieran McCarty, *Desert Documentary*, p. 6; Dobyns, *Spanish Colonial Tucson*, p. 58.

5. Greenleaf and Wallace, "Tucson," p. 18; James Rodney Hastings and Raymond M. Turner, *The Changing Mile*, p. 3.

6. The name Papago was a Spanish invention. Kino did not use it, but his successors did. O'odham (or Ootam) was the name the Papagos used for themselves. The relationship between the Hohokam and the O'odham is uncertain. Charles DiPeso, in *The Upper Pimas of San Cayetano and Tumacacori: An Archaeohistorical Reconstruction of the Ootam of Pimería Alta*, p. 34, thinks the Pimas were in the country before and after the Hohokam "intrusion." For differing opinions see Paul H. Ezell, "Is There a Hohokam Continuum?" *American Antiquity*, vol. 29 (Spring, 1963), p. 61–66; Emil W. Haury, *The Hohokam: Desert Farmers and Craftsmen*, pp. 265, 321, 351–56; Isabel T. Kelly et al., *The Hodges Ruin: A Hohokam Com-*

munity in the Tucson Basin, ed. Gayle Harrison Hartmann, p. 126; Linda M. Gregonis and Karl J. Reinhard, *Hohokam Indians of the Tucson Basin*, 1979.

7. Fay Jackson Smith, John L. Kessell, and Francis J. Fox, *Father Kino in Arizona*, pp. 14, 44.

8. *Ibid.*, p. 14; Harry J. Karns, ed. and trans., *Unknown Arizona and Sonora*, p. 92; Bonaventure Oblasser, "Papaguería: The Domain of the Papagos," *Arizona Historical Review*, vols. 6–7 (April, 1936), pp. 3–9. Oblasser calls the temporary settlements "emergency villages." Charles DiPeso, in *The Upper Pimas*, discusses the adjustment from various points of view.

9. Smith et al., *Father Kino in Arizona*, p. 14.

10. Rufus Kay Wyllys, "Padre Luis Velarde's *Relación* of Pimeria Alta, 1716," *New Mexico Historical Review*, vol. 16 (April, 1931), pp. 132ff. The Pima lifeway is well described in Daniel S. Matson and Bernard L. Fontana, *Friar Bringas Reports to the King*, pp. 23–25; and in Bernard L. Fontana, *Of Earth and Little Rain*, pp. 32–44.

11. Herbert Eugene Bolton used *Rim of Christendom* as the title of his most famous book. Theodore E. Treutlein discusses the phrase in "Father Gottfried Bernhardt Middendorff, Pioneer of Tucson," *New Mexico Historical Review*, vol. 32 (October, 1957), p. 311, n. 3.

12. Dobyns, *Spanish Colonial Tucson*, p. 57.

13. Charles W. Polzer, "Long Before the Blue Dragoons," *Military History of the Spanish-American Southwest*, p. 9.

14. John L. Kessell, *Mission of Sorrows*, p. 82; Dobyns, *Spanish Colonial Tucson*, pp. 12–13; John Augustine Donahue, *After Kino*, pp. 141–143; Juan Nentvig, *Rudo Ensayo*, p. 79.

15. DiPeso, *The Upper Pimas*, p. 129.

16. John L. Kessell, *Friars, Soldiers, and Reformers*, p. 5; Dobyns, *Spanish Colonial Tucson*, pp. 12–13.

17. Kessell, *Mission of Sorrows*, p. 5.

18. Jack D. Forbes, *Apache, Navajo, and Spaniard*, pp. 283–84: "Prior to 1693–97, the Pimas and Sobaipuris were friends and allies of the Apaches. This friendly relationship was purposely destroyed as part of the Hispanic policy of 'divide and conquer.'"

19. Kieran Robert McCarty, "Franciscan Beginnings in the Arizona-Sonora Desert," p. 1; Herbert E. Bolton, *The Mission as a Frontier Institution*, p. 3.

20. Bolton, *The Mission*, pp. 4, 23; Charles DiPeso, "The Sobaipuris: Defenders of the San Pedro Valley," *Military History of the Spanish-American Southwest*, p. 3.

21. Victor R. Stoner, "Spanish Missions in the Santa Cruz Valley," *Kiva*, vols. 1–4 (May, 1936), p. 3.

22. Matson and Fontana, *Friar Bringas Reports*, pp. 25, 31.

23. *Ibid.*

24. For example, "Forgotten Frontiers, A Film Portrayal of the Missions," televised by Station KUAT, Tucson, Saturday, May 19, 1979. Bolton (*The Mission as a Frontier Institution*, p. 1) comments on "the romance that hovers round the mission ruins."

25. DiPeso, "The Sobaipuris," pp. 20–21.

26. George P. Hammond, "Pimería Alta after Kino's Time," *New Mexico Historical Review*, vol. 4 (July, 1929), p. 221; Edward H. Spicer, *Cycles of Conquest*, pp. 128, 130; John Francis Bannon, "The Mission as a Frontier Institution," *Western Historical Quarterly*, vol. 10 (July, 1979), pp. 303–22; Charles W. Polzer, *Rules and Precepts of the Jesuit Missions of Northwestern New Spain*.

27. Russell C. Ewing, "The Pima Outbreak of November, 1751," *New Mexico Historical Review*, vol. 4 (October, 1938), pp. 337–46.

28. Dobyns, *Spanish Colonial Tucson*, p. 13.

29. Daniel S. Matson translates the name Cuitabagu (interview, June 4, 1979); Ernest J. Burrus, *Kino and Manje*, "Place Finder," inserted by Ronald Ives. Ives locates Santa Catalina de Cuitabagu about thirty miles downriver (north) of Tucson.

30. Theodore E. Treutlein, "Father Gottfried Bernhardt Middendorff, S.J., Pioneer of Tucson," *New Mexico Historical Review*, vol. 32 (October, 1957), p. 316.

31. Bernard L. Fontana, "Biography of a Desert Church," Tucson Corral of the Westerners, *Brand Book No. 1*, p. 7. Fontana considers Espinosa "the most remarkable Jesuit at San Xavier del Bac since Kino," but quotes J. Augustine Donohue ("The Unlucky Jesuit Mission of Bac, 1732–1767," *Arizona and the West*, vol. 2 [Summer, 1960], pp. 134–35), who notes that "his physical ailments were complicated by the spiritual disease of scruples." In a recent Papago autobiography, Peter Blaine's *Papagos and Politics*, pp. 19–20, Blaine notes that in his youth the people of San Xavier went to Magdalena, Sonora, every October for Saint Francis' Day. Father Bonaventure tried to stop them because he "didn't like the drinking that went on down there." The Papagos legalized their drinking by proving that the cactus liquor was used for ceremonial purposes.

32. Dobyns, *Spanish Colonial Tucson*, pp. 16–17. Kessell (*Mission of Sorrows*, pp. 140–41) questions Dobyns's conclusions about Espinosa's part in starting the rebellion. Donohue (*After Kino*, p. 141) thinks Middendorff at Tucson helped set it off. Father Velarde (Rufus K. Wyllys, *Arizona*, p. 136) discusses the ceremonial intoxication. Compare Kessell, *Mission of Sorrows*, p. 55.

33. Dobyns, *Spanish Colonial Tucson*, p. 15; Kessell, *Mission of Sorrows*, pp. 140–41; Donohue, *After Kino*, pp. 132–40; Max L. Moorhead, *The Apache*

Frontier, pp. 115–23; John L. Kessell, *Friars, Soldiers, and Reformers*, p. 137.

34. DiPeso ("The Sobaipuris," p. 28) and Wyllys ("Padre Luis Velarde," p. 38) note that the ranks of the Apaches were swelled by Indians from other tribes who wished to share the spoils.

35. Kessell, *Mission of Sorrows*, p. 165.

36. DiPeso, "The Sobaipuris, p. 28; John L. Kessell, ed., "San José de Tumacacori—1773: A Franciscan Reports from Arizona," *Arizona and the West*, vol. 6 (Winter, 1964), pp. 310–11.

37. Janet R. Fireman, *The Spanish Royal Corps of Engineers*, pp. 74–77; Sidney B. Brinckerhoff and Odie B. Faulk, *Lancers for the King*, pp. 83–89.

38. Lawrence Kinnaird, *The Frontiers of New Spain*, pp. 23–24.

39. Max L. Moorhead, *The Presidio*, p. 88; Odie B. Faulk, *The Leather Jacket Soldiers*, p. 28; Fireman, *The Spanish Royal Corps of Engineers*, p. 78.

40. The great histories of the Jesuits cover the expulsion: Xavier Alegre, *Historia de la Compania de Jesus*; Gerard Decorme, *La Obra de los Jesuitas Mexicanos durante la Epoca Colonial*; Alberto Francisco Pradeau, *La Expulsion de los Jesuitas*. Contemporary accounts include Francis J. Fox, "Expulsion of the Jesuits from New Spain, "Studies in *Medievalia and Americana*, pp. 113–28; Magnus Hörner, *Expulsion of the Jesuits*.

41. Matson and Fontana, *Friar Bringas Reports*, pp. 17–18.

42. Kessell, *Friars, Soldiers, and Reformers*, p. 8.

43. *Ibid.*, p. 20; McCarty, "Franciscan Beginnings," pp. 73, 77–78, 83. Father McCarty points out that the few secular priests in the field did their best to fill the gaps left by the departing Jesuits. For a thorough study of the Franciscan takeover see Kieran McCarty, *A Spanish Frontier in the Enlightened Age: Franciscan Beginnings in Sonora and Arizona, 1767–1770*.

44. John L. Kessell, "The Making of a Martyr: Young Francisco Garcés," *New Mexico Historical Review*, vol. 45 (July, 1970), pp. 181–96.

45. Herbert E. Bolton, *Anza's California Expedition*, vol. 1, p. 46.

46. Dobyns, *Spanish Colonial Tucson*, p. 27.

47. Bolton, *Anza's California Expedition*, vol. 4 (*Font's Complete Diary*), p. 121.

48. Dobyns, *Spanish Colonial Tucson*, p. 29.

49. Bolton, *Anza's California Expedition*, vol. 1, p. 47; John E. Kessell, "The Making of a Martyr," p. 182. See Kessell, *Friars, Soldiers, and Reformers*, p. 56, for a sample of their squabbles.

50. Kessell, "Anza Damns the Missions," *Journal of Arizona History*, vol. 13 (Spring, 1972), pp. 57, 59; McCarty, "Franciscan Beginnings," pp. 98–99.

51. Dobyns, *Spanish Colonial Tucson*, p. 31.

52. McCarty, *Desert Documentary*, p. 140.

53. Polzer, "Clarification."

54. Bolton, *Anza's California Expedition*, vol. 4, pp. 59, 195 n. 27.

Chapter 2
The Presidio and the Pueblito

1. Henry F. Dobyns, *Spanish Colonial Tucson*, pp. 59–60.

2. Alfred Barnaby Thomas, *Forgotten Frontiers*, pp. ix–x; J. W. Bowman and R. F. Heizer, *Anza and the Northwest Frontier of New Spain*, pp. 45–47.

3. Dobyns, *Spanish Colonial Tucson*, pp. 59–60.

4. Herbert E. Bolton, *Anza's California Expedition*, vol. 4, p. 510.

5. John L. Kessell, *Friars, Soldiers, and Reformers*, p. 131; Dobyns, *Spanish Colonial Tucson*, p. 63.

6. Kessell, *Friars, Soldiers, and Reformers*, pp. 128, 132; Sidney B. Brinckerhoff and Odie B. Faulk, *Lancers for the King*, p. 93.

7. Kieran R. McCarty, *Desert Documentary*, p. 29.

8. Kessell, *Friars, Soldiers, and Reformers*, pp. 127–128.

9. Garcés to Pineda, August 20, 1775, Southwest Mission Research Center, University of Arizona, Tucson; hereafter cited as SWMRC.

10. Dobyns, *Spanish Colonial Tucson*, pp. 66–67; Alfred Barnaby Thomas, *Teodoro de Croix*, p. 14; Oakah L. Jones, *Los Paisanos: Spanish Settlers on the Northern Frontier of New Spain*, p. 194.

11. Dobyns, *Spanish Colonial Tucson*, p. 113.

12. Charles W. Polzer, "Tucson Before the Territory," p. 7; Dobyns, *Spanish Colonial Tucson*, p. 73. A. S. Reynolds ("Description of the Old Walled Pueblo of Tucson, 1926," MS), Arizona Historical Society, Tucson (hereafter cited as AHS), quotes Samuel Hughes's statement that the mission and the Indian pueblo were where "the two branches of the Santa Cruz came together near the old church."

13. Kessell, *Friars, Soldiers, and Reformers*, p. 135.

14. McCarty, *Desert Documentary*, p. 50; Dobyns, *Spanish Colonial Tucson*, p. 63.

15. McCarty, *Desert Documentary*, p. 50.

16. Dobyns, *Spanish Colonial Tucson*, pp. 64, 198 n. 74.

17. Brinckerhoff and Faulk, *Lancers for the King*, pp. 86–87; Jones, *Los Paisanos*, p. 347.

18. Dobyns, *Spanish Colonial Tucson*, p. 66; Jones, *Los Paisanos*, p. 246.

19. Thomas, *Teodoro de Croix*, pp. 12, 152.

20. *Ibid.*, pp. 17–30.

21. *Ibid.*, pp. 66–68.

22. *Ibid.*, pp. 21, 31.

23. *Ibid.*, p. 31.

24. Dobyns, *Spanish Colonial Tucson*, p. 68.

25. *Ibid.*, p. 69.

26. *Ibid.*, pp. 70, 96; Kessell, *Friars, Soldiers, and Reformers*, p. 135.

27. Dobyns, *Spanish Colonial Tucson*, pp. 72–78. Polzer, in "Tucson Before the Territory," also tells the story.

28. Dobyns, *Spanish Colonial Tucson*, pp. 84, 158 (table 7).

29. *Ibid.*, p. 61.

30. Rex E. Gerald, *Spanish Presidios of the Late Eighteenth Century in Northern New Spain*, p. 16; Moorhead, *The Presidio*, pp. 166–67.

31. George W. Chambers, "The Old Presidio of Tucson," *Kiva*, vol. 20 (December–February, 1955), pp. 15–16.

32. McCarty, *Desert Documentary*, pp. 41–46.

33. Dobyns, *Spanish Colonial Tucson*, pp. 83–84.

34. McCarty, *Desert Documentary*, p. 42.

35. Dobyns, *Spanish Colonial Tucson*, p. 91.

36. McCarty, *Desert Documentary*, pp. 47–50, 57–59.

37. *Ibid.*, pp. 58–59.

38. Max L. Moorhead, *The Presidio*, pp. 84–85.

39. Donald F. Worcester, trans. and ed., *Instructions for Governing the Interior Provinces of New Spain, 1786, by Bernardo de Gálvez*, pp. 23–24, 47–49.

40. Matson and Fontana, *Friar Bringas Reports*, p. 122.

41. McCarty, *Desert Documentary*, pp. 61–63; Dobyns, *Spanish Colonial Tucson*, pp. 100–101; Sidney B. Brinckerhoff, "The Last Years of Spanish Arizona, 1786–1821," *Arizona and the West*, vol. 19 (Spring, 1967), pp. 12–13.

42. Dobyns, *Spanish Colonial Tucson*, pp. 102–103.

43. *Ibid.*, pp. 103–105.

44. George P. Hammond, "The Zúñiga Journal, Tucson to Sante Fe: The Opening of a Spanish Trade Route, 1788–1795," *New Mexico Historical Review*, vol. 61 (January, 1931), pp. 40–49.

45. Jack Holterman, "José Zúñiga, Commandant of Tucson," *Kiva*, vol. 22 (November, 1956), pp. 1–2.

46. Hammond, "The Zúñiga Journal," pp. 49–50; Dobyns, *Spanish Colonial Tucson*, p. 107.

47. Hammond, "The Zúñiga Journal," p. 62.

48. Jones, *Los Paisanos*, p. 244; Dobyns, *Spanish Colonial Tucson*, pp. 110–12.

49. McCarty, *Desert Documentary*, p. 92; Jones, *Los Paisanos*, p. 244.

50. McCarty, *Desert Documentary*, p. 92.

51. *Arizona Citizen*, June 21, 1873.

52. McCarty, *Desert Documentary*, pp. 93–110; Dobyns, *Spanish Colonial Tucson*, pp. 108–109.

53. Brinckerhoff, "Last Years," p. 15; Thomas, *Teodoro de Croix*, p. 19; Moorhead, *The Presidio*, pp. 224–42; Ray H. Mattison, "Early Spanish Settlement in Arizona," *New Mexico Historical Review*, vol. 21 (October, 1946), pp. 279–80.

54. Dobyns, *Spanish Colonial Tucson*, p. 107.

55. Victor R. Stoner, "Fray Pedro de Arriquibar," *Arizona and the West*, vol. 1 (Spring, 1959), pp. 71–79.

56. Albert Stagg, *The First Bishop of Sonora, Antonio de los Reyes*, pp. 37–39.

57. Greenleaf and Wallace, "Tucson," pp. 20–21; Julio Betancourt, "Cultural Resources Within the Proposed Santa Cruz Riverpark Archaeological District" (MS), pp. 68–70.

58. Karen Sikes Collins, "Fray Pedro de Arriquibar's Census of Tucson, 1820," *Journal of Arizona History*, vol. 11 (Spring, 1970), pp. 14–22; Henry F. Dobyns, "The 1797 Population of the Presidio of Tucson," *Journal of Arizona History*, vol. 13 (Autumn, 1972), pp. 205–209. Stoner and Collins mistakenly assign Arriquibar's census and inventory to the year 1820. Dobyns shows that the date must have been 1797.

59. Stoner, "Fray Pedro de Arriquibar," pp. 71–75.

60. Kessell, *Friars, Soldiers, and Reformers*, p. 134.

61. *Ibid.*, p. 77.

62. *Tucson Citizen*, July 8, 1871, quoted in *San Diego Union*, July 20, 1871; Hilario Gallego, "Reminiscences of a Pioneer," *Arizona Historical Review*, vol. 6 (January 1935), p. 77.

Chapter 3
The Yanqui Invasion

1. A. P. K. Safford and Samuel Hughes, The Story of Mariana Díaz," *Arizona Citizen*, June 21, 1873.

2. Charles C. Cumberland, *Mexico: The Struggle for Modernity*, pp. 116–26.

3. Jones, *Los Paisanos*, pp. 194, 248–55: "Apparently the civilian settlers and presidial families of Tucson were a dissolute lot."

4. Dobyns, *Spanish Colonial Tucson*, pp. 127–30.

5. *Ibid.*, p. 129.

6. *Ibid.*, pp. 124–25.

7. Ignacio Zúñiga, *Rapida Ojeada*, pp. 45–73.

8. Joaquín Quiroga, "Report to the Secretary of the Department of Sonora" (MS). See also Arizona State Museum Archives A–H, correspondence of Rev. Victor R. Stoner, e.g., John F. Farson to Harold Steinfeld, April 5, 1945, describing attempts in the 1940s to preserve the ruins of the convento; see also Bernard L. Fontana, "Synopsis of the History of Tucson," (MS).

9. Henry F. Dobyns, "Indian Extinction in the Middle Santa Cruz Valley, Arizona," *New Mexico Historical Review*, vol. 38 (April, 1963), pp. 163–81;

Polzer, "Tucson Before the Territory," p. 8. Polzer thinks many of the Indians were "absorbed."

10. George William Beattie, "Development of Travel Between Southern Arizona and Los Angeles as It Related to the San Bernardino Valley," *Annual Publications of the Historical Society of California*, vol. 7 (1925), pp. 228–57.

11. Harlan Hague, *The Road to California*, pp. 228–57.

12. David J. Weber, *The Taos Trappers: The Fur Trade in the Far Southwest, 1540–1846*, p. 67.

13. James Ohio Pattie, *Pattie's Personal Narrative*, pp. 90–108; Joseph J. Hill, "New Light on Pattie and the Southwestern Fur Trade," *Southwestern Historical Quarterly*, vol. 26 (April, 1923), pp. 251–54; David J. Weber, "Mexico and the Mountain Men," *Journal of the West*, vol. 8 (July, 1969), pp. 368–78; Hague, *The Road to California*, pp. 159–66.

14. Jedediah S. Smith, *The Southwest Expedition of Jedediah S. Smith*, pp. 83–85.

15. Hague, *The Road to California*, p. 181.

16. J. J. Warner, "Reminiscences of Early California," *Annual Publications of the Historical Society of Southern California*, vol. 7 (1907–1908), p. 178.

17. Carl D. W. Hays, "David E. Jackson," in Leroy R. Hafen, ed., *Mountain Men and the Fur Trade of the Far West*, vol. 9, pp. 232–35; Weber, *The Taos Trappers*, pp. 147–48.

18. Howard R. Lamar, *The Far Southwest 1846–1912*, p. 415; Benjamin Thomas, "Recent Historiography of the Origins of the Mexican War," *New Mexico Historical Review*, vol. 54 (July, 1979), pp. 168–81.

19. B. H. Roberts, *The Mormon Battalion: Its History and Achievements*, pp. 6–11.

20. Charles S. Peterson, John F. Urtinus, David E. Atkinson, and A. Kent Powell, *Mormon Battalion Trail Guide* (includes maps of the route).

21. Frank A. Golder, Thomas A. Bailey, and J. Lyman Smith, *The March of the Mormon Battalion*, pp. 192–93; Robert W. Whitworth, "From the Mississippi to the Pacific," *Arizona and the West*, vol. 7 (Summer, 1965), pp. 127, 149–50.

22. Christopher Layton, *Autobiography of Christopher Layton*, pp. 76–79. The Mormon diarists all mention the Battle of the Bulls; e.g., Robert W. Bliss, "The Journal of Robert W. Bliss," *Utah State Historical Quarterly*, vol. 4 (July 1931), p. 80; Rebecca M. Jones, "Extracts from the Life Sketch of Nathaniel M. Jones," *Utah State Historical Quarterly*, vol. 4 (January, 1931), p. 8.

23. Philip St. George Cooke, "Cooke's Journal of the March of the Mormon Battalion," in Ralph P. Bieber and Averam B. Bender, eds., *Exploring Southwestern Trails 1846–1854*, vol. 7, p. 149.

24. Roberts, *The Mormon Battalion*, p. 40. Cooke first heard that 230 soldiers, including detachments

from Tubac and Santa Cruz, had been concentrated at El Paso. Later reports brought the number down to 130. See Hamilton Gardner, "Report of Lt. Col. P. St. George Cooke," *Utah State Historical Quarterly*, vol. 22 (January, 1954), p. 27. Nathaniel Jones (Jones, "Extracts," p. 9), counted eighty presidials.

25. Cooke, *Cooke's Journals*, p. 147.

26. Nathaniel Jones (Jones, "Extracts," p. 7) observes significantly, "The Indians brought into camp a large quantity of mescal to sell, it being the most part of their living, but our good Col. Cooke would not allow us to buy any of it." For Foster see Paul Bailey, *The Armies of God*, p. 162. Foster became the first American mayor of Los Angeles.

27. Whitworth, "From the Missouri to the Pacific," p. 151.

28. Cooke, *Cooke's Journal*, p. 149.

29. *Ibid.*, p. 1.

30. *Ibid.*, pp. 150–52.

31. Daniel Tyler, *A Concise History of the Mormon Battalion*, p. 227.

32. Whitworth, "From the Missouri to the Pacific," p. 150.

33. Tyler, *Concise History*, p. 227; Bliss "Journal," p. 51.

34. Tyler, *Concise History*, p. 227.

35. Golder, *March*, p. 196. Jones ("Extracts," p. 9) says that the men obtained supplies "by selling our clothing."

36. Tyler, *Concise History*, pp. 230–31; Wyllys, *Arizona*, p. 100. Cooke, in his official report, revealed: "I intended attacking him [the enemy] at Bac under favorable circumstances" (Gardner, "Report of Lieut. Col. P. St. George Cooke,"). *Utah State Historical Quarterly*, vol. 22 (January, 1954), pp. 27–28).

37. Judge F. Adams, "Tucson in 1847," *Arizona Historical Review*, vol. 1 (January, 1929), pp. 83–85. Greenleaf and Wallace ("Tucson," p. 23) refer to the Adams story as "unverified."

38. Lamar, *The Far Southwest*, p. 419.

39. Cave J. Couts, *Hepah, California!* p. 62.

40. Samuel E. Chamberlain, *My Confession*, pp. 258–59.

41. Couts, *Hepah, California!* p. 69.

42. Wyllys, *Arizona*, pp. 240–41.

43. James G. Bell, "A Log of the Texas-California Cattle Trail, 1854," *Southwest Historical Quarterly*, vol. 35 (October, 1931), p. 209.

44. *Ibid.*, pp. 315–16. See Michael Erskine, *The Diary of Michael Erskine*, pp. 19, 80–81, for the views of another Texas cowman who saw Tucson in 1854. David J. Weber, in "Failure of a Frontier Institution," *Western Historical Quarterly*, vol. 12 (April, 1981), pp. 125–43, comments on the collapse of the frontier Catholic Church at this time.

45. John E. Durivage, "Through Mexico to California," in Ralph P. Bieber, ed., *Southern Trails to California*, vol. 5, p. 207.

46. *Ibid.*, pp. 209–10.

47. A. B. Clarke, *Travels in Mexico and California*, p. 86.

48. *Ibid.*, pp. 86–87. For the history of the Tucson meteorite see *Arizona Citizen*, January 15, April 8, 1876; P. J. McGough, "References on the Early History of the Tucson, Arizona, Meteorite," *Journal for the Society for Research on Meteorites*, vol. 5 (November, 1946), pp. 108–47.

49. C. C. Cox, "From Texas to California in 1849," part 2, *Southwestern Historical Quarterly*, vol. 29 (October, 1925), pp. 143–44; Lorenzo D. Aldrich, *A Journal of the Overland Route to California*, p. 52.

50. Robert Eccleston, *Overland to California on the Southwestern Trail, 1849: The Diary of Robert Eccleston*, pp. 201–203. Eccleston's editors, George P. Hammond and Edward H. Howes, think that "Torrey" was David S. Terry, a former Texas Ranger who settled in California and was involved in a famous killing. It is uncertain whether he set up his store at Bac or at Tucson.

51. John Russell Bartlett, *Personal Narrative*, p. 296.

52. *Ibid.*, pp. 294–97.

53. "Mr. Leon's Conversation" (undated interview), Hayden file, AHS; *Arizona Days and Ways* (*Arizona Republic*, Phoenix), August 5, 1956 (interview with Cirilo's son Frank).

54. Hilario Gallego, "Reminiscences of an Arizona Pioneer," *Arizona Historical Review*, vol. 6 (January, 1935), pp. 75–81.

55. "Reminiscences of Juan I. Tellez," *Arizona Historical Review*, vol. 7 (January, 1936), pp. 85–89.

56. Louis Ivan Deitch, "Changing House Styles in Tucson, Arizona" (MS), pp. xi–xii; John Spring, *John Spring's Arizona*, p. 46.

57. Cecil Robinson, *With the Ears of Strangers*, p. 16.

58. David J. Weber, *Foreigners in Their Native Land*, p. 19.

59. Louis Bernard Schmidt, "Manifest Opportunity and the Gadsden Purchase," *Arizona and the West*, vol. 3 (Autumn, 1961), p. 245; Paul Neff Garber, *The Gadsden Treaty*, p. 4; Frank C. Lockwood and Donald W. Page, *Tucson: The Old Pueblo*, p. 34.

60. B. Sacks, "The Origins of Fort Buchanan: Myth and Fact," *Arizona and the West*, vol. 7 (Autumn, 1965), p. 217.

61. "Reminiscences of Mrs. Carmen R. Lucero, as Interpreted by Miss Maggie Brady to Mrs. Geo. F. Kitt, 1928," Hayden File, AHS.

Chapter 4
The Great Transition

1. Waterman L. Ormsby, *The Butterfield Overland Mail*, p. 96

2. Rosemary Gipson, "The Mexican Performers," *Journal of Arizona History*, vol. 13 (Winter, 1972), pp. 235–38. J. Ross Browne encountered "a noisy band of Sonorian buffoons" in Tucson in 1864 (*A Tour Through Arizona*, p. 133).

3. "Tucson a Hundred Years Ago," *Arizona Citizen*, June 31, 1873, reprinted in *Tucson Daily Citizen*, June 26, 1965.

4. William Duffen, ed., "Diary of Phocion R. Way," in "Overland via Jackass Mail in 1858," part 2, *Arizona and the West*, vol. 2 (Summer, 1960), pp. 157–62.

5. *Ibid.*, p. 159.

6. Ormsby, *The Butterfield Overland Mail*, p. 96; Roscoe P. Conkling and Margaret B. Conkling, *The Butterfield Overland Mail 1857–1869*, vol. 2, pp. 164–65.

7. Thomas H. Peterson, Jr., "The Buckley House: Tucson Station for the Overland Mail," *Journal of Arizona History*, vol. 7 (Winter, 1966), pp. 155–57; Conkling, *Butterfield Overland Mail*, p. 158; Bernice Cosulich, *Tucson*, p. 147.

8. *Arizona Daily Citizen*, December 29, 1893.

9. *Ibid.*

10. Raphael Pumpelly, *My Reminiscences*, vol. 1, pp. 187–88.

11. *Weekly Arizonan* (Tucson), March 5, 1870.

12. Cosulich, *Tucson*, p. 147.

13. Frank C. Lockwood, *Life in Old Tucson*, p. 203; *Arizona Daily Star*, May 28, 1912, June 20, 1917.

14. *Star*, November 18, 1956.

15. Lockwood, *Life in Old Tucson*, p. 202.

16. *Ibid.*, p. 206.

17. *Ibid.*, p. 200.

18. Duffen, "Diary of Phocion R. Way," p. 159.

19. John Coleman Reid, *Reid's Tramp*, p. 186.

20. *Sacramento Union*, October 5, 1859; *Star*, December 22, 1940 ("Early Arizona Characters"); March 28, 1893 (obit.); correspondence and records in Hayden File, AHS.

21. "Memorandum: Mark A. Aldrich," Hayden File, AHS; Lockwood, *Life in Old Tucson*, pp. 16–23.

22. José de Castillo, "Solomon Warner," Hayden File, AHS; Joseph Fish, "History of Arizona" (MS), AHS, p. 275; *Citizen*, October 13, 1875; November 14, 1899 (obit.).

23. Cornelius C. Smith, Jr., *William Sanders Oury*, pp. xii, 1–84.

24. Francis P. Brady, "Portrait of a Pioneer: Peter R. Brady 1825–1902," *Journal of Arizona History*, vol. 16 (Summer, 1975), pp. 171–80.

25. Biographical sketch, Hayden File, AHS; *Citizen*, September 13, 1899; *Star*, May 5, July 30, 1909; January 5, 1937.

26. *Weekly Arizonan*, February 7, 1869; "Anecdotes of Early Days," Robinson folder, Hayden File, AHS; *Star*, October 2, 1879; March 22, 28, 31, 1893; *Citizen*, May 4, 1889; March 21, 22, 1893; March 25, 1898; *Tucson Post*, September 12, 1902; items in Hayden File, AHS. Petra appears in the 1960 census as Stevens's wife.

27. *Citizen*, May 4, 1889; March 25, 1898; *Star*, September 19, 1903; December 29, 1910; Lockwood, *Life in Old Tucson*, pp. 159–68; items in Hayden File, AHS.

28. A. W. Gressinger, *Charles D. Poston: Sunland Seer*, pp. 22–27; Frank Love, "Poston and the Birth of Yuma," *Journal of Arizona History*, vol. 19 (Spring, 1978), pp. 403–16; Constance Wynn Altshuler, "Poston and the Pimas," *Journal of Arizona History*, vol. 18 (Spring, 1977), pp. 23–42.

29. *Arizona Enterprise* (Florence), August 9, 1890 (obit. of Burke); *Arizona Citizen*, February 28, 1874; *Citizen*, March 15, 16, 1898 (obit. of Van Alstine); Carl T. Hayden, *Charles Trumbull Hayden, Pioneer*; Joseph Fish, "History of Arizona" MS). Jay J. Wagoner (*Early Arizona*, p. 100) adds names of Americans present in 1858: Edward Miles, William and Alfred Rowlett, Joe Cummings, Alfred Friar, Asa McKinzie, "and a handful of others."

30. J. B. Salpointe, *Soldiers of the Cross*, pp. 224–27.

31. Yginio F. Aguirre, "The Last of the Dons," *Journal of Arizona History*, vol. 10 (Winter, 1969), pp. 239–55; "Echoes of the Conquistadores," *Journal of Arizona History*, vol. 16 (Autumn, 1975), pp. 267–86.

32. Lockwood, *Life in Old Tucson*, pp. 234–55; *Arizona Citizen*, October 29, 1888; *Star*, October 31, 1888; items in Hayden File, AHS; Elizabeth Albrecht, "Estevan Ochoa: Mexican-American Businessman," *Arizoniana*, vol. 4 (Summer, 1963), pp. 34–40.

33. Rudy Pacheco, "A Case Study of a Pioneer Family" (MS).

34. Ana María Comaduran Coenen, "Fiestas at Old Plaza Recalled by Mrs. Coenen" (interview).

35. Mrs. Samuel Hughes, "Reminiscences, 1930," *Arizona Historical Review*, vol. 6 (April, 1935), pp. 66–74; *Star*, May 20, 1912; May 16, 1928; November 6, 1934; Lockwood, *Life in Old Tucson*, pp. 5–15.

36. John Upton Terrell, *Apache Chronicle*, p. xii.

37. Transcript of MS by John A. Rockfellow, Hayden File, AHS; *Arizona Weekly Citizen*, April 8, 1883; *Arizona Weekly Enterprise*, January 14, 1892; other items in Hayden File.

38. *Citizen*, November 14, 1899 (obit.); Joseph Fish, "History of Arizona," p. 275; José de Castillo, biographical sketch of Warner in Hayden File, AHS; Lockwood, *Life in Old Tucson*, pp. 50–56.

39. *Star*, June 14, 1899 (obit.); *Citizen*, June 13, 14, 1899; Wyllys, *Arizona*, p. 128; Wagoner, *Early Arizona*, p. 397.

40. Microfilm, AHS.

41. *Citizen*, November 14, 1899.

42. *Citizen*, March 22, 1893; *Star*, March 21, 22, 1893.

43. *Citizen*, October 29, 1888; *Star*, October 31, 1888.

44. Gressinger, *Charles D. Poston*, pp. 185–88.

45. B. Sacks, *Be It Enacted*, pp. 42–43.

46. B. Sacks, "Charles Debrille Poston," *Smoke Signal*, Spring, 1963, p. 9.

47. Biographical sketch, Hayden File, AHS; *Territorial Expositor* (Phoenix), January 20, 1880; Isaac Polhamus, Yuma, letter to Herbert Brown, Tucson, Hayden File, AHS; Mowry, letter to Bicknall, Yuma, October 29, 1855 (mentioning Indian and Spanish mistresses). E. S. Wallace folder, Hayden file, AHS.

48. Sacks, *Be It Enacted*, pp. 24–30, 69.

49. *Ibid.*, pp. 39–40.

50. Ronstadt went to Arizona in 1854 with the Sonora Exploration and Mining Company, based at Ajo. He had a long career in Mexico, became a colonel in the Sonora National Guard, and settled in Tucson permanently in 1885.

51. For what little is known about Cook see *San Francisco Herald*, October 28, 1856, and items in the Hayden File, AHS. W. Turrentine Jackson (*Wagon Roads West*, pp. 221–25) calls him an "explorer, surveyor and engineer."

52. Jackson, *Wagon Roads West*, pp. 219–26.

53. Sylvester Mowry, *Memoir of the Proposed Territory of Arizona*, p. 22. Henry Alexander Crabbe led a party into Sonora in 1857, expecting to receive colonizing and mining concessions. He and his men were massacred at Caborca on April 7, 1847.

54. *Ibid.*

55. *Ibid.*, pp. 25–30.

56. Sacks, *Be It Enacted*, pp. 17–23.

57. *Ibid.*, p. 35.

58. *Ibid.*, p. 40.

Chapter 5
The Tides of War

1. John Russell Bartlett, *Personal Narrative*, p. 296.

2. U.S., Congress, Senate, Federal Census, Territory of New Mexico and Territory of Arizona, excerpts, 89th Cong., 1st sess., 1912, Doc. 13.

3. *Weekly Arizonian*, June 26, 1869.

4. *Weekly Arizonian*, October 27, 1859 (the Rowletts had just installed "the most improved milling stones" and were ready for business).

5. Samuel W. Cozzens, *The Marvelous Country*, p. 20.

6. Constance Wynn Altshuler, ed., *Latest from Arizona*, p. 140.

7. Gilbert J. Pederson, "A Yankee in Arizona," *Journal of Arizona History*, vol. 16 (Summer, 1975), pp. 129–30.

8. *Ibid.*, p. 136.

9. *Ibid.*, p. 137.

10. *Ibid.*, p. 139. Grant was awarded $77,989.33 by Congress on January 25, 1898.

11. "Statement of Samuel Hughes, July 3, 1862," War Department Records, copy in AHS; Sacks, *Be It Enacted*, p. 63. Poston's brother was killed, and Poston himself, with his engineer, Raphael Pumpelly, barely escaped from Tubac. The mining enterprise was abandoned.

12. Sacks, *Be It Enacted*, p. 63. Thompson W. Turner, in a dispatch from Tucson to the *St. Louis Republican*, printed on April 18, 1861, declared that "the great mass of our citizens are in favor of the Union" (Altshuler, ed., *Latest from Arizona*, p. 168).

13. The letter is reproduced in *Arizoniana*, vol. 1 (Winter, 1960), p. 27. For new light on the Bascom incident see B. Sacks, "New Evidence on the Bascom Affair," *Arizona and the West*, vol. 4 (Autumn, 1962), pp. 261–78; Constance Wynn Altshuler, *Chains of Command*, pp. 15–17.

14. Boyd Finch, "Sherod Hunter and the Confederates in Arizona," *Journal of Arizona History*, vol. 10 (Autumn, 1969), pp. 158–63. Baylor thought that California was "on the eve of revolution" (W. H. Watford, "The Far Western Wing of the Rebellion, 1861–1865," *California Historical Quarterly*, vol. 34 [June, 1955], p. 133). Confederate leaders also had designs on northern Mexico. "The South must have Chihuahua and Sonora," wrote Colonel James Reily to James H. Reagan (Charles S. Walker, "Causes of the Confederate Invasion of New Mexico," *New Mexico Historical Review*, vol. 8 [January, 1933], p. 77).

15. Finch, "Sherod Hunter," pp. 140–42, 148–50, 159–62; Statement of Hiram S. Stevens, October 3, 1862, M. Aldrich and M. G. Gay, witnesses, *Official Records of the War of the Rebellion*, 1st ser., vol. 50, part 2, pp. 151–52; hereafter cited as *Official Records*.

16. *Arizona Graphics*, March 3, 1900, copy in Hayden File, AHS; Carl T. Hayden, *Charles Trumbull Hayden*, pp. 9–10.

17. Lockwood, *Life in Old Tucson*, pp. 237–38; José de Castillo, undated interview with Sam Hughes, José de Castillo Collection, AHS.

18. Lockwood, *Life in Old Tucson*, pp. 237–38; Albrecht, "Estevan Ochoa," p. 39.

19. John Spring, *John Spring's Arizona*, pp. 83–95, 128–37.

20. Brady, "Portrait of a Pioneer," p. 181.

21. Finch, "Sherod Hunter," p. 175; Robert Lee Kerby, *The Confederate Invasion of New Mexico and Arizona 1861–1862*, pp. 77–81.

22. Wagoner, *Early Arizona*, p. 454. For another encounter see Bert M. Fireman, "How Far Westward the Civil War?" Denver Posse of the Westerners *Brandbook* (1964), pp. 163–70.

23. Finch, "Sherod Hunter," p. 179.

24. Wagoner, *Early Arizona*, pp. 454–55; David L. Hughes, "A Sketch of the Skirmish at Picacho, Arizona, Between the Union and Confederate Troops During the Civil War as Related by George Brandes [Brandon], Saddler D, 1st California Cavalry, written by D. L. Hughes" (MS), D. L. Hughes Collection, AHS.

25. *San Francisco Evening Bulletin*, April 28, 1862, quoted in Finch, "Sherod Hunter," p. 178.

26. "A Conversation Between General James H. Carleton and Sam Hughes in 1862," *Arizoniana*, vol. 4 (Fall, 1963), p. 29.

27. Carleton to Drum, May 25, 1862, Calvin Horn and W. S. Wallace, *Union Army Operations in the Southwest*, 1961, p. 39.

28. *Alta California*, June 8, 1862, quoted in Aurora Hunt, *The Army of the Pacific*, pp. 109–10.

29. Wagoner, *Early Arizona* pp. 455–56; Ray C. Colton, *The Civil War in the Western Territories*, pp. 103–108.

30. George O. Hand, "Diary," entries for August 22, October 10, 11, 26, 1862 (typescript in AHS).

31. Wagoner, *Early Arizona*, pp. 456–58; transcripts of court proceedings, Mowry file, AHS; Lamar, *The Far Southwest*, p. 429.

32. Bert Fireman, "What Comprises Treason?" *Arizoniana*, vol. 1 (Winter, 1960), pp. 5–10; Constance Wynn Altshuler, "The Case of Sylvester Mowry: the Charge of Treason," and "The Case of Sylvester Mowry: The Mowry Mine," *Arizona and the West*, vol. 15 (Spring and Summer, 1973), pp. 63–82, 149–74.

33. *Sacramento Union*, August 9, 1862, copy in Hayden File, AHS.

34. *Official Records*, 1st ser., vol. 50, part 1, pp. 196–97, 1127.

35. Wagoner, *Early Arizona*, p. 456; Constance Wynn Altshuler, "Military Administration in Arizona 1854–1865," *Journal of Arizona History*, vol. 10 (Winter, 1969), pp. 225–30.

36. Horn and Wallace, *Union Army Operations in*

the Southwest, pp. 51–52; G. W. Oaks, *George Washington Oaks, Man of the West*, pp. 24–25.

37. Charles Byars, "The First Map of Tucson," *Journal of Arizona History*, vol. 7 (Winter, 1966), pp. 189–95; Thomas F. Saarinen, Introduction to "Territorial Tucson" (typescript), in possession of Donald H. Bufkin, pp. 11–12.

38. Sacks, *Be It Enacted*, pp. 69–75.

39. *Ibid.*, pp. 79–80.

40. *Ibid.*, pp. 87–95.

41. Charles D. Poston, *Building a State in Apache Lane*, pp. 112–13.

42. W. W. H. Davis, *El Gringo*, pp. 24–26; Norman M. Whalen, "The Catholic Church in Arizona" (MS), pp. 53–55.

43. Interview with George W. Chambers and G. T. Urias, Tucson, October, 1927, copy in AHS.

44. Whalen, "Catholic Church in Arizona," p. 56.

45. Biographical material on Aloysius Bosco and Charles Messea, collected by Charles W. Polzer, Southwestern Mission Research Center, SFX-Bac, University of Arizona, Tucson. These Jesuits were "recalled by their superior," leaving no priest in Arizona.

46. J. B. Salpointe, *Soldiers of the Cross*, pp. 248–49.

47. Jerry Wallace, *The Episcopal Church Comes to Arizona*, p. 1.

48. Wagoner, *Arizona Territory*, p. 26.

49. *Ibid.*, pp. 21, 26–27; Robert L. Spude, "A Land of Sunshine and Silver: Silver Mining in Central Arizona, 1871–1885," *Journal of Arizona History*, vol. 16 (Spring, 1975), pp. 32–35.

50. J. George Hilzinger, *Treasure Land*, p. 60.

51. Wagoner, *Arizona Territory*, p. 31.

52. *Ibid.*, pp. 31–33.

53. J. Ross Browne, *Adventures in the Apache Country*, pp. 137–39; B. Sacks, *Arizona's Angry Man: United States Marshal Milton B. Duffield*, p. 19.

54. Wagoner, *Arizona Territory*, p. 47.

55. *Ibid.*, p. 36.

56. *Ibid.*, p. 41.

57. John S. Goff, "The Arizona Career of Coles Bashford," *Journal of Arizona History*, vol. 10 (Spring, 1969), pp. 19–36.

58. *Weekly Arizona Miner* (Prescott), June 22, 1864; Loomis Morton Ganaway, "New Mexico and the Sectional Controversy," part 6, *New Mexico Historical Review*, vol. 19 (January, 1944), pp. 64–66; items in Hayden File, AHS.

59. *San Diego Union*, September 9, 1914; *Star*, March 22, 1911; *Citizen*, October 14, 1910, February 4, 1906; items in Hayden File, AHS.

60. Edward D. Tuttle, "Arizona Begins Law Making, *Arizona Historical Review*, vol. 1 (April, 1928),
pp. 50–62; Gilbert J. Pedersen, "The Founding First," *Journal of Arizona History*, vol. 7 (Summer, 1966), pp. 52–57.

61. Wagoner, *Arizona Territory*, pp. 61–62.

62. Pedersen, "The Founding First," p. 45.

63. *Ibid.*, p. 57.

64. Wagoner, *Arizona Territory*, pp. 61–62.

65. John Bret Harte, "The Strange Case of Joseph C. Tiffany," *Journal of Arizona History*, vol. 16 (Winter, 1975), pp. 383–404; Hunter Ingram, *Fort Apache*, p. 44.

66. *Weekly Arizonian*, October 1, 1870.

67. *Weekly Arizonian*, January 31, 1869; *Star*, December 25, 1908; "Reminiscences of Augustus Brichta" (MS), AHS; items in Hayden File, AHS.

68. George W. Chambers and C. L. Sonnichsen, *San Agustín*, pp. 14–16; Sister Monica Corrigan, "Trek of the Seven Sisters" (diary), in Sister Aloysia Ames, C.S.J., *The St. Mary's I Knew*, pp. 131–50.

Chapter 6
Roads to Civilization

1. For changing attitudes toward the Indian see Vine Deloria, Jr., *God Is Red*; T. C. McLuhan, *Touch the Earth*. For changing attitudes toward the Mexican see Cecil Robinson, *With the Ears of Strangers*.

2. J. Ross Browne, *Adventures in the Apache Country*, pp. 22, 138.

3. John G. Bourke, *On the Border with Crook*, pp. 63–64. Sam Hughes's report is in the *Weekly Citizen*, March 11, 1871.

4. J. H. Marion, *Notes of Travel Through the Territory of Arizona*, ed. Donald M. Powell, p. 42. The *Citizen* for March 11, 1871, reported that the chain gang was now making adobes so they could pay their way, "as they ought to do."

5. C. C. Smith, "Some Unpublished History of the Southwest," *Arizona Historical Quarterly*, vol. 6 (January, 1935), p. 61.

6. Bernice Cosulich, *Tucson*, pp, 185–87.

7. George W. Chambers and C. L. Sonnichsen, *San Agustín*, p. 14.

8. George H. Kelly, *Legislative History of Arizona 1864–1912*, p. 40.

9. Jay J. Wagoner, *Arizona Territory*, p. 73.

10. Thomas H. Peterson, Jr., "Fort Lowell, A. T.: Army Post During the Apache Campaigns," *Smoke Signal* (Tucson Corral of the Westerners), no. 8 (fall, 1963), p. 5. For a soldier's life at Camp Lowell see Constance Wynn Altshuler, ed., "Interviews with Henry I. Yohn," *Journal of Arizona History*, vol. 16 (Summer, 1975), pp. 119–26; James T. King, *War Eagle: A Life of General Eugene A. Carr*, pp. 136–38.

11. John A. Turcheneske, Jr., "The Arizona Press and Geronimo's Surrender," *Journal of Arizona History*, vol. 14 (Summer, 1979), pp. 133–34.

12. Robert H. Forbes, *The Penningtons: Pioneers of Early Arizona*.

13. Wagoner, *Arizona Territory*, pp. 101–103; John S. Vosburg, "Conversations," Hayden File, AHS.

14. Wagoner, *Arizona Territory*, p. 103; Kelly, *Legislative History*, p. 45.

15. *Arizona Miner*, March 3, 1871; *Arizona Citizen*, April 15, 1876; *Memorials and Affidavits Showing the Outrages Perpetrated by the Apache Indians in the Territory of Arizona During the Years 1869 and 1870*.

16. James R. Hastings, "The Tragedy at Camp Grant in 1871," *Arizona and the West*, vol. 1 (Summer, 1959), pp. 149–50.

17. Books on the Camp Grant story include Don Schellie, *Vast Domain of Blood* (nonfiction) and *Me, Cholay & Co* (fiction); Elliott Arnold, *The Camp Grant Massacre* (fiction).

18. Hastings, "The Tragedy at Camp Grant," pp. 155–58. The best evaluation of the facts is that by Constance Wynn Altshuler in *Chains of Command*, pp. 190–96.

19. Randy Kane, "An Honorable and Upright Man," *Journal of Arizona History*, vol. 19 (Autumn, 1978), pp. 297–314.

20. Hayden File, AHS.

21. Mrs. Samuel Hughes, "Reminiscences," *Arizona Historical Review*, vol. 6, (April, 1935), pp. 71–73. James H. Cady wrote later in *Arizona's Yesterday* (pp. 94–96): "We suffered no qualms . . . what we had done was right."

22. John A. Spring, "Troublous Days in Arizona" (MS); B. Sacks, *Arizona's Angry Man*, pp. 51–52.

23. *Arizona Citizen*, August 9, 1873; Spring, "Troublous Days"; John G. Bourke, "A Lynching in Tucson in 1873," *New Mexico Historical Review*, vol. 19 (July, 1941), pp. 233ff.; Hubert Howe Bancroft, *Popular Tribunals* (*Works*, vol. 36), pp. 730–31.

24. Tucson-Pima County Historical Commission, *Tucson the Old Pueblo: A Chronology*, pp. 6–7. A description of the courthouse is in J. H. Marion, *Notes of Travel*, p. 41. For competition among stagecoach companies see Bert M. Fireman and Lillian Theobald, "Imprudent Enterprise: The Arizona and New Mexico Express Company," *Journal of Arizona History*, vol. 17 (Winter, 1976), pp. 415–30. Tucson in the fall of 1874 is the subject of a photographic essay, "A Tour of Tucson—1874," by Thomas H. Peterson, Jr., in *Journal of Arizona History*, vol. 11 (Autumn, 1970), pp. 160–201.

25. Estelle Luttrell, "Arizona Frontier Press," *Arizona Historical Review*, vol. 6 (January, 1935), pp. 14–26; Don Schellie, *The Tucson Citizen*, pp. 22–23;

Kenneth Hufford, "P. W. Dooner: Pioneer Editor of Tucson," *Journal of Arizona History*, vol. 10 (Spring, 1960), pp. 34–41.

26. Safford earned his title, "Father of Education." See Judith Ellen Tobias, "Governor Safford and Education in Arizona" (MS), pp. 8–16; Wagoner, *Arizona Territory*, pp. 107–10; John J. Vosburg, "Conversation," Hayden File, AHS.

27. John Spring, *John Spring's Arizona*, pp. 238–43.

28. Elmer Flaccus, interview, Tucson, June 3, 1981; Cooper, *The First Hundred Years*, pp. 14–19.

29. James Officer, "Historical Factors in Interethnic Relations in the Community of Tucson," *Arizoniana*, vol. 1 (Summer, 1960), pp. 12, 14, 16; Richard Griswold del Castillo, "Tucsonenses and Angelenos," *Journal of the West*, vol. 18 (January, 1979), p. 61.

30. *Weekly Arizonan*, June 19, September 4, 1869; January 8, February 26, March 5, April 16, May 21, 1870; April 1, 1876; March 24, June 30, 1877; December 7, 1878; April 4, June 7, 1883; items in Hayden File, AHS. Levin dissolved his partnership with Goldtree after a year, and the firm name became Levin & Hopkins. John Spring, Levin's brother-in-law, was associated with the company.

31. *Citizen*, July 21, 1953; David F. Brinegar, Introduction, "Prostitution in Arizona," (MS).

32. Don Bufkin, "The Broad Pattern of Land Use Change in Tucson, 1862–1912," in Thomas F. Saarinen, ed, "Territorial Tucson" (MS), p. 6.

33. *Ibid.*, p. 3.

34. Gilbert J. Pedersen, "The Townsite Is Now Secure: Tucson Incorporates, 1871," *Journal of Arizona History*, vol. 11 (Autumn, 1970), p. 154.

35. Thomas Edwin Farish, *History of Arizona*, vol. 5, p. 328.

36. *Star*, December 12, 1914; *Arizonan*, December 23, 1869; items in Hayden File, AHS.

37. *Weekly Star*, April 11, 1878; *Arizona Citizen*, February 13, 1875, November 22, 1906; note by Edith Kitt, August 16, 1962, in Hayden File, AHS.

38. Floyd S. Fierman, "The Goldberg Brothers: Arizona Pioneers," *American Jewish Archives*, vol. 18 (April, 1966), p. 4; items in Hayden File, AHS.

39. *Arizonan*, February 11, 1871.

40. Diane Tully Tretschek, "Pinckney Randolph Tully and Charles Hoppin Tully, Arizona Pioneers" (MS), AHS, p. 2.

41. *Ibid.*

42. Randy Kane, "An Honorable and Upright Man," *Journal of Arizona History*, vol. 19 (Autumn, 1978), p. 299.

43. Hayden File, AHS.

44. Wagoner, *Arizona Territory*, p. 148. Robert M. Utley is skeptical: "Whether or not such a ring really

existed, Kautz, like his successors, fulminated against it" (*Frontier Regulars: The United States Army and the Indians*, p. 367).

45. Wagoner, *Arizona Territory*, p. 129.

46. *Ibid.*, p. 77.

47. Tretschek, "P. R. Tully," p. 3; items in Hayden File, AHS.

48. John Bret Harte, "The Strange Case of John C. Tiffany," *Journal of Arizona History*, vol. 16 (Winter, 1975), p. 384. Most historians take the existence and infamy of the ring for granted; for example, Farish, *History of Arizona*, vol. 5, pp. 304–16; Wagoner, *Arizona Territory*, pp. 147–48.

49. For example, Hunter Ingram, *Fort Apache*.

50. *Star*, September 3, 1950; Fierman, "The Goldberg Brothers," p. 4; items in Hayden File, AHS.

51. J. S, Mansfeld, "Literature in the Territory of Arizona in 1870," *Arizoniana*, vol. 2 (Fall, 1961), p. 32.

52. William H. Lyon, "The Corporate Frontier in Arizona," *Journal of Arizona History*, vol. 9 (Spring, 1968), p. 7.

53. *Ibid.*, p. 9.

54. *Ibid.*, pp. 3–4.

55. Estelle Luttrell, "Arizona's Frontier Press," *Arizona Historical Review*, vol. 6 (January, 1935), pp. 14–26; Douglas C. McMurtrie, "The Beginnings of Printing in Arizona, *Arizona Historical Review*, vol. 5 (October, 1932), pp. 176–77; David F. Brinegar, "The Arizona Daily Star" (MS).

56. Lyon, "The Corporate Frontier," p. 2.

57. Hiram C. Hodge, *Arizona as It Is*, pp. 42–43; Patrick Hamilton, *The Resources of Arizona*, p. 140.

58. Lyon, "The Corporate Frontier," p. 2.

59. Jay J. Wagoner, *History of the Cattle Industry in Southern Arizona*, pp. 38–39.

60. Lyon, "The Corporate Frontier," pp. 6–7.

61. Copy in Hayden File, AHS.

62. Jon Nicholson, *The Arizona of Joseph Pratt Allen*, p. 16.

63. Odie B. Faulk, *Tombstone*, pp. 160–85; Lyon, "The Corporate Frontier," pp. 13–16; Morris J. Elsing and Robert E. S. Heinemann, *Arizona Metal Production*.

64. Richard J. Hinton, *The Hand Book to Arizona*, pp. 266–67. Carrillo owned much property, but his special interest was in a plot of land at Main and Simpson streets, where he developed the springs and had a lush garden. A terrific storm in July, 1877, cost him "a thousand dollars worth of peaches, grapes and melons" (*Arizona Citizen*, July 21, 1877). In 1886 he further developed his property into Carrillo Gardens, eight acres of greenery and flowers with a dancing pavilion, a restaurant and bar, pools of water large enough to be called "lakes," and a small zoo (*Citizen*,

June 2, 1886). In 1903, Emanuel Drachman acquired the gardens and renamed them Elysian Grove. In 1921 the grove became a city subdivision. See *Star*, October 26, 1958; Roy P. Drachman, *Just Memories*, pp. 24–26, 64–66; C. C. Wheeler, "History and Facts Concerning Warner and Silver Lake and the Santa Cruz River" (MS).

65. The Presbyterian and Congregational groups combined to build a community church in 1878. For church organizations see the *Star* and *Citizen* for April 9, 1876, October 12, 1879, May 1, 1880; Earl S. Bell, "Pioneer Protestant Churches in Arizona, 1859–1879" (MS); History Committee of the First Congregational Church, *A Century in the Life of the First Congregational United Church of Christ, Tucson, Arizona* (Tucson: N.p., 1981). The bathhouse was noted in the *Star*, September 23, 1879; the ice-machine, hospital, and real-estate boom were mentioned in the *Citizen* on February 14, 17, 28, 1880.

66. Will C. Barnes, *Apaches and Longhorns*, pp. 17–21.

67. Lansing B. Bloom, ed., "Bourke on the Southwest, IV," *New Mexico Historical Review*, vol. 9 (July, 1934), pp. 284–85.

Chapter 7
Chariot of Fire

1. Bernice Cosulich, *Tucson*, pp. 240–43; Robert H. Forbes, unmailed letter to *Reader's Digest*, Tucson, October 6, 1944, in the Forbes Collection, Box 5, folder 8, AHS.

2. *Arizona Citizen*, January 18, 1880.

3. David F. Myrick, *Railroads of Arizona Vol. I: The Southern Roads*, p. 49.

4. *Arizona Weekly Star*, March 18, 1880.

5. *Arizona Weekly Star*, March 25, 1880.

6. *Ibid.*

7. Myrick, *Railroads of Arizona*, pp. 50–51.

8. Cosulich, *Tucson*, p. 244. According to Mose Drachman ("Reminiscences," MS), the author of the joke was Tom Fitch, a well-known local lawyer.

9. *Arizona Weekly Star*, March 25, 1880.

10. Myrick, *Railroads of Arizona*, p. 55.

11. *Arizona Citizen*, February 28, 1880.

12. Diane Tully Tretschek, "Pinckney, Randolph Tully" (MS), p. 5; *Star*, March 25, 1902.

13. Hayden File, AHS.

14. *Star*, April 3, 1884; Jay J. Wagoner, *Arizona Territory, 1863–1912*, p. 97, n. 60, quoting *Arizona Champion*, August 8, 1885; items in Hayden File.

15. *Star*, June 22, 24, 1884.

16. *Arizona Weekly Star*, March 25, 1880.

17. *Star*, February 1, 10, 1884; *Citizen*, February 4, 1884 (account of the proceedings); Arizona Pi-

oneers Historical Society Register, 1888–1895, p. 390 (Poston's call); Odie B. Faulk, *The Arizona Historical Society*, pp. 1–6.

18. APHS Register, 1888–1895, "Certificate of Incorporation of the Society of Arizona Pioneers," "Institution and Incorporation, Arizona Historical Society," p. 1.

19. *Ibid.*, p. 3.

20. APHS, Minute Book no. 1, p. 94.

21. Donald H. Bufkin, "The Broad Pattern of Land Use Change in Tucson" (MS), p. 5.

22. *Ibid.*, p. 8.

23. *Arizona Citizen*, October 29, 1882.

24. *Arizona Citizen*, March 15, 1884, noting the presence of "a green lawn in front of the Cosmopolitan Hotel."

25. Harris J. Sobin, "From Vigas to Rafters," *Journal of Arizona History*, vol. 16 (Winter, 1975), pp. 357–82; Janet Ann Stewart, "The Mansions of Main Street," *Journal of Arizona History*, vol. 20 (Summer, 1979), pp. 200–201. The *Citizen*, October 29, 1882, reported that brick was replacing adobe.

26. *Star*, March 20, 1882; February 22, 1935.

27. *Star*, January 31, 1952.

28. *Citizen*, July 22, 1902, January 2, 1931; *Star*, July 27, 1969; July 1, 1971; *Arizona Weekly Star*, July 7, 1881.

29. *Star*, February 23, 1940.

30. *Star*, August 16, 1951; *Arizona Weekly Star*, June 30, July 7, 1881; *Tucson Weekly Citizen*, December 18, 1881; "History of the Tucson Fire Department" (MS).

31. C. C. Wheeler, "History and Facts Concerning Warner Lake" (MS); James Rodney Hastings and Raymond M. Turner, *The Changing Mile*, pp. 40–46.

32. Clark Manuscript, transcript of testimony of the May, 1885, trial (MS), AHS.

33. Hayden File, AHS.

34. The *Citizen* of May 29, 1885, noted that the case was still being tried.

35. Clara Ferren, "The Vegetable Chinamen" (MS), May 6, 1897, AHS.

Chapter 8
Renegades and Desperadoes

1. For the Cibecue affair see Thomas Cruse, *Apache Days and After*, pp. 102–45; Sidney B. Brinckerhoff, "Aftermath of Cibecue: Courtmartial of the Apache Scouts, 1881," *Smoke Signal*, (Tucson Corral of the Westerners), no. 36 (Fall, 1978); Lori Davisson, "New Light on Cibecue: Untangling Apache Identities," *Journal of Arizona History*, vol. 20 (Winter, 1979), pp. 423–44.

2. Dan L. Thrapp, *The Conquest of Apacheria*, pp. 251–53; *Star*, June 20, 30, 1882.

3. *Star*, July 13, 15, 1882; John G. Bourke, *On the Border with Crook*, pp. 433–35; Dan L. Thrapp, *General Crook and the Sierra Madre Adventure*, pp. 103–17; General George Crook, *Autobiography*, pp. 241–45.

4. Cruse, *Apache Days*, pp. 184–85; Odie B. Faulk, *The Geronimo Campaign*, p. 36.

5. Thrapp, *General Crook and the Sierra Madre Adventure*, pp. 175–76.

6. Britton Davis, *The Truth About Geronimo*, pp. 83–101.

7. *Star*, June 20, 21, 1884.

8. Thrapp, *Conquest*, pp. 311–12.

9. *Ibid.*, p. 353.

10. Faulk, *The Geronimo Campaign*, pp. 70–73.

11. Thrapp, *Conquest*, p. 335.

12. *Ibid.*, p. 336.

13. *Ibid.*, pp. 343–47; Bourke, *On the Border with Crook*, pp. 474–79.

14. *Arizona Republic* (Phoenix), August 18, 1935 (obit. of S. J. Tribolet); *Star*, October 27, 1929.

15. Grace McCool, "First Sierra Vista Businessman Was Shot in Mexico," undated, unidentified clipping, Hayden File, AHS.

16. Charles F. Lummis, *General Crook and the Apache Wars*, p. 28; Angie Debo, *Geronimo: The Man, His Time, His Place*, pp. 264–69.

17. Thrapp, *Conquest*, p. 346; Charles Fletcher Lummis, *Dateline Fort Bowie*, p. 75. Editor L. C. Hughes himself, in a *Star* editorial on April 1, 1887, was still blasting "the Indian Ring in Washington"—not in Tucson.

18. Faulk, *The Geronimo Campaign*, pp. 97–131. For the heliograph see Bruno J. Rolak, "General Miles' Mirrors," *Journal of Arizona History*, vol. 16 (Summer, 1975). pp. 145–60.

19. Faulk, *The Geronimo Campaign*, pp. 132–51.

20. *Ibid.*, pp. 177–78. The letter is in the Gatewood File, AHS.

21. The ceremonies are described in detail by the *Star* and the *Citizen* for November 8, 9, 1887.

22. General Nelson A. Miles, *Personal Recollections and Observations*, p. 532.

23. James H. McClintock, *Arizona: Prehistoric—Aboriginal—Pioneer—Modern*, vol. 2, pp. 266–67.

24. William F. Hogan, "William Morgan: First Village Marshal of Tucson," *Arizoniana*, vol. 3 (Fall, 1962), pp. 46–50.

25. William F. Hogan, "John Miller: Pioneer Lawman," *Arizoniana*, vol. 4 (Summer, 1963), pp. 41–45.

26. William F. Hogan, "Adolph George Buttner: Tucson's First Chief of Police," *Arizoniana*, vol. 5

(Summer, 1964), pp. 26–31; George Hand, "Diary" September 3, 1882, (MS), AHS.

27. Mose Drachman, "The Tucson Gamblers," *Journal of Arizona History*, vol. 14 (Spring, 1973), pp. 1–9.

28. Journals of the Ninth Arizona Legislative Assembly, 1877, quoted in Wagoner, *Arizona Territory*, p. 113; *Arizona Weekly Star*, August 22, 1878.

29. *Florence Citizen*, August 2, 9, 16, 23, 1878.

30. Henry P. Walker, "Retire Peacefully to Your Abodes: Arizona Faces Martial Law, 1882," *Journal of Arizona History*, vol. 10 (Spring, 1969), p. 1; Wagoner, *Arizona Territory*, p. 191.

31. Walker, "Retire Peacefully," p. 18.

32. Wagoner, *Arizona Territory*, p. 199.

33. Douglas D. Martin, *An Arizona Chronology: The Territorial Years, 1846–1912*.

34. *Star*, April 29, 1887.

35. Clara T. Woody and Milton L. Schwartz, *Globe, Arizona*, pp. 101–86.

36. Odie B. Faulk, *Tombstone*, p. 155; Alford E. Turner, *The Earps Talk*, pp. 103–104, 114.

37. Woody and Schwartz, *Globe, Arizona*, pp. 183, 225–26.

38. Hand, "Diary."

39. Nancy Tisdale Clark, "The Demise of the Demon Rum in Arizona," *Journal of Arizona History*, vol. 18 (Spring, 1977), p. 71; Hand, "Diary," March 30, 1883.

40. *Star*, July 15, 1881.

41. The one book-length study of the robbery— Otto Miller Marshall's *The Wham Paymaster Robbery*— argues for the complete innocence of the accused and for the existence and responsibility of the outlaw gang. The case was followed with great interest by the newspapers (*Star*, November 12, December 13–15, 1889). See also Donald N. Bentz, "The Wham Robbery," *Golden West*, vol. 7 (November, 1970), pp. 12–15, 46–50.

Chapter 9
Growing Pains

1. *Report of the Governor of Arizona, September 1, 1893*, p. 3; Charles H. Dunning and Edward Peplow, *Rocks to Riches*, pp. 99–100.

2. Jay J. Wagoner, *History of the Cattle Industry in Arizona*, pp. 53–54; Edward L. Vail, "The Diary of a Desert Trail," *Texasland*, vol. 6 (May, 1926), pp. 5–7; vol. 6 (June, 1926), pp. 13–14; vol. 6 (July, 1926), pp. 8–9, 17; *Star*, February 1, 1890.

3. Ed Vail's "Diary" was reproduced in part in *Arizona Cattlelog*, vol. 26 (February, March, 1970). See also Bernice Cosulich, "Empire Ranch and Total Wreck Mine," *Star*, March 6, 1932.

4. Larry D. Ball, "This High-handed Outrage," *Journal of Arizona History*, vol. 17 (Summer, 1976), pp. 219–32; *Star*, August 11–15, 1887; February 24–25; March 2, 9, 20, 1888.

5. Eugene B. Block, *Great Train Robberies of the West*, pp. 54–65; *Citizen*, February 22, 1888; *Star*, February 24, 1888.

6. *Star*, September 11, 1889; Block, *Great Train Robberies*, p. 300.

7. *Arizona Silver Belt* (Globe), January 29, 1895; *Star*, February 1, 2, 1895.

8. *Citizen*, February 16, 1900.

9. J. Evetts Haley, *Jeff Milton: A Good Man with a Gun*, pp. 322–27.

10. *Star*, September 27, October 3, 1891; *Los Angeles Evening Herald and Express*, November 1, 1937; Haley, *Jeff Milton*, p. 183; Mose Drachman, "Reminiscences" (MS), pp. 34–37; C. L. Sonnichsen, *Billy King's Tombstone*, pp. 34–37; Thomas E. Gibson, "George E. Goodfellow," *Surgery, Gynecology, and Obstetrics*, vol. 54 (April, 1936), pp. 716–18.

11. A. S. Reynolds, "Reminiscences" (MS), 1936, AHS; John Hubner, "Just One Goodfellow in Tombstone," *Arizona Highways*, vol. 52 (September, 1976), p. 14; Miley B. Wesson, "Early History of Urology on the West Coast," reprinted from *History of Urology*, vol. 1, (1933), copy in AHS.

12. *Phoenix Gazette*, July 20, 1893.

13. *Citizen*, April 8, 1893; *Star*, April 23, 1893; Jo Ann Schmitt, *Fighting Editors*, pp. 164–67.

14. "Curly-headed John Dunbar," born in Maine, came to Arizona in 1876, bought the *Gazette* ten years later, started his own legend, and kept it going. See *Phoenix Republican*, September, 1892 (special edition); June 19, 20, 21, 1895; *Gazette*, October 12, 19, 1893; *Star*, June 19, 20, 1895; *Tombstone Prospector*, June 26, 1913; December 23, 1919; February 8, 9, 1923; *Tombstone Epitaph*, October 15, 1929; Richard E. Sloan, *Memories of an Arizona Judge*, pp. 126–27.

15. *Star*, January 5, 1897; January 5, 1899.

16. Walter S. Logan, *Arizona and Some of Her Friends*, quoted in Wagoner, *Arizona Territory*, p. 294.

17. George Hilzinger, *Treasure Land*, p. 115.

18. Don Bufkin, "The Broad Pattern of Land Use Change in Tucson: 1862–1912" (MS), pp. 8–13.

19. Drachman, "Reminiscences," pp. 88ff.

20. The argument was revived as late as 1949 ("Legalized gambling proposed as New Source of Revenue," *Star*, December 1, 1949). The measure was actually submitted to the people and soundly de-

feated. See Edward H. Peplow, *History of Arizona*, vol. 2, p. 518.

21. Mose Drachman, "The Tucson Gamblers," *Journal of Arizona History*, vol. 14 (Spring, 1973), pp. 1–7. Compare C. C. Wheeler, "Some of the Many Changes That Have Taken Place in the Old Pueblo" (MS), AHS; James H. McClintock, *Arizona*, vol. 2, pp. 383–84; Wagner, *Arizona Territory*, p. 441.

22. Wagoner, *Arizona Territory*, p. 439.

23. "Mayor Manning's Message," *Star*, January 3, 1905; Drachman, "The Tucson Gamblers," pp. 8–9.

24. *Star*, January 12, April 4, 1926; November 27, 1928; August 2, 1935 (Manning's obit.).

25. *Star*, January 9, 1908.

26. *Star*, December 23, 1936; November 26, 1951.

27. *Star*, November 29, 1951.

28. *Star*, April 17, 1951.

29. Nancy Tisdale Clark, "The Demise of the Demon Rum in Arizona," *Journal of Arizona History*, vol. 18 (Spring, 1977), p. 71; C. Louise Boehringer, "Josephine Brawley Hughes—Crusader, State Builder," *Arizona Historical Review*, vol. 2 (January, 1930), pp. 98–107.

30. Clark, "Demise of the Demon Rum," pp. 73–85.

31. Robert H. Forbes, *The Penningtons*, p. 31.

32. Drachman, "Reminiscences," p. 63.

33. *Ibid.*, pp. 62–63; *Citizen*, March 10, 12, 18, 1885; Estelle Luttrell, "History of the University of Arizona 1885–1926" (MS), p. 27.

34. Two of the six regents (the secretary of the territory and the superintendent of public instruction), were ex officio. For the acquisition of the site see Douglas D. Martin, *The Lamp in the Desert*, pp. 25–26.

35. Wagoner, *Arizona Territory*, p. 312.

36. Martin, *The Lamp in the Desert*, p. 30; *Star*, October 30, 1887.

37. Martin, *The Lamp in the Desert*, p. 32.

38. *Ibid.*, pp. 38–40; *Report of the Acting Governor of Arizona for 1891*, pp. 28–33.

39. Luttrell, "History of the University," pp. 41–42; Martin, *The Lamp in the Desert*, pp. 38–39.

40. Martin, *The Lamp in the Desert*, p. 38.

41. *Ibid.*, p. 56.

42. *Star*, May 30, 1895.

43. Bufkin, "The Broad Pattern of Land Use," pp. 7–8.

44. Rosemary Gipson, "Tom Fitch's Other Side," *Journal of Arizona History*, vol. 16 (Autumn, 1975), pp. 287–96.

45. *Star*, May 21, 1882.

46. Bufkin, "The Broad Pattern of Land Use," p. 13.

47. Drachman, "Reminiscences," p. 108.

48. *Ibid.*, p. 110.

49. Mary Huntington Abbott, "Papagos, Presbyterians and the Indian Training School" (MS), pp. 1–5, 13–14; C. C. Wheeler, untitled, undated account of the Indian School, C. C. Wheeler Collection, AHS; *Star*, May 18, 1929; February 23, 1950; June 18, 1964; Howard Billman, Letter to Mrs. C. E. Walker, Tucson, December 10, 1888, Tucson Indian Training School Papers, 1888–1953, box 1, Book 1, p. 44, AHS.

50. Abbott, "Papagos, Presbyterians," pp. 22–23; *Star*, April 23, 1950.

51. *Star*, April 23, 1893.

52. Haddington C. Brown, *Historical Circular of Indian Training School*, p. 7.

53. Abbott, "Papagos, Presbyterians," pp. 11–12; Elsie Prugh Herndon, "Indian Training School at Tucson, *La Aurora* (Albuquerque), March 26, 1903.

54. *Star*, February 23, 1950.

55. *Star*, May 22, 1929; May 12, 1935.

56. *Star*, February 23, 1950; Martin L. Girton, "Glimpses of Our Work at Tucson" (MS), Indian Training School Papers, box 5 (published in *Home Mission Monthly*, December 11, 1918).

57. *Star*, February 23, 1950.

58. Abbott, "Papagos, Presbyterians," pp. 18–22.

59. James Officer, "Historical Factors in Interethnic Relations in the Community of Tucson," *Journal of Arizona History*, vol. 1 (Summer, 1960), pp. 1, 14; Richard Griswold del Castillo, "Tucsonenses and Angelenos," *Journal of the West*, vol. 18 (January, 1929), pp. 62–65.

60. Tomás Serrano Cabo, *Crónicas Alianza Hispano-Americana*, pp. 278–79.

61. *Ibid.*, p. 23.

62. *Star*, May 26, 1929.

63. *Star*, January 13, 14, 1944.

64. Officer, "Historical Factors," p. 14.

65. *Star*, October 1, 1966.

66. *Star*, February 13, 1926; January 24, 1960; *Citizen*, July 8, 1931.

67. *Citizen*, May 17, 1932; *Star*, July 20, 1932.

68. *Star*, September 28, October 7, 1966.

69. Billy M. Jones, *Health-Seekers in the Southwest, 1817–1900*, pp. 82, 93–97, 150–51, 169–72; Hugh J. Smith and Frederick J. Brady, "Arizona's Desert as a Health Resort" (MS), AHS, chap. 4, pp. 1–2.

70. *Star*, January 16, 1891.

71. Reprint in AHS.

72. *Star*, June 18, 1895.

73. *Star*, April 6, 1892.

74. *Star*, January 31, 1890.

75. *Star*; Dick Hall, "Ointment of Love," *Journal of Arizona History*, vol. 19 (Summer, 1978), p. 113.

76. Hall, "Ointment," pp. 111–12.

77. *Ibid.*, p. 112.

78. "St. Luke's in the Desert," *Magazine Tucson*, vol. 5 (January, 1952), pp. 12–13; Bernice Cosulich, "Pima County Celebrates Fiftieth Anniversary," *Arizona Medicine*, vol. 3 (October, 1926), pp. 9, 36.

79. C. H. Condon, "Tucson Progress," *Progressive Arizona*, vol. 3 (October, 1926), pp. 9, 36.

80. Thomas C. Langdon, "Harold Bell Wright: Citizen of Tucson," *Journal of Arizona History*, vol. 16 (Spring, 1975), pp. 82–83.

81. Hall, "Ointment," pp. 122–23.

82. *Star*, April 2, 1928; February 13, 1936; January 10, 1954; Hall, "Ointment," pp. 123–24.

83. Marilyn Drago, "VA Hospital Beginnings Recalled," *Sunday Star-Citizen*, July 26, 1970.

84. David F. Brinegar, "New Day for the Star," *Journal of Arizona History*, vol. 18 (Winter, 1977), pp. 422–23.

85. *Star*, September 11, 1917; Hall, "Ointment," p. 129.

Chapter 10
Great Events

1. In 1910 the Tucson corporate area counted 13,193 residents; Phoenix, 11,134. In 1920, Tucson had 20,292; Phoenix, 29,353.

2. The background of the war is covered in such books as Russell A. Alger's *The Spanish-American War* and Frank Freidel's *The Splendid Little War*.

3. *Star*, February 22, 1898; Charles Herner, *The Arizona Rough Riders*, p. 11.

4. *Star*, December 7, 1897, March 18, 1898; Herner, *Arizona Rough Riders*, pp. 4–5.

5. *Star*, October 7, 28, November 18, December 19, 1897; January 25, February 10–12, 1898; Dale L. Walker, *Death Was the Black Horse*, p. 119.

6. *Star*, February 16–18, 1898.

7. *Star*, February 22–26, March 8–9, 1898.

8. *Star*, March 9, 1898.

9. *Star*, May 6, 1898.

10. *Citizen*, August 11, 1898.

11. *Star*, April 29, 1898.

12. Mose Drachman, "Reminiscences" (MS), p. 86.

13. Herner, *Arizona Rough Riders*, p. 33.

14. Theodore Roosevelt, *The Rough Riders*, p. 15.

15. Hermann Hagedorn, *Leonard Wood: A Biography*, p. 152.

16. Herner, *Arizona Rough Riders*, p. 39. For shifts in organization and command see James H. McClintock, *Arizona*, vol. 2, pp. 514–16.

17. Herner, *Arizona Rough Riders*, p. 38.

18. *Citizen*, August 9, 1898.

19. Roosevelt, *The Rough Riders*, pp. 12–14; Edward Marshall, *The Story of the Rough Riders*, pp. 25–27. See Thomas H. Rynning, *Gun Notches*, pp. 138–44, for early experiences of the Rough Riders.

20. A. D. Webb, "Arizonians in the Spanish-American War," *Arizona Historical Review*, vol. 1 (January, 1929), p. 56.

21. *Citizen*, August 15, 23, 1898.

22. *Citizen*, September 23, 1898.

23. *Citizen*, August 9, 1898.

24. David L. Hughes, "A Story of the 'Rough Riders,' as Related by David L. Hughes" (MS), Hughes Collection, AHS.

25. *Citizen*, August 15, 1898.

26. *Citizen*, June 3, 1899.

27. *Citizen*, December 11, 1925; May 4, 1929.

28. *Citizen*, March 25, June 2, 1952; Thomas H. Peterson, "Danger Sound Klaxon: The Automobile Comes to Territorial Arizona," *Journal of Arizona History*, vol. 15 (Autumn, 1974), p. 252.

29. Peterson, "Danger," p. 251. Oldfield won the Los Angeles–Phoenix race in 1914. See Richard Yates, "The Great Cactus Derby of 1914," *Arizona Highways*, vol. 45 (June, 1969), pp. 2–9. He was definitely in Tucson in November, 1915, and raced at the fairgrounds on November 6 (*Star*, November 5, 1915).

30. *Star*, June 18, 1894.

31. *Citizen*, April 8, 1913; Judy Donovan, "Traffic Problem Wild in Old Tucson," *Star*, September 18, 1972.

32. John A. Haney and Cirino G. Scavone, "Cars Stop Here," *Smoke Signal*, Tucson Corral of the Westerners, no. 23 (Spring, 1971).

33. David F. Myrick, *Railroads in Arizona*, vol. 1: *The Southern Roads* pp. 313–19.

34. *Ibid.*, pp. 196–244; *Citizen*, November 10, 1924; June 30, 1976; *Star*, December 2, 1968; May 1, 1979; Mose Drachman, "Reminiscences" (MS), pp. 42–49.

35. *Citizen*, February 17, 18, 1910.

36. *Citizen*, February 19, 21, 1910; Ruth M. Reinhold, "The Old Douglas International Airport," *Journal of Arizona History*, vol. 15 (Winter, 1974), p. 326.

37. *Star*, October 29, 31, November 1, 2, 5, 1911; *Citizen*, November 5, 6, 1915.

38. Stacy C. Hinkle, *Wings over the Border*, pp. 4–10; Reinhold, "The Old Douglas International Airport," p. 326; *Citizen*, July 26, 1919.

39. Judith C. Wilder, "The Years of the Desert Laboratory," *Journal of Arizona History*, vol. 8 (Autumn, 1967), pp. 179–99; Judith Ratliff, "Botanist Writes of Desert Lab," *Star*, May 9, 1981; William McGinnies, *Discovering the Desert*, pp. 1–16.

40. George Ernest Webb, "The Indefatigable As-

tronomer: A. E. Douglass," *Journal of Arizona History*, vol. 19 (Summer, 1978), pp. 169–88.

41. *Citizen*, February 12, 14, 1904; *Star*, November 18–21, 1919.

42. Stone Avenue was macadamized in 1911. Asphalt paving started in 1913. A *Citizen* headline on April 9 reads: "Women Protest Against Stone Avenue Paving." They had paid for macadamizing, they said, "two years ago."

43. William R. Mathews, "Agnes and the Summer Bachelors," *Star*, August 1, 1965.

44. *Star*, June 1, 1906; Robert L. Thomas, "Outdoorsman Recalls Trek up Mount Lemmon," *Arizona Republic*, May 21, 1977.

45. Glenton Sykes, "The First Mount Lemmon Road" (MS), AHS; Sykes, interview, July 2, 1980.

46. *Citizen*, December 9, 1915; September 3, 1930; October 13, 1931; *Star* February 8, 1928; October 13, 1931; August 5, 1935 (Hitchcock obit.); Don Schellie, *The Tucson Citizen*, pp. 83–85; Marilyn Evans, "Amid Problems, Summerhaven Celebrates" (Mount Lemmon centennial), *Citizen*, May 25, 1981.

47. *Citizen*, February 25, 1933.

48. *Star*, February 23, 1940; August 25, 27, 1948.

49. *Ibid.*, October 2, 1957; Don Bufkin, interview, July 5, 1980. The Woman's Club celebrated its eightieth birthday in 1980 (J. C. Martin, "Woman's Club Lighting 80 Candles," *Star*, September 22, 1980).

50. Frederick Ronstadt, "Music in Tucson, 1880's" (MS), November 13, 1943, AHS; J. George Hilzinger, *Treasure Land*, p. 123, *Citizen*, May 13, 1928.

51. *Star*, November 8, 1924.

52. *Citizen*, January 22, 26, 27, 1910.

53. Ann-Eve Johnson, interview, July 17, 1980.

54. *Ibid.*

55. *Star*, November 11, 1926; March 11, 1940.

56. *Star*, November 11, 1926; October 22, 23, 1927; Souvenir Dedication Program, Fine Arts Association of Tucson, Temple of Music and Art, October 21, 1927, AHS.

57. *Star*, November 11, 1926; October 22, 23, 1927.

58. *Star*, May 12, 1929; May 1, 1940; October 4, 1943. For the later history of the temple see Jacqui Tully, "Visionary Hutchinson Not Giving Up on Tottering Temple," *Star*, September 28, 1980.

59. Jay J. Wagoner, *Arizona Territory*, p. 250.

60. *Ibid.*, pp. 249–50.

61. *Ibid.*, pp. 316–17.

62. *Citizen*, October 13, 14, 1909.

63. Michael S. Wade, *The Bitter Issue*, pp. 14–15.

64. Wagoner, *Arizona Territory*, pp. 480–82.

65. *Ibid.*, p. 475.

66. *Citizen*, February 14, 1912.

67. Wagoner, *Arizona Territory*, p. 472.

68. *Citizen*, January 1, 1915.

69. Nancy Tisdale Clark, "The Demise of the Demon Rum in Arizona," *Journal of Arizona History*, vol. 18 (Spring, 1977), p. 70.

70. *Ibid.*, p. 75.

71. *Ibid.*, p. 84.

72. *Citizen*, January 1, 1915.

73. *Ibid.*

Chapter 11
Tucson at War

1. Harrison W. Baldwin, *World War I*, p. 71; *Citizen*, February 14, 26, 27, March 14, 1917.

2. *Citizen*, March 20, 1917; Cyril Falls, *The Great War*, pp. 174–176.

3. *Citizen*, March 17, 23, 1917.

4. *Citizen*, March 30, 1917; Marshall Trimble, *Arizona*, p. 369; Dick Hall, "Sixty Years of a Misspent Life" (MS), in possession of C.L.S.

5. *Citizen*, April 20, 21, May 2, 1917; Espinel folder, Ronstadt Collection, Box 2, AHS; Edward Ronstadt, interview with C.L.S., August 21, 1981. Louise Ronstadt studied in Spain, became a well-known concert artist, and adopted the name Espinel as an aid to her career. Yndia Smalley Moore, director of the Arizona Historical Society, 1959–64, was a civic leader.

6. *Citizen*, March 31, April 2, 1917.

7. *Citizen*, April 2, 1917.

8. *Citizen*, April 11, 1917.

9. *Citizen*, May 5, 1917; *Star*, May 30, June 1, 1917; S. L. A. Marshall, *World War I*, p. 308. Marshall notes that there were no conscientious objectors but that 1,697 "reasonable facsimiles" were dealt with. In 1980, Mexico was still a refuge for men who wished to avoid registering for the draft. See *El Paso Herald-Post*, July 28, 1980. The Reverend Henry van Dyke advocated hanging all pacifists (Mark Sullivan, *Our Times*, vol. 5, p. 467). Mountanans asked for the death penalty in 1918 (*Star*, March 10, 1918).

10. *Citizen*, March 30, April 21, July 13, 1917; Trimble, *Arizona*, p. 355.

11. James A. Sandos, "The Plan of San Diego," *Arizona and the West*, vol. 14 (Spring, 1972), pp. 5–24; Barbara W. Tuchman, *The Zimmerman Telegram*, pp. 195–200; *Star*, March 2, 1917.

12. *Star*, April 6, 7, 1917.

13. *Citizen*, April 26, May 1, 1917.

14. James W. Byrkit, "The I. W. W. in Wartime Arizona," *Journal of Arizona History*, vol. 18 (Summer, 1978), pp. 149–70; "True Copy of the Notes of

Hon. Thomas E. Campbell" (MS, no. 132), Thomas Campbell Papers, S. 8, AHS.

15. *Citizen*, April 10, May 18, 1917; *Star*, May 30, 1917.

16. *Citizen*, April 6, 1917; *Star*, May 30, 1917.

17. *Citizen*, May 14, 1917.

18. *Citizen*, April 24, 1917.

19. *Citizen*, April 25, 1917.

20. *Citizen*, June 1, 1917.

21. *Citizen*, April 19, 1917.

22. *Citizen*, April 20, 1917; *A Record of the Activities of the Arizona State Council of Defense from Foundation April 18 1917 to Dissolution June 1919*. The National Defense Council was formed in August, 1916. In Arizona county councils and defense committees were organized.

23. *Citizen*, April 26, 30, May 5, 1917; *Star*, June 18, 22, 1918.

24. *Star*, May 9, 1917. Samuel P. Martin is not to be confused with druggist Andy Martin, who led the first draft contingent from Tucson.

25. *Citizen*, May 11, 1917; Glenton Sykes, interview, Tucson, July 23, 1980.

26. *Citizen*, May 9, 10, 1917; *Star*, May 20, 1917; Orville S. McPherson, interview, Tucson, August 25, 1980.

27. *Citizen*, May 18, 1917; *Star*, May 20, 1917.

28. *Star*, June 15, 1917; Sullivan, *Our Times*, vol. 5, pp. 424–28.

29. *Star*, June 2, 6, 11, 12, 1917. The *Star* noted on September 16 that Mexican consul R. R. Domínguez in Tucson had issued about 900 certificates of Mexican citizenship to men born in Arizona of Mexican parents. This was in accordance with Mexican government policy. Major-metals production in Arizona in 1916: $190,806,170; in 1917: $209,393,802.

30. *Star*, June 5, 1917.

31. *Ibid.*, June 8, 16, 23, 28, November 12, 1917; Falls, *The Great War*, pp. 352–54.

32. *Star*, July 11, 15, 16, 26, 1917.

33. *Star*, September 5, 11, 21, October 17, 1917; July 4, 1952.

34. *Ibid.*, November 3, 11, 1917; May 9, 1943; Helen C. Land, interview, Tucson, August 29, 1980.

35. *Star*, June 2, 1917; March 24, 1978.

36. *Star*, June 10, 15, 25, 1917.

37. The second Liberty Loan, with merchant Leo Goldschmidt in charge, was announced on August 1 and was covered in the *Star* on August 1, September 19, and October 2, 3, 7, 24, 25, 28, 1917.

38. *Star*, September 11, 1917.

39. *Citizen*, April 20, 1917.

40. *Ibid.*

41. *Star*, August 9, 1917.

42. *Star*, October 27, 1917.

43. *Star*, October 30, November 1, 1917.

44. *Star*, December 18, 1917.

45. *Star*, January 15, 1918.

46. *Star*, February 2, 3, 6, 14, 17, 1918.

47. *Star*, June 28, 1917; *Citizen*, July 8, 23, 1917.

48. *Star*, January 7, 1918; Frederick Lewis Allen, *Only Yesterday*, pp. 77–78.

49. *Star*, December 30, 1917; January 3, 9, 18, 19, 20, February 5, August 1, 1918.

50. *Star*, March 13, 1918.

51. *Star*, April 7, May 18, June 5, 1917; Sullivan, *Our Times*, vol. 5, pp. 416–19.

52. *Star*, July 22, 27, 31, August 2, 9, 1917; Andrew Sinclair, *Prohibition: The Era of Excess*, pp. 148–49.

53. *Citizen*, February 12, 20, 1917.

54. *Star*, June 12, 14, July 4, 1917; July 3, 8, 1918.

55. *Star*, November 27, 1917.

56. *Star*, July 12, August 31, 1917.

57. *Star*, February 14, 21, March 15, 1918.

58. *Star*, February 22, March 1, 8, 14, 21, 22, June 5, August 17, 1918.

59. Sullivan, *Our Times*, vol. 5, pp. 424–29.

60. *Star*, April 14, 1918.

61. *Star*, May 1, June 4, 7, 1918; John S. Goff, *George W. P. Hunt and His Arizona*, pp. 114–15. Hunt also sued Fred S. Breen, of the *Coconino Sun*, but lost the suit.

62. *Star*, May 5, 19, 22, 1918.

63. *Star*, June 29, July 3, 10, 1918.

64. *Citizen*, July 13, 1918.

65. *Star*, June 4, 1918.

66. *Star*, September 10, 1917; March 9, 1918.

67. *Star*, March 9, 12, 13, 15, 26, 31, April 3, 1918. Yndia Smalley Moore, interview, Tucson, August 19, 1980.

68. *Star*, April 3, 1918.

69. *Star*, April 5, 7, 19, 1918; *Citizen*, March 24, 26, April 1, 4, 6, 1918; Orville S. McPherson, interview.

70. *Star*, December 21, 1970; Glenton Sykes, interview, August 20, 1980.

71. *Star*, May 24, 1918.

72. *Star*, March 10, 1918.

73. *Sullivan, Our Times*, vol. 5, pp. 652–54; Marshall, *World War I*, p. 450.

74. *Star*, October 1–November 1, 1918.

75. *Citizen*, November 10, 1918.

76. Estelle Luttrell, "The University of Arizona in World War I 1917–1918" (MS), Special Collections, University of Arizona, p. iii.

77. *Citizen*, November 11, 1918.

78. *Citizen*, November 13, 1919.

Chapter 12
The Gold-plated Decade

1. Roger Butterfield, "Introduction," in Frederick Lewis Allen, *Only Yesterday*, pp. ix–x: " . . . the most delightful decade that has occurred in the lifetime of anyone present."

2. *Star*, May 10, 1919.

3. *Citizen*, May 25, 1919; June 25, 1920.

4. *Citizen*, June 22, 24, 1920.

5. *Citizen*, July 11, 1920.

6. *Citizen*, November 2, 1919.

7. *Star*, August 10, 12, 14, 15, 17, 20, 21, 23, 24, 28, 31, 1919.

8. *Star*, February 6, 19, April 27, August 15–17, 19–21, 23, 24, 28, 1919.

9. *Star*, February 6, 19, April 22, 1919; *Citizen*, December 2, 1919; March 12, 17, 24, 1920.

10. *Star*, February 6, 8, 1919; *Citizen*, May 16, 19, 1919; Thomas E. Navin, *Copper Mining and Management*, pp. 125–27.

11. *Citizen*, May 17, 1919; November 26, 1920; *Star*, February 7–9, 11, 14, 15, March 29, 1919.

12. James W. Byrkit, "The I. W. W. in Wartime Arizona," *Journal of Arizona History*, vol. 18 (Summer, 1977), pp. 149–70.

13. *Star*, November 22, 23, 1919; Harvey Wish, *Contemporary America*, pp. 274–77.

14. Copy in Special Collections, University of Arizona.

15. *Star*, July 12, 1919.

16. Frank Freidel, *America in the Twentieth Century*, p. 225.

17. Michael S. Wade, *The Bitter Issue*, pp. 16–18.

18. *Citizen*, June 25, 1920.

19. *Ibid.*

20. *Ibid.*; *Star*, February 7–9, 1919; Wish, *Contemporary America*, pp. 274–81.

21. *Citizen*, June 25, 1920.

22. *Citizen*, June 26, 29, 30, 1920.

23. *Star*, June 11, 1922.

24. *Star*, April 11, June 11, 1922; Sue Wilson Abbey, "The Ku Klux Klan in Arizona," *Journal of Arizona History*, vol. 14 (Spring, 1973), pp. 17, 21.

25. *Tombstone Prospector*, March 23, 28, April 11, May 22, 1922; *Arizona Gazette* (Phoenix), June 9, 1922; *Arizona Republican* (Phoenix), March 22, 23, 25, 26, 28, 1922; Kenneth T. Jackson, *The Ku Klux Klan in the City*, pp. xv, 188–95; David M. Chalmers, *Hooded Americanism*, pp. 222–23.

26. *Star*, February 6, 1919.

27. Dick Hall, "Jesus Camacho: The Mayor of Meyer Street," *Journal of Arizona History*, vol. 20 (Winter, 1979), pp. 453–54; Andrew Sinclair, *Prohibition*, pp. 396–98; Allen, *Only Yesterday*, pp. 252–55.

28. *Citizen*, June 10, 13, 1920.

29. Hall, "Jesus Camacho," pp. 449–52; Richard Spring Le Garra, "Son of Pioneers Recalls His Teenage Years on Convent Street" (MS), AHS; Roy F. Drachman, *Just Memories*, p. 23.

30. "Report of the Police Department for the Entire Year of 1926," January 1, 1927, AHS.

31. *Citizen*, April 1, 1919. The great auto show ignited editorial enthusiasm.

32. *Star*, February 3, June 4, 1920; Douglas D. Martin, *The Lamp in the Desert*, pp. 135–37.

33. *Citizen*, May 8, 10, 15, 1919.

34. *Citizen*, May 18, 1919; Evo DeConcini, *Hey! It's Past 80!* pp. 153–58.

35. Glenton Sykes, interview, September 3, 1980. The craze returns intermittently. See "Oil Fever Moves to Tombstone," *Star*, May 16, 1981.

36. *Citizen*, May 10, 17, 1919.

37. "Address by J. F. 'Pop' McKale, . . . November 14, 1964" (MS), AHS.

38. *Citizen*, April 3, 1919.

39. *Star*, November 2, 1919.

40. C. L. Sonnichsen, *Tularosa*, p. 196.

41. *Star*, November 3, 4, 1919.

42. *Star*, February 15, May 17, 18, June 13, 1919.

43. *Citizen*, June 27, 1920.

44. *Citizen*, June 16, 18, 20, 1920.

45. *Citizen*, June 15, 20, 1920; March 11, 1921 (road-appropriation bill passed by legislature), April 23, 1922 (good-roads convention); *Star* February 6 (memberships for Good Roads Association "flooding in"), February 9 ("Senate Passes Postoffice Bill Carrying Huge Funds for Roads"), 1919; *Arizona Republican*, April 23, 24 (National Good Roads Association meeting in Phoenix).

46. *Citizen*, June 10, 1920.

47. Rufus Kay Wyllys, *Arizona*, p. 343.

48. *Citizen*, June 23, 1920.

49. *Star*, August 18, 1920.

50. *Star*, July 10, 1924.

51. *Citizen*, October 18, 1923.

52. *Star*, October 3, 1937.

53. Yndia S. Moore, interview, August 19, 1980.

54. *Citizen*, May 1, 1920.

55. *Citizen*, August 11, 1921.

56. Gladys Sarlat Public Relations, News Release, "El Con Shopping Center," 1969, AHS; *Citizen*, April 5, 1925.

57. *Star*, March 7, November 22, 1928; February 20, 1929.

58. Gladys Sarlat, "El Con" (news release).

59. *Star*, December 18, 1930 (opening); April 26, 1965; June 16, 1974; Christopher Square: Nancy Sortore, "A Relaxed Tucson Home for a 'Family' of Guests," *Star*, January 7, 1973.

60. "The New Pueblo's First Skyscraper," *Citizen*, September 30, 1928; *Citizen*, October 10, 27, 1929. For the bank's problems and sale to the Valley National Bank see *Star*, September 20, 23, 1934; February 12, 1935. For the Pioneer Hotel opening see *Star*, December 12, 1929.

61. *Star*, December 20, 1970.

62. Charles H. Broman, ed., *The Story of Tucson Airport Authority, 1948–1966*, pp. 5–6; *Star*, September 21, 23, 1924; *Citizen*, September 22, 1924.

63. *Star*, September 22–24, 1927.

64. *Star*, March 16, 1928.

65. *Broman, Tucson Airport* p. 6; Sue Abbey, "The Man Who Lived to Fly," *Journal of Arizona History*, vol. 15 (Winter, 1974), pp. 380–86.

66. Jerome L. Rodnitzky, "Recapturing the West," *Arizona and the West*, vol. 10 (Summer, 1968), pp. 116, 118.

67. Nancy Sortore, "Where Did the Dude Ranch Go," *Star*, October 17, 1971; *Tucson*, vol. 12 (September, 1939), Dude Ranch Issue, pp. 11–13.

68. Sortore, "Where Did the Dude Ranch Go?"

69. Rodnitzky, "Recapturing the West," p. 122, quoting Hal G. Evarts, "Dude Wranglers," *Saturday Evening Post*, vol. 192, p. 34.

70. Sybil Ellinwood, "East Meets West in the Field of Education," *Journal of Arizona History*, vol. 15 (Autumn, 1974), pp. 269–96.

71. *Tucson*, vol. 12 (September, 1939), p. 11.

72. J. C. Martin, "Dude Ranches," *Star*, August 15, 1976.

73. Sybil Ellinwood, "City's Present Rich Interest in Music Started Unpretentiously Way Back in 1895," *Star*, September 12, 1948. For Van Hulse see *Citizen*, April 7, 1925; September 30, 1972; August 16, 1975; *Star*, September 16, 1931; February 7, 1933; April 11, 1943; September 22, 1978; April 27, May 1, 1981.

74. *Star*, January 14, 1927; Souvenir Program, Dedication of the Temple of Music and Art, Tucson Fine Arts Association, AHS.

75. *Star*, October 2, 1957; May 2, 1975; June 26, 1978.

76. For activities of the Scribblers Club see *Star*, November 4, 1925; January 13, 1926; April 21, 25, November 10, 1927; January 20, February 19, March 22, April 22, May 3, December 14, 1928; October 12, 1930.

77. Abe Chanin, *They Fought like Wildcats*, pp. 27–33, 53–57.

78. David F. Brinegar, "A New Day for the *Star*," *Journal of Arizona History*, vol. 18 (Winter, 1977), pp. 425–30.

79. *Star*, July 24, 1927; November 6, 26, 1928; February 17, September 21, 1929; June 10, 1931; *Citizen*, May 7, 1929.

Chapter 13
Hard Times in Tucson

1. Evo A. DeConcini, *Hey! It's Past 80!* pp. 171–72. For the onset of the Depression see Murray H. Rothbard, *Depression*; Robert T. Patterson, *The Great Boom and Panic, 1921–1929*.

2. William E. Leuchtenberg, *Frankline D. Roosevelt and the New Deal*, p. 1.

3. *Star*, May 11, December 18, 1930 (first official report).

4. *Star*, January 1, 1930.

5. *Star*, January 3, 4, 5, March 6, July 17, 1930; Thomas C. Langdon, "Harold Bell Wright," *Journal of Arizona History*, vol. 16 (Spring, 1975), pp. 86–88.

6. *Star*, February 22, 1930.

7. *Star*, February 21, 22, 1930.

8. *Star*, February 16, March 2, May 11, June 12, July 6, 31, September 2, 1930.

9. *Star*, February 29, September 21, October 15, 16, November 5, 1930.

10. *Star*, December 17, 1930 (Sam Bailey, manager of the Arizona Automobile Association, speaking at a luncheon on December 6).

11. Douglas D. Martin, *The Lamp in the Desert*, p. 158.

12. *Star*, December 19, 22, 1930. The crime wave continued—see *Star*, February 23, 1931 (fourteen robberies in thirteen days).

13. *Star*, December 21, 1930; April 19, 1932.

14. *Star*, December 17, 18, 24, 1930.

15. *Star*, December 23, 1930.

16. *Star*, December 18, 1930.

17. *Star*, December 24–26, 1930.

18. *Star*, January 17, 1931.

19. *Star*, December 21, 1931; Dixon Wechter, *The Age of the Great Depression*, pp. 72–74.

20. Wechter, *The Age of the Great Depression*, p. 62.

21. *Ibid.*

22. Ernest J. Hopkins, *Financing the Frontier*, pp. 221–22; *Star*, June 23, 1931.

23. Hopkins, *Financing the Frontier*, pp. 240–43; *Star*, September 30, 1934; *Citizen*, October 27, 1929; Evo DeConcini, "Early Days in Tucson," lecture, Tucson Literary Club, January 19, 1981.

24. *Star*, February 27, 1937.

25. William H. Jervey, Jr., "When the Banks Closed," *Arizona and the West*, vol. 10 (Summer, 1968), p. 143.

26. David F. Brinegar, "The Arizona Daily Star" (MS), 1974, pp. 173–74.

27. *Ibid.*, pp. 180–81.

28. *Citizen*, February 2, 1927; *Star*, May 15, 1929; May 27, 1930; August 9, 1931; August 28, 1933.

29. Report of the Organized Charities of Tucson for 1929, May, 1929, AHS.

30. *Star*, May 15, 1929.

31. *Citizen*, February 2, 1927; June 29, 1930; *Star*, January 11, April 10, 1932.

32. *Star*, October 14, 1951.

33. George C. Kiser and David Silverman, "Mexican Reptriation During the Great Depression," in George C. Kiser and Martha Woody Kiser, eds., *Mexican Workers in the United States*, pp. 54–55; *Star*, May 2, 1931; April 10, 1932.

34. *Star*, April 10, 1932.

35. Edward H. Spicer, *Pascua: A Yaqui Village in Arizona*; Edward H. Spicer *The Yaquis: A Cultural History*; Jonathan H. Kress, "A Surviving Breed: The Yaquis of Tucson," *Tucson Weekly News*, vol. 1 (October 15–21, 1980), pp. 7–10. The Yaquis were given tribal status on September 18, 1978, a century after their first arrival.

36. Leo M. Jacques, "Have Quick More Money Than Mandarins," *Journal of Arizona History*, vol. 17 (Summer, 1976), pp. 212–13; Evelyn Hu-DeHart, "Immigrants to a Developing Society," *Journal of Arizona History*, vol. 21 (Autumn, 1980), pp. 275–312; R. F. Torrance, interview, October 15, 1980.

37. Letter addressed to Mrs. Tom Davenport, AHS; *Star*, April 27, 1935; April 21, 1937; May 5, 1960; June 7, 1974.

38. *Star*, January 9, 1940; May 5, 1960, July 6, November 9 1974 (obit.); *Citizen*, June 30, 1935; January 8, 1940; November 9, 1974 (obit.).

39. Glenton Sykes, interview, October 15, 1980; *Star*, January 21, 30, March 17, April 4, 1930; April 4, 1932; July 23, 1964; December 22, 1965 (obit.); *Citizen*, March 8, 1933; Don Bufkin, interview, October 15, 1980.

40. *Star*, July 14, 29, 1930; August 13, September 16, 26, October 2, 4, 6, 1932.

41. *Star*, September 26, October 2, 6, December 3, 1932.

42. Roger Daniels, *The Bonus March*, pp. 65–75; *Star*, June 4, 5, 13, 14, 1932.

43. *Star*, June 6, 7, 12, 15–17, 1932.

44. *Star*, June 18, 1932.

45. Daniels, *The Bonus March*, pp. 136–40; Henry Bartlett, *The Bonus March and the New Deal*, pp. 31–40; *Star*, June 19–21, 1932.

46. *Star*, all issues, January and February, 1934; August 18, October 27 (Sabino Canyon), December 17, 1934; March 1, 1935 (university); July 18, 1935 (CCC); February 27, March 9, 21, 28, 31, April 16, June 25, July 4, 1937 (PWA works and workers); October 22, 1936; September 28, 1937.

47. Martin, *The Lamp in the Desert*, pp. 165–69; *Star*, February 15, 1933; February 8, March 30, 1934; March 1, 1935; January 15, July 11, September 14, 24, October 11, 1936; June 4, 1938.

48. *Star*, September 14, 24, 1936.

49. *Star*, February 22, 24, April 20, May 5, 13, 30, June 3, 22, July 26, 1932; January 21, 1934; January 18, 30, 1936; C. E. Houston, interview, October 29, 1980.

50. *Star*, April 28, 1931, and following issues; DeConcini, *Hey! It's Past 80!* pp. 203–205.

51. *Star*, April 28, 29, September 20, 1931; Nancy Sortore, "What Is the Marshall Foundation?" *Star*, June 6, 1975.

52. *Citizen*, April 27, May 21, 1931; September 11, 1957 (obit.).

53. Evo DeConcini, interview, October 26, 1980; C. E. Houston, interview.

54. *Citizen*, April 27, 1931.

55. *Citizen*, September 18, 1931; *Star*, September 16, 1931.

56. *Star*, April 29, 1931.

57. *Star*, September 11, 1931.

58. *Star*, September 17, 1931; C. E. Houston, interview.

59. *Star*, September 24, 1931.

60. Sortore, "What Is the Marshall Foundation?"

61. C. E. Houston, interview.

62. Dick Hall, "Jesus Camacho," *Journal of Arizona History*, vol. 20 (Winter, 1979), pp. 445–86; *Star*, February 5, 6, 14, March 2, April 1–3, 23, May 2–10, 12, 17, 25, 26, June 1, 2, 1932; November 27, 1941; *Citizen*, January 16, December 27, 1934; January 26, 1935; J. F. Weadock, "Desert Notebook," undated clipping in Yuma Mine File, AHS. Henry Juliani suffered condemnation for taking the Adkins case, but he was convinced that Clifford was better than his record showed. He had refused to reveal the name of the third kidnapper (a Tucsonan) and had been deserted by his father, the real criminal (Mrs. Harry Juliani, interview, Tucson, February 5, 1982).

63. *Citizen*, April 25–30, 1934.

64. *Citizen*, May 10, 1934.

65. *Star*, May 15, 1934; Roy Drachman, *Just Memories*, pp. 109–10.

66. *Star*, April 28, 1934; November 25, 1936.

67. *Star*, December 16–19, 1936; C. E. Houston, interview; Drachman, *Just Memories*, pp. 109–10.

68. *Star*, January 24, 1934.

69. C. A. Wollard and Jack Weadock, "Clark! Makley! Pierpont!" *True Detective Mysteries*, June, 1934, pp. 13, 80–83; Al Speers, "The Dillinger Story" (six-part series), *Star*, December 17–22, 1978.

70. Bill Shaw, "Retired Detective Recalls Chase," *Star*, December 21, 1978; Don Schellie, "On View in Tucson," *Citizen*, September 15, 1975; "Exclusive! The True Story of Tucson Realty and Dillinger!" *Territorial Days Dispatch*, April, 1974, AHS; J. F. Wea-

dock, "Desert Notebook, *Star*, undated clipping, AHS; John Toland, *The Dillinger Days*, pp. 176–93.

71. Evo DeConcini, *Hey! It's Past 80!* pp. 174–76.

72. John Bret Harte, *Tucson*, p. 130.

73. Peter Bermingham, *The New Deal in the Southwest*.

74. *Star*, September 1, 1933; August 11, 30, October 26, 1936. In 1980, South Tucson was again under pressure from the mayor and city council to disincorporate. See Joe Burchell and Bob Levin, "City Cancels Aid Pact, Asks South Tucson to Merge," *Star*, October 28, 1980; John Bret Harte, "A Feisty Town Grows up," *Citizen*, June 6, 1975. In 1982, as a result of a $4 million judgment against the municipality in favor of a Tucson policeman shot and permanently crippled by a South Tucson officer, the town was about to declare itself bankrupt (*Star*, April 15, 1982).

75. *Citizen*, June 3, 1935; *Star*, October 30, 31, 1936; July 13, 22, 1939.

Chapter 14
War Again

1. Cabell Phillips, *The 1940's*, pp. 174–75; Douglas D. Martin, *The Lamp in the Desert*, p. 175.

2. For background see Phillips, *The 1940's*, pp. 3–10; Harvey Wish, *Contemporary America*, pp. 534–69; Mark Arnold Forster, *The World at War*, pp. 1–78; James L. Stokesbury, *A Short History of World War II*, pp. 1–20.

3. *Star*, July 19, 20, 26, August 1–3, 9, September 15, 1940; Phillips, *The 1940's*, pp. 188–90 (role of radio).

4. *Star*, July 11, 19, 1940.

5. *Star*, August 4, 5, 10, 15, 1940.

6. *Star*, July 15, August 5, 1940.

7. *Star*, August 24, September 4, 1940; Wish, *Contemporary America*, pp. 564–565.

8. *Star*, August 11, 1940; Phillips, *The 1940's*, p. 139.

9. *Star*, August 13, 16, 17, 1940.

10. *Star*, August 23, 24, 1940.

11. *Star*, July 15, August 4, September 2, 1940.

12. *Star*, August 7, 25, 29, November 1, 1940.

13. *Star*, July 24, 27, August 3, 1940.

14. *Star*, July 12, August 2, 25, 1940.

15. *Star*, August 14, 15, 1940.

16. *Star*, August 3, September 1, 15, 22, 23, 30, October 13, 1940.

17. *Star*, August 9, September 24, 29, 1940; Charles H. Broman, *The Story of the Tucson Airport Authority*, p. 5.

18. *Star*, August 16, 18, 1940.

19. *Star*, August 24, 30, September 15, 1940.

20. *Star*, August 18, 23, September 13, November 1, 1940.

21. *Star*, November 14, 15, 17, 1940.

22. *Star*, August 7, 27, September 10, October 18, 1940.

23. *Star*, August 7, September 10, 1940; Phillips, *The 1940's*, pp. 106–108, 114–38.

24. *Star*, August 11, 1940.

25. *Star*, September 26, 1940.

26. *Star*, May 20, 21, 28, 1940; Elmer W. Flaccus, "Arizona's Last Great Indian War," *Journal of Arizona History*, vol. 22 (Spring, 1981), pp. 5, 9.

27. *Star*, October 17, 1940.

28. *Star*, May 21, 28, July 20, 1941; Flaccus, "Arizona's Last Great Indian War," pp. 15–19.

29. *Star*, October 9, 20, 29, 1940; May 1, 5, 11, 1941; *Citizen*, September 15, 1941; Phillips, *The 1940's*, pp. 56, 66–67.

30. *Star*, December 5, 1940.

31. *Star*, April 20, August 3, 1941; *Citizen*, March 1, 1977; *Arizona Highways*, vol. 18 (June, 1937), pp. 14–15.

32. *Star*, August 6, September 29, October 7, 1940.

33. *Star*, October 10, November 7, 12, December 10, 13, 1940; January 31, February 8, 1941; January 1, 1981.

34. *Star*, September 27, October 4, 1940; November 8, 10–12, 1941; *Citizen*, December 1, 1941.

35. *Star*, November 17, 18, December 3, 1941; Wish, *Contemporary America*, pp. 598–600.

36. *Star*, December 6, 1941.

37. *Star*, December 8–12, 1941; *Citizen*, December 8–12, 1941.

38. *Star*, December 8, 11, 1941.

39. *Star*, December 9, 1941.

40. *Star*, December 8, 9, 1941.

41. *Star*, December 10, 12, 1941.

42. *Star*, December 9, 10, 1941.

43. *Star*, December 10, 14, 1941; Phillips, *The 1940's*, pp. 191–93.

44. *Star*, December 19, 1941.

45. *Star*, December 8, 9, 11, 21, 1941.

46. *Star*, December 10, 22, 25, 1941.

47. *Star*, December 27, 28, 1941.

48. *Arizona (Arizona Republic)*, December 3, 1978; George W. Howard, "Bridges in the Desert," *Journal of Arizona History*, vol. 17 (Winter, 1976), pp. 431–68.

49. *Star*, September 2, 1945.

50. *Arizona (Arizona Republic)*, December 3, 1978.

51. *Star*, January 2, August 4, 1944.

52. *Star*, July 27, 1945.

53. *Arizona (Arizona Republic)* December 3, 1978.

54. Richard A. Harvill, interview, December 15, 1980; *Citizen*, July 11, 1970; Wish, *Contemporary America*, 597–98; George E. Mowry, *The Urban Nation, 1920–1960*, p. 198.

55. *Arizona* (*Arizona Republic*), December 3, 1978; Phillips, *The 1940's*, p. 176.

56. Margaret Bret Harte, interview, January 2, 1981; Cecil Stambrough, interview, January 2, 1981.

57. *Star*, January 3, 1943; Phillips, *The 1940's*, pp. 176–77.

58. *Star*, January 1, 1943.

59. *Star*, January 3, 1943.

60. *Star*, July 14, August 2, 1943.

61. *Star*, January 3, 1943.

62. *Star*, August 4, 1945; Louise Spencer Reid, "Guerrilla Wife," *Ladies' Home Journal*, vol. 62 (August, 1945), pp. 17, 64–87, 89–91. A Mrs. Spencer, wife of another mining engineer, escaped by submarine with fifty-eight other Americans in April, 1944.

63. *Star*, July 27, 1945.

64. *Star*, July 11, 12, August 2, 9, 1945.

65. Forster, *The World at War*, pp. 155–85; Wish, *Contemporary America*, pp. 572–77, 583–86.

66. *Star*, August 15, 16, 19, 1945.

67. *Star*, August 27, 29, 31, September 1, 2, 1945.

Chapter 15
The Price of Progress

1. *Star*, September 12, 1944; January 12, May 7, 1945; May 5, 1946; March 3, 1948; December 30, 1979.

2. *Star*, February 2, 3, March 3, 12, 26, 30, June 27, 1951.

3. Evo A. DeConcini, *Hey! It's Past 80!* pp. 178–79.

4. George E. Mowry, *The Urban Nation*, p. 197; Melvin R. Levin, *The Urban Prospect*, pp. 19–20.

5. City Council Planning Department, *General Land Use Plan*, 1960, pp. 11, 19; Tucson Area Transportation Planning Agency, *Land Development: Planning Series Report no. 2, Land Status in Eastern Pima County*, 1967, pp. 12–15; "Accumulative Population and Area Growth of the Tucson Region," U.S. Census information assembled by Don Bufkin (MS); Don Bufkin, "From Mud Village to Modern Metropolis: The Urbanization of Tucson," *Journal of Arizona History*, vol. 22 (Spring, 1981), pp. 90–91; *Citizen*, February 14, 1952; Edward N. Bassett, "Tucson Nears 'Magic Mark' of 500,000," *Citizen*, December 21, 1977.

6. C. W. Griffin, Jr., *Taming the Last Frontier*, pp. 212–13; *Citizen*, May 14, 1953; *New York Times*, December 14, 1979; *Star*, October 1, 1940.

7. *Star*, September 12, 1944.

8. *Star*, September 13, 1944.

9. *Star*, May 1, 1979; DeConcini, *Hey! It's Past 80*, p. 179.

10. City-County Planning Department, *General Land Use Plan: A Part of the Master Plan* (1960), p. 1; Pima County Planning Department, City of Tucson Planning Division, Town of South Tucson, Pima Association of Governments, Tucson Greater Transportation Planning Agency, *General Land Use Planning*, Comprehensive Report no. 3, November, 1972, sec. 2; Gary M. Muncinger, "A Bridge from the Past to the Future," *Tucson: Town Hall on Community Development, June 23–25, 1974*, p. 14, Donald H. Bufkin, interview, January 26, 1981.

11. City of Tucson Planning Division et al., *Community Responses*, August, 1974, pp. 1–14. For Green Valley, Oro Valley, and Marana see *Citizen*, May 15, 1963; December 12, 1979; *Star*, April 17, 1976; December 7, 1977.

12. *Citizen*, June 15, 1951; June 19, 1978 (obit.); Vicki Thompson, *Across the Dry Rillito*, pp. 1–3, 5–7, 15–18.

13. City of Tucson Planning Division et al., *Comprehensive Planning Process*, phase 4, December 8, 1976, p. 8; City of Tucson et al., *Summary of Tucson's Land Use*, 1960, p. 11.

14. *Star*, March 13, 1946; February 22, 25, May 13, October 3, November 28, 1956; September 29, 1957; *Citizen*, April 15, 1954; January 22, March 15, October 5, 1958; April 18, November 29, December 2, 1960; August 4, 10, November 9, 16, 1965; September 19, 1967. El Con was the first regional shopping center; Park Mall on Broadway was the second. A third, at Oracle and Wetmore, opened in March, 1982 (*Star*, March 22, 1982).

15. *Summary of Tucson's Land Use*, 1960, p. 11; *Star*, March 13, 1948; September 4, 1952; April 20, May 6, July 1, December 10, 16, 1960; August 22, 1962; August 8, 1963; October 7, 1978; January 7, September 18, 22, 1979; June 12, 1980; Donald H. Bufkin, interview, February 4, 1981.

16. *Star*, September 28, 1975; October 2, 9, 1980; "Tucson Meet Yourself," program, October 7–9, 1977, AHS.

17. Lay James Gibson, "Where Have We Been and Where Are We Heading," *Tucson Town Hall*, 1974, p. 15; *Star*, April 20, May 6, July 1, December 10, 16, 1960; August 22, 1962; May 15, August 3, 8, 1963; June 10, 11, 25, 26, July 14, 27, 30, August 19, 1965; *Citizen*, December 12, 1979; January 7, 1981.

18. "Copper: Changing Faces, Changing Times,"

Star, November 30, 1976.

19. George Ernest Webb, "The Indefatigable Astronomer," *Journal of Arizona History*, vol. 19 (Summer, 1978), p. 186; *Star*, March 16, 1946; *Citizen*, June 14, 15, 1951; May 15, 1954; May 4, 1963; February 17, 1966.

20. *Star*, June 7, 1966; March 31, 1978; "Tucson's Bigger Size," *Sun Dancer* (Los Angeles), April, 1974.

21. *Citizen*, January 6, 8, 1965; June 26, 1970; July 4, 1974; September 26, October 16, 1976; June 11, 13, 15, July 15, October 5, 11, 25, 1969; March 20, June 15, 1980; *Star*, November 13, December 3, 9, 1977; March 14, 1978; February 11, 18, June 11, December 29, 1979; February 21, March 30, October 16, December 3, 17, 1980; February 28, 1981 (Motorola negotiating again).

22. *Star*, December 29, 1954; August 2, 1979.

23. *Star*, September 26, December 6, 1963; July 9, 1964; March 27, 1966.

24. *Star*, September 18, 1954.

25. *Star*, February 18, 21, November 8, December 3, 1941; February 11, 1942; October 9, 1957; Blake McKelvey, *American Urbanization*, pp. 130–31.

26. "Report of the Citizens Low-Cost Housing Committee to the Mayor and Council, December 16, 1949" (MS), AHS; *Star*, May 7, 1962; March 10, 1964; August 15, October 7, 1967; August 26, 1971; February 8, June 6, September 3, 1980; *Citizen*, December 12, 18, 1970. La Reforma was closed in December, 1979.

27. *Star*, October 3, 9, 1957; May 1, October 5, 1958; March 1, April 25, May 8, June 28, 1962; February 11, December 6, 1963; December 12, 1970; July 31, September 7, 1971; July 19, 1972; March 8, 23, 25, 1979; November 4, 1980; *Citizen*, March 8, 1962; January 11, November 9, 1966; May 3, 1974; March 14, 1975; July 22, 1976; July 17, 1980.

28. *Citizen*, May 7, 8, 1962.

29. *Citizen*, October 9, 1957; March 1, April 25, June 28, 1962; March 10, 1964; February 2, November 9, 23, 1965; January 13, 1966.

30. *Citizen*, October 5, 1967; August 26, 1971; November 25, 1979; July 17, November 14, 1980; *Star*, May 7, 1962; February 2, 1965; October 8, 1967; July 6, October 17, 1969; March 14, 1975; March 23, November 25, 1979.

31. *Star*, December 10, 12, 1978; *Citizen*, June 30, October 7, 1966; December 12, 1970.

32. *Star*, August 6, 1970; March 4, September 1, 29, October 16, 1971; June 30, 1975; *Citizen*, October 7, December 22, 1970; January 9, February 5, April 13, 20, June 22, 1971; June 30, 1975; *New Model Cities Program*, Tucson, November 1, 1970; *Pueblo Center Notes*, no. 6, February 19, 1968.

33. *Star*, February 9, 1942; October 16, 1974; September 11, 1977; April 11, 1980.

34. *Star*, May 5, 10, 1979; February 6, 1981; *Citizen*, January 12, 1966.

35. *Star*, January 11, 1979; March 23, April 1, 11, 18, 20, May 7, August 21, November 4, December 21, 1980; May 15, 1981 (flood control to come in fall).

36. "Report and Information on the John C. Frémont House, 'Casa del Gobernador,' Prepared for the Dedication of the Home by Mrs. Richard M. Nixon, Friday, April 7, 1972" (MS), AHS; *Citizen*, May 17, 1973.

37. *Star*, February 9, July 19, 1972; February 11, November 30, 1973; July 22, 1976; March 23, November 25, 1979; July 14, 1980; *Citizen*, March 25, May 12, 1971; July 17, 1980.

38. Mrs. Jay Sternberg, "Outline History of the Tucson Museum of Art" (MS, Tucson Museum of Art; Dorcas Worsley and Tina Lyons, interviews, February 9, 1981; *Star*, July 3, 1965, January 19, June 5, 9, 1970; December 23, 1971; January 26, November 21, 1973; May 4, 1975; June 4, 1978; April 11, 1980; *Citizen*, July 1, 1972; December 13, 1974; April 2, 1977.

39. *Star*, June 28, October 8, 1978; August 9, 1979; May 30, 1980; *Citizen*, June 8, 1978; William A. Caldwell, *How to Save Urban America*, pp. 199–201; Donald H. Bufkin, interview, December 30, 1980.

40. *Citizen*, September 24, 1976; Caldwell, *How to Save Urban America*, pp. 6–7; Lewis Mumford, *The Urban Prospect*, p. ix.

41. Downtown Advisory Committee, *Plan for Downtown Tucson*, 1978, pp. 43–61; *Star*, August 11, 1975; January 31, July 6, October 12, 1976; May 6, 19, 1977; August 3, 1979; *Citizen*, August 11, 1975; January 31, July 6, October 12, 1976; May 6, 1977; March 14, 21, 1978.

42. *Star*, April 21, 1978; March 8, 1979; *Citizen*, February 4, 1980. See *Star*, April 21, 1970, for Steve Emerine's summary of revitalization history.

43. *Star*, July 8, 1979; January 7, September 23, 1979; July 10, 1980.

44. *Star*, March 23, 1973; Griffith, *Taming the Last Frontier*, pp. 222–25 ("The Subtle Evils of Sprawl"); H. P. Walker, interview, March 11, 1981.

45. *Star*, April 2, 1973; July 17, 1977; December 10, 30, 1979; Donald H. Bufkin, letter to author, February 11, 1981.

46. *Star*, September 6, 1979; Frank Lloyd Wright, *The Living City*, p. 31.

47. *Star*, September 23, 1971; May 3, 1973; May 11, 1974; May 2, 9, September 30, 1979; January 2, July 27, 1980; January 26, 27, 30, 31, February 3, 1981; *Citizen*, July 28, 1975.

48. *Star*, April 10, 1979; February 18, March 16, 1980; Suzanne T. Gary, "Arizona's Favorite Child," *Tucson*, February, 1979, p. 19.

49. *Star*, October 29, 1978; Tom Danehy, "Who Is This Man and Why Is He So Important to You?" *Tucson*, August, 1979, p. 19.

50. *Star*, September 15, 1946; March 1, 24, April 25, 1951; *Citizen*, June 28, 1956 (obit.).

51. *Star*, April 2, 1958; August 25, 1971; January 1, 1972; *Citizen*, January 3, 1957.

52. *Citizen*, February 24, November 1, 1950; January 15, 29, February 16, October 8, 11, 1951.

53. *Citizen*, March 12, 1952; July 25, 1954; September 12, 1955; January 3, March 1, 1957.

54. *Citizen*, July 24, August 2, 1967; September 11, 1970; *Star*, October 21, 1970.

55. *Citizen*, September 7, 1968; March 14, 1973.

56. *Citizen*, July 7, 1968; October 20, 25, 1973.

57. *Citizen*, January 24, June 11, July 6, August 2, 1968; January 5, 11, 15, 22–25, 1971; Richard H. Harvill, interview, January 19, 1981.

58. *Citizen*, February 26, 27, 1973.

59. For the Arizona Inn see *Citizen*, October 17, 1967; November 16, 1973; January 29, June 29, September 24, 1974; August 12, 1977; April 15, 1978; *Star* December 14–17, 1980. For Christopher Square see Nancy Sortore, "A Relaxed Tucson Home for a Family of Guests, *Star*, January 7, 1975.

60. *Citizen*, January 17, 1969; February 9, 1972; June 2, 1973; April 30, 1976; April 11, December 1, 1977; July 23, 24, August 2, 22, 24, September 24, 1979; *Star*, July 31, 1979.

61. *Citizen*, April 2–4, 1951; April 30, 1976; *Star*, April 19, 28, September 5, 18, November 4, 15, 1979; July 3, 24, August 2, September 3, 13, October 2, December 20, 1980; January 23, 30, 1981.

62. *Star*, May 30, September 18, 23, 1979.

63. *Star*, August 4, 1979, February 15, September 14, 1980.

64. Tom Danehy, "Who Is This Man?" p. 24.

65. *Star*, September 23, 1979; January 12, 1980 (rape-crisis group organizes).

66. *Star*, March 11, 1981.

67. *Star*, February 18, 1969; April 6, 1977; September 14, 1980; *Phoenix Gazette*, May 12, 1977; "Tucson: A Soaring Decade of Crime," *Tucson Weekly News*, October 15–21, 1980; *Star*, March 27, 1981.

Chapter 16
. . . But, on the Other Hand

1. On waste disposal: Howard G. Applegate, *Environmental Problems of the Borderlands*, pp. 6–9; on

school segregation, white flight: *Star*, September 8, October 12, November 15, 1979; January 30, 1980. On south Tucson: *Star*, August 30, 1979; May 16, August 2, 9, 10, 1980; on elderly indigents: *Star*, July 8, 10–13, 1979.

2. William H. Carr, *The Desert Speaks*; Hal and Natie Gras, interview, April 21, 1981; Watson Smith, interview, April 30, 1981. Joseph Wood Krutch named the *Desert Ark*.

3. Tucson Festival of the Arts, March 25–April 8, 1951, announcement, AHS; Murray Sinclair, "Tucson Festival," *Star*, undated clipping. AHS; Mrs. Robert H. Foster, letter to the public, February 6, 1980, AHS.

4. "Tucson Festival 81, Celebrating Southern Arizona's Multi-Cultural Heritage," program, AHS; Murray Sinclair, interview, March 16, 1981.

5. Dorothy Gaines, "Forum's Founder Retires," *Star*, March 28, 1976; J. C. Martin, "Tucson: Sunday Evening Forum," *Star*, April 7, 1974; Lawrence Cheek, "Musical Giants," *Star*, May 18, 1980.

6. *Star*, November 8, 1979; September 28, 1980.

7. *Citizen*, February 4, 1950; J. C. Martin, "Tucson Boys Chorus," *Star*, March 14, 1974.

8. Michael Keating, "Friends of Music Launch 31st Year with Tokyo Quartet," *Citizen*, October 11, 1978; George Rosenberg, interview, March 16, 1981. Among the many groups which might be mentioned are the Philharmonia Orchestra, Orchestai, Junior Strings, the Tucson Pops Orchestra, and the Tucson Jazz Society.

9. Kenneth La Fave, "Tucson Opera Company on Its Way to Big Time," *Star*, September 26, 1976; "Opera Problems Result of Debts," *Star*, February 3, 1980; "Opera Sings a Happier Tune," *Star*, October 1, 1980; "Opera Pays off $99,000 Debts," *Star*, December 4, 1980; "Opera Is Cleaning Up Its Act," *Star*, December 23, 1980; "Arizona Opera Optimistic About 2d Decade," *Star*, January 10, 1982; Tucson Opera Company, announcement, 1974–75 season, AHS.

10. *Star*, September 15, 1977; October 25, 1978; November 16, 1980; March 31, 1981; Kenneth La Fave, "Living Dance: The Beginning of the End for Tucson Arts?" *Star*, April 12, 1981.

11. Artist File, Tucson Museum of Art Library; J. C. Martin, "Tucson Art Center," *Star*, May 20, 1973; "Tucson Museum of Art Reflects Heritage," *Highroads* (American Automobile Association), January–February, 1981.

12. *Acceptance of the Statue of Francisco Eusebio Kino . . .*, 89th Cong., 1st sess., H. Doc. 158, pp. 16, 22–24; *Star*, April 2, May 20, 1975 (obit.)

13. Tucson Festival of the Arts, "Theatres," an-

nouncement, 1951, AHS; Tucson Community Theater announcement, September 25, 1957, AHS; Arizona Civic Theater, *In the Act*, vol. 1 (October, 1975),
AHS; *Star*, July 22, 1952; May 21, 1978; November
27, 1979; September 28, 1980; *Citizen*, September
14, December 1, 1977; Broadway Dinner Theater,
announcement, 1975, AHS; *Star*, April 1, 1982
(Tucson loses its last dinner theater); Invisible Theater, announcement, December 1975–76, AHS.

14. Tucson Festival of the Arts, "Writers," announcement, 1951; Elliott Arnold: *Arizona Republic*,
October 22, 1950; *Citizen*, May 10, 1979; *Star*, May
15, 1980 (obit.). On Charles Finney: *Star*, July 6,
1935; March 7, 1936; *Citizen*, September 22, 1979;
David F. Brinegar, "The Newspaper Guy" (MS), copy
in possession of David F. Brinegar.

15. On Margaret Sanger Slee: *Star*, October 6,
1934; April 13, 1936; September 14, 1950; February
22, September 20, 1952; May 21, 1961; September
7, 1966 (obit.); *Citizen*, November 23, 1934; February 12, 1935; March 13, 1936; January 22, 1940;
Don Schellie, "No More the Sleepy Cowtown, *Citizen*, May 10, 1979.

16. On Westbrook Pegler: *Star*, June 25, 1969;
Citizen, June 24, 1968 (obit.). On Joseph Wood
Krutch: *Citizen*, May 22, 23 (obit.), 25, 1970; May
4, 1977; Don Schellie, "He Lives Again," *Citizen*,
May 23, 1970. Krutch's friend and student Gerald
Green made him the central figure in *An American
Prophet*.

17. On Ann Nolan Clark: *Citizen*, March 6, 1970;
May 27, 1973. On John Creasey: *Citizen*, November
13, 1971. On Clarence Budington Kelland: *Star*,
January 29, 1942; February 19, 1962 (obit.); *Arizona
Republic*, February 19, 1964.

18. *On Evangeline Ensley: J. C. Martin, "Author
Adept at Going Back in Time," Star*, May 15, 1977. On
Jeanne Williams: J. C. Martin, "Book Markets Covered with Arizonan's Fiction," *Star*, September 15,
1980. On Lorenzo Zavala: *Star*, March 1, 1881.

19. J. C. Martin, The Face of Poetry," *Star*, March
1, 1977; "Poetry Center" (MS), AHS; Laurence Muir,
interview, March 16, 1981; Laverne Harrell Clark,
interviews, May 4, 21, 1981; Murray Sinclair, interview. On Richard Shelton: *Los Angeles Times*, February
19, 1978.

20. On Richard Summers: *Star*, February 2, 1936;
October 26, 1969 (obit.). On Edith Heal: *Citizen*,
June 16, 1940; October 14, 1943.

21. On Byrd Baylor: *Star*, August 28, 1977.

Chapter 17
Back to the Bowl and Pitcher

1. For the CAP see Rich Johnson, *The Central
Arizona Project 1918–1968*.

2. Sol Resnick, interview, March 2, 1981.

3. Ellsworth Huntington, *The Climatic Factor*, p.
99.

4. Arizona Bureau of Mines, *Mineral and Water
Resources of Arizona*, pp. 527, 581; H. C. Schwalen
and R. J. Shaw, *Water in the Santa Cruz Valley*, pp. 1–
2; John Harshbarger, "Use of Groundwater in Arizona," in Teran L. Smiley, ed., *Climate and Man in the
Southwest*, p. 64; James Rodney Hastings and Raymond M. Turner, *The Changing Mile*, p. 42.

5. *Star*, December 25, 1977; July 2, 1978 (quoting Edward S. Davidson, of the University of Arizona
Geology Department).

6. Harshbarger, "Use of Groundwater," p. 64.

7. Peter C. Duisberg, "Prologue," in Smiley, ed.,
Climate and Man in the Southwest, p. 1.

8. *Star*, May 7, 1960; November 20, 27, December 18, 1977; January 6, September 17, 1978; May
2, 1979.

9. Charles C. Colley, "Water Under the Earth,"
Journal of Arizona History, vol. 16 (Autumn, 1975),
pp. 245–64; Howard G. Applegate, "A Survey of
Environmental Problems Along the Border," *Environmental Problems Along the Border*, p. 29.

10. Colley, "Water under the Earth," pp. 260–64.

11. *Star*, January 2, 12, February 24, May 21,
June 12, September 30, November 26, 1978; *Citizen*, January 19, February 19, 1977.

12. Maurice M. Kelso, William E. Martin, and
Lawrence E. Mack, *Water Supplies and Economic Growth
in an Arid Environment: An Arizona Case Study*, pp.
26–27; *Star*, March 17, December 18, 1977; November 26, 1978 November 25, 1981; *Citizen*, January 19, February 19, 1977.

13. Charles Bowden, *Killing the Hidden Waters*, pp.
135–36.

14. *Star*, November 17, 27, 1977; September 17,
1978.

15. Edward Abbey, *Good News*, p. 3.

16. Mabel Dodge Luhan, *Edge of Taos Desert*, p.
295; Vine Deloria, Jr., *God Is Red*, p. 55.

17. Bernard L. Fontana, "Sonoran Heritage: Where
Are We?" *Tucson* (April, 1979), pp. 25–29.

18. Edward Abbey, *The Journey Home*, p. 157.

19. Jon Manchip White, *A World Elsewhere*, p. 7.

Sources

MISCELLANEOUS INTERVIEWS

Ana María Comaduran Coenen. Interview with George W. Chambers and G. T. Urias, Tucson, October, 1927. Arizona Historical Society.

Samuel Hughes. Undated interview with José de Castillo, Tucson. Arizona Historical Society.

Cirilo Leon. "Mr. Leon's Conversation." Undated interview with Cirilo Leon, Tucson. Hayden Biographical File, Arizona Historical Society.

Joseph Frank Leon (son of Cirilo). *Arizona Days and Ways (Arizona Republic)*, August 15, 1956.

Mrs. Carmen P. Lucero. "Reminiscences as Interpreted by Miss Maggie Brady to Mrs. George F. Kitt, 1928." Hayden File, Arizona Historical Society.

INTERVIEWS WITH AUTHOR

Margaret BretHarte, Tucson, January 2, 1980.

Sidney B. Brinckerhoff, Tucson, December 31, 1980.

Donald H. Bufkin, Tucson, July 5, February 28, 1980; January 19, 26, February 2, 4, 1981.

Laverne Harrell Clark, May 4, 21, 1981.

Lori Davisson, Tucson, December 24, 1980.

Evo DeConcini, Tucson, January 19, 1981.

Elmer Flaccus, Tucson, June 3, 1981.

Hal Gras, Tucson, April 25, 1981.

Gordon Gordon, Tucson, February 21, 1981.

Richard A. Harvill, Tucson, December 15, 1980; January 19, 1981.

Albert Hesselberg, Tucson, February 13, 1981.

Ann-Eve Johnson, September 10, 1980.

Helen Land, Tucson, September 1, 1980.

Tina Lyons, Tucson, February 9, 1981.

Orville McPherson, Tucson, August 25, 1980.

Daniel Matson, Tucson, June 4, 1979.

Yndia Moore, Tucson, August 19, 1980.

Lawrence Muir, Tucson, March 16, 1981.

Helen Murphy, Tucson, May 6, 1981.

Charles W. Polzer, Tucson, June 4, 1979.

Sol Resnick, Tucson, March 2, 1981.

Edward Ronstadt, Tucson, August 21, 1981.

George Rosenberg, Tucson, March 16, 1981.

Murray Sinclair, Tucson, March 16, 1981.

Watson Smith, Tucson, April 26, 1981.

Harris Sobin, Tucson, August 29, 1980.

Cecil Stambrough, Tucson, January 2, 1981.

Glenton Sykes, Tucson, July 2, August 20, September 3, October 15, December 31, 1980; April 1, 1981.

Robert F. Torrance, Tucson, October 15, 1980.

Henry P. Walker, Tucson, March 11, 1981.

Adina Wingate, Tucson, March 16, 1981.

Dorcas Worsley, Tucson, February 9, 1981.

LETTERS

Howard Billman to Mrs. C. E. Walker, Tucson, December 10, 1888. Tucson Indian School Papers, 1883–1953, box 1, p. 44, Arizona Historical Society.

Donald H. Bufkin to author, Tucson, February 11, 1981.

John F. Farson to Harold Steinfeld, Tucson, April 5, 1945. Correspondence of the Rev. Victor R. Stoner, A–H, Arizona State Museum Archives, Tucson.

Mrs. Robin A. Foster, President, Tucson Festival Society, to the Public, February 6, 1980. Arizona Historical Society.

Father Francisco Garcés to Governor Juan de Pineda, San Xavier, August 20, 1775. Transcript in Southwest Mission Research Center, University of Arizona, Tucson.

Sylvester Mowry to ——— Bicknall, Fort Yuma, October 29, 1855. E. S. Wallace folder, Hayden File, Arizona Historical Society.

Donald W. Page to Eleanor Sloan, Director, Arizona Historical Society, Berkeley, California, March 6, 1954. Arizona Historical Society.

NEWSPAPERS

Arizona Daily Star (variations, e.g., *Weekly Star*, appear as they occur).
Arizona Enterprise (Florence).
Arizona Miner (Prescott).
Arizona Mining Index (Tucson).
Arizona Republic (Phoenix).
Arizona Silver Belt (Globe).
El Paso Herald-Post.
La Aurora (Albuquerque).
Los Angeles Evening Herald and Express.
Phoenix Gazette.
Territorial Expositor (Phoenix).
Tombstone Epitaph.
Tombstone Prospector.
Tucson Daily Citizen (variations, e.g., *Arizona Citizen*, appear as they occur).
Tucson Post.
Tucson Weekly News.
Sacramento Union.
San Diego Union.
San Francisco Herald.
Sun Dancer (Los Angeles).

MANUSCRIPTS, DOCUMENTS, ARCHIVAL MATERIAL

Abbott, Mary Huntington. "Papagos, Presbyterians, and the Indian Training School." Course paper, History 596A, University of Arizona, Fall, 1979. MS. Copy in Arizona Historical Society.

Acceptance of the Statue of Francisco Eusebio Kino. . . . 89th Cong., 1st sess., H. Doc. 158. Washington, D.C.: Government Printing Office, 1965.

Arizona Pioneers Historical Society. Minute Book no. 1. Arizona Historical Society.
———. Register, 1888–96. Arizona Historical Society.

Arizona State Council of Defense. *A Record of the Activities of the Arizona State Council of Defense from Foundation April 18 1917 to Dissolution June 1919.* [Phoenix, 1919].

Barragua, Manuel, Francisco Castro, and Antonio Romero. Letter to Captain Don Pedro de Allende y Saavedra, November 24, 1777. 33d Cong., 2d sess., H. Exec. Doc. 91, 1857.

Baylor, George Wythe. "Historical Stories of the Southwest." MS. El Paso Public Library.

Bell, Earl S. "Pioneer Protestant Preachers, 1859–1879, Arizona Territory." Seminar paper, University of Arizona, Spring, 1964. MS., Arizona Historical Society.

Brinegar, David F. "The Arizona Daily Star: A History." MS. In possession of Brinegar.
———. "The Newspaper Guy." MS. Copy in possession of Brinegar.
———. "Prostitution in Arizona." Introduction. MS. In possession of author.

Broadway Dinner Theatre. Announcement, 1979. Arizona Historical Society.

Donald H. Bufkin. "Accumulative Population and Area Growth of the Tucson Region." U.S. Census information assembled by Donald H. Bufkin. MS. In possession of Bufkin.
———. "The Broad Pattern of Land Use Change in Tucson, 1862–1912." In "Territorial Tucson." Edited by Thomas F. Saarinen. MS. Copy in possession of DHB.
———. "Tucson: An Urban History. Patterns of Growth." Lecture, Sonoran Heritage Series, Tucson Public Library, Winter, 1971. Notes in possession of author.

Campbell, Thomas E. "True Copy of the Notes of Hon. Thomas E. Campbell." Thomas Campbell Papers, MS 132, S.B. Arizona Historical Society.

de Castillo, José. "Solomon Warner." Hayden File, Arizona Historical Society.

DeConcini, Evo. "Early Days in Tucson." Lecture, Tucson Literary Club, January 19, 1981. Notes in possession of author.

Deitch, Louis Ivan. "Changing House Styles in Tucson, Arizona." Master's thesis, University of Arizona, 1966.

Downtown Advisory Committee [Tucson]. *Plan for Downtown Tucson.* Tucson, 1938.

Drachman, Mose. "Reminiscences." MS. Arizona Historical Society.

Emory, William H. *Report on the United States and Mexican Boundary Survey Made Under the Direction of the Secretary of the Interior.* Vol. 1. 34th Cong., 1st sess., H. Exec. Doc. 135, 1857.

Ferren, Clara. "The Vegetable Chinamen," May 6, 1897. MS. Arizona Historical Society.

Fine Arts Association of Tucson. Souvenir Dedication Program, Temple of Music and Art, October 21, 1927. Arizona Historical Society.

Fish, Joseph. "History of Arizona." MS. Arizona Historical Society.

Fontana, Bernard L. "Synopsis of Early History of Tucson," 1975. MS. Arizona State Museum.

Girton, Martin L. "Glimpses of Our Work at Tucson." Tucson Indian Training School Papers, 1888–1955, box 2. Typescript, transcribed from *Home Mission Monthly,* December 11, 1918. Arizona Historical Society.

Hall, Dick. "Sixty Years of a Misspent Life: The Story of My Early Days in Tucson," 1977. MS. Copy in possession of CLS.

Hand, George O. "Diary." MS. Arizona Historical Society.

Hughes, David L. "A Sketch of the Skirmish at Picacho, Arizona, Between the Union and Confederate Troops During the Civil War as Related by George Brandes (Brandon), Saddler D, 1st California Cavalry, Written by D. L. Hughes." MS. D. L. Hughes Collection, Arizona Historical Society.

———. "A Story of the 'Rough Riders' as Related by David L. Hughes." MS. D. L. Hughes Collection, Arizona Historical Society.

Hughes, Samuel. "Reminiscences, 1838–1885, Dictated to J. W. Olds at Tucson About February 6, 1885, Transcribed and Annotated by Donald W. Page." Donald W. Page Collection, Arizona Historical Society.

———. "Statement of Samuel Hughes, July 3, 1862." War Department Records, Provost Marshal General, Confederate Citizens File, National Archives. Copy in Arizona Historical Society.

Invisible Theater. Announcement, December, 1975–76. Arizona Historical Society.

Leach, James R. *Itinerary of the El Paso and Fort Yuma Wagon Road Expedition Under the Superintendence of James B. Leach.* Records of the Office of the Secrtary of the Interior Relating to Wagon Roads. Washington, D.C., 1858.

Le Garra, Richard Spring. "Son of Pioneers Recalls His Teenage Years on Convent Street," November, 1967. MS. Arizona Historical Society.

Luttrell, Estelle. "History of the University of Arizona, 1885–1926." MS. Special Collections, University of Arizona.

McCarty, Kieran Robert. "Franciscan Beginnings on the Arizona-Sonora Desert 1767–1770." Ph.D. dissertation, Catholic University of America, 1973. Microfilm. Arizona Historical Society.

McCool, Grace. "First Sierra Vista Businessman Was Shot in Mexico." Undated, unidentified clipping. Hayden File, Arizona Historical Society.

McKale, J. F. "Address of J. F. 'Pop' McKale at the Annual Meeting of the Arizona Pioneers Historical Society, November 14, 1964." MS. Arizona Historical Society.

Pacheco, Rudy. "A Case Study of a Pioneer Family." Course paper, History 26, University of Arizona, September 27, 1965. Copy in possession of Sidney B. Brinckerhoff.

Pima County, City of South Tucson, City of Tucson, Town of Oro Valley. Introduction ("Problems"). *The Comprehensive Plan—Policies.* Hearing draft, January, 1977.

Pima County Planning Department, City of Tucson Planning Division, Town of South Tucson, Pima Association of Governments, Tucson Greater Transportation Planning Agency. *General Land Use Planning.* Comprehensive Planning Report 3, Tucson, November, 1972.

Polzer, Charles W. Biographical material on Fathers Bosco and Messea. Southwest Mission Research Center files, SFX-Bac, University of Arizona, Tucson.

———. "Tucson Before the Territory." In "Territorial Tucson." Edited by Thomas F. Saarinen. MS. In possession of Donald H. Bufkin.

Purcell, Margaret Kathleen. "Life and Leisure in Tucson Before 1880." Master's thesis, University of Arizona, 1969.

Quiroga, Joaquín, Subprefect of San Ignacio, Cucurpe. "Report to the Secretary of the Department of Sonora in Guaymas on Mission Temporalities in the Area of Tucson–San Xavier del Bac." MS. Copy in Southwest Mission Research Center, University of Arizona.

Reynolds, A. S. "Description of the Old Walled Pueblo of Tucson, 1926." MS. Arizona Historical Society.

———. "Reminiscences," 1936. MS. Arizona Historical Society.

Rockfellow, John A. Untitled MS Hayden File, Arizona Historical Society.

Ronstadt, Frederick. "Music in Tucson, 1880's." MS. Arizona Historical Society.

Saarinen, Thomas F., ed. Introduction. "Territorial Tucson." MS. Copy in possession of DHB.

Sarlat, Gladys, Public Relations. "El Con Shopping Center," 1969, "Tucson Trends," 1978. News releases. Arizona Historical Society.

Smith, Hugh J., and Frederick J. Brady. "Arizona's Desert as a Health Resort," 1977. MS. Copy in possession of author.

Spring, John A. "Troublous Days in Arizona," 1903. MS. Arizona Historical Society.

Sternberg, Mrs. Jay. "Outline History of the Tucson Museum of Art and Its Background." MS. Tucson Museum of Art.

Stevens, Hiram. "Anecdotes of Early Days." Hayden File, Arizona Historical Society.

Sykes, Glenton. "First Mount Lemmon Road." MS. Arizona Historical Society.

Tobias, Judith Ellen. "Governor Safford and Education in Arizona, 1869–1877." Seminar paper, University of Arizona, January 14, 1965. Copy in Arizona Historical Society.

Tretschek, Diane Tully. "Pinckney Randolph Tully and Charles Hoppin Tully, Arizona Pioneers." Term paper, History 216, University of Arizona, May 12, 1965. Copy in Arizona Historical Society.

Tucson, City of. "History of the Tucson Fire Department." MS. Arizona Historical Society.

———. "Report of the Police Department for the Entire Year of 1926," January 1, 1927. Arizona Historical Society.

———. Tucson City Council Minutes, June 6, 1881. Arizona Historical Society.

———, Planning Department, City of South Tucson Planning Department, Pima Association of Governments. *Comprehensive Planning*

Process, Phase IV (Metro Land Use), December 8, 1976.

———, City-County Planning Departments. *Summary of Tucson's Land Use Plan: A Part of the Master Plan.* Tucson, 1960.

———, Planning Division, Town of South Tucson, Pima County Planning Department, Pima Association of Governments, Tucson Area Transportation Planning Agency. *Comprehensive Planning Report No. 4 . . . : A Report for Community Discussion.* [Tucson, 1970].

———, Planning Division, Town of South Tucson, Pima County Planning Department, Pima Association of Governments, Tucson Area Transportation Planning Agency. *Comprehensive Planning Report No. 5: A Report for Community Discussion,* February, 1973, pt. 1.

———, Tucson Area Transportation Planning Area. *Forecast Review and Data Inventories,* August, 1972.

———, Tucson Area Transportation Planning Agency. "Land Status in Eastern Pima County." *Land Development.* Planning Series Report 2, Tucson, March, 1967.

Tucson Festival of the Arts. Announcement ("Theatre," "Writers"), March 15–April 8, 1951. Arizona Historical Society.

Tucson Festival Society. *Tucson Festival 81, Celebrating Southern Arizona's Multi-Cultural Heritage.* Program, 1981. Arizona Historical Society.

Tucson Indian Training School Papers, 1888–1953. Arizona Historical Society.

Tucson Meet Yourself. Program, October 7–9, 1977. Arizona Historical Society.

U.S. Government. Federal Census, 1860. 37th Cong., 2d sess., H. Exec. Doc. 116.

———. Federal Census, Territory of New Mexico and Territory of Arizona. Excerpts. 89th Cong., 1st sess., S. Doc. 13, 1912.

———. *Official Records of the War of the Rebellion.* 1st ser., vol. 50, pt. 2.

Wainer, J. J. "Early Transportation in California," 1888. MS. Arizona Historical Society.

Wasson, John. *Memorial of Governor A. P. K. Safford.* Tucson, 1892.

Whalen, Norman M. "The Catholic Church in Arizona." Master's thesis, University of Arizona, 1966.

Wheeler, Charles C. "History and Facts Concerning Warner and Silverlake and the Santa Cruz

River." MS. C. C. Wheeler Collection, Arizona Historical Society.

———. "Some of the Many Changes That Have Taken Place in the Old Pueblo." MS. C. C. Wheeler Collection, Arizona Historical Society.

———. ["Tucson Indian Training School"]. Untitled, undated account. C. C. Wheeler Collection, Arizona Historical Society.

Williams, Norman. "Zoning and Preservation." Paper read at the Arizona Historical Convention, Tucson, April 27, 1979. Notes in possession of author.

BOOKS AND ARTICLES

Abbey, Edward. "The Blob Comes to Arizona." In *The Journey Home*. New York: Dutton, 1977.

———. *Good News*. New York: Dutton, 1980.

Abbey, Sue Walton. "The Ku Klux Klan in Arizona." *Journal of Arizona History*, vol. 14 (Spring, 1973), pp. 10–30.

———. "The Man Who Lived to Fly: The Story of Charley Mayse—Arizona Pioneer Aviator." *Journal of Arizona History*, vol. 15 (Winter, 1974), pp. 373–90.

Abrams, Charles. *The City as Frontier*. New York: Harper & Row, 1965.

Adams, F. "Tucson in 1847: Reminiscences of Judge F. Adams—Description of the Fort, and So Forth." *Arizona Historical Review*, vol. 1 (Winter, 1929), pp. 83–85.

Aguirre, Yjinio F. "The Last of the Dons." *Journal of Arizona History*, vol. 10 (Winter, 1969), pp. 239–55.

Albrecht, Elizabeth. "Estevan Ochoa: Mexican-American Businessman." *Arizoniana*, vol. 4 (Summer, 1963), pp. 34–40.

Alegre, Xavier. *Historia de la Campañia de Jesús*. 3 vols. Mexico City, 1841.

Alger, Russell A. *The Spanish-American War*. New York: Harper, 1901.

Allen, Frederick Lewis. *Only Yesterday: An Informal History of the Nineteen-Twenties*. New York: Harper & Row, 1957 (first publication, 1931).

Altshuler, Constance Wynn. "The Case of Sylvester Mowry: The Charge of Treason." *Arizona and the West*, vol. 15 (Spring, 1973), pp. 63–82.

———. "The Case of Sylvester Mowry: The Mowry Mine." *Arizona and the West*, vol. 15 (Summer, 1973), pp. 149–74.

———. *Chains of Command*. Tucson: Arizona Historical Society, 1981.

———. *Latest from Arizona: The Hesperian Letters, 1859–1861*. Tucson: Arizona Pioneers Historical Society, 1969.

———. "Military Administration in Arizona, 1854–1865." *Journal of Arizona History*, vol. 10 (Winter, 1969), pp. 215–38.

Ames, Sister Aloysia, C.S.J. *The St. Mary's I Knew*. Tucson: Privately printed, 1970 ("Trek of the Seven Sisters," diary of Sister Monica Corrigan, pp. 131–50).

Applegate, Howard G. *Environmental Problems Along the Border*. Border-States Consortium for Latin America, Occasional Paper no. 7, San Diego, Calif.: Institute of Public and Urban Affairs, San Diego State University, Winter, 1979.

Arizona (*Arizona Republic* magazine), December 3, 1978 (World War II issue).

Arizona Bureau of Mines. *Mineral and Water Resources of Arizona*. Bulletin no. 180. Tucson: University of Arizona, 1969.

Arizona Civic Theatre. *In the Act*, vol. 1 (October, 1973). Arizona Historical Society.

Arizona Daily Star, Tucson Citizen, and Valley National Bank of Arizona. *Tucson Trends*, Tucson, 1978.

Arizona State Council of Defense. *A Record of the Activities of the Arizona State Council of Defense from Formation, April 18, 1917, to Dissolution, June, 1918*. Phoenix, 1919.

Arizona Territory. *Memorial and Affidavits Showing Outrages Perpetrated by the Apache Indians in the Territory of Arizona for the Years 1869 and 1870: Published by Authority of the Legislature of the Territory of Arizona*. San Francisco: Francis & Valentine, Printers, 1871.

———. *Report of the Acting Governor of Arizona to the Secretary of the Interior, 1891*. Washington, D.C.: Government Printing Office, 1891.

———. *Report of the Governor of Arizona, September 1, 1893*. Phoenix, 1893.

Arnold, Elliott. *The Camp Grant Massacre*. New York: Simon & Schuster, 1976.

Arricivita, Juan Domingo. *Crónica Seráfica y Apostólica del Colegio de Propaganda Fide de la Santa Cruz de Querétaro en la Nueva España*. Pt. 2. Mexico City: Felipe de Zúñiga y Ontiveros, 1792.

Aster, Sidney. *1939: The Making of the Second World War*. New York: Simon & Schuster, 1973.

Bailey, Paul. *The Armies of God*. Garden City, N.Y.: Doubleday, 1968.

Baldonado, Luis. "Missions San José de Tumacacori and San Xavier del Bac in 1774." *Kiva*, vol. 24 (April, 1959), pp. 21–24.

Baldwin, Hanson W. *World War I: An Outline History*. New York: Harper & Row, 1962.

Ball, Larry D. "This High-handed Outrage: Marshal William Kidder Meade in a Mexican Jail." *Journal of Arizona History*, vol. 17 (Summer, 1976), pp. 219–32.

Bancroft, Hubert Howe. *History of Arizona and New Mexico, 1530–1888*. Vol. 17 of *Works*. San Francisco: History Co., 1889.

Bannon, John Francis. "The Mission as a Frontier Institution: Sixty Years of Interest and Research." *Western Historical Quarterly*, vol. 10 (July, 1979), pp. 303–22.

Barnes, Will C. *Apaches and Longhorns: The Reminiscences of Will C. Barnes*. Los Angeles: Ward Ritchie, 1941.

Bartlett, John Henry. *The Bonus March and the New Deal*. Chicago: M. A. Donohue, 1937.

Bartlett, John Russell. *Personal Narrative of Explorations and Incidents in Texas, New Mexico, California, Sonora, and Chihuahua Connected with the United States and Mexico Boundary Commission During the Years 1850, '51, '52, and '55*. Vol. 2. New York: D. Appleton, 1854.

Bassett, Edward W. "Tucson Nears 'Magic Mark' of 500,000." *Tucson Daily Citizen*, December 21, 1977.

Bean, Lowell John, and William Marvin Mason. *Diaries and Accounts of the Romero Expedition in Arizona and California, 1823–1826*. Palm Springs, Calif.: Palm Springs Desert Museum; Los Angeles: Ward Ritchie Press, 1962.

Beattie, George William. "Development of Travel Between Southern Arizona and Los Angeles as It Related to the San Bernardino Valley." *Historical Society of Southern California Publications*, vol. 7 (1925), pp. 228–57.

Beckinsale, R. P., and J. M. Houston, eds. *Urbanization and Its Problems*. New York: Barnes & Noble, 1968.

Bell, James G. "A Log of the Texas-California Cattle Trail, 1854." Edited by J. Evetts Haley. *Southwest Historical Quarterly*, vol. 35 (October, 1932), pp. 290–316.

Benjamin, Thomas. "Recent Historiography of the Origins of the Mexican War." *New Mexico Historical Review*, vol. 54 (July, 1979), pp. 169–81.

Bentz, Donald N. "The WHAM Robbery." *Golden West*, vol. 7 (November, 1970, pp. 12–15, 46–50.

Bermingham, Peter. *The New Deal in the Southwest: Arizona and New Mexico: An Exhibition Organized by the University of Arizona*. [Tucson, 1980].

Betancourt, Julio. *Cultural Resources Within the Proposed Santa Cruz Riverpark Archaeological District*. Cultural Resource Management Section, Arizona State Museum. Archaeological Series, no. 125, September, 1978.

Blaine, Peter, as told to Michael Adams. *Papagos and Politics*. Tucson: Arizona Historical Society, 1981.

Bliss, Robert S. "The Journal of Robert S. Bliss, with the Mormon Battalion." *Utah Historical Quarterly*, vol. 4 (July, 1931), pp. 67–96, 110–28.

Block, Eugene B. *Great Train Robberies of the West*. New York: Coward, McCann, 1959.

Bloom, Lansing B., ed. "Bourke on the Southwest, VI." *New Mexico Historical Review*, vol. 9 (July, 1934), pp. 273–89.

Bobb, Bernard E. *The Vice-Regency of Antonio María Bucareli in New Spain, 1771–1779*. Austin: University of Texas Press, 1962.

Boehringer, C. Louise. "Josephine Brawley Hughes—Crusader, State Builder." *Arizona Historical Review*, vol. 2 (January, 1930), pp. 98–107.

Bolton, Herbert Eugene. *Anza's California Expedition*. Vol. 4, *Font's Complete Diary of the Second Anza Expedition*. Berkeley: University of California Press, 1930.

———. *Kino's Historical Memoir of Pimería Alta: A Contemporary Account of the Beginnings of California, Sonora, and Arizona by Father Eusebio Francisco Kino, S. J., Pioneer Missionary, Explorer, Cartographer, and Ranchman*. Berkeley and Los Angeles: University of California Press, 1948.

———. *The Mission as a Frontier Institution*. El Paso: Texas Western College Press, 1962 (reprinted from *American Historical Review*, vol. 23 [October, 1917]).

———. *Rim of Christendom*. New York: Russell & Russell, 1960 (first publication, 1936).

Bourke, John G. "A Lynching in Tucson in 1873." Edited by Lansing B. Bloom. *New Mexico His-*

torical Review, vol. 19 (April, July, 1944), pp. 233–42, 312–28.

———. *On the Border with Crook*. New York: Scribner's, 1902.

Bowden, Charles. *Killing the Hidden Waters*. Austin: University of Texas Press, 1977.

Bowman, J. N., and R. F. Heizer. *Anza and the Northwest Frontier of New Spain*. Los Angeles: Southwest Museum, 1967.

Brady, Francis P. "Portrait of a Pioneer: Peter R. Brady, 1925–1902." *Journal of Arizona History*, vol. 16 (Summer, 1975), pp. 171–86.

Brandes, Ray. *Frontier Military Posts of Arizona*. Globe, Ariz.: Dale Stuart King, 1960.

BretHarte, John. "A Feisty Town Grows Up." *Tucson Daily Citizen*, June 6, 1975.

———. "The Strange Case of Joseph C. Tiffany." *Journal of Arizona History* vol. 16 (Winter, 1975), pp. 383–404.

———. *Tucson: Portrait of a Desert Pueblo*. Woodland Hills, Calif.: Windsor Publications, 1980.

Brinckerhoff, Sidney B. "Aftermath of Cibecue: Courtmartial of the Apache Scouts, 1881." *Smoke Signal*, Publication of the Tucson Corral of the Westerners, no. 36, Fall, 1978.

———. "The Last Years of Spanish Arizona 1786–1821." *Arizona and the West*, vol. 9 (Spring, 1967), pp. 5–20.

———, and Odie B. Faulk. *Lancers for the King: A Study of the Frontier Military System of Northern New Spain, with a Translation of the Royal Regulations of 1772*. Phoenix: Arizona Historical Foundation, 1965.

Brinegar, David F. "A New Day for the Star: The Ellinwood-Mathews Partnership." *Journal of Arizona History*, vol. 18 (Winter, 1977), pp. 405–30.

Broman, Charles H., ed. *The Story of Tucson Airport Authority, 1948–1966*. Tucson, December 31, 1966. Arizona Historical Society.

Brown, Haddington C. *Historical Circular of the Indian Training School*. Tucson: Citizen Printing and Publishing Co., 1905.

Browne, J. Ross. *Adventures in the Apache Country: A Tour Through Arizona and Sonora, 1864*. Tucson: University of Arizona Press, 1974.

Bufkin, Don. "From Mud Village to Modern Metropolis: The Urbanization of Tucson." *Journal of Arizona History*, vol. 22 (Spring, 1981), pp. 63–98.

Burchell, Joe, and Bob Levin. "City Cancels Aid Pact, Asks South Tucson to Merge." *Arizona Daily Star*, October 28, 1980.

Burrus, Ernest J. *Kino and Manje, Explorers of Sonora and Arizona*. St. Louis: Jesuit Historical Institute, 1971.

———. *Kino Reports to Headquarters: Correspondence of Eusebio F. Kino, S.J., from New Spain with Rome*. St. Louis: Jesuit Historical Institute, 1954.

Bury, John Charles. *The Historical Role of Arizona's Superintendent of Public Instruction*. Flagstaff: Northern Arizona University, 1974.

Byars, Charles. "The First Map of Tucson." *Journal of Arizona History*, vol. 7 (Winter, 1966), pp. 188–95.

Byrkit, James W. "The IWW in Wartime Arizona." *Journal of Arizona History*, vol. 18 (Summer, 1977), pp. 149–70.

Cady, John H. *Arizona's Yesterday: Being the Narrative of John H. Cady, Pioneer, Revised and Rewritten by Basil Dillon Woon, 1915*. N.p., n.d. Copyright by John H. Cady.

Caldwell, William A., ed. *How to Save Urban America: Regional Plan Association Choice for 1976*. New York: New American Library, 1973.

Calvo Berber, Laureano. *Nociones de Historia de Sonora*. Mexico City: Manuel Porrúa, 1958.

Campa, Arthur L. *Hispanic Culture in the Southwest*. Norman: University of Oklahoma Press, 1978.

Cargill, Andrew Hays. "The Camp Grant Massacre: Reminiscences of Andrew Hays Cargill, 1907." *Arizona Historical Review*, vol. 7 (July, 1936), pp. 73–79.

Carr, William H. *The Desert Speaks*. 3d ed. Tucson: Arizona-Sonora Desert Museum, 1973 (first publication, 1953).

Castetter, Edward F., and Willis H. Bell. *Pima and Papago Indian Agriculture*. Albuquerque: University of New Mexico Press, 1942.

Chalmers, David M. *Hooded Americanism*. New York: Doubleday, 1965.

Chamberlain, Samuel. *My Confession*. New York: Harper, 1956.

Chambers, George W. "The Old Presidio of Tucson." *Kiva*, vol. 20 (December–February, 1955), pp. 15–16.

———, and C. L. Sonnichsen. *San Agustín: First Cathedral Church in Arizona*. Tucson: Arizona Historical Society and Arizona Silhouettes, 1974.

Chanin, Abe. *They Fought Like Wildcats*. Tucson: Midbar Press, 1974.

Cheek, Lawrence. "Musical Giants." *Arizona Daily Star*, May 18, 1980.

Clarke, A. B. *Travels in Mexico and California: Comprising a Journal of a Tour from Brazos Santiago, Through Central Mexico by Way of Monterey, Chihuahua, the Country of the Apaches, and the River Gila to the Mining Districts of California*. Boston: Wright and Hasty's Steam Press, 1852.

Clark, Nancy Tisdale. "The Demise of the Demon Rum in Arizona." *Journal of Arizona History*, vol. 18 (Spring, 1977), pp. 69–92.

Colley, Charles C. "Water Under the Earth: Robert H. Forbes and the Fight for Control." *Journal of Arizona History*, vol. 16 (Autumn, 1970), pp. 14–22.

Collins, Karen Sikes. "Fray Pedro de Arriquibar's Census of Tucson, 1820." *Journal of Arizona History*, vol. 11 (Spring, 1970), pp. 14–22.

Colton, Ray C. *The Civil War in the Western Territories: Arizona, Colorado, New Mexico, and Utah*. Norman: University of Oklahoma Press, 1959.

Condron, A. H. "Tucson Progress." *Progressive Arizona*, vol. 3 (October, 1926), pp. 7–9.

Conkling, Roscoe P., and Margaret B. Conkling. *The Butterfield Overland Mail, 1857–1869*. 3 vols. Glendale, Calif.: Arthur H. Clark Co., 1947.

Cooke, Philip St. George. "Cooke's Journal of the Mormon Battalion." In *Exploring Southwestern Trails 1846–1854*. Vol. 7. Edited by Ralph P. Bieber and Averam B. Bender. Glendale, Calif.: Arthur H. Clarke Co., 1938.

Cooper, James F. *The First Hundred Years: The History of Tucson School District 1, Tucson, Arizona, 1867–1967*. Edited by Joseph H. Fahr. Tucson, 1967.

"Copper: Changing Faces, Changing Times." *Arizona Daily Star*, November 30, 1976 (special section).

Cosulich, Bernice. "Empire Ranch and Total Wreck Mine." *Arizona Daily Star*, March 6, 1932.

———. "Pima County Celebrates Fiftieth Anniversary." *Arizona Medicine*, vol. 12 (March, 1955), pp. 126–30.

———. *Tucson*. Tucson: Arizona Silhouettes, 1953.

Coues, Elliott. *On the Trail of a Spanish Pioneer: The Diary and Itinerary of Francisco Garcés (Missionary Priest) in His Travels Through Sonora, Arizona, and California, 1775–1776*. 2 vols. New York: Francis P. Harper, 1900.

Couts, Cave J. *Hepah, California! The Journal of Cave Johnson Couts from Monterey, Nuevo Leon, Mexico, to Los Angeles, California, During the Years 1848–1849*. Edited by Henry F. Dobyns. Tucson: Arizona Pioneers Historical Society, 1961.

Cox, C. C. "From Texas to California in 1849." Pt. 2. Edited by Mabel Eppard Martin. *Southwestern Historical Quarterly*, vol. 29 (October, 1925), pp. 128–46.

Cozzens, Samuel. *The Marvelous Country: Explorations and Adventures in Arizona and New Mexico*. Boston: Lee & Shepard, 1876.

Crook, General George. *General George Crook: His Autobiography*. Edited by Martin F. Schmitt. Norman: University of Oklahoma Press, 1946.

Cruse, Thomas. *Apache Days and After*. Caldwell, Idaho: Caxton Printers, 1941.

Danehy, Tom. "Who Is This Man and Why Is He So Important to You?" *Tucson*, August 1, 1979, pp. 19–24.

Daniels, Roger. *The Bonus March: An Episode of the Great Depression*. Westport, Conn.: Greenwood, 1971.

Davis, Britton. *The Truth About Geronimo*. New Haven, Conn.: Yale University Press, 1929.

Davis, W. W. H. *El Gringo: New Mexico and Her People*. Chicago: Rio Grande Press, 1962 (first publication, 1851).

Davisson, Lori. "New Light on the Cibecue Fight: Untangling Apache Identities." *Journal of Arizona History*, vol. 20 (Winter, 1979) pp. 423–44.

"The Dead Broke Rich Men of Tucson." *Arizona Mining Index* (Tucson), July 3, 1886. Copy in Hayden File, Arizona Historical Society.

Debo, Angie. *Geronimo: The Man, His Time, His Place*. Norman: University of Oklahoma Press, 1976.

DeConcini, Evo A. *Hey! It's Past 80: A Biography of a Busy Life*. Edited by John Spalding. Tucson: Privately printed, 1981.

Decorme, Gerard. *La obra de los Jesuitas mexicanos durante la Epoca Colonial*. Mexico City: José Porrúa e llijos, 1941.

del Castillo, Richard Griswold. "Tucsonenses and Angelenos: A Socio-Economic Study of Two Mexican American Barrios, 1860–1863." *Journal of the West*, vol. 18 (January, 1979), pp. 58–66.

Deloria, Vine, Jr. *God Is Red*. New York: Delta

Books, 1975 (first publication, 1973).

Díaz, Mariana. "Tucson a Hundred Years Ago." *Arizona Citizen*, June 21, 1873.

DiPeso, Charles C. *The Sobaipuri Indians of the Upper San Pedro Valley*. Dragoon, Ariz.: Amerind Foundation, 1953.

———. "The Sobaipuris: Defenders of the San Pedro Valley Frontier." In *Military History of the Spanish-American Southwest: A Seminar*. Edited by Bruno J. Rolak. Fort Huachuca, Ariz.: U.S. Army Communications Command, 1976, pp. 20–30.

———. *The Upper Pimas of San Cayetano del Tumacacori: An Archaeohistorical Reconstruction of the Ootam of Pimería Alta*. Dragoon, Ariz.: Amerind Foundation, 1956.

Dobyns, Henry F. "Indian Extinction in the Middle Santa Cruz River Valley, Arizona." *New Mexico Historical Review*, vol. 38 (April, 1963), pp. 163–81.

———. *Lance Ho! Containment of the Western Apaches by the Royal Spanish Garrison at Tucson*. Lima: Estudios Andinos, 1964.

———. *Pioneering Christians Among the Perishing Indians of Tucson*. Lima: Estudios Andinos, 1962.

———. "The 1797 Population of the Presidio of Tucson." *Journal of Arizona History*, vol. 13 (Autumn, 1972), pp. 205–209.

———. *Spanish Colonial Tucson: A Demographic History*. Tucson: University of Arizona Press, 1976.

Donohue, J. Augustine. *After Kino: Jesuit Missions in Northwestern New Spain, 1711–1767*. St. Louis: Jesuit Historical Institute, 1969.

———. "The Unlucky Jesuit Mission at Bac." *Arizona and the West*, vol. 2 (Summer, 1960), pp. 127–39.

Donovan, Judy. "Traffic Problem Wild in Old Tucson." *Arizona Daily Star*, September 18, 1972.

Douskey, Franz. "Tucson." In *Southwest: A Contemporary Anthology*. Albuquerque, N. Mex.: Red Earth Press, 1978.

Drachman, Mose. "The Tucson Gamblers." *Journal of Arizona History*, vol. 14 (Spring, 1973), pp. 1–9.

Drago, Marilyn. "VA Hospital Beginnings Recalled." *Sunday Star-Citizen* (Tucson), July 26, 1970.

Duffen, William A., ed. "Overland via 'Jackass Mail' 1858: The Diary of Phocion R. Way." *Arizona and the West*, vol. 2 (Spring–Winter, 1960), pp. 35–53, 147–64, 279–92, 353–70.

Duisberg, Peter C. "Prologue." In *Climate and Man in the Southwest*. Edited by Terah L. Smiley. Program in Geochronology; Contribution no. 6. Tucson: University of Arizona Press, 1958.

Dunning, Charles H., and Edward H. Peplow, Jr. *Rocks to Riches: The Story of American Mining*. Phoenix: Southwest Publishing Co., 1959.

Durbin, Carolyn B. *History of the Tucson Medical Center*. Tucson: Privately printed, 1965.

Durivage, John E. "Through Mexico to California; Letters and Journal of John E. Durivage." In *Southern Trails to California in 1849*. Edited by Ralph P. Bieber. Southwest Historical Series, no. 5. Glendale, Calif.: Arthur H. Clark Co., 1937.

Eccleston, Robert. *Overland to California on the Southwestern Trail, 1849*. Edited by George P. Hammond and Edward W. Howes. Berkeley and Los Angeles: University of California Press, 1950.

Ellinwood, Sybil. "City's Present Rich Interest in Music Started Unpretentiously Way Back in 1895." *Arizona Daily Star*, September 12, 1948.

———. "East Meets West in the Field of Education." *Journal of Arizona History*, vol. 15 (Autumn, 1974), pp. 269–318.

Emerine, Steve. "Downtowners Accessories After the Fact in Slow Death of Their Area." *Arizona Daily Star*, April 21, 1980.

Erskine, Michael. *The Diary of Michael Erskine*. Edited by J. Evetts Haley. Midland, Texas: Nita Stewart Haley Memorial Library, 1979.

Ewing, Russell C. "The Pima Outbreak of November, 1751." *New Mexico Historical Review*, vol. 13 (October, 1938), pp. 337–46.

Ezell, Paul H. "Is There a Hohokam-Pima Cultural Continuum?" *American Antiquity*, vol. 39 (Spring, 1963), pp. 61–66.

Falls, Cyril. *The Great War*. New York: Putnam, 1959.

Farish, Thomas Edwin. *History of Arizona*. 8 vols. San Francisco: Filmer Brothers, 1914–18 (published by the State of Arizona, Phoenix).

Faulk, Odie B. *The Arizona Historical Society*. Tucson: Arizona Pioneers Historical Society, 1966.

———. *The Geronimo Campaign*. New York: Oxford University Press, 1969.

———. *The Leather Jacket Soldiers: Spanish Military Equipment and Institutions of the Late Eighteenth*

Century. Pasadena, Calif.: Socio-Technical Publications, 1971.

———. *Tombstone: Myth and Reality*. New York: Oxford University Press, 1972.

Fierman, Floyd S. "The Goldberg Brothers: Arizona Pioneers." *American Jewish Archives*, vol. 18 (April, 1966), pp. 3–19.

Finch, Boyd. "Sherod Hunter and the Confederates in Arizona." *Journal of Arizona History*, vol. 10 (Autumn, 1969), pp. 137–206.

Bert Fireman. "How Far Westward the Civil War?" Denver Posse of the Westerners *Brandbook*, 1963. Denver, 1964.

———. "What Comprises Treason?" *Arizoniana*, vol. 1 (Winter, 1960), pp. 5–10.

———, and Lillian Theobald. "Imprudent Enterprise: The Arizona & New Mexico Express Company." *Journal of Arizona History*, vol. 17 (Winter, 1976), pp. 415–30.

Fireman, Janet. *The Spanish Royal Corps of Engineers in the Western Borderlands: Instrument of Bourbon Reform, 1764–1815*. Glendale, Calif.: Arthur H. Clark Co., 1977.

First Congregational Church History Committee. *A Century in the Life of the First Congregational United Church of Christ, Tucson, Arizona*. Tucson, [1981].

Flaccus, Elmer W. "Arizona's Last Great Indian War: The Saga of Pia Machita." *Journal of Arizona History*, vol. 22 (Spring, 1981), pp. 1–21.

Fontana, Bernard L. *Biography of a Desert Church: The Story of Mission San Xavier del Bac*. Tucson: Tucson Westerners, 1961.

———. "Calabasas on the Rio Rico." *Smoke Signal*, vol. 24 (1971), pp. 66–68.

———. "Where Are We?" *Tucson*, November, 1979, pp. 25–29.

Forbes, Jack D. *Apache, Navajo, and Spaniard*. Norman: University of Oklahoma Press, 1960.

———. "Development of the Yuma Route Before 1846." *California Historical Quarterly*, vol. 43 (June, 1964), pp. 99–118.

Forbes, Robert H. *The Penningtons: Pioneers of Early Arizona*. Tucson: Arizona Archaeological and Historical Society, 1919.

Forster, Mark Arnold. *The World at War*. New York: Stein & Day, 1973.

Fox, Francis J. "Expulsion of the Jesuits from New Spain." In *Studies in Medievalia and Americana: Essays in Honor of William Lyle Davis, S.J.* Edited

by Gerard D. Steckler and Leo Donald Davis. Spokane, Wash.: Gonzaga University Press, 1973.

Freeman, M. P. *The City of Tucson: Its Foundation and Origin of Its Name*. Tucson: Acme Printing Co., 1931.

Freidel, Frank. *America in the Twentieth Century*. 2d ed. New York: Knopf, 1966.

———. *The Splendid Little War*. Boston: Little, Brown, 1958.

Froebel, Julius. *Seven Years' Travel in Central America, Northern Mexico, and the Far West of the United States*. London: Richard Bentley, 1859.

Gaines, Dorothy. "Forum Founder Retires." *Arizona Daily Star*, March 28, 1976.

Gallego, Hilario. "Reminiscences of an Arizona Pioneer." *Arizona Historical Review*, vol. 4 (Spring, 1935), pp. 75–87.

Gálvez, Bernardo de. *Instructions for Governing the Interior Provinces of New Spain, 1786*. Translated and edited by Donald E. Worcester. Berkeley: Quivira Society, 1951.

Garber, Paul Neff. *The Gadsden Treaty*. Philadelphia: University of Pennsylvania Press, 1923.

Gardiner, Arthur D., trans. "Letter of Father Middendorf, S.J., Dated 3 March 1757." *Kiva*, vol. 22 (June, 1957), pp. 1–10.

Gardner, Hamilton. "The Command and Staff of the Mormon Battalion in the Mexican War." *Utah State Historical Quarterly*, vol. 20 (July, 1952), pp. 331–51.

———, ed. "Report of Lieut. Col. P. St. George Cooke on the March from Sante Fe, New Mexico, to San Diego, Upper California." *Utah State Historical Quarterly*, vol. 22 (January, 1954), pp. 15–40.

Gary, Suzanne T. "Arizona's Favorite Child: Battered but Not Beaten, Tucson Faces the Year 2000." *Tucson*, February, 1979, pp. 27–34.

Gerald, Rex E. *Spanish Presidios of the Late Eighteenth Century in Northern New Spain*. Museum of New Mexico Research Records, no. 7. Sante Fe: Museum of New Mexico Press, 1968.

Getty, Harry T. "People of the Old Pueblo." *Kiva*, vol. 17 (November–December, 1951), pp. 1–6.

Gibson, Lay James. "Where Have We Been and Where Are We Heading?" *Tucson Town Hall*, 1974.

Gibson, Thomas E. "George A. Goodfellow." *Surgery, Gynecology, and Obstetrics*, vol. 54 (April,

1936), pp. 716–18.

Gipson, Rosemary. "The Mexican Performers." *Journal of Arizona History*, vol. 13 (Winter, 1972), pp. 235–52.

———. "Tom Fitch's Other Side." *Journal of Arizona History*, vol. 16 (Autumn, 1975), pp. 287–94.

Glasscock, C. B. *Bandits on the Southern Pacific*. New York: Frederick A. Stokes, 1929.

Goff, John S. "The Arizona Career of Coles Bashford." *Journal of Arizona History*, vol. 10 (Spring, 1969), pp. 19–36.

———. *George W. P. Hunt and His Arizona*. Pasadena, Calif.: Socio-Technical Publications, 1973.

Goldberg, Isaac. "Original Manuscript." *Arizona Historical Review*, vol. 6 (April, 1935), pp. 74–82.

Golder, Frank Alfred, Thomas H. Bailey, and J. Lyman Smith. *The March of the Mormon Battalion from Council Bluffs to California, Taken from the Journal of Henry Standage*. New York: Century, 1928.

Granaway, Loomis Morton. "New Mexico and the Sectional Controversy." Pt. 6. *New Mexico Historical Review*, vol. 19 (January, 1944), pp. 55–79.

Green, Gerald. *An American Prophet*. Garden City, N.Y.: Doubleday, 1977.

Greenleaf, Cameron, and Andrew Wallace. "Tucson, Pueblo, Presidio, and American City: A Synopsis of Its History." *Arizoniana*, vol. 3 (Summer, 1962), pp. 18–27.

Gregonis, Linda M., and Karl J. Reinhard. *Hohokam Indians of the Tucson Basin*. Tucson: University of Arizona Press, 1979.

Gressinger, A. W. *Charles D. Poston: Sunland Seer*. Globe, Ariz.: Dale Stuart King, 1961.

Griffin, C. W., Jr. *Taming the Last Frontier: A Prescription for the Urban Crisis*. New York: Pitman Publishing Co., 1974.

Hagedorn, Hermann. *Leonard Wood: A Biography*. New York: Harper, 1931.

Hague, Harlan. *The Road to California: The Search for a Southern Overland Route, 1540–1848*. Glendale, Calif.: Arthur H. Clark Co., 1978.

Haley, J. Evetts. *Jeff Milton: A Good Man with a Gun*. Norman: University of Oklahoma Press, 1948.

Hall, Dick. "Jesus Camacho: The Mayor of Meyer Street." *Journal of Arizona History*, vol. 20 (Winter, 1979), pp. 445–66.

———. "Ointment of Love: Oliver E. Comstock and Tucson's Tent City." *Journal of Arizona History*, vol. 19 (Summer, 1978), pp. 111–30.

Hamilton, Patrick. *The Resources of Arizona*, 2d ed. San Francisco: A. L. Bancroft & Co., 1883.

Hammond, George P. "Pimeria Alta After Kino's Time." *New Mexico Historical Review*, vol. 4 (July, 1929), pp. 220–38.

———. "The Zúñiga Journal, Tucson to Santa Fe: The Opening of a Spanish Trade Route, 1788–1795." *New Mexico Historical Review*, vol. 6 (January, 1931), pp. 40–65.

Handlin, Oscar, and John Burchard, eds. *The Historian and the City*. Cambridge: Massachusetts Institute of Technology Press, 1963.

Haney, John A., and Cirino Scavone. "Cars Stop Here: A Brief History of Street Railways in Tucson, Arizona." *Smoke Signal* (Tucson Corral of the Westerners), no. 23 (Spring, 1971).

Harris, Benjamin Butler. *The Gila Trail: The Texas Argonauts and the California Gold Rush*. Edited by Richard H. Dillon. Norman: University of Oklahoma Press, 1960.

Hastings, James P. "The Tragedy at Camp Grant in 1871." *Arizona and the West*, vol. 1 (Summer, 1959), pp. 146–60.

Hastings, John Rodney, and Raymond M. Turner. *The Changing Mile*. Tucson: University of Arizona Press, 1965.

Haury, Emil W. *The Hohokam: Desert Farmers and Craftsmen: Excavations at Snaketown, 1964–1965*. Tucson: University of Arizona Press, 1970.

Hayden, Carl Trumbull. *Charles Trumbull Hayden, Pioneer*. Tucson: Arizona Historical Society, 1972.

Hays, Carl D. W. "David E. jackson." In *The Mountain Men and the Fur Trade of the Far West*. Vol. 9. Edited by Leroy R. Hafen. Glendale, Calif.: Arthur H. Clark Co., 1972.

Heinemann, Robert E. S. *Arizona Metal Production*. Arizona State Bureau of Mines Bulletin 140. Tucson: University of Arizona, 1936.

Henry, Robert Selph. *The Story of the Mexican War*. New York: Frederick Ungar, 1950.

Herndon, Elsie Prugh. "Indian Training School at Tucson." *La Aurora* (Albuquerque), March 26, 1903.

Herner, Charles. *The Arizona Rough Riders*. Tucson:

University of Arizona Press, 1973.

Hess, John W. "John W. Hess with the Mormon Battalion." Edited by Wanda Wood. *Utah Historical Quarterly*, vol. 4 (April, 1931), pp. 47–55.

Hill Joseph J. "New Light on Pattie and the Southwestern Fur Trade." *Southwestern Historical Quarterly*, vol. 26 (April, 1923), pp. 243–54.

Hilzinger, J. George. *Treasure Land 1897: A Handbook to Tucson and Southern Arizona*. Glorieta, N. Mex.: Rio Grande Press, 1969 (first publication, 1897).

Hinkle, Stacy C. *Wings over the Border*. El Paso: Texas Western College Press, 1970.

Hinton, Richard J. *The Handbook to Arizona: Its Resources, History, Towns, Mines, Ruins, and Scenery*. Glorieta, N. Mex.: Rio Grande Press, 1970 (first publication, 1878).

Hodge, Hiram E. *Arizona as It Was*. Albuquerque: Rio Grande Press, 1962 (first publication, 1877).

Hofstadter, Richard. *The Age of Reform: From Bryan to F.D.R.* New York: Knopf, 1955.

Hogan, William F. "Adolph George Buttner: Tucson's First Chief of Police." *Arizoniana*, vol. 5 (Summer, 1964), pp. 26–31.

———. "John Miller: Pioneer Lawman." *Arizoniana*, vol. 4 (Summer, 1963), pp. 41–45.

———. "William Morgan: First Village Marshal of Tucson." *Arizoniana*, vol. 3 (Fall, 1962), pp. 47–50.

Holterman, Jack. "José Zúñiga." *Kiva*, vol. 22 (November, 1956), pp. 1–4.

Hopkins, Ernest J. *Financing the Frontier*. Phoenix: Arizona Printers, 1950.

Horn, Calvin, and W. S. Wallace, [comps.]. *Union Army Operations in the Southwest*. Albuquerque, N. Mex.: Horn and Wallace, 1961.

Hörner, Magnus. *Expulsion of the Jesuits*. New York: Knopf, 1965.

Howard, George W. "Bridges in the Desert: Early Days of the Yuma Proving Ground." *Journal of Arizona History*, vol. 17 (Winter, 1976), pp. 431–68.

Hubner, John. "Just One 'Goodfellow' in Tucson." *Arizona Highways*, vol. 52 (September 1976), pp. 8–15.

Hu-De Hart, Evelyn. "Immigrants to a Developing Society: The Chinese in Northern Mexico." *Journal of Arizona History*, vol. 21 (Autumn, 1980), pp. 275–312.

Hufford, Kenneth. "P. W. Dooner: Pioneer Editor of Tucson." *Arizona and the West*, vol. 10 (Spring, 1968), pp. 25–42.

Hughes, Sam. "A Conversation Between General James H. Carleton and Sam Hughes in 1862." *Arizoniana*, vol. 4 (Fall, 1963), pp. 26–32.

Hughes, Mrs. Samuel. "Mrs. Samuel Hughes, Tucson, Reminiscences, 1930." *Arizona Historical Review*, vol. 6 (April, 1935), pp. 66–74.

Hughes, Samuel, et al. "Our Roads and Streets." *Arizona Citizen*, March 11, 1871.

Hunt, Aurora. *The Army of the Pacific: Its Operations in California, Texas, Arizona, New Mexico, Utah, Nevada, Washington, Plains Region, Mexico, etc., 1860–1866*. Glendale, Calif.: Arthur H. Clark Co., 1951.

———. *James Henry Carleton, 1814–1873: Western Frontier Dragoon*. Glendale, Calif.: Arthur H. Clark Co., 1958.

Huntington, Ellsworth. *The Climatic Factor as Illustrated in Arid America*. Washington, D.C.: Carnegie Institution of Washington, 1914.

Indian Training School. *Historical Circular of Indian Training School, Tucson, Arizona*. Tucson: Citizen Printing and Publishing Co., 1905.

Ingram, Hunter. *Fort Apache*. New York: Ballantyne Books, 1975.

Iturralde, Francisco. *Visita de las misiones . . . , 1797*. Rome: Franciscan Archives, n.d.

Jackson, Kenneth T. *The Ku Klux Klan in the City, 1915–1930*. New York: Oxford University Press, 1967.

Jackson, W. Turrentine. *Wagon Roads West: A Study of Federal Road Surveys and Construction in the Trans-Mississippi West, 1846–1864*. Berkeley and Los Angeles: University of California Press, 1952.

Jacques, Leo M. "Have Quick More Money than Mandarins: The Chinese in Sonora." *Journal of Arizona History*, vol. 17 (Summer, 1976), pp. 201–18.

Jervey, William H., Jr. "When the Banks Closed: Arizona's Bank Holiday, 1933." *Arizona and the West*, vol. 10 (Summer, 1968), pp. 127–52.

Johnson, Rich. *The Central Arizona Project, 1918–1968*. Tucson: University of Arizona Press, 1977.

Johnston, William Preston. *The Life of General Albert Sidney Johnston*. New York: D. Appleton, 1878.

Jones, Billy M. *Health Seekers in the Southwest,*

1817–1900. Norman: University of Oklahoma Press, 1967.

Jones, Nathaniel V. "The Journal of Nathaniel V. Jones, with the Mormon Battalion." *Utah Historical Quarterly*, vol. 4 (January, 1931), pp. 6–24.

Jones, Oakah L., Jr. *Los Paisanos: Spanish Settlers on the Northern Frontier of New Spain.* Norman: University of Oklahoma Press, 1978.

Kane, Randy. "An Honorable and Upright Man: Sidney R. DeLong as Post Trader." *Journal of Arizona History*, vol. 19 (Autumn, 1978), pp. 297–314.

Karns, Harry J., ed. and trans. *Unknown Arizona and Sonora, 1693–1721, from the Francisco Fernandez del Castillo Version of Luz de Tierra Incognita by Captain Juan Mateo Manje.* Tucson: Arizona Silhouettes, 1954.

Keating, Michael. "Friends of Music Launch 31st Year with Tokyo Quartet." *Tucson Daily Citizen*, October 11, 1978.

Kelly, George H. *Legislative History of Arizona, 1864–1912.* Phoenix: Manufacturing Stationers, 1926.

Kelly, Isabel T., James E. Officer, and Emil W. Haury. *The Hodges Ruin: A Hohokam Community in the Tucson Basin.* Edited by Gayle Harrison Hartmann. Tucson: University of Arizona Press, 1978.

Kelso, Maurice M., William E. Martin, and Lawrence E. Mack. *Water Supplies and Economic Growth in an Arid Environment: An Arizona Case Study.* Tucson: University of Arizona Press, 1973.

Kerby, Robert Lee. *The Confederate Invasion of New Mexico and Arizona, 1861–1862.* Los Angeles: Westernlore Press, 1952.

Kessel, John L. "Anza Damns the Missions: A Spanish Soldier's Criticism of Indian Policy, 1772." *Journal of Arizona History*, vol. 13 (Spring, 1972, pp. 53–63.

———. *Friars, Soldiers, and Reformers: Hispanic Arizona and the Sonoran Mission Frontier.* Tucson: University of Arizona Press, 1976.

———. "The Making of a Martyr: Young Francisco Garcés." *New Mexico Historical Review*, vol. 45 (July, 1970), pp. 181–96.

———. *Mission of Sorrows: Jesuit Guevavi and the Pimas, 1691–1767.* Tucson: University of Arizona Press, 1970.

———, ed. "San José de Tumacacori—1773: A

Franciscan Reports from Arizona." *Arizona and the West*, vol. 6 (Winter, 1964), pp. 303–12.

King, James T. *War Eagle: A Life of General Eugene A. Carr.* Lincoln: University of Nebraska Press, 1963.

Kinnaird, Lawrence. *The Frontiers of New Spain: Nicolás de la Fora's Description, 1766–1768.* Quivira Society Publications, vol. 13. Berkeley, Calif.: Quivira Society, 1958.

Kiser, George C., and Martha Woody Kiser. *Mexican Workers in the United States: Historical and Political Perspectives.* Albuquerque: University of New Mexico Press, 1979.

Kress, Jonathan H. "A Surviving Breed: The Yaquis of Tucson." *Tucson Weekly News*, vol. 1 (October 15–21, 1980), pp. 7–10.

La Fave, Kenneth. "Mayan Work to Be Featured." *Arizona Daily Star*, April 27, 1981.

———. "Opera Cleaning Up Its Act." *Arizona Daily Star*, December 23, 1980.

———. "Opera Pays Off $99,000 Debt." *Arizona Daily Star*, December 4, 1980.

———. "Opera Problems Result of Debts." *Arizona Daily Star*, February 3, 1980.

———. "Opera Sings a Happier Tune." *Arizona Daily Star*, October 1, 1980.

———. "Tucson Opera Company on Its Way to Big Time." *Arizona Daily Star*, September 26, 1976.

Lamar, Howard Roberts. *The Far Southwest, 1846–1912: A Territorial History.* New Haven, Conn.: Yale University Press, 1966.

Langdon, Thomas C. "Harold Bell Wright: Citizen of Tucson." *Journal of Arizona History*, vol. 16 (Spring, 1975), pp. 77–98.

Lasch, Christopher. *The New Radicalism in America, 1889–1963.* New York: Knopf, 1965.

Layton, Christopher. *Autobiography of Christopher Layton, with an Account of the Funeral, a Personal Sketch, etc., and Genealogical Appendix.* Salt Lake City, Utah: Deseret News, 1911.

Leuchtenberg, William E. *Franklin D. Roosevelt and the New Deal, 1932–1940.* New York: Harper & Row, 1963.

Levin, Melvin R. *The Urban Prospect: Planning, Policy, and Strategies of Change.* North Scituate, Mass.: Duxbury Press, 1977.

Lewis, Oscar. *The War in the Far Southwest.* New York: Doubleday, 1961.

Lockwood, Frank C. "American Hunters and Trappers in Arizona." *Arizona Historical Review*, vol.

2 (July, 1929), pp. 70–85.

———. *Life in Old Tucson, 1854–1864, as Remembered by the Little Maid Atanacia Santa Cruz*. Los Angeles: Ward Ritchie, 1943.

———, and Donald W. Page. *Tucson, the Old Pueblo*. Phoenix: Manufacturing Stationers, n.d.

Love, Frank. "Poston and the Birth of Yuma." *Journal of Arizona History*, vol. 19 (Spring, 1978), pp. 403–16.

Luhan, Mabel Dodge. *Edge of Taos Desert*. New York: Harcourt, 1937.

Lummis, Charles Fletcher. *Dateline Fort Bowie: Charles Fletcher Lummis Reports on an Apache War*. Edited by Dan L. Thrapp. Norman: University of Oklahoma Press, 1979.

Luttrell, Estelle. "Arizona's Frontier Press." *Arizona Historical Review*, vol. 6 (January, 1935), pp. 14–26.

———. *Newspapers and Periodicals of Arizona, 1859–1911*. Tucson: University of Arizona Press, 1950.

Lyon, William H. "The Corporate Frontier in Arizona." *Journal of Arizona History*, vol. 9 (Spring, 1968), pp. 1–18.

McCarty, Kieran Robert. *Desert Documentary*. Tucson: Arizona Historical Society, 1976.

McClintock, James H. *Arizona: Prehistoric—Aboriginal—pioneer—Modern*. 3 vols. Chicago: S. J. Clark, 1916.

McCormick, Richard C. "The First Arizona Historical Society—A Letter from Richard C. McCormick." *Journal of Arizona History*, vol. 6 (Summer, 1965), pp. 90–91.

———. "There Is No Humbug About the Gold: McCormick Writes from Arizona." *Arizoniana*, vol. 5 (Fall, 1961), pp. 61–62.

McGinnies, William. *Discovering the Desert*. Tucson: University of Arizona Press, 1981.

McGough, P. J. "References on the Early History of the Tucson, Arizona, Meteorite: The 'Irwin Ainsa' and the 'Carleton' Irons." *Journal of the Society for Research on Meteorites*, vol. 5 (November, 1925), pp. 108–47.

McKelvey, Blake. *American Urbanization: A Comparative History*. Glenview, Ill.: Scott, Foresman, 1973.

McLuhan, T. C. *Touch the Earth*. New York: Outerbridge & Dienstfrey, 1971.

McMurtrie, Douglas C. "The Beginning of Printing in Arizona." *Arizona Historical Review*, vol. 5 (October, 1932). pp. 173–87.

Mahon, Emmie Giddings, and Chester V. Kielman. "George H. Giddings and the San Antonio-San Diego Mail Line." *Southwestern Historical Quarterly*, vol. 61 (Summer, 1957), pp. 220–39.

Mansfeld, J. S. "Literature in the Territory of Arizona in 1876: A Reminiscence." *Arizoniana*, vol. 2 (Autumn, 1961), pp. 31–43.

Marion, J. H. *Notes of Travel Through the Territory of Arizona: Being the Account of the Trip Made by General George Stoneman and Others in the Autumn of 1870*. Edited by Donald M. Powell. Tucson: University of Arizona Press, 1965.

Marshall, Edward. *The Story of the Rough Riders: 1st U.S. Volunteer Cavalry*. New York: Dillingham, 1899.

Marshall, Otto Miller. *The Wham Paymaster Robbery*. Pima, Ariz.: Pima Chamber of Commerce, 1967.

Marshall, S. L. A. *World War I*. New York: American Heritage Press, 1971 (first publication, 1964).

Martin, Douglas D. *An Arizona Chronology: The Territorial Years, 1846–1912*. Tucson: University of Arizona Press, 1963.

———. *The Lamp in the Desert*. Tucson: University of Arizona Press, 1960.

Martin, J. S. "Author Adept at Going Back in Time." *Arizona Daily Star*, May 15, 1977.

———. "Book Markets Covered with Arizonan's Fiction." *Arizona Daily Star*, September 15, 1980.

———. "Dude Ranches." *Arizona Daily Star*, August 15, 1976.

———. "The Face of Poverty." *Arizona Daily Star*, March 1, 1977.

———. "Tucson: Sunday Evening Forum." *Arizona Daily Star*, April 7, 1974.

———. "Tucson Boys Chorus." *Arizona Daily Star*, March 14, 1974.

———. "Woman's Club Lighting 80 Candles." *Arizona Daily Star*, September 22, 1980.

Mathews, William R. "Agnes and the Summer Bachelors." *Arizona Daily Star*, August 1, 1965.

Matson, Daniel S., and Bernard L. Fontana. *Friar Bringas Reports to the King*. Tucson: University of Arizona Press, 1878.

Mattison, Ray H. "Early Spanish Settlement in Arizona." *New Mexico Historical Review*, vol. 21 (October, 1946), pp. 273–327.

Miles, General Nelson A. *Personal Recollections and*

Observations of General Nelson A. Miles. . . . Chicago: Werner Co., 1897.

Miller, Sherman R. *Tropic of Tucson.* Tucson: Rutz Press, 1964.

"Miracle Mile: Safety-Plus Thoroughfare." *Arizona Highways,* vol. 18 (June, 1937), pp. 14–15.

Moore, Mary Lu, and Delmar L. Beene. "The Interior Provinces of New Spain: The Report of Hugo O'Conor, January 30, 1776." *Arizona and the West,* vol. 13 (Autumn, 1971), pp. 265–82.

Moorhead, Max L. *The Apache Frontier: Jacobo Ugarte and Spanish-Indian Relations in Northern New Spain, 1769–1781.* Norman: University of Oklahoma Press, 1968.

———. *The Presidio: Bastion of the Spanish Borderlands.* Norman: University of Oklahoma Press, 1975.

Mowry, George E. *The Urban Nation, 1920–1960.* New York: Hill & Wang, 1965.

Mowry, Sylvester. *Arizona and Sonora: The Geography, History, and Resources of the Silver Region of North America.* 3d ed. New York: Harper & Brothers, 1871.

———. *Memoir of the Proposed Territory of Arizona.* Washington, D.C.: Henry Polkinghorn, Printer, 1857.

Mumford, Lewis. *The Urban Prospect.* London: Secker & Warburg, 1968.

Muncinger, Gary M. "A Bridge from the Past to the Present." In *Tucson: Town Hall on Community Development, June 23–25, 1974.* Tucson: Tucson Chamber of Commerce, 1874.

Myrick, David F. *Railroads of Arizona.* Vol. 1, *The Southern Roads.* Berkeley, Calif.: Howell-North Books, 1975.

Navarro García, Luís. *Don José de Gálvez y la Comandancia General de las Provincias Internas del Norte de Nueva España.* Seville: Consejo Superior de Investigaciones Científicas, 1964.

Navin, Thomas R. *Copper Mining and Management.* Tucson: University of Arizona Press, 1978.

Nentvig, Juan. *Rudo Ensayo.* Tucson: Arizona Silhouettes, 1951.

Nicolson, John, ed. *The Arizona of Joseph Pratt Allen: Letters from a Pioneer Judge: Observations and Travels, 1863–1866.* Tucson: University of Arizona Press, 1974.

Oaks, George Washington. *Man of the West.* Edited by Ben Jaastad and Arthur Woodward. Tucson: Arizona Pioneers Historical Society, 1956.

Oblasser, Bonaventure. "Papaguería, the Domain of the Papagos." *Arizona Historical Rview,* vols. 6–7 (April, 1936), pp. 3–9.

Officer, James. "Historical Factors in Interethnic Relations in the Community of Tucson." *Journal of Arizona History,* vol. 1 (Summer, 1960), pp. 12–16.

Patterson, R. T. *The Great Boom and Panic.* Chicago: Henry Regnery, 1965.

Pattie, James Ohio. *Pattie's Personal Narrative of a Voyage to the Pacific and in Mexico: June 20, 1824–August 30, 1830.* Vol. 18 in Early Western Travels Series. Edited by Reuben Gold Thwaites. Cleveland: Arthur H. Clark Co., 1905.

Pedersen, Gilbert J. "The Founding First." *Journal of Arizona History,* vol. 7 (Summer, 1966), pp. 45–58.

———. "The Townsite Is Now Secure: Tucson Incorporates, 1871." *Journal of Arizona History,* vol. 2 (Autumn, 1970), pp. 151–74.

———. "A Yankee in Arizona: The Misfortunes of William S. Grant, 1860–1861." *Journal of Arizona History,* vol. 16 (Summer, 1975), pp. 127–44.

Peplow, Edward H. *History of Arizona.* 3 vols. New York: Lewis Historical Publishing Co., 1958.

Peterson, Charles H., John F. Urtinus, David E. Atkinson, and A. Kent Powell. *Mormon Battalion Trail Guide.* Salt Lake City: Utah Historical Society, 1972.

Peterson, Thomas H., Jr. "The Buckley House: Tucson Station for the Butterfield Overland Mail." *Journal of Arizona History,* vol. 7 (Winter, 1966), pp. 153–67.

———. "Danger, Sound Klaxon." *Journal of Arizona History,* vol. 15 (Autumn, 1974).

———. "A Tour of Tucson—1874." *Journal of Arizona History,* vol. 11 (Autumn, 1970), pp. 23–33.

Phillips, Cabell. *The 1940's: Decade of Triumph and Trouble.* New York: Macmillan, 1975.

Polzer, Charles W. "Clarification." *Arizona Daily Star,* December 3, 1973.

———. "Long Before the Blue Dragoons: Spanish Military Operations in Pimeria Alta." In *Military History of the Spanish-American Southwest: A Seminar.* Edited by Bruno J. Rolak. Fort Huachuca, Ariz., U.S. Army Communications Command, 1976.

———. *Rules and Precepts of the Jesuit Missions of Northwestern New Spain.* Tucson: University of Arizona Press, 1976.

Poston, Charles D. *Building a State in Apache Land.* Edited by John Myers Myers. Tempe, Ariz.: Aztec Press, 1963 (first published in *Overland Monthly,* July–October, 1894).

Pradeau, Alberto Francisco. *La expulsión de los Jesuitas de las Provincias de Sonora, Ostimuri, y Sinaloa en 1767.* Mexico City: José Porrúa e Hijos, 1959.

Pumpelly, Raphael. *My Reminiscences.* Vol. 1. New York: Henry Holt, 1918.

Reid, John Coleman. *Reid's Tramp: A Journal of the Incidents of Ten Months' Travel Through Texas, New Mexico, Arizona, Sonora, and California. . . .* Selma, Ala.: John Hardy & Co., 1858.

Reinhold, Ruth M. "The Old Douglas International Airport." *Journal of Arizona History,* vol. 15 (Winter, 1974), pp. 325–48.

Roberts, Brigham Henry. *The Mormon Battalion: Its History and Achievements.* Salt Lake City, Utah: Deseret News, 1919.

Robinson, Cecil. *With the Ears of Strangers: The Mexican in American Literture.* Tucson: University of Arizona Press, 1963 (republished, 1978, under the title *Mexico and the Hispanic Southwest in American Literature*).

Rochlin, Jay. "Yaquis Still Waiting." *Tucson Weekly News,* vol. 1 (October 15–21, 1980), p. 11.

Rodnitzky, Jerome L. "Recapturing the West: The Dude Ranch in American Life." *Arizona and the West,* vol. 10 (Summer, 1968), pp. 111–26.

Rolak, Bruno. "General Miles' Mirrors." *Journal of Arizona History,* vol. 16 (Summer, 1975), pp. 145–60.

Roosevelt, Theodore. *The Rough Riders.* New York: Scribner, 1899.

Rothbard, Murray N. *Depression.* Princeton, N.J.: D. Van Nostrand, 1963.

Roland, Charles P. *Albert Sidney Johnston: Soldier of Three Republics.* Austin: University of Texas Press, 1964.

Rynning, Captain Thomas H. *Gun Notches: The Life Story of a Cowboy Soldier.* New York: Frederick A. Stokes, 1931.

Sacks, B. *Arizona's Angry Man: United States Marshal Milton B. Duffield.* Tempe: Arizona Historical Foundation, 1970.

———. *Be It Enacted: The Creation of the Territory of Arizona.* Phoenix: Arizona Historical Foundation, 1964.

———. "Charles Debrille Poston: Prince of Arizona Pioneers." *Smoke Signal,* publication of the Tucson Corral of the Westerners (Spring, 1963), pp. 1–12.

———. "New Evidence in the Bascom Affair." *Arizona and the West,* vol. 4 (Autumn, 1962), pp. 261–78.

———. "The Origins of Fort Buchanan: Myth and Fact." *Arizona and the West,* vol. 7 (Autumn, 1965), pp. 207–26.

Schmidt, Louis Bernard. "Manifest Opportunity and the Gadsden Purchase." *Arizona and the West,* vol. 3 (Autumn, 1961), pp. 245–64.

Schmitt, Jo Ann. *Fighting Editors.* San Antonio, Texas: Naylor, 1958.

Sheretta, Stephen E. "Black Shale Rumor Could Fit Piece into Arizona Oil Puzzle." *Arizona Daily Star,* October 8, 1980.

Schwalen, H. C., and R. J. Shaw. *Water in the Santa Cruz Valley.* Agricultural Experiment Station Bulletin 288 (October, 1957). Tucson.

Shaw, Bill. "Retired Detective Recalls Chase." *Arizona Daily Star,* December 21, 1978.

Sinclair, Andrew. *Prohibition: The Era of Excess.* Boston: Little, Brown, 1962.

Sloan, Richard E. *Memoirs of an Arizona Judge.* Stanford, Calif.: Stanford University Press, 1932.

Smiley, Terah L., ed. *Climate and Man in the Southwest.* University of Arizona Bulletin, vol. 28, no. 4 (November, 1957), Program in Geochronology, Contribution no 6. Tucson: University of Arizona, 1958.

Smith, Cornelius C. "Some Unpublished History of the Southwest." *Arizona Historical Review,* vol. 4 (July, 1931), p. 22.

———. *William Sanders Oury: History Maker of the Southwest.* Tucson: University of Arizona Press, 1967.

Smith, Fay Jackson, John Kessell, and Francis Fox. *Father Kino in Arizona.* Phoenix: Arizona Historical Foundation, 1966.

Smith, Jedediah S. *The Southwest Expedition of Jedediah S. Smith: His Personal Account of His Journey to California, 1826–1827.* Edited by Geroge R. Brooks. Glendale, Calif.: Arthur H. Clark Co., 1977.

Sobin, Harris J. "From Vigas to Rafters." *Journal of Arizona History,* vol. 18 (Winter, 1975), pp. 357–82.

Sonnichsen, C. L. *Billy King's Tombstone.* Tucson: University of Arizona Press, 1972 (first published, 1941).

———. *Pass of the North: Four Centuries on the Rio Grande.* 2 vols. El Paso: Texas Western Press, 1980 (first published, 1968).

———. *Tularosa: Last of the Frontier West.* New York: Devin-Adair, 1972 (first published, 1960).

Sortore, Nancy. "A Relaxed Tucson Home for a 'Family' of Guests." *Arizona Daily Star*, January 7, 1973.

———. "What Is the Marshall Foundation?" *Arizona Daily Star*, June 6, 1975.

———. "Where Did the Dude Ranch Go?" *Arizona Daily Star*, October 17, 1971.

Speers, Al. "The Dillinger Story." 6 pts. *Arizona Daily Star*, December 17–22, 1978.

Spencer, Louise Reid. "Guerrilla Wife." *Ladies Home Journal*, vol. 62 (August, 1945), pp. 17, 64–87, 89–91.

Spicer, Edward H. *Cycles of Conquest: The Impact of Spain, Mexico, and the United States on the Indians of the Southwest, 1533–1960.* Tucson: University of Arizona Press, 1962.

———. *Pascua: A Yaqui Village in Arizona.* Chicago: University of Chicago Press, 1940.

———. *The Yaquis: A Cultural History.* Tucson: University of Arizona Press, 1980.

Spring, John F. *John Spring's Arizona.* Edited by A. M. Gustafson. Tucson: University of Arizona Press, 1966.

———. "Teaching School in the Early Days." Address at Teachers Institute, Tucson, December 31, 1895. MS. State Archives, Phoenix. Quoted in John Charles Bury. *The Historical Role of Arizona's Superintendent of Public Instruction.* Flagstaff, Ariz.: State Department of Public Instruction, 1974.

———. "With the Regulars in Arizona in the Sixties." *Washington National Tribune*, November 20, 1902.

Spude, Robert L. "A Land of Sunshine and Silver: Silver Mining in Central Arizona, 1871–1885." *Journal of Arizona History*, vol. 6 (Spring, 1975), pp. 32–76.

Stagg, Albert. *The First Bishop of Sonora: Antonio de los Reyes, O.F.M.* Tucson: University of Arizona Press, 1976.

Standage, Henry. "Journal of Henry Standage." In *The March of the Mormon Battalion from Council Bluffs to California.* Edited by Frank Alfred

Golder, Thomas A. Bailey, and J. Lyman Smith. New York: Century, 1928.

Stewart, Janet Ann. "The Mansions of Main Street." *Journal of Arizona History*, vol. 20 (Summer, 1979), pp. 193–222.

Stokesbury, James L. *A Short History of World War II.* New York: Morrow, 1980.

Stoner, Victor R. "Fray Pedro de Arriquibar, Chaplain of the Royal Fort at Tucson." Edited by Henry F. Dobyns. *Arizona and the West*, vol. 1 (Spring, 1959), pp. 71–79.

Sullivan, Mark. *Our Times.* Vol. 5, *Over Here.* New York: Scribner, 1972.

Téllez, Juan I. "Reminiscences." *Arizona Historical Review*, vol. 7 (January, 1936), pp. 85–89.

Terrell, John Upton. *Apache Chronicle.* New York: World, 1972.

Thomas, Alfred Barnaby, trans. and ed. *Forgotten Frontiers: A Study of the Spanish Indian Policy of Don Juan Bautista de Anza, Governor of New Mexico, 1777–1783.* Norman: University of Oklahoma Press, 1969 (first publication, 1932).

———, trans. and ed. *Teodoro de Croix and the Northern Frontier of New Spain, 1776–1783.* Norman: University of Oklahoma Press, 1968 (first publication, 1941).

Thomas, Robert L. "Outdoorsman Recalls Trek up Mount Lemmon." *Arizona Republic*, May 21, 1977.

Thompson, Vicki. *Across the Dry Rillito: An Informal History of Casas Adobes.* Tucson: Territorial Publishers, 1979.

Thorn, Lee. "Tucson: A Soaring Decade of Crime." *Tucson Weekly News*, vol. 1 (October 15–21, 1980), pp. 3, 6.

Thrapp, Dan L. *The Conquest of Apacheria.* Norman: University of Oklahoma Press, 1967.

———. *General Crook and the Sierra Madre Adventure.* Norman: University of Oklahoma Press, 1973.

———, ed. *Dateline: Fort Bowie: Charles F. Lummis Reports on an Apache War.* Norman: University of Oklahoma Press, 1979.

Toland, John. *The Dillinger Days.* New York: Random House, 1963.

Treutlein, T. E., ed. and trans. "Father Gottfried Bernhardt Middendorf, S.J., Pioneer of Tucson." *New Mexico Historical Review*, vol. 32 (October, 1957), pp. 310–18.

Trimble, Marshall. *Arizona: A Panorama History of*

a Frontier State. Garden City, N.Y.: Doubleday, 1977.

Tuchman, Barbara W. *The Zimmerman Telegram.* New York: Macmillan, 1978 (first publication, 1958).

Tucson-Pima County Historical Commission. *Tucson, the Old Pueblo: A Chronology.* Tucson, 1971.

Tucson Realty. "Exclusive! The True Story of Tucson Realty and Dillinger." *Territorial Days Dispatch: The Official Publication of Tucson Realty and Trust Co.*, April, 1974. Dillinger Collection, Arizona Historical Society.

Tully, Jacqui. "Visionary Hutchinson Not Giving Up on Tottering Temple." *Arizona Daily Star*, September 28, 1980.

Turcheneske, John A. "The Arizona Press and Geronimo's Surrender." *Journal of Arizona History*, vol. 14 (Summer, 1973), pp. 133–48.

Turner, Alfred E. *The Earps Talk.* College Station, Texas: Creative Publishing Co., 1980.

Tuttle, Edward D. "Arizona Begins Law Making." *Arizona Historical Review*, vol. 1 (April, 1928), pp. 50–62.

Tyler, Daniel. *A Concise History of the Mormon Battalion in the Mexican War, 1846–1847.* Salt Lake City, Utah, 1881.

Utley, Robert M. *Frontier Regulars: The United States Army and the Indian, 1866–1890.* New York: Macmillan. 1973.

Vail, Edward L. "The Diary of a Desert Trail." *Texasland*, vol. 6 (May, 1926), pp. 5–7; (June, 1926), pp. 13–14; (July, 1926), pp. 8–9, 17.

Vigness, David M. "Don Hugo Oconor and New Spain's Northeastern Frontier." *Journal of the West*, vol. 6 (January, 1967), pp. 28–35.

Wade, Michael S. *The Bitter Issue: The Right to Work Law in Arizona.* Tucson: Arizona Historical Society, 1976.

Wagoner, Jay J. *Arizona Territory, 1863–1912: A Political History.* Tucson: University of Arizona Press, 1970.

———. *Early Arizona: Prehistory to Civil War.* Tucson: University of Arizona Press, 1974.

———. *The History of the Cattle Industry in Southern Arizona, 1540–1940.* Tucson: University of Arizona Press, 1952.

Walker, Charles S. "Causes of the Confederate Invasion of New Mexico." *New Mexico Historical Review*, vol. 8 (January, 1933), pp. 76–97.

Walker, Dale L. *Death Was the Black Horse: The Story of Rough Rider Buckey O'Neill.* Austin: Madrona Press, 1975.

Walker, Henry P. "Freighting from Guaymas to Tucson, 1850–1880." *Western Historical Quarterly*, vol. 1 (July, 1970), pp. 291–304.

———. "Retire Peaceably to Your Abodes: Arizona Faces Martial Law, 1882." *Journal of Arizona History*, vol. 10 (Spring, 1969), pp. 1–18.

Wallace, Jerry. *The Episcopal Church in Arizona.* Tucson: Grace Episcopal Church, 1974.

Warner, J. J. "Reminiscences of Early California from 1831 to 1846." *Annual Publications of the Historical Society of Southern California*, vol. 7, pts. 2, 3 (1907–1908), pp. 176–93.

Watford, W. H. "The Far Western Wing of the Rebellion, 1861–1865." *California Historical Society Quarterly*, vol. 34 (June, 1955), pp. 125–48.

Webb, A. D. "Arizonans in the Spanish-American War," *Arizona Historical Review*, vol. 1 (January, 1929), pp. 50–68.

Webb, George Ernest. "The Indefatigable Astronomer: A. E. Douglass and the Founding of the Steward Observatory." *Journal of Arizona History*, vol. 19 (Summer, 1978), pp. 169–88.

Weber, David J. "Failure of a Frontier Institution: The Secular Church in the Borderlands Under Independent Mexico, 1821–1846." *Western Historical Quarterly*, vol. 12 (April, 1981), pp. 125–43.

———. *Foreigners in Their Native Land: Historical Roots of the Mexican-American.* Albuquerque: University of New Mexico Press, 1973.

———. "Mexico and the Mountain Men." *Journal of the West*, vol. 8 (July, 1969), pp. 369–78.

———. *The Taos Trappers: The Fur Trade in the Far Southwest, 1540–1846.* Norman: University of Oklahoma Press, 1971.

Wechter, Dixon. *The Age of the Great Depression, 1929–1941.* New York: Macmillan, 1948.

Wesson, Miley B. *Early History of Urology on the West Coast.* Reprinted from *History of Urology*, vol. 1 (1933). Arizona Historical Society.

White, Jon Manchip. *A World Elsewhere: One Man's Fascination with the American Southwest.* New York: Crowell, 1976.

Whitworth, Robert W. "From the Mississippi to the Pacific: An Englishman in the Mormon Battalion." Edited by David B. Gracy II and Helen J. H. Rugely. *Arizona and the West*, vol. 7 (Summer, 1965), pp. 127–60.

Wilder, Judith C. "The Years of the Desert Laboratory." *Journal of Arizona History*, vol. 8 (Autumn, 1967), pp. 179–99.

Wish, Harvey. *Contemporary America*. 4th ed. New York: Harper & Row, 1966 (first publication, 1945).

Woody, Clara T., and Milton L. Schwartz. *Globe, Arizona*. Tucson: Arizona Historical Society, 1977.

Wright, Frank Lloyd. *The Living City*. New York: Morrison, 1958.

Wyllys, Rufus K. *Arizona: The History of a Frontier State*. Phoenix: Hobson & Herr, 1950.

———. "Padre Luis Velarde's Relacion . . . , 1716," *New Mexico Historical Review*, vol. 6 (April, 1931), pp. 111–57.

Yates, Richard. "The Great Cactus Derby of 1914." *Arizona Highways*, vol. 45 (June 1969), pp. 2–9.

Young, Otis E., Jr. *The West of Philip St. George Cooke, 1809–1895*. Glendale, Calif.: Arthur H. Clark, 1955.

Zúñiga, Ignacio. *Rapido ojeada al estado de Sonora, dirijida y dedicada al Supremo Gobierno de la Nación por el C. Ignacio Zúñiga . . . , 1835*. Mexico City: Juan Ojeda, 1835.

Index

Tucson,

designed by Ed Shaw and Bill Cason, was set in various sizes of Garamond by Graphic Composition, Inc., with display type on the title page in handset Caslon Antique by the University of Oklahoma Press. The book was printed offset on 60-pound Glatfelter by Christian Board of Publication and bound by Becktold Company.